WHEN MEDIA ARE NEW

Joseph Turow
SERIES EDITOR

Broadcasting, Voice, and Accountability: A Public Interest Approach to Policy, Law, and Regulation
Steve Buckley, Kreszentia Duer, Toby Mendel, and Seán Ó Siochrú, with Monroe E. Price and Marc Raboy

Owning the Olympics: Narratives of the New China
Monroe E. Price and Daniel Dayan, editors

The Hyperlinked Society: Questioning Connections in the Digital Age
Joseph Turow and Lokman Tsui, editors

When Media Are New: Understanding the Dynamics of New Media Adoption and Use
John Carey and Martin C. J. Elton

DIGITALCULTUREBOOKS is an imprint of the University of Michigan Press and the Scholarly Publishing Office of the University of Michigan Library dedicated to publishing innovative and accessible work exploring new media and their impact on society, culture, and scholarly communication.

When Media Are New

UNDERSTANDING THE DYNAMICS OF NEW MEDIA ADOPTION AND USE

John Carey AND *Martin C. J. Elton*

The University of Michigan Press AND *The University of Michigan Library*
ANN ARBOR

Published in the United States of America by
The University of Michigan Press and
The University of Michigan Library
Manufactured in the United States of America
♾ Printed on acid-free paper

2013 2012 2011 2010 4 3 2 1

A CIP catalog record for this book is available from the British Library.

Library of Congress Cataloging-in-Publication Data

Carey, John, 1946–
When media are new : understanding the dynamics of new media adoption and use / John Carey and Martin C. J. Elton.
p. cm. — (The new media world)
Includes bibliographical references and index.
ISBN 978-0-472-07085-5 (cloth : alk. paper) — ISBN 978-0-472- 05085-7 (pbk. : alk. paper)
1. Digital media—Social aspects. I. Elton, M. C. J. II. Title.

HM851.C3665 2010
302.23'1—dc22 2010004475

To Eileen
—JC

•

To Sarah
—MCJE

Preface

There is certainly no shortage of recent literature on the subject of new media; in fact, it has become somewhat difficult to avoid it. However, this book aims to be rather different. It is about electronic media when they are new—not only the media of today but also media introduced earlier, in the past 40 or so years. All were made available to users and went through a process of adoption (or rejection). Some established themselves, some are still trying to do so (even after decades), and some fell by the wayside. Our premise is that it is valuable for those working in the field to have an understanding that ranges both across the wide varicty of new electronic media and back through time. While dramatic changes have occurred—not least the acceleration of the implementation and adoption processes—many more similarities exist between what happens today and what happened in the pre-Web era than many people realize. We have synthesized past and current experience in a way that will be useful to both practitioners and academics. We offer an integrated treatment of a variety of media at the time each was introduced, set the introduction of each in historical and technological context, and, as relevant fill in what happened after it established itself.

Some of the mistakes made in the past have been repeated many times over and are still made today. This phenomenon is reflected in our lighthearted working title for the book, "Making New Mistakes." In a field that is moving so fast and for which the development of theory lags far behind current developments, mistakes are inevitable. New mistakes can offer a wonderful potential for learning: what a shame to waste time on old ones!

Individually and jointly, our main interest has always lain in the actions and experiences of media users rather than in the industries that provide the associated products and services, the technologies themselves, impacts on society as a whole, or the role of government, all of which the literature already covers extensively. We started working together in the mid-1970s and have had many opportunities to do so since. Each of us is fortunate to have started research on new media close to the turning point when services going far beyond broadcast television or the simple telephone were knocking loudly at the door—which opened rather slowly at first. Today, we find much of what we learned in earlier years very helpful in understanding contemporary new media. In one sense, this book is about that learning and how it applies in today's much less tranquil environment.

A great deal of our research has been undertaken within interdisciplinary teams. Our collaboration with one another—one coming from mass communication and anthropology, the other from management science and mathematics—has necessarily been interdisciplinary. As a result, in our professional work, we generally have to write to be accessible to the intelligent layperson, and we adopt that style here. The book is written from a transdisciplinary perspective, making no assumptions about readers' prior disciplinary backgrounds but at the same time attempting to avoid sacrificing the conceptual rigor of constructs imported from diverse disciplines.

It is more than clear by now that new media are very far from an exclusively American concern; indeed, this was already clear enough four decades ago, when one of us began to research then emerging media from a base in the United Kingdom. Accordingly, we set out to write a book that was not overly focused on the United States, and we have covered a good proportion of the important innovations that have taken place elsewhere. Nevertheless, as we look over the result, we are ruefully aware of how much more could have been written about important developments in other countries if only we had had both the time to gather the information and the space to provide it.

We have drawn heavily on research for which we received funding over the years from the National Science Foundation, the Corporation for Public Broadcasting, the Markle Foundation, and the Freedom Forum Media Studies Center as well as from a number of other organizations on both sides of the Atlantic. We are grateful for their financial support and for the generous encouragement and advice offered us by the officers who administered it. For their valued comments on draft chapters or helpful information on specific topics, we are particularly indebted to Gary Arlen, Elizabeth Carey, Brian Champness, Robert Cowan, Gali Einav, Elliot Gold, David Kamien, Martin Nisenholtz, A. Michael Noll, Jules Tewlow, and Bertil Thorngren as well as to an unnamed reviewer of an early partial draft of the manuscript, who made a number of very helpful and insightful suggestions. We are grateful to Eileen Connell for her substantial contribution to the creation of the graphical components of the book and to Devyani Mehta and Jonathan Weidman for their assistance. Naturally, we alone are responsible for any errors of fact or interpretation on the following pages.

Finally, our heartfelt thanks go to our wives, whose patience and support have always meant so much to us but never more than during the long hours we spent closeted away writing the book.

Contents

Introduction

This book is about understanding new media. For many, the term has become a loose but voguish way of referring to the latest or hottest new offerings from a growing miscellany of digital devices used for communication, entertainment, and information purposes. We, however, will avoid discussion of what's hot and what's not in new media along with predictions of what the new media landscape will look like in the future. Many other books cover these topics, though they often do not do it well.

Our use of the term *new media* is set in a broader historical context: a media service or product is new from the point when the underlying concept starts to be implemented until the service or product can be regarded as established in the marketplace (in the sense that the product or service is very unlikely to be withdrawn as a failure). The amount of time from concept to established presence can range between a few years and many decades; we regard the video telephone, which first came onto the American market in the 1960s, as still an example of new media. The title of the book, *When Media Are New*, conveys our intent to examine both current new media and earlier media, such as online services when they were first introduced. The subtitle of the book, *Understanding the Dynamics of New Media Adoption and Use*, indicates that we focus primarily on users' reactions to new media and their determinants.

A new media product or service may be broadcast, person-to-person, or—increasingly, these days—a combination of the two. A clear-cut dichotomy no longer exists. Its content may be created for distribution to an audience, as in conventional broadcasting, or it may be the interaction among two or more users, as in conventional telephony or simple e-mail. The innovation may be radical (as when the telephone first enabled people to engage in conversation despite not being within earshot of one another) or a matter of substantial improvement in the quality of the communication that is provided (as in the transition from conventional to high-definition television).

It is helpful to distinguish individual communication products and services from platforms. We regard neither the Internet nor today's mobile phones as examples of new media. It is better to treat them as platforms, each of which can be used in the provision of a variety of media—clearly, an increasing variety. We will treat them in this way and focus on some but not all of the new media they have come to support.

Some new media do not require their users or audiences to acquire a product that embodies new technology or to use a newly introduced service, or both. *User-developed media* come into being when users fashion a new application for themselves using technology that is *already* (even if only recently) available and *without* a purpose-designed service having been provided for them. An important case in point is early blogs, formerly weblogs—how quickly language can change! Generally, however, new media have required the introduction of new communication products or services.

This book is written from a standpoint that balances guarded optimism with measured skepticism and balances theory with practice in a way that is useful to both professional and academic readers. A variety of people are professionally concerned with questions such as whether the start-up or field trial of a new service is likely to succeed, at what price and on what timescale; what issues need to be addressed to maximize the chances of success; how research can play a useful part in the process; and how, by whom, in what order, and to what ends the service is likely to be taken up. These people principally are found in firms, large and small, that are trying to make a success of new ventures in this field, but they also include those in the public and private sectors who are planning and implementing the use of new media in a diverse range of organizational settings, such as government agencies, education institutions, and community organizations as well as businesses. The policymakers and regulators who set rules that affect the take-up and use of new services and technologies are involved as well. All the foregoing comprise one of the intended audiences for this book.

The other principal audience comprises academics who teach and conduct research in this area and students who seek to learn the history of new media start-ups along with the associated planning and implementation processes. Journalists who cover technology and general readers with an interest in new media will also find the volume useful. While our analysis is anchored in several areas of media theory and draws inferences to further those areas, the book is not intended as a primer on media theory that uses new media as examples to teach the theory. In focusing on the current new media environment and on useful lessons from when earlier media were new, we do not offer a cultural critique of new media. Other researchers (e.g., Brian Winston) claim this territory and cover it much better than we could.[1]

We discuss failures as well as successes. These terms have their customary meanings: success or failure relative to the goals when a new product was introduced. In places, however—principally in chapter 6, when we discuss the "failures" that preceded the Web—we question the use of these terms. Kenneth Lipartito's radical critique of the concept of success and failure is particularly relevant.[2] Failures can provide useful and important lessons, and something would be seriously wrong in any large, contemporary industrial economy in which most launches of new media products and services succeeded. Since there are increasingly compelling reasons to bring innovations to market before there can be certainty—if ever there can be—as to their success, too few failures would signal too little dynamism.

New media may fail at a particular time, but the underlying concept may go on to succeed at some future time—maybe after more than one false start in the interim. Facsimile transmission provides an example: except for limited purposes, such as sending weather maps, it had several false starts after first being demonstrated in the middle of the nineteenth century, before the telephone was invented. (Transmission originally occurred over telegraph lines.) We explore difficulties that arise when new media are introduced into markets or organizational settings. There are many difficulties; mistakes are inevitable. Too often, however, we have noticed that people unwittingly make mistakes that others have made before. If knowledge of what has gone wrong in the past helps some readers working in the industries concerned at least to make new mistakes, then their successors can learn something new from them.

A well-known companion of many publicity campaigns in support of new media is hype—unwarranted exaggeration about the wonders of some new technology. It can be harmful in a number of ways. It can set false expectations among end users, who are then disappointed by the reality of the new media technology or service. It can mislead those providing the necessary investment into underestimating costs. Planners may come to believe their publicists' hype and make poor decisions about marketing and service development. In addition, if the bar of expectations is set too high for journalists who cover the media or analysts on Wall Street, good performance may be judged as weak performance.

Fortunately, hype is not inevitable. It did not, for example, feature in the introduction of e-mail. Nor did it surround the transition from the Arpanet to the Internet; the *Information Superhighway* and similar terms came later, helped along by American politicians—especially a future vice president—who seem to have had in mind something even grander than the Internet has yet become.

Uncertainty is a core characteristic associated with new media. Will the technology work as intended? Do people want it? How do you communicate about a product that is very new? Many far-from-obvious lessons can be learned from those who have already traveled down this road. While they cannot eliminate uncertainty, they can certainly reduce it.

As the next section describes in more detail, part 1 of the book examines processes that occur at two different levels. At the concrete level (what actually happens), one chapter looks at users' adoption of new media, while another explores suppliers' implementation of new media. At the abstract level (understanding what really happens or is expected to happen), one chapter examines research, and another examines forecasting.

To provide in-depth examples illustrating these processes and to add detail to them, part 2 of the book provides a set of case studies of particular media or families of closely related media. Most of the chapters in this section examine how particular media or families of media progressed to success or failed to do so. One chapter, however, focuses on an established medium, broadcast television, describing how it was affected by subsequent media innovations, and another shows how much a highly successful family of media—those delivered via the Internet—owes to a series of earlier new media that failed to live up to expectations.

Part 1: Processes

Successful new media affect individuals, families, firms, industries, government, and society as a whole only as a result of the host of decisions by different people to adopt them. Because of the centrality of the adoption process, it forms the subject of the opening chapter, which describes common patterns that occur as one looks at the field across new media and through time. Many of these patterns exist—patterns in growth rates, the relationship between price and household income, trends in price over time, and the characteristics of early adopters. Most successful technologies reach a critical mass where growth becomes self-sustaining, but the path to critical mass can differ from one technology to another. Further, an examination of adoption patterns produces a number of surprises: for example, the role of serendipity in helping many technologies to become broadly adopted. Accepted wisdom holds that success requires a new technology to meet an identifiable need. However, many of the most successful technologies entered a marketplace where no apparent need existed. In some cases, latent needs existed. For example, color television met a latent need to see visuals that more closely resembled the real world, even though millions of people had embraced black-and-white television with few complaints about the lack of color. In other cases, new media created demand. For example, it may be argued that video games met a latent need for more entertainment, but it may also be argued that they really created a demand for a new form of entertainment that previously did not exist.

Chapter I covers not just successes but also failures. They are of interest both to avoid repeating previous mistakes—not always easy to diagnose even with the benefit of hindsight—and to find candidates for successful future products and services among the near misses of the past. Unfortunately, we have relatively few reasonably detailed accounts of failures on which to draw not least because those responsible often try to bury the evidence. Also covered is the search for the Holy Grail of many technologists, "killer applications"—content or services that are so compelling that people rush out to adopt the new medium in question. More commonly, however, content and/or services must come together to generate sufficient appeal that people will adopt the technology.

In chapter 2, we turn to forecasting. As the term is commonly used, a forecast is presumed to be based on research and a scientific process that yields quantitative estimates of future adoption rates. In general, forecasting methods, whether they deal with the weather or advertising revenue, have been getting better. There are exceptions, of course, and they can occur even when professional forecasters deal with well-known products or events and have many data points at their disposal.

Forecasts about new media have been highly unreliable. Most have overestimated adoption rates, though some have grossly underestimated the market for a new technology. An example of the former comes from 1998, when a consensus of Wall Street media analysts forecast 30 million satellite telephone subscribers by 2006. In fact, the company that launched satellite telephone service in 1998 went bankrupt the following year. The service was reorganized by two other operators and by 2006 had developed a modest group of approximately half a million users, including emergency workers and people living or working in very remote areas such as oil rigs in the North Atlantic.

A classic example of underestimating demand is McKinsey and Company's reported forecast for AT&T during the 1980s that the total market for mobile phones by the year 2000 would be 900,000 subscribers. On the basis of this forecast and an internal analysis, AT&T pulled out of the mobile phone market, only to reenter it about a decade later by purchasing McCaw Communications at an overall cost of $16 billion.[3] This example illustrates the most obvious reason why forecasts are necessary: to make sound business decisions. Forecasts are also needed in the development and implementation of public policy.

For some decision-making purposes, it may be possible to get by with something less precise than a forecast: a simple prediction about whether a projected new media service will establish itself in the marketplace within a certain time frame. But even these much simpler binary predictions frequently prove incorrect. Of course, if a forecasting team is wrong in such a prediction (whether implicit or explicit), its forecast will inevitably be completely wrong.

Chapter 2 discusses practitioners' poor track record in forecasting the demand for new media products and services, methods used to create the forecasts, and how the business context in which forecasts are often produced appears to contribute to their biases. Even with improvements in practice, however, one would be unwise to expect substantial improvements in accuracy in the foreseeable future, so we also consider how to make the best of a bad job. To readers with practical interests in the field, the relevance of these issues will be obvious; we expect other readers, aware of how the inability to make accurate forecasts has clearly been a major determinant of how new media have developed during the past half century, to have an interest in understanding the limitations of the process.

Chapter 3 deals with the implementation process. In connection with new media, implementation usually means either putting into effect a plan for the market introduction of a new product or service or—as in a field trial—putting into effect a plan to get a new service into use in a particular organizational or community context. It may sound like a dull, low-level, technical process, stretching from the approval of funding for an exciting concept to the concrete realization of a new service with satisfied users. It often turns out, however, to be a complex, broadly defined, multiphased process encompassing social, technical, and organizational components that, in addition to the installation of a technical system, include managing relationships with partners, dealing with end users, marketing, interacting with equipment suppliers or manufacturers, overcoming a variety of obstacles, managing costs, and much more.

Whether or not one is interested in the implementation process as such, one should recognize that although it has received relatively little attention in the literature about new media, it is more difficult than is generally appreciated and therefore offers many opportunities for failure. Numerous services with strong potential have crashed in flames as a result of poor planning and implementation—for example, many of the trial telemedicine services of the 1970s. After one or more failures in some new media initiative, an important but difficult question has often been to what extent failure indicated that the concept was not viable or that the timing of the initiative was wrong and to what extent it reflected no more than poor implementation.

Implementation of a field trial or the launch of a new product or service almost invariably takes longer than those managing it expect. When it is a matter of bringing new media to the marketplace, the longer-than-anticipated time frames required for implementation also stretch out growth rates and eventual profits, putting more pressure on promises about return on investment for outside investors or parent organizations. Managers then often make compromises regarding critical features of a new service, such as the user interface, to overcome the delays. But these compromises can reduce a new product's appeal and hence its prospects for success. End-user skill levels also come into the picture. The weaker the design of a new media product, the more skill is required of an end user.

Sometimes a new media technology or service must be implemented at a particular site or set of sites—perhaps for the purpose of a trial—in which case the challenges differ somewhat. In addition to the chain reactions of effects that can be caused by allowing insufficient time, these challenges can include turf issues, staff turnover and training, product champions, and budget cycles.

Implementation is generally not for the fainthearted. Chapter 3 seeks both to show why this is the case and to point to some of the more generalizable lessons that have been learned about how to avoid the often seemingly mundane errors that too frequently lead to failure. Some of these errors occur at high levels in organizations and doom the implementation process even before it begins.

Chapter 4, the final chapter in part 1 of the book, concerns the research process. Research on new media has been undertaken from within many disciplines—communication, psychology, economics, and sociology, for example—and on an interdisciplinary basis. Some research is better categorized as belonging to a particular field in which new media may be applied—telemedicine, telecommuting, and distance education, for instance. Doing justice to all of these fields in a single chapter would be impossible, so we focus on *user research* on new media—i.e., research that centers specifically on actual or potential users of new media. (The term should not be confused with *usability testing*, which may be regarded as one of many component activities in the much larger field of user research.) This focus is in keeping with the book's emphasis on users. Moreover, whatever kind of research is undertaken on new media, questions addressed by user research—such as what kinds of people use the products or services in question, how they do so and to what effect, and how better to serve them—are likely to be central.

There have been three eras of user research. The first was devoted largely to two types of topic: ergonomics (*human factors*) relating mainly to the telephone and the effectiveness of new media in education. The second era, starting at the end of the 1960s and lasting roughly a quarter of a century, was devoted largely to teleconferencing, two-way cable television, telemedicine, videotex, and teletext—on the whole, services that fell far short of establishing themselves within the time frames their proponents expected. With hindsight, the second era of user research can be seen as the calm before the storm. Even though the new services whose prospects drove the research were not particularly successful, valuable research results were obtained and methodological lessons learned. The storm arrived with the explosion of new Web-based services and to a lesser extent mobile services. Rather than showing any signs of ending, the storm is continuing with increasing force. The context for user research in its third era differs radically from that in the second era. The amount and variety of research activity are expanding very fast; users' media environments are changing rapidly; research agendas—whoever's they may be—are changing quickly; and the conclusions of much applied research that might well have been of value in a calmer period are quite likely to have been overtaken by events by the time they are available.

There is little value to trying to examine this storm while we are still in it. Research is changing too rapidly; too much of it has not yet been digested. Conversely, much that remains relevant emerged from user research conducted during the preceding calm and apparently is not widely known. Therefore, our coverage of user research in this chapter concentrates on the second era of it; a number of the case studies, however, draw on research results from the third era.

Part 2: Case Studies

In her outstanding book, *When Old Technologies Were New*, Carolyn Marvin provides a model for trying to understand new media: examining specific new media services of the past.[4] It examines the past as if we were living in it and provides a fresh perspective on technologies (the telephone and electricity) that are more than a hundred years old. This model strongly influences our approach to the six case studies that form the second part of the book, placing an emphasis on how people actually used new media as well as on the strategies employed to encourage adoption and the obstacles that hindered it. These case studies provide in-depth illustrations of many of the ideas explained in part 1.

The first case study provides an example of the interactions between new media and established media, showing how technology, user behavior, and content are interlinked. Specifically, it deals with how new television technologies such as digital video recorders (DVRs), high-definition television (HDTV), video on demand (VOD), and video for mobile phones have affected television viewing behavior and how these changes in behavior are, in turn, leading to changes in programming. Clues about what may happen with the latest generation of new television technologies may be found in an understanding of the history of earlier technologies that affected viewing behavior and subsequently content.

In the earliest days of television, set size and the location of TVs affected viewing behavior and content. Later, remote controls, larger TV sets, color TVs, cable television, multiple TV sets in homes, and the video cassette recorder further affected both behavior and content. These earlier lessons are combined with new research to provide a perspective on the ways in which today's new media alter television viewing behavior.

New media are changing the composition, location, size, and placement in time of audiences as well as their relationship with content. Old mass media models of communication treated audiences as large, passive groups that received content from a relatively few sources at predetermined points in time. The models needed to be revised when large cable television systems began to develop niche audiences for specialized content, and these models need to be revised again now that very large digital cable and satellite systems have begun to destroy the concept of a mass audience while technologies such as DVRs, VOD, and Web video sites free audiences from fixed schedules and allow them to consume content at any time.

The second case study deals with services in which content is generally created by interaction among users rather than for consumption by audiences: video telephones and teleconferencing. The video telephone was anticipated in some of the earliest experiments with television in the 1920s and was offered as a service in Germany during the 1930s. It was demonstrated with great fanfare by AT&T at the 1964 World's Fair (under the trademark Picturephone), and service was introduced in limited markets by the late 1960s. It failed both in the consumer market and as a business service, though some promising applications were developed in criminal justice and health care.[5] Video telephones were reintroduced a few times over the next three decades, failing each time.

Teleconferencing has two primary forms. One is a variation on video telephones—group-to-group video teleconferencing. This service was launched in the late 1960s and early 1970s in the United States and the United Kingdom. Early services were very expensive and had limited success. Over time, however, prices declined, and a modest market emerged by the 1990s.[6] The second form is audio teleconferencing—voice communication among three or more people at two or more sites. The most important form is the now familiar conference call, but initially this service was expensive, and the associated technology was not always reliable. Later, however, prices dropped sharply, technology improved, and it was widely adopted, so much so that it is now taken for granted in business settings and in many homes (e.g., three-way calling).

The value in understanding the history of video telephones and teleconferencing is first that they were subjected to a great deal of research that has widespread applicability and demonstrates how common sense can lead one astray. Second, video telephones keep returning every few years, often introduced by organizations that seem to be ignorant of the product's history; the latest iteration is the Web-based video call. The research reveals why video telephones failed in the past and what obstacles must be overcome if they are to be widely accepted in the future.

We turn next to the Web—or, more accurately, toward the Web. There are two stories about how it developed. One is well known; the other not. The well-known version focuses narrowly on the *technological* development of the Internet as a U.S. Defense Department project that began with the Arpanet in the late 1960s and then expanded to include many universities and research laboratories. Later, key advances in software technology at CERN in Europe and the development of the Mosaic browser at the University of Illinois led to the World Wide Web. The much less well-known version has a broader focus that includes both development of content and attraction of users as well as technology. The content that eventually populated the Web—information, shopping, communication, games, and advertising—already had a long history of development, mainly in the context of videotex and teletext.

Videotex and teletext are now largely forgotten or considered irrelevant failures by those who know about them, although teletext was moderately successful in certain European countries. Both are or were electronic information services. For transmission, videotex used the telephone network, and teletext uses a portion of the broadcast television signal. They began in Britain and spread to a number of other countries in Europe as well as to North America, Japan, and South America. Nearly all of the early services failed (the Ceefax and Oracle teletext services in Britain are notable exceptions; the Minitel videotex service was a limited exception in France), but a few U.S. videotex services eventually emerged with modest success, led by AOL.

From the late 1970s through the mid-1990s, videotex and teletext were the experimental field laboratories for content development. The names of the associated services are largely forgotten—CompuServe, Gateway, Prodigy, The Source, Time Teletext, and Viewtron, among others. Between them, however, they developed advertising, news services, games, shopping, and even auctions; videotex furthered the development of e-mail and forums, which had been introduced on earlier online platforms. All these services led the way to models of content on the Web today. Through the industry leader, AOL, they also brought millions of users to the Web in the mid-1990s. In these ways, videotex can certainly be seen as having played a significant part in the explosive early growth of the Web. Moreover, the reasons why most of these services failed and what was learned in the extensive research with consumers are very relevant to the current new media environment.

Interactive television (ITV), the subject of the fourth case study, offers a good example of a set of new media technologies that failed dozens of times before finally gaining marketplace acceptance. One of the very first demonstrations of television in the 1920s was a form of interactive television. ITV was tried again in the 1950s and in each decade of the twentieth century thereafter, failing in almost all cases. These failures provided many lessons, but subsequent proponents of the technology often did not know those lessons and repeatedly made the same mistakes.

In the early 2000s, ITV started to gain acceptance, first in Europe and then in the United States, through a broad range of applications, including interactive advertising, movies on demand, interactive program guides, and voting about who should be thrown off a reality TV program. Still, many uncertainties remain, such as the best platform on which to offer ITV, what services people want, and how to design interactive content. A core question about whether people want to interact with television has largely been answered, however: people want to interact with TV content, but some want to interact a lot, and some want to interact only a little, as in ordering a movie and then watching it passively for two hours. It is also unclear whether the core attractiveness of ITV is interaction with content or the control, convenience, and customization its services can provide.

Satellite radio provides another revealing case study about the adoption process for new media. The technology was developed originally to provide radio service to remote parts of Africa. In the early 2000s, it entered the U.S. market through two companies, XM and Sirius. Pundits greeted satellite radio with much skepticism, declaring that people would not pay for radio and that radio is a local medium with which a national service could not compete. The pundits were proved wrong, in part because they underestimated the negative attitudes toward terrestrial radio engendered by incessant commercials (as much as 23 minutes per hour); satellite radio has no commercials on its music channels. Doubters also underestimated the appeal of breadth of content and depth in the playlists within each content category. (Many commercial radio stations in the United States play only a couple of dozen songs, all middle of the road, to appeal to the widest audience.)

Satellite radio overcame the "radio is local" mantra in two ways. First, for many terrestrial radio stations, that mantra already no longer held true: they had abandoned local content years ago and carried no local news. Further, some stations were programmed and operated from other cities with no local DJs or content at all. Second, *local* implies *community*. Satellite radio created community in new ways, such as among fans of a particular genre of music or people who grew up in a certain period and identify with content from that period—satellite radio has "decades channels" that offer music, news, and talk about the 1960s, 1970s, 1980s, and so on.

Satellite radio provides concrete illustrations of the adoption process. When early satellite radios were expensive, the operators had to find a group of adopters who were willing to pay the high initial price. Members of a few groups had a strong need for the service—for example, long-distance truck drivers and people who lived in rural areas where there was little radio. As the price came down, second and third waves of adopters emerged among such people as those with long commutes and owners of luxury cars. Sirius and XM eventually merged, and on the cusp of becoming a mass media service, satellite radio then became a target for other competitors, including Web radio and portable MP-3 players, and found itself weighed down by the high cost it paid for programming stars.

The final case study focuses on the integration of mobile phones into everyday life. Mobile phones have become ubiquitous around the world. Further, their capabilities have expanded well beyond making phone calls—e.g., mobile phones that take photos and motion video as well as play songs, access the Web, and display television programming.

What are the implications of this new mobile phone (or mobile multimedia) environment? At a personal level, many people decorate and wear mobile phones, treating them, like clothing, as extensions of an individual's personality. In addition, some people, mostly the younger generation, have come to depend so much on mobile phones that they abandon traditional wired telephone service. The spread of mobile phones also means that whenever newsworthy events occur in a public setting, someone is likely to capture those happenings in photographs or on video and later share them with news organizations or post them on the Web. Mobile phones have wrought not only changes in lifestyles but also, and more important, changes in perceptions about the world we live in, our sense of time, and the expectation that information and communication should be available anywhere, anytime. For many people, these changes in perception have also led to a new sense of space and the microcoordination of location with others.

Mobile phones also exemplify the need to develop an international perspective on the adoption of new media. A first step in this process is to recognize that there are many differences among countries in adoption rates and in attitudes about and uses of new media. It is not simply the case that some countries lag others in adoption. The technological landscape in each country is affected by cultural and lifestyle differences, regulatory climates, preexisting telecommunication and broadcasting infrastructures, economic differences, and the pricing of services, among other factors.

These differences can make it difficult to know whether a new communication technology or service that is broadly accepted in one country will be readily accepted in another. The broad context for technology adoption in each country must be examined carefully. There were, for example, several reasons why Europe led the United States in mobile phone text messaging: text messages were much cheaper relative to voice calls in Europe than in the United States; no obstacles prevented European users from exchanging messages with users of other networks, as was initially the case in the United States; and the ready availability of economical prepay models encouraged many European parents to provide mobile phones to their children much earlier than U.S. parents did.

Theory

Some readers may seek an understanding of the state of relevant theory about new media and this book's position in relation to it. We have not set out to create a work about media theory, but this volume is built on and can help to extend a number of theoretical constructs.

By far the most widely known and accepted theory useful in understanding new media is sociologist Everett Rogers's theory on the diffusion of innovations.[7] Rogers's work provides a sound foundation for our treatment of the adoption process. We illustrate a variety of different ways that successful new media can diffuse in accordance with Rogers's theory: for example, the sociodemographic characteristics of innovators and early adopters for one innovation may differ from those for another.

Broad as Rogers's theory is, some factors and issues fall outside it. One of these, considered in chapter 1, is the relevance to the adoption process of the relationship between price and household income. Another is the potential role of seemingly small chance effects in determining the fate of a new product. This is explained by Brian Arthur's theory of positive feedback, which also makes the case that early providers of a new media service have an advantage over later entrants.[8] We demonstrate that this hypothes is true—sometimes. A third issue falling outside Rogers's theory is the at times devastating impact of an innovation undergoing a process of successive improvements on other products that are already established in a particular market. This is explained by Clayton Christensen's construct of disruptive technologies.[9] The disruption is a dramatic impact as a result of a certain type of reinvention process. The process of reinvention, which occurs when an innovation is changing at the same time as it is diffusing, is an important component of Rogers's theory. Examples of it will be found in a number of the case studies as well as in the chapters on adoption and implementation.

Naturally, some practitioners have hoped that the theory of the diffusion of innovations would provide a basis for forecasting the demand for new media before they have established themselves in use. Attempts to employ it in this way have not, however, succeeded. One reason appears to be the impossibility of making a good estimate of comparative advantage—another of Rogers's key constructs—at an early enough stage.

Another set of basic questions concerns media effectiveness—that is, how well new media compare with established media or other configurations of new media in serving particular purposes of particular types of users. At the start of the 1970s, social psychologists at the Communications Studies Group in London initiated an important stream of research, investigating different forms of real-time, person-to-person business communication—primarily, in-person, two-way video, and audio-only communication. The main research method was the controlled experiment.[10] In the United States, Robert Johansen and his colleagues at the Institute for the Future[11] and others conducted complementary studies. This research has provided us with a much better understanding of the effectiveness of new media relative to established media for purposes of interpersonal communication. This work is covered in chapter 4, and results obtained from it inform the case study on video telephones and teleconferencing (chapter 6).

Byron Reeves and Clifford Nass expanded our social psychological understanding of media in their classic book, *The Media Equation.*[12] They argue that many people equate a media experience with real life and that interactions with media technology are fundamentally social and natural. We draw from this theory in the case studies about interactive television (chapter 8) and mobile phones (chapter 10). A related theory about social presence, or how a mediated experience can be perceived in the same way as face-to-face experience, was first put forward by John Short et al., in the 1970s[13] but did not gain widespread acceptance in the field. It planted a seed, however, for a large number of studies in the 1990s and 2000s about social presence, identity, and interaction with technology through avatars, multiuser dungeons (MUDs), and social networks on the Web and mobile phones.[14] We draw from this work in the case studies about the Web (chapter 7) and mobile phones (chapter 10).

Some theories from the field of mass communication are very relevant to the study of new media, while others are outdated and need significant modification. Functional analysis theory, which examines the core sociological and psychological functions of media in people's lives, is very relevant to the study of new media. Harold Mendelsohn,[15] Leo Bogart,[16] and Lynn Spigel[17] studied the core functions of television in people's lives, and we draw on their work in our chapters about early online services (chapter 7), how new media affect television viewing (chapter 5), and satellite radio (chapter 9). More recent functional analysis by James Katz[18] about telephones reinvigorated this theoretical paradigm and influenced our chapter on mobile phones (chapter 10). Uses and gratifications theory, rooted in functional analysis and advanced by Jay Blumler and Elihu Katz,[19] emphasizes an active audience that selects what content to view and how they interact with media to fulfill basic needs such as escape, entertainment, and formation of personal identity. This theoretical model is very relevant to all forms of new interactive media. Some theoretical models from mass media research fall short in the conceptualization of audiences, however. In many models, audiences are conceptualized as large, passive collections of people who are acted on by the media. We prefer the term *users* over *audiences* to signify that people actively engage with media.

Economics theory has much to contribute about new media, though it is not central to our book. By the late 1960s, Bertil Thorngren, a Swedish economist, soon joined by John Goddard, a geographer in England, started to develop empirically grounded theory relating to the geographical patterns of communication by firms and government agencies. This idea quickly came to be seen as potentially useful for projecting the impacts that new telecommunication technologies could be expected to have on transportation and office location, which opened an avenue of research that other economists expanded to include consumers and a larger set of economic issues.

Naturally, considering the high and growing significance of the information sector in national economies, economists have done much work on related issues during the past two decades or so. While many of the issues they have studied, such as those concerning policy, regulation, and industry structure, are not directly related to the subject of this book, others—including, for example, standards, pricing, online auctions, and network effects—are directly relevant to users of new media products and services, as Carl Shapiro and Hal Varian very clearly demonstrated in their celebrated book, *Information Rules: A Strategic Guide to the Network Economy*.[20] More recently, Per Andersson, Ulf Essler, and Bertil Thorngren[21] at the Center for Information and Communications Research in Stockholm have conducted elegant research on the wireless market, and we draw on their work in chapter 10. Eli Noam and colleagues at the Columbia Institute for Tele-Information have conducted wide-ranging economic research about consumer behavior with new media that informs our work in chapter 1.[22]

At the core of our book is how users adopt or fail to adopt new media and, if they adopt a new technology or service, how they integrate it into their everyday lives. A large literature on the sociology of everyday life has grown out of the pioneering work of Erving Goffman.[23] Later, Roger Silverstone[24] and Shaun Moores[25] focused on media use in everyday life, and most recently, Rich Ling[26] has tackled this set of issues in relation to mobile phones. We draw on this research in a number of our case studies. A related body of theory has emerged from the work of historians and political scientists who have examined the introduction of earlier media when they were new from a user perspective. Carolyn Marvin has done excellent work in this area, as have Ithiel de Sola Pool and colleagues[27] and Claude Fischer.[28]

For readers who seek more about new media theory, we suggest Rogers, along with James Katz,[29] and Leah Lievrouw.[30]

// PART 1 // · Processes

// ONE //

Adoption of New Media

How do new media make their way into users' hands? This chapter reviews several common patterns, both recent and in the past, associated with the adoption of new media products and services and suggests ways in which these patterns can inform the development and introduction of new media. In assessing patterns of development, the chapter examines price trends, rate of adoption, categories of early and later adopters, the attainment of critical mass, applications that drive adoption, replacement cycles, failures, cyclical technologies, and lifestyle issues, among other topics. Contrary to popular wisdom that the present new media environment differs completely from that of the past, many parallels exist in the adoption processes for the telephone and advanced mobile phones, for TV and HDTV, for VCRs and DVRs, and for dial-up and broadband Web access.

Everett Rogers and the Diffusion of Innovations

The late Everett Rogers is a seminal figure in the study of how individuals and organizations adopt innovations, and his theory provides a foundation for this chapter. His work is broad in scope, covering farming, health campaigns, and changes in the workplace as well as consumer adoption of new media technologies.[1] He made several key contributions to our understanding of the diffusion of innovations in general and of the adoption of media in particular that are relevant here. Rogers has pointed out that the diffusion of an innovation is a process that takes place over time; it involves people who learn about the innovation in different ways and who operate in a social context into which the new technology or way of doing things may or may not fit easily. He raises a series of questions that are useful in assessing what barriers must be overcome for an innovation to be accepted and at what rate it will diffuse if they are overcome. For example, how much complexity is involved—do people understand what a new technology does, and must they learn or be trained how to use it? Is the new technology or the new way of doing things compatible with the existing values, past experiences, and needs of prospective adopters, or does it require them to make significant changes in their values or behavior? Is the adoption a matter for individuals or for organizations? In the latter case, many bureaucratic and political processes may enter into the process. For example, schools have hierarchies of decision makers, budget cycles, and even union rules that may affect the adoption of a new computer network.

Rogers has also pointed out that exposure to information about a new technology or other innovation can be direct or indirect. People can learn about it from mass media, such as advertising, or by word of mouth. Both generally are present, but advertising is typically a stronger force early in the rollout of a new technology, when few people own it, and word of mouth typically becomes stronger later, when more people are likely to own it. Further, some products generate a lot of word of mouth, positive (e.g., the iPod) or negative (e.g., early DSL service), while other products sneak under the radar, thereby affecting the relative impact of advertising and word of mouth.

A concept to which Rogers ascribes particular importance, especially in the case of interactive technologies, is critical mass—when adoption reaches this level, additional promotion becomes unnecessary because diffusion is propelled by the innovation's own social momentum. Many variations on this concept have emerged in the academic and popular business literature—for example, takeoff point, tipping point, and (a misnomer) inflection point.[2] Attaining critical mass is clearly a major goal of those who introduce a new technology.

Rogers has emphasized the importance of examining the entire adoption process and all groups of adopters, not just those who are the first to use a technology. Early users and later users often differ substantially, but how many categories of adopters are necessary to capture a complete picture? Figure 1.1 presents his model of adopters at different stages in the process. Drawing on a number of studies, he makes some generalizations about each group. It must be borne in mind that these are generalizations, and the type as well as the

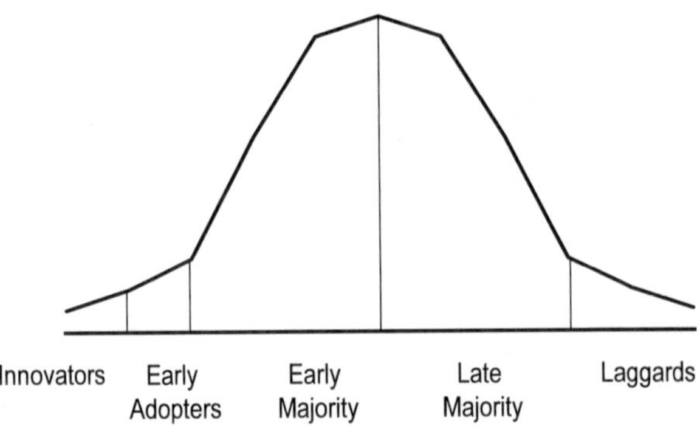

Fig. 1.1. Rogers's categorization of adopters. (Data from Everett Rogers, *Diffusion of Innovations,* 4th ed. [New York: Free Press, 1995].)

number of groupings can vary depending on the technology, the social or organizational context, and the time frame.

In Rogers's framework, Innovators often are willing to take risks and accept uncertainty. As individuals, they tend to have higher incomes, communicate with other innovators, and act as gatekeepers for those who will adopt later but who are not part of the innovator group. Early Adopters are respected opinion leaders who advise others in their peer and near-peer network of contacts. They are not as daring as Innovators but are willing to try new products before they are widely accepted. The Early Majority is a large group whose members are deliberative, not likely to be opinion leaders, and often, after waiting a while, follow the advice of early adopters. The members of the Late Majority are generally skeptical and cautious and require that the uncertainties associated with new technologies or other innovations are substantially reduced before adopting them. Frequently, they wait until sufficiently motivated to adopt for economic reasons or as a result of pressure from peers. Laggards have traditional values and are reluctant to change. They have limited resources, are often isolated from social networks, and take a long time to come to decisions.

Rogers emphasizes that a term such as *Laggards* is not intended to be pejorative. In fact, he argues that insufficient research has examined why people fail to adopt innovations and that there has been a bias in much of the research implying that adoption is inherently the wiser course of action.

We turn now to a series of factors that complement and build on Rogers's model of the diffusion of innovation, focusing on new media adoption patterns.

Price Trends

Media Products

The price of consumer electronic products has played an important role in their rate of adoption by the public and in determining the overall size of their market. Historically, new media technologies have been introduced at high prices, which drop over time, as shown in table 1.1. Early manufacturing of such a product is generally expensive, largely because it cannot realize the economies of scale that are possible in mass production, and demand is often unknown, which can lead companies to try to maximize revenue from the first group of purchasers, many of whom are willing to pay high prices to be among the first to get it. Alternatively, companies can subsidize the price to try to build a user base rapidly and gain the benefits of the network effect (see The Network Effect and the Chicken-and-Egg Problem below), where the value of a service such as mobile phones is increased as more people acquire and use the technology.

RAPID DECREASES IN COSTS

Production costs generally decline dramatically in the early years of a successful new technology for two reasons: the volume of production and the time since production started. The first is the well-known effect of economies of scale. Especially when the fixed costs of production are very high but the marginal costs are very low—as is the case, for example, with technologies reliant on purpose-developed chips—the average cost of a unit of the technology falls very dramatically as the volume of production rises. The other reason is the learning curve effect—the idea that accumulating experience makes possible substantial cumulative improvement in the efficiency of manufacturing processes in the early years of a new technology. Naturally, the rate of this improvement generally declines with time.

The price of successful consumer electronic technologies almost always drops sharply over time, spurring adoption by the mass public. Dozens of products have followed this pattern, including radios, black and white TVs, color TVs, VCRs, CD players and DVD players, as illustrated in Table 1.1. More recently, HDTVs and DVRs were introduced at high prices which were reduced sharply within a few years.

It is revealing to translate these actual price figures into a common element that spans time. Table 1.2 expresses the prices in terms of weekly household income—that is, for an average U.S. household, how many weeks of income were required to purchase the technology? (Data are not available for income prior to 1929.) Notice the similarity of costs to households in terms of weekly household income when radio, black and white TV, and color TV were entering half of U.S. households: 1.8 or 1.9 weeks of household income. Also, notice the very high cost of early black and white TVs, color TVs, and VCRs: approximately 6 weeks of household income. More recent technologies such as CD and DVD players were introduced at lower costs in terms of household income (1.8 and 0.8 weeks of household income, respectively) and declined to much lower costs (0.2 and 0.1 weeks of household income, respectively) at the point when they entered half of U.S. households.

Manufacturers of more recent technologies face greater pressure to introduce them at a lower price and then to drive the price down rapidly. This development is partly a consequence of the greater number of electronic products in the marketplace compared to the 1920s or 1950s, together with greater competition for the information and entertainment dollars of the household budget. CD and DVD players offered simple enhancements to competitive predecessors (audiocassettes and VCRs), which had been in the marketplace for some time and had already reduced their prices, thereby putting considerable price pressure on manufacturers of CD and DVD players.

Rapid decreases in the price of recent new media technologies also occur because of advances in the design and manufacturing of chip sets, which lie at the heart of these new technologies. Chips are more reliable than the tubes and transistors that were at the heart of earlier generations of radios and TV sets and in high volume are, on average, much cheaper to manufacture. Further, chip sets can be redesigned multiple times after a product is introduced, reducing their cost, size, weight, and heat emission and thereby enabling the product's cost to be brought down more rapidly than was possible with earlier electronic products.

The same pattern has occurred with many telecommunication devices—for example, fax machines, which declined in price dramatically between the early 1980s and late 1990s. During the 1980s and early 1990s, fax machines were

TABLE 1.1. Average Price of Selected Electronic Products (in the United States, current dollars)

Year[a]	Radio Set	B&W TV	Color TV	VCR	CD	DVD
1925	83					
1930	78					
1935	55					
1940	38					
1945	40					
1947		279				
1950		190				
1955		138	500			
1960		132	392			
1965			356			
1970			317			
1975			341	1,140		
1980				1122		
1983				572	733	
1985				494	310	
1989				382	218	
1993					180	
1997						760
1999						360
2001						210
2003						145

Source: Christopher Sterling and Timothy Haight, *The Mass Media: Aspen Institute Guide to Communication Industry Trends* (New York: Praeger Publishers, 1978); John Carey, "The First 100 Feet for Households: Consumer Adoption Patterns," in Deborah Hurley and James Keller (eds.), *The First 100 Feet* (Cambridge, MA: MIT Press, 1978), 39–58; Electronic Industries Association, *Electronic Market Data Book* (Washington, DC, multiple years).

[a]Variable intervals between successive rows.

predominantly a technology for business. They began to enter some homes in the 1990s, although they still served mainly business. Early fax machines had to overcome not only a price barrier but also slow transmission speeds and the lack of a single standard, which meant that a given fax machine could communicate only with another fax machine that employed the same standard. Only after a single standard (the Group 3 standard) was adopted in 1983 did fax machines become interoperable. This development also helped to lower their costs through greater economies of scale in manufacturing and made them much more useful to businesses and consumers. By the 1990s, it was cheaper in most cases to send a fax than to send a single-page letter through the postal service. Fax machines became so widely accepted that most businesspeople put their fax numbers on their business cards.[3]

Personal computers (PCs) have followed a different price trajectory. Rather than reduce their price, the industry for a long time increased their capabilities each year. This approach was an appropriate response to the early market for PCs, represented by office workers and working professionals who used

TABLE 1.2. Average Price of Selected Electronic Products in Weekly Household Income (in the United States)

Year[a]	Radio Set	B&W TV	Color TV	VCR	CD	DVD
1929	1.8[b]					
1930						
1935						
1940						
1945						
1947		5.3				
1950		3.3				
1955		1.8[b]	6.6			
1960			4.1			
1965			3.1			
1970			1.9[b]			
1975				6.2		
1980				3.3		
1983				1.4	1.8	
1985				1.1[b]	0.7	
1989					0.4	
1993					0.2[b]	
1997						0.8
1999						0.3
2001						0.2
2003						0.1[b]

[a]Variable intervals between successive focus.
[b]Point by which the technology had entered half of U.S. households.

FAX MACHINES VERSUS E-MAIL

For the transmission of text, fax machines more than held their own against emerging e-mail service for much longer than many experts expected. Faxes remained popular despite the fact that use of e-mail is far more efficient than use of fax machines for this purpose; many more bits must be transmitted when alphanumeric characters are treated as images than when they are treated as symbols. Indeed, some champions of the digital age complained that the miserable analog fax machine was holding back progress: in the words of one member of the digerati, "The fax machine was a serious blemish on the information landscape, a step backward, whose ramifications will be felt for a long time."[1]

Why did fax machines remain resilient for so long? While the time society needed to adjust to the absence of personal signatures may have been one factor, two others were almost certainly much more important: (1) the incompatibility of many e-mail systems which could not be interconnected at the time (which was not fully overcome until the Internet came into widespread use) and (2) the simplistic meaning given to efficiency. It was a serious mistake to see this situation solely in engineering terms. From the standpoint of most users, it was more significant that, in sharp contrast to the e-mail systems of those days, fax machines were extremely easy to use—a temporary office worker could learn to use a previously unfamiliar fax machine in only a few minutes, if that; and even a boss could do so relatively quickly. (Many of today's office fax machines make much greater use of "intelligence" than did their predecessors, meaning that it now takes much longer to learn to use them. So, in the end, the digerati have had their revenge!) Both interconnection and ease of use have arisen time and again as crucial factors in the success—or lack thereof—of new media services.

1. Nicholas Negroponte, *Being Digital* (New York: Alfred Knopf, 1995), 186.

them at home. Consumers received the benefits of technological advances and economies of scale in the form of improved performance rather than as a decline in price. In the early and mid-1980s, some companies (for example, Acorn in the United Kingdom and Atari and Commodore in the United States) offered low-end computers to try to reach households but they met with limited success. In late 1997, personal computers had not yet entered half of U.S. households, and some research indicated that the penetration of PCs into households was hitting a wall of resistance.[4] This barrier appeared to be related to price. Responding to this perception, the industry began to offer low-end computers at lower prices for mass market adoption in homes and schools. As a result, the average price dipped below $1,000, a new group of users adopted personal computers, and the PC surpassed the 50 percent penetration mark in homes. The lower price also helped to bring many more computers into schools.

Media Services

The price of media services often drops over time, but the pattern is not as strong as in the case of media products. Telephone service provides a good example. The adoption of telephone service in households was linked to reductions in the cost of both basic service and long distance calls. In 1896, the fee for basic telephone service in New York City was $20 per month; in 1902, the cost of a three-minute call between New York and Chicago was more than $5—a week's wages for some households.[5] In 2005, the cost of basic telephone service in New York was approximately the same—$20—and the cost of a three-minute call between New York and Chicago had dropped to 30 cents under a typical calling plan (see figure 1.2).

Table 1.3 provides examples of some media services where the price dropped over time and others where it did not. The key variable distinguishing between the two groups is content. Where there is no content or the service provider does not have to pay for content (as when users create it), the cost of the service has fallen. When the service provides and pays for content, the costs of talent

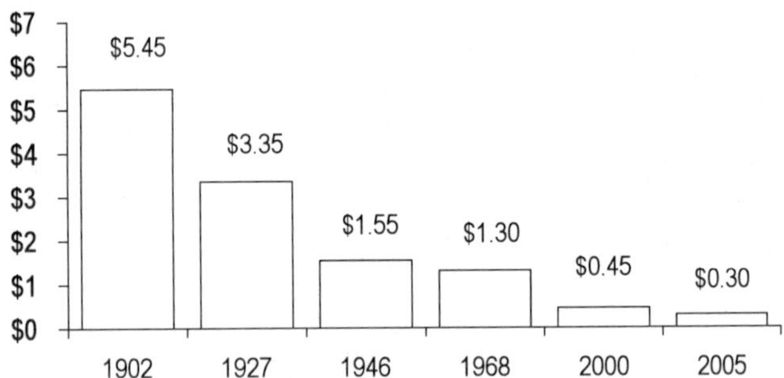

Fig. 1.2. Pricing of telephone service, three-minute call, New York to Chicago, in current dollars. (Data from *Historical Statistics of the United States* [Washington, DC: Bureau of the Census, 1975], 784; and AT&T rate cards, multiple years.)

TABLE 1.3. Services Where the Price Dropped or Did Not Drop over Time

Price Dropped over Time	Price Did Not Drop over Time
Long distance telephone	Cable TV
Dial-up online	Satellite TV
Broadband DSL	Satellite radio
Mobile phone service	Video-on-demand
DVR service	

and production increase over time. Further, competition and demands from end users often require that the supplier expand service offerings, which leads to greater costs. For example, while the price of cable TV increased over time, so did the number of channels offered. Many other factors, such as regulations, can intervene and affect the price of a service.

A new technology or service must attract initial users who are able and willing to pay a relatively high price for it to move toward the economies of scale in manufacturing that will reduce the price for the general public. (Most new services have required the manufacture of new technology components.) Who purchases new products and services when they are expensive? The answer varies somewhat by product, but the initial group of consumer purchasers is often wealthy, has an insatiable desire for the product, or loves electronic gadgets and is willing to pay a high price to be one of the first to own "the latest." In addition to individual consumers, many of the purchasers are businesses or schools that need the product. The adoption of new media technology first by businesses and later by consumers is illustrated in the case of mobile phones (see chapter 10).

The S-Curve

The cumulative purchases of a new technology over time typically take the form of an S-curve—a curve that rises slowly at first, then much faster after reaching some threshold, and finally slows down as a saturation level is approached. The elements required to reach the threshold are not the same for all technologies, and the timetable for reaching the threshold can vary from a few years to many decades. Indeed, the crucial question associated with these S-curves is the time required to move from the launch of a new technology to the threshold point

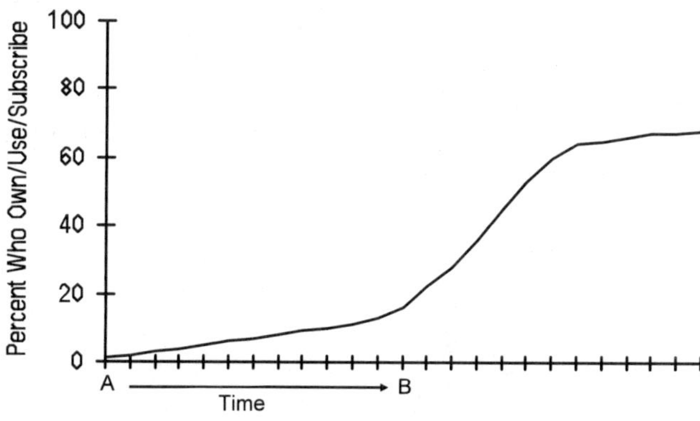

Fig. 1.3. S-curve pattern of adoption

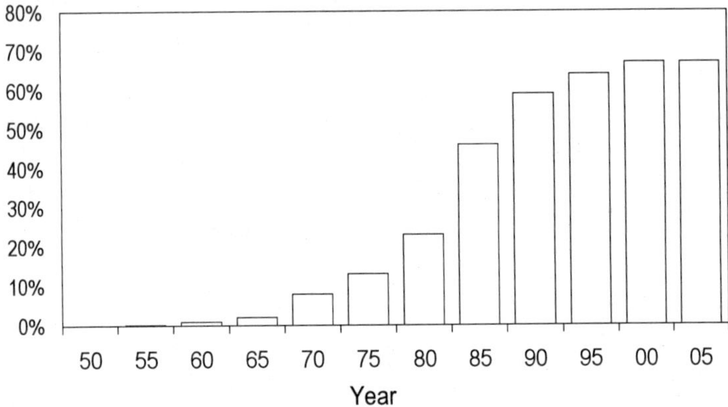

Fig. 1.4. Percentage of TV households subscribing to cable, 1950–2005. (Data from Christopher Sterling and Timothy Haight, *The Mass Media: Aspen institute Guide to Communication Industry Trends* [New York: Praeger Publishers, 1978]; and U.S. Census Bureau, *Statistical Abstract of the United States* [Washington, DC: U.S. Department of Commerce, multiple years].)

where rapid growth begins (from point A to point B in figure 1.3). The many technologies that do not succeed in the marketplace simply fail to gain any acceptance or never reach the point at which rapid growth occurs.

Of course, the ceiling at which the S-curve levels off does not necessarily represent all households. While TV, radio, and telephones reached nearly all U.S. households at their peaks (98, 99, and 95 percent, respectively), cable TV appears to have reached the top of its S-curve with approximately two-thirds of U.S. households (figure 1.4). The penetration of personal computers may fall well short of all households, though computing technology will likely enter all households in the form of appliances that have microprocessors. It is too soon to know where DVRs, MP-3 players, and satellite radio will top out.

Many successful products and services are characterized by curves showing their adoption rates—e.g., annual adoption—that take the familiar bell-shaped form suggested by figure 1.1. However, curves showing the annual adoption rates of others—in particular, those discussed later in this volume that are failures or fads or that have cyclical patterns of adoption—may be very different, even though the curves showing their diffusion (i.e., cumulative adoption) will typically be broadly S-shaped.

Start-Up Issues

What is involved in getting to critical mass—that is, the takeoff point on the S-curve? Here a distinction must be made between interactive technologies

THE NETWORK EFFECT AND THE CHICKEN-AND-EGG PROBLEM

The network effect refers to the fact that the more people who are on a network, the more valuable the network is to all of them, for the simple reason that there is then a greater number of others with whom any of them can communicate. An associated and important start-up problem is whether a rational incentive to connect to a network exists when it first becomes available. In part, the answer is that decisions to join may not be independent decisions by the individual users concerned: in the early days of e-mail, much of the use occurred on relatively small intraorganizational networks that were set up by a single central decision. Another example would be when a family buys a pair of picture telephones because grandparents want to communicate with grandchildren far away.

Networked services generally do not require professionally created content, unlike, for example, broadcast television and DVDs. Those services that need third-party professional content often have a somewhat comparable start-up problem: why should the third parties risk creating content until there are enough owners of the associated technology, but why should people buy the technology until enough content exists?

In the case of VCRs and DVDs, the greater the number of people who have players (operating to the same standard), the more attractive it is for third parties to provide content. So even though no telecommunication networks are involved, the value of ownership of a player increases with the total number of players in use; the same holds true for fax machines. Economists refer to this, too, as a network effect—more specifically, an *indirect network effect.*

The stronger the perception that a new service will succeed—by prospective purchasers in the first case, by prospective creators of content in the second—the more likely it is that people will make decisions that will give the service a better chance to succeed. This is a major inducement to hype. Hal R. Varian, Joseph Farrell, and Carl Shapiro note that when two standards competed for the 56 kbps modem market in the United States, each of the producers advertised that it had an 80 percent market share.[1] But many other factors also lead to hype (see chapter 2).

1. Hal R. Varian, Joseph Farrell, and Carl Shapiro, *The Economics of Information Technology: An Introduction* (New York: Cambridge University Press, 2004), 39.

(e.g., telephones, e-mail, and text messaging) that link people together and technologies that are used by people individually (e.g., an iPod or a satellite radio). In the case of products that stand alone, critical mass can be achieved when enough users talk about a product in a positive way, people see others using it in many settings, newspapers and TV proclaim it to be a hit, and so on, with the result that many nonusers want to acquire it. In the case of communication technologies that link people together, the core value of the product is associated with how many people are already using it. For example, a telephone has less value when only a small number of people have it as compared with when millions have it. This is called the network effect.

Some innovations achieve critical mass more easily than others. We consider three cases: when the innovation is an enhancement of an existing service, when it can piggyback on replacement cycles, and a third category which we call "charmed lives."

How New Is New?

A difference exists between enhancing existing technologies and developing entirely new services. Introducing qualitative enhancements to existing technologies often provides a good path for the development of new media technologies. Consumers have responded positively to enhancements such as adding color to black and white television, higher fidelity for recordings, stereo sound for television, touch-tone telephones for rotary dial telephones, and broadband Internet access as a replacement for dial-up service. From a supply-side perspective, consumers were adopting new technologies and services. From a demand-side perspective, they were simply upgrading to a better version of a familiar and desirable technology or service.

Sometimes the introduction of new services does not mean that users need to acquire new technology. This was the case with telephone-based voice services (sometimes called audiotex), used, for example, to check a bank balance through an automated voice system, and more recently with streaming audio and video on the Web. Often, however, new services as well as enhancements require new user technology. Table 1.4 illustrates four different possibilities.

TABLE 1.4. New/Existing Technologies for New/Enhanced Applications

Application or Experience	Technology in Home or Office	
	Already in Place	New
Enhanced	Software update	Color TV Touch-tone telephone
New	Automated voice services Streaming audio/video on Web	Videotex[a] Interactive TV Prerecorded videocassettes

[a]Videotex is a generic term for online services before the Web.

The combination of new services with new user technologies is the most problematic of the four cells in the table. High cost and uncertainty occur when, as is often the case, new content must be created (for example, for early online services and interactive television) or even when existing content must be bought from outside sources or distributed in new ways, as in the case of prerecorded videocassette movies, which, while successful, required several years to achieve significant usage.

Then there are the uncertainties surrounding whether the new technology will work well enough and whether consumers will pay for it. There are also issues associated with the necessity of consumers changing how they use media. For example, a person watching HDTV uses the content in the same way as someone watching standard-definition television even though there is a qualitative difference in their experiences. However, a teenager acquiring a video game console for the first time in 1985 or an adult using the Web for the first time in 2000 needed to learn and employ new behaviors. These changes were all the more significant because they required that users alter existing media habits. Such change often requires time. Indeed, both the growth in hours per week spent on the Web and the rise in time spent on video games have spanned a considerable number of years.

Piggybacking on Replacement Cycles

Sometimes, the adoption of one technology is linked to the purchase of another. For example, while few people in the 1980s bought a TV set or a VCR just to obtain a remote control device or stereo sound, many consumers chose these features as options when they purchased new VCRs or replaced old TV sets. Thus, replacement cycles for existing technologies may provide an important opportunity to introduce new technologies. In U.S. households, color TVs are replaced after an average of eight years, personal computers are replaced after two years, and mobile phones last a little more than one year before owners seek new models (or replace lost or broken ones). In the case of both mobile phones and PCs, the replacement cycle has shortened considerably over just the past few years to the levels shown in table 1.5. This more rapid rate of replacement has provided an opportunity for providers of new hardware and services to introduce their technologies more quickly. This is a conservative model of adoption in which new technologies piggyback on replacement cycles. It provides one way in which Rogers's Late Majority and Laggards acquire new electronic technologies.

In the mid-1970s, a variation of this process was associated with a cultural quirk in the United Kingdom in the years following the launch of teletext there (see chapter 7). At the time, the majority of consumers still rented their TV sets

TABLE 1.5. Replacement Cycles for Electronic Products

Product	Average Life (years)
Cordless telephone	8
Color TV	8
CD player	6
Telephone answering machine	6
VCR	5
Camcorder	5
Fax	4
Personal computer	2
Mobile phones	1

Source: Appliance, September issue, multiple years.

from local stores. Upgrading the sets occurred relatively frequently since it required little if any effort or outlay by users. This provided a highly favorable context for the rapid diffusion of teletext in the U.K. market.

New models of an existing technology are purchased for at least four reasons: to replace an existing model that no longer works; to obtain an additional unit of the technology; to upgrade an existing model that works but does not have a desired feature or is of lower quality than the upgrade model; or as a by-product of another purchase. Upgrade purchases have been very important to products for which the pace of technological change has been rapid. For example, in the late 1980s, very few personal computers had modems, the technology necessary to link the computer to the telephone network, primarily for use of online services. While people who wanted to go online could purchase stand-alone modems that connected computers to telephone jacks, relatively few did so. In the late 1980s, the industry began building modems into most computers. Then, with people's purchases of new or replacement computers, the number of computer-owning households that had modems grew from less than 10 percent of the total in 1988 to more than 60 percent in early 1997. This was one of the vital elements that made it possible for people to use the Web. The building of modems into nearly all computers by 1995 helped this key peripheral device to cycle through the population of PC owners. CD drives and DVD drives were later introduced into households in the same way.

Charmed Lives

On some occasions, a new service or technology seems to have come from nowhere and to have enjoyed an effortless ride to spectacular success, to the amazement even of those introducing it—and of independent analysts. The original Sony Walkman was one such product. Mobile phones have provided the platform for more recent examples: mobile phones incorporating still cameras, text messaging (SMS), and applications (Apps) such as maps or games. Far from being user-friendly, the user interface of early mobile phones for creating text was positively user-hostile, and before SMS took hold, it seemed bizarre to believe that people would find uses for it that would justify the effort involved. But they certainly did—billions of text messages are sent each month. It would be a serious mistake to regard these surprise successes as no more than lucky flukes. The phenomenon has important implications for large corporations that introduce new products or services as well as for makers of public policy (see chapter 3).

There is a variation of "charmed lives" in the dynamic relationship between a dazzling but initially disappointing new service and a humdrum but commercially successful counterpart—for example, the Prestel videotex service (dazzler that disappointed) and teletext (humdrum success) in the United Kingdom (see chapter 7). Does the publicity surrounding the dazzler help promote its lesser counterpart? Very probably. Does the Cinderella service spoil the market for the dazzler? Over the years we have certainly come across bitter remarks to this effect from marketing executives who were failing to make sufficient progress with one of the former. Does the Cinderella service help prepare the market for the successful entry of the more powerful version at a later time? Possibly, but it is unlikely that the technology of the more powerful version will stand still in the interim.

Rate of Adoption

Although it is common knowledge that, over recent decades, the pace at which consumers take up new technologies has been accelerating, it is worth quantifying the phenomenon by examining how many years it took different media to reach the point at which the median household decided that they were affordable—that is, to reach levels of penetration of 50 percent of U.S. households. Newspapers were introduced in the precolonial America, and more than 100 years passed before half of U.S. households read them regularly—in the 1890s. The slow growth resulted from high costs of production and distribution as well as low literacy rates among the American population. Telephones were introduced in the late 1870s and did not enter half of U.S. households until 1946. High early costs of telephone service (figure 1.2) were a major factor in the slow adoption.

Radio achieved a 50 percent penetration of U.S. homes in 1929, nine years after becoming widely available. Black and white TV achieved a 50 percent penetration in 1955, eight years after it became readily available to the public.[6] Color television reached this level of penetration in 1972 after seventeen years. VCRs achieved a 50 percent penetration at the end of 1987, and CD players did so at the end of 1993, each ten years after becoming widely available. DVD players grew at a rate faster than any other new media technology, entering half of U.S. households in 2003, just six years after entering the marketplace (table 1.6).

Why did the market penetration of DVDs increase so rapidly? From a pricing perspective, manufacturers introduced the technology at a lower price point, in terms of weekly household income, than many other technologies and were able to bring the price down very rapidly. DVDs also entered a marketplace where VCRs had already established a strong demand for movie rentals and sales. They offered better quality than videocassettes but could not record. Why didn't this limitation reduce interest in them? At the time when DVDs were introduced, most households did not use the recording function of VCRs (only one in five households with VCRs did any recording), so the lack of a recording feature was not a major obstacle. Further, the movie studios saw DVDs as a major source of income (they quickly surpassed movie theaters) and released thousands of movies on DVDs in just a few years. From a consumer perspective, in addition to providing better picture quality, DVDs took up less space than videocassettes; lasted longer (at least in theory; in practice, durability depends on how people handle and store them); had extra features, such as outtakes; quickly became affordable; and soon had a large inventory of movies. All of these factors came together to make U.S. homes quickly adopt DVDs.

TABLE 1.6. Number of Years to Reach a 50 Percent Penetration of U.S. Households

Technology/Medium	Years
Newspapers	100+
Telephone	70
Phonograph	55
Cable TV	39
Personal computer	17
Color TV	17
VCR	10
CD player	10
Radio	9
Black & white TV	8
DVD player	6

Source: Christopher Stelling and Timothy Haight, *The Mass Media: Aspen Institute Guide to Communication Industry Trends* (New York: Praeger Publishers, 1978); U.S. Census Bureau, *Statistical Abstract of the United States* (Washington, DC: U.S. Department of Commerce, multiple years).

In entering the market at high prices that drop over time, DVD players and DVRs have followed the same pattern as earlier technologies. However, a compression factor appears to be developing in which the introductory price is not as high relative to earlier technologies and the price drops more rapidly and to a lower level than with earlier technologies. This trend appears to hold for recently introduced new media technologies more generally, though some exceptions, such as HDTV, exist.

False Starts

Some successful new services or technologies suffered from false starts or languished for a long time on the initial, low-growth part of the S-curve. For example, television was launched as a commercial service in the late 1930s, but the high price of TV sets ($600) and the disruption caused by World War II led to a suspension of most service. The technology was reintroduced after the war and grew rapidly. Similarly, two home video recording technologies were launched and then withdrawn in the early 1970s (CBS's EVR system and Avco's Cartrivision system) before the modern VCR finally took hold in the mid-1970s. Fax technology wins the prize for false starts. It was invented in the 1840s and tested in the 1860s, with no significant adoption; reintroduced unsuccessfully in the 1930s and the 1950s; then achieved widespread adoption in the business market during the 1980s; and finally entered a moderate numbers of households in the 1990s.[7]

The Advantages and Pitfalls of Being First

There has been a long-running debate about the advantages and disadvantages associated with early entry into the media marketplace. Brian Arthur makes the case for early entry.[8] He starts by noting that economists generally view competition in terms of equilibrium. For example, a hydroelectric power company that gains an advantage in the marketplace will eventually run out of good locations to build new plants, thereby providing an opportunity for power companies using other sources of energy to compete effectively and thus restore equilibrium. He then argues that this classic economic model does not adequately explain what happens with new media technologies. Here, small competitive advantages gained early often escalate over time and lead to market dominance. Arthur describes this process in terms of positive feedback, citing many examples. From this perspective, a technology with a small marketplace advantage may benefit from positive market feedback that strengthens the advantage and generates more positive feedback, with the process continuing until market leadership is established. For example, when VHS and Beta formats were competing for the videocassette market, VHS had a longer recording capability and developed better marketing agreements with electronics manufacturers and movie distributors. These advantages, in turn, attracted more retailers to market VHS. With this positive feedback, VHS's small advantage grew larger and larger over time, and Beta was essentially eliminated from the consumer marketplace even though many observers argued that it was technically superior.

A technology's small early advantage over its competition may arise from chance, a favorable geographic location, or a seemingly inconsequential event, such as favorable coverage in a magazine story. The importance of lucky breaks has been overlooked by many who have studied the adoption of media, in part, quite possibly, because the involvement of luck suggests that the process of adoption cannot be fully analyzed in advance and that the growth rate for a new service cannot be forecast. However, there are many examples of chance playing a crucial role in the adoption process, from the mom-and-pop videocassette rental shops that emerged spontaneously during the development of the VCR marketplace to the development of cybercafés that brought Internet service to millions of people worldwide who might not otherwise have experienced it.

Arthur's model of positive economic feedback can be used to support the case for early market entry as a means of generating positive feedback. Indeed, many instances of early market entry have escalated into market dominance. AM radio preceded FM into the marketplace and dominated radio for fifty years; HBO was the first to develop a national pay-cable service and quickly dominated the market; and the three broadcast networks that entered television in the late 1940s achieved a lock on the market that was not challenged for 30 years.

However, for each example of early entry that led to marketplace dominance, there is an example of early entry that led to failure or weak market performance. Among other examples, a 45-RPM automobile record player developed in the 1950s (the "Highway HiFi") failed to achieve any significant market; two-way video trials and services in the 1970s for business meetings and medical applications were largely unsuccessful; and a broadcast pay-TV service developed by Zenith in the 1950s failed. Yet each of these cases was followed by technologies and services for somewhat similar purposes that succeeded. There are many reasons why early market entrants fail. In some cases, the technology simply does not work properly: for example, the 45-RPM automobile record player skipped whenever the car hit a bump. In other cases, the costs associated with marketing and launching a service overwhelm an early entrant: several groups that planned to launch direct broadcast satellite services in the early 1980s abandoned their plans as they faced the huge costs associated with launching the services. In still other cases, an inhospitable regulatory climate can cripple an early entrant, or consumers' lack of skill in using the new technology can lead to failure. Those who enter a market later may find that their technology works better, costs are lower, consumers have improved their skills in using the technology, the regulatory climate is more hospitable, and so on.

A historical review of new media technologies suggests that early entry is an advantage in some cases and a disadvantage in others. It is an advantage when all the pieces are in place (or soon will be) to launch the technology successfully. It is a disadvantage when the technology suffers from one or more serious weaknesses. XM Satellite Radio is an example of the former, a new service that grew rapidly even though it was missing a number of vital pieces during its prelaunch planning phase. For example, satellite radio sets did not exist, and the company had no agreements with automobile manufacturers to place receivers in cars. However, the company put these pieces into place before or shortly after the actual launch of the service (see chapter 9).

How Applications Can Change over Time

Another example of the valuable concepts that Rogers introduced is reinvention, which he defined as "the degree to which an innovation is changed or modified by a user in the process of its adoption and implementation."[9] Reinvention occurs far more frequently than is generally acknowledged. Mobile phones are a good example. When first introduced, they were intended for dispatching police and emergency calls. Later, usage evolved into general business calls and then to social chitchat by consumers. In the case of new media, modifications to an innovation can be introduced by the industry concerned as well as by users. In this sense, we would expand the definition of reinvention to include industry modification. The various combinations include new purposes (maybe associated with new types of user) but unchanged technology, new technology but unchanged purposes, and new purposes together with new technology. This definition can cause confusion: since the associated changes may be gradual rather than abrupt, it is not always clear whether and when a new product or service should be regarded as having become a different entity. For example, is a new model of a personal computer with an upgraded central processor a new product? In some cases, the upgrades are minor; in other cases, the new CPU adds significant capacity, such as the ability to use the PC for watching and editing video or playing fast-action games.

In addition to the time-based distinctions that Rogers introduced between adopters (Innovators and so on), another type of time-based difference is associated with reinvention. There is a broad generalization that applies to many new technologies: the *early uses* as well as the *early users* for a new product or service often differ substantially from the *later uses* and *later users*. This difference may be explained with a staircase analogy.

A Staircase Analogy

For a technology to be adopted, several steps must be climbed. The first step represents one group of users and uses, but the group or mix of groups at the second and third steps may change. It follows that there must be a first step if a technology is to reach the second step. Ideally, those who are introducing a technology will anticipate the mix of users and uses at each step. Since doing so is very difficult, however, they must be prepared to shift strategies as they climb each new step. VCRs illustrate this process. When VCRs were first introduced in the United States, they were quite expensive—approximately $1,200. Early users included businesses and schools that had been using 3/4 inch U-Matic recorders, costing $2,000 or more, for training and education. For them, a $1,200 VCR was a cheaper alternative. The early adopters also included some high-income households, especially those with an interest in the latest electronic gadgets. Household usage included time-shift viewing of television programs and a considerable amount of pornography; a majority of videocassettes sold and rented in the late 1970s featured pornography.[10] Pornography or risqué content also played a part in the early adoption of books, films, 900 pay-telephone services (often called premium telephone services outside the United States), and various other media.[11]

Businesses, schools, people who were willing to pay a high price for time-shift viewing of programs, and those who wanted to see pornography comprised the first step of users and uses. They made it possible for a second step of adoption to occur, at a lower price and with a different mix of users (more middle-income households) and uses (more videocassette rentals of Hollywood movies and later sales). This example suggests that some services might appeal to a mass market at the second or third step in the adoption process but never have the opportunity to test the mass market because no group is prepared to pay the higher price at the first step or because of some other early barrier. Teletext in the United States is an example. When tested in a number of markets during the early and mid-1980s, teletext generated positive consumer reactions, but few were willing to spend more than $150 for a teletext decoder attached to or built into a TV set. However, service providers and television set manufacturers were not able to agree on a standard, and the Federal Communications Commission (FCC) declined to set one. In the absence of a single standard, early teletext receivers cost approximately $700. At that price, there was no user group or application that could be used to climb the first step in the adoption process and bring the price down for a mass market.

In the case of VCRs, some important unanticipated events also occurred. One was the emergence of local shops set up by individuals who purchased copies of videocassette movies and then rented them to the public. (Blockbuster and other large chains later replaced many of these small shops.) The major movie distributors tried to prevent these mom-and-pop rental shops from doing business independently, suing to stop them but losing in court under the "first sale doctrine," which held that a store could buy a copy of a movie on videocassette and rent it to consumers. Ironically, this defeat led to tens of billions of dollars in revenue for those major distributors.

These shops were critical for the second and third steps of VCR adoption to occur, suggesting that the growth of a technology is often a fragile, changing process. Early use can differ from later use, and the elements that are critical to success at various steps along the way can come from unplanned and unanticipated sources.

Killer Applications or a Confluence of Factors?

The staircase analogy does not preclude the possibility that a "killer application" can get a new media technology beyond the first and second steps to mass market acceptance. But how often does it happen? Those who develop and market new media technologies often herald killer applications and magic bullets that will lead to a decisive home run for a new technology or service. Indeed, some very popular applications helped technologies to gain quick acceptance in millions of American homes. For example, a few very popular radio programs drove the sale of radio sets, and a few early video games drove the adoption of video game consoles. Within the business community, spreadsheet programs played a similar role in the early days of personal computers.

More commonly, however, a confluence of several factors is required for a new media technology to take off and gain widespread acceptance. This confluence may take only a few years, but a technology sometimes has rested on the first step for decades. DVDs and black and white TV (when reintroduced after World War II) provide examples of the former—they grew very rapidly after their introduction. Cable television and FM radio provide examples of the latter—they were in the marketplace for many years before they experienced a period of rapid growth.

Cable television was introduced in Oregon and Pennsylvania during 1948. From 1948 to 1972, cable television grew from no penetration of U.S. households to 10 percent penetration.[12] In other words, it required more than 20 years to achieve a 10 percent penetration level. From 1972 to 2005, cable grew from 10 percent penetration to more than 65 percent penetration (figure 1.4). Why did penetration jump so rapidly in the 1970s and 1980s? The cause was not a single factor or killer application.

In the 1950s and 1960s, cable TV represented a way to improve reception of over-the-air broadcast signals in communities that could not otherwise watch television or could not get a good signal. Generally, these were small rural towns and some suburban areas 50 or more miles from a broadcast transmitter. Cable offered very few extra channels or services, so it had little appeal in areas where the over-the-air reception was good. Indeed, one of the most common cable-originated channels during this early period was a channel that showed a clock 24 hours a day. While practical, such "programming" was not likely to attract new subscribers. In the 1970s, a confluence of several new elements acted as a starter motor for a powerful growth engine to kick in. For the first time, it appeared that cable could be profitable in large cities; at the same time, the FCC lifted a freeze on franchise awards in major markets. As a result, major media companies competed fiercely to win franchises in Boston, Cincinnati, Pittsburgh, Dallas, San Diego, and elsewhere and built large cable systems where none existed previously. In addition, satellite transmission made national cable program distribution easier and less costly, which gave rise to the launch of many basic channels, such as superstation WTBS, and significantly improved the distribution of the pay-movie channel HBO, which had previously mailed tapes of movies to cable outlets, a process called bicycling. Then, in the late 1970s, several popular new channels with specialized programming—for example, Nickelodeon and MTV—were developed as a result of a flurry of experimentation with program formats triggered by interest in interactive cable services.[13] This confluence of elements provided a powerful engine for growth.

Similarly, FM radio experienced slow growth for many years before a period of rapid expansion kicked in. It was introduced in the 1930s and widely available to the public in the 1940s. For 30 years, audience share grew very slowly, but in the 1970s, a dramatic growth in audience share began. Between 1973 and 1985, FM's share of the radio audience climbed from 28 percent to 72 percent. In other words, the FM/AM share of audience changed from approximately 30/70 to 70/30. Why did such a dramatic change occur over this period? The answer appears to be related not to any single element but (in the United States at least) to a confluence of elements that triggered a growth spurt.

A variety of barriers and potholes along the way had created problems in the start-up of FM broadcasting. In 1945, the FCC changed its spectrum allocation for FM, with the result that FM radios purchased before that date were useless and the industry essentially had to start the adoption process over again. During the 1940s and 1950s, most FM stations were co-owned by an AM station operator, which carried the same programming on both stations. In addition, FM receivers were expensive, and there were decidedly fewer FM stations than AM stations. In 1960, for example, there were four AM stations for every FM station. With relatively few stations on the air, little original programming, and expensive receivers, consumers were reluctant to adopt FM even though it was technically superior to AM. Nonetheless, FM gained a foothold thanks largely to classical music devotees who valued its superior sound quality.

Beginning in the late 1950s, a series of events helped FM gain strength in the marketplace. In 1958, AM frequency allocation reached a saturation level in major markets, thereby encouraging new groups that wanted to launch stations to apply for FM licenses in those markets. In 1961, FM stereo was launched, and in 1965 the FCC ruled that co-owners of AM and FM stations in the same market could not transmit the same content on both of them. Stereo provided a qualitative enhancement to FM, while the requirement to offer original programming led many FM stations to explore new formats. In addition, the price of FM receivers declined, and many manufacturers began to offer combined AM/FM receivers for both homes and cars. Many households then moved to acquire FM receivers. By 1970, the ratio of AM/FM stations was 3/2, and 74 percent of households had FM receivers. This confluence of elements placed FM in a strong position to challenge AM.

Disruptive Technologies

A dramatic example of the dynamics of changing uses and users is provided by what Clayton Christensen has termed a disruptive technology.[14] Sometimes a technology is introduced at substantially lower levels of price and performance than technologies already available in the market and creates a new market for itself among those who are particularly price conscious. Because of its low performance, it initially poses no threat to suppliers already in the market. However, with the positive feedback resulting from direct or indirect network effects, together with economies of scale, significant improvements in performance are progressively implemented without commensurate increases in price (as with personal computers). As it improves, the new technology attracts new types of users. At some point, it invades and takes an existing market away from its incumbents. Calculators were a disruptive technology for the makers of slide rules; other disruptive technologies have included low-cost photocopiers, ink-jet printers, and, in the corporate computing market, personal computers.

Natural Selection—when a Better Format Comes Along

Recorded music illustrates how adoption of new media can take place when a new format is introduced. Long-playing records (LPs) were the format of choice for a few decades. They were replaced by audiocassettes, which were replaced by CDs, which are being replaced by digital downloads. Figure 1.5 shows the transitions from one format to another.

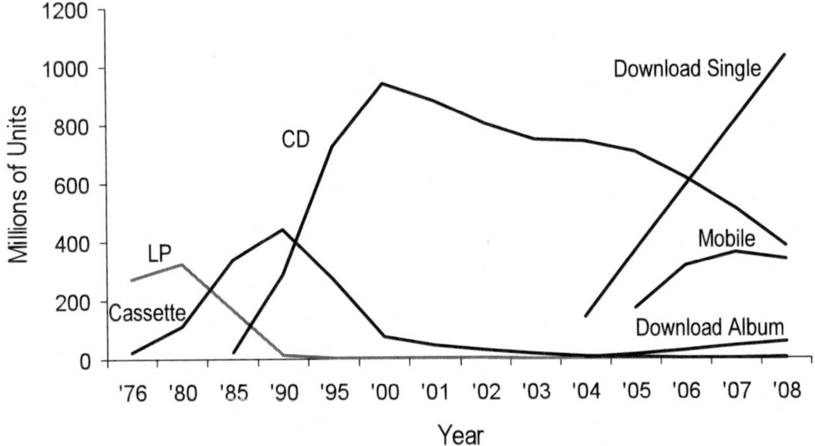

Fig. 1.5. Transitions as platforms change: Shipments of recorded media. (Data from Recording Industry Association of America, *Year-End Shipment Statistics* [Washington, DC, multiple years].)

CDs were challenged by the MP-3 format in the early 2000s. However, attempted transitions to a new format do not always succeed. In the 1960s, prerecorded music on reel-to-reel tape was technically superior to LPs but it was difficult to use (the tape could spill onto the floor if not handled carefully) and achieved little acceptance in the home market. Eight-track cartridges were introduced in the mid-1960s as a more user-friendly tape format. They were offered first for cars and later for homes. Eight-track cartridges competed for market share with LPs. They achieved modest success by the mid-1970s, but at that point, audiocassettes were growing in popularity, and they replaced both LPs and eight-track.

For a new format to be adopted, end users must perceive advantages (more capacity, better quality, valued extra features, and so forth) sufficient to overcome the hurdles of purchasing new hardware and accepting the eventual obsolescence of recordings in the older format. More recently, high-definition DVDs challenged standard-definition DVDs and faced the same obstacles.

Demographic Characteristics and Lifestyle Issues Associated with Adoption

Adoption of new media technologies is associated with age (generally, younger and middle-aged groups are more likely to adopt a new technology), income (those with higher incomes adopt technology sooner), education (those with more education adopt technology more readily), gender (while evidence is mixed and patterns may be changing, a greater proportion of males were early users of household personal computers, VCRs, and the Web), and in some cases, moving patterns (moving to another location appears to trigger a reevaluation of what technologies or services are desirable). In a large metastudy of computer adoption research, William Dutton and his colleagues have argued convincingly that among all the demographic factors positively associated with adoption, income is the most important.[15]

One of the barriers to mass adoption of many new media technologies is distribution of income. The distribution of income in the United States has been characterized as a fishbowl, with a small top, small bottom, and large middle section where most of the fish swim. To a large degree, this image is correct and has been supported by the income data collected since the 1920s. The typical middle-income American household has also been characterized as a family unit in the suburbs with the husband working and the wife taking care of the house while raising their children. This latter image was accurate for many households in the 1950s and 1960s. However, as more women entered the workforce in the 1970s, 1980s, and 1990s, some characteristics of the typical American household unit began to change. From the perspective of technology adoption, the most important changes have been increasing wealth at the top of the fishbowl and increasing poverty at the bottom, along with the characteristics of those who compose these groups. At the top, a large group has annual incomes of $100,000 or more. This group of households consists predominantly of married couples in which both spouses work. They are generally middle-aged (35 to 55), are well educated, and have children. This is a very important target group for early adoption of new media technologies. At the bottom, a large group lives in greater poverty than did so a few decades ago. This group cannot afford many of the new technologies until their prices have dropped a long way but may experience these technologies in schools, libraries, the workplace, and other locations outside the home.

Age is another important demographic characteristic that affects adoption. A distinction must be made, however, between age and generation. That is, when one age group has adopted a technology, did they do so because of their age or because they were a new generation? For example, it is reasonable to assume that young people have adopted MP-3 players because people between 15 and 30 like to hear music as they move from one setting to another, just as young people in past decades adopted portable radio, Walkman audiocassettes and portable CD players. However, what about young people's preference to get news from the Web rather than newspapers? Does this phenomenon relate to their age, or is it a generational shift in which this generation has adopted the Web and will continue to prefer it even as it gets older?

Among the many lifestyle issues that affect adoption of new media are hectic schedules, home offices, mobility, and individualism. Two-income households with children are prime candidates for early adoption of new media. However, adult members of these households are also characterized by very hectic schedules and a feeling that they are pressed for time.[16] The evidence is mixed about how much free time they actually have but it clearly shows that they believe that they have too little. This is particularly true for working women, who have responsibilities for child rearing and household chores on top of work obligations. A key issue for this group is whether a new technology takes up or saves time. Further, does it take time to learn, and can it easily fit into their schedule, or must they change their schedule to use it? Some of the appeal of MP-3 players and the Web is that they are schedule-free; part of the appeal of the DVR is that it frees users from the restrictions of a television schedule.

Households with home offices are also associated with early adoption of many new media. They include people who operate businesses from their homes, telecommuters who work part-time at home and part-time at regular offices, and professionals such as teachers or lawyers who maintain an office at home to complement their regular place of work. The number of home offices has grown sharply from about 20 million in 1990 to more than 50 million by the mid-2000s. Households with home offices have a need for many new media technologies. For example, they were among the first households to have two or more telephone lines, fax machines, Web access, and broadband. This example also highlights some of the limitations of the categories we use to classify types of adopters. A "business" category encompasses many different types of users.

Two social trends, mobility and individualism, are coming together to encourage the adoption of new media. Mobility involves the greater use of cars, more air travel, jobs that are farther from home, and more activities outside the home. Individualism (as the term is coming to be used in the sociodemographic field) is a long-term social trend in which people are participating less in groups. In politics, citizens have been identifying less and less with political parties. In communities, fewer people identify closely with social organizations such as the Lions Club or the Kiwanis. This development carries over to media. In print media, general-interest magazines have declined, and special-interest magazines have increased. In television, ratings for general-interest programs that appear on the major networks have declined, and ratings for special-interest cable channels have increased. Individualism and mobility have combined to lead many people to consume personalized media anywhere and at any time. This long-term trend began with households acquiring multiple units of technologies such as radio, TV, and the telephone, thereby encouraging personal access to and usage of media. Walkman radios, mobile phones, PDAs, MP-3 players, and laptop computers later strengthened the habit of using personalized and customized media in any setting.

With multiple units of technology in homes and many personalized and portable media, where do people put all this equipment? Part of the answer is that miniaturization of electronics allows more equipment to fit into smaller spaces than were necessary in earlier decades. Perhaps more important is a changing social pattern in using media. More technology has been integrated into the social fabric of everyday life, especially in mobile settings, where many people wear technology such as mobile phones or MP-3 players in a manner similar to clothing (see chapter 10).

Failures, Fads, and Cyclicals

So far, we have been concerned primarily with new technologies that became successes. Inevitably, however, failures are much more numerous than successes, and much of value can be learned from them. Many analysts have noted that new technologies are often created by engineers who have little knowledge about whether there is a demand for these technologies.[17] In this sense, new services often result from "technology push" rather than "demand pull." This practice has been correctly cited as a reason why many technologies fail. While the criticism is correct, it would be facile to leave it at that: many of the most successful communication technologies of the past 125 years—telephones, motion pictures, radio, phonographs, and television—entered the marketplace as technology push, in a context of uncertain demand. Technologies do not falter simply because they represent technology push; they fail because they cannot meet the challenge of finding or creating applications that people want. As one of the pioneers of videotex in the United Kingdom presciently asked, Will we succeed in reaching takeoff speed before we run out of runway?

After a short discussion of failures, we turn to fads and cyclical technologies, which have patterns of adoption that differ from those of either successes or failures.

Failures

A common pattern is associated with the marketing of many unsuccessful products and services—a phantom S-curve. These technologies frequently languish with low consumer acceptance while their advocates proclaim that they are about to take off and project rapid near-term growth based on an S-curve pattern of adoption. Videotex, eight-track audio cartridges, and over-the-air subscription television (STV) are among the technologies that have followed this pattern.

STV was a form of movie channel available by subscription, like HBO, but delivered by means of a scrambled broadcast signal. STV was tried in the

1950s and 1960s with little success. Again in 1977, a few companies launched STV services and achieved modest penetration of homes. By 1980, more than 600,000 people subscribed to these services; two years later, that number had topped 1.3 million.[18] At this time, some media analysts projected that STV was about to take off. However, at the same time, cable TV was entering major markets across the United Service offering technically superior service and multiple channels, not just one. STV soon faded away.

More generally, many lessons can be learned from technologies that failed in the marketplace or lost ground after achieving a significant penetration of households. First, many technologies have failed because the benefit they offered was at best superficial. For example, quadraphonic sound (four-channel sound) was introduced in the 1970s but did not represent a significant advance in technology for the consumer market. Rather, it represented an attempted transfer of existing industrial technology (multitrack recording and playback) that provided a genuine benefit in an industrial setting (control of editing) to a home market in which no benefit could be demonstrated. In addition, very few recordings took advantage of the new system, thus further reducing its appeal to consumers. From a consumer's point of view, quadraphonic sound offered no advantage over existing stereophonic sound. Though its failure could have been anticipated, proponents ignored its weaknesses and instead tried to market advantages that were ephemeral from a consumer's perspective. Videophones (see chapter 6) and Smell-O-Vision are illustrative examples of failure. Smell-O-Vision was a 1950s gimmick to try to bring more people into movie theaters in the face of competition from television. The concept was to introduce scents into the theater that complemented the scene in the movie—for example, the smell of the sea in a scene on an island. It was short-lived. The problem was not so much introducing the scents but getting them out of the theater before the next scene, which might require an entirely different scent.

In general, companies have ignored failures and the many lessons that can be derived from them. In addition to the fact that an understanding of failures can help technology start-ups avoid making the same mistakes as in the past, it is also possible for a phoenix to arise from the ashes of failure. For example, the failed videotex trials of the 1970s and 1980s offered many clues about how online services could succeed (see chapter 7). Unfortunately, when a technology or service fails, the company that initiated it often lays off the personnel who gained the learning and literally throws out the records showing what happened, including the research. Many years ago, communication researcher Harold Mendelsohn suggested that a good way to identify potentially successful new media services and applications is to look for near misses of the past.[19]

Fads

Some seemingly successful technologies prove to be fads. We are familiar with fads in leisure products such as hula hoops, yo-yos, tamagotchis, and pet rocks. Consumer electronic technologies and services, too, may be fads or have a faddish component. A good example is citizens band (CB) two-way radio, which in the early 1970s had a steady population of approximately 200,000 users. CB became a fad in the mid-1970s, and many consumers bought CB radios for their car or home. The population of users grew to a peak of 10 million in 1976 before declining rapidly and leveling off at approximately 1 million by the early 1980s (see chapter 10). Other media fads have included boom boxes, beepers for teenagers, and minidisc players.

Cyclical Adoption

Some technologies exhibit a cyclical pattern of adoption: strong adoption, followed by decline in usage, followed by periodic returns to popularity. 3-D movies, for example, were popular during the mid-1950s then faded away, experiencing renewed interest in the 1960s and for brief periods in each decade thereafter. 3-D movies are essentially a one-trick pony. They are appealing when an object comes at the audience—an arrow, perhaps, or the hand of a monster—but have little value for most scenes. They found a niche market in exhibitions at amusement parks such as DisneyWorld and for some large-screen IMAX movies. 3-D technology has also been tried a number of times on television with the same results as in movie theaters.

Video game consoles are another cyclical technology that has had much more success than 3-D movies. These consoles and associated software surged in the early 1980s, collapsed in the mid-1980s, and were resurrected in the late 1980s. From the 1990s onward, they have experienced cyclical growth and decline, although the fluctuations have been less extreme than in the 1980s. These peaks and valleys are associated with the introduction of new generations of equipment—8-, 16-, 32-, and 64-bit microprocessors, each of which was replaced by faster processors after a few years.

Cyclical patterns of adoption and decline can sometimes be anticipated, as in the case of console video games. After two phases of the cyclical pattern, it could be anticipated that the pattern would continue. Cyclical phases can sometimes be controlled. For decades, the Walt Disney Company built cyclical phases into the distribution of its children's movies. The company released a movie into theaters and later showed it a few times on television before withdrawing it, only to reintroduce it several years later when a subsequent generation of children would perceive it as new. When videocassettes and DVDs were introduced, Disney followed a similar pattern, distributing the movie on videocassette or DVD for a fixed period of time, withdrawing it, and redistributing it several years later.

Some Practical Implications for Those Introducing New Media

How can an understanding of patterns of adoption be applied to the introduction of a new media technology or service? The first step is to identify which lessons are likely to be relevant. A technical standard is important in some instances but not others. The initial price for a technology may be completely beyond the reach of consumers, meaning that businesses, schools, or government must be the early adopters or that the group introducing it must subsidize the price. An existing technology may be present in most homes, allowing the new technology or service to piggyback on the replacement cycle for the existing technology, or the new service may involve disruptive adoption and change in behavior. A close parallel may exist between a new technology and one that entered the marketplace in the past, so that several lessons apply, or there may be no close match, in which case it is necessary to pick and choose relevant lessons from several earlier technologies.

The Context for Adoption

It is important to understand the broad social, media, and business contexts in which a technology or service must take hold. What are the likely competitive technologies? (Those investing in satellite telephony did not see cellular telephony as a threat but they miscalculated as cellular services expanded very rapidly throughout the world.) What social trends support adoption or present a barrier to adoption? Which organizations might be appropriate partners in the marketing of a new technology? Many social, economic, and demographic trends are likely to affect the demand for new media services, including the aging of the population, more work at home, and a harried lifestyle of middle-aged, middle-income households. In assessing these and other trends, it is important to ask what content needs may arise because of a change in population demographics or social lifestyle and what are the implications for the technology or service that is under development or in a planning stage. For example, will professionals working at home need new multimedia information services, and will households need more bandwidth coming into the home to receive new services? In addition, what long-term media technology and service needs does an aging population have?

At present, perhaps the most intriguing social trend that can inform the planning of future technologies and services is the combination of mobility and individualism. These ingrained habits and desires have already had a major impact on society through the widespread adoption of mobile phones, laptop computers, MP-3 players, and portable video game players. What new media technologies and services are likely to follow? Will people carry even more devices around with them, or will new services be built into existing technology as has happened with mobile phones? With individualism have come more personal and customized media and associated values of control, convenience, and links between technology and social identification. How much further will mobile devices go in the direction of being integrated with clothing and becoming fashion statements as well as functional devices? Taken together, they provide a road map for many new media devices that will emerge in the future. At the moment, the map is incomplete, and much more research is needed to fill it in.

General Lessons

A review of consumer adoption patterns for new media technologies and services suggests a number of general lessons that may help us to understand how consumers are likely to respond to new electronic technologies and services.

1. *Service matters more than technology.* The technology used in delivering a service is far less important to ordinary consumers than the service itself and how they perceive it. Therefore, it is important to emphasize the services that will be delivered rather than the way they will be delivered. Similarly, consumers may not distinguish services in terms of technological characteristics such as the bandwidth or storage capacity, even though those characteristics are very important to network providers, equipment manufacturers, and the engineers who designed and built the technology. Consumers are certainly able to distinguish a text Web page with sports scores from a video sports segment on a PC or TV. They are more likely to think, however, about advantages such as convenient access, timeliness of information, and fun in watching video clips of games rather than about the bandwidth of the distribution channel or storage requirements for the file.
2. *Experiencing the new media product or service before adopting it is very important in some cases.* This was clearly the case with early DVRs such as TiVo. Many people did not understand what the product did. On hearing a description, they thought it was a glorified VCR. However, experiencing it in a friend's home turned many into adopters. It can also be argued that this was a problem in the early marketing of HDTV. Most people had never seen it, and television set manufacturers did a poor job of placing it in public locations where many people could see it. Even in electronics stores, many early HDTV sets displayed regular television signals that did not convey the true character-

istics of high-definition television. Those who did see true HDTV were impressed. The remaining hurdle was price, which declined over time and led to widespread adoption.

Transparency

Design transparency is crucial if consumers are to adopt and use new media technologies and services. In the past, the term *user friendly* was employed to convey the idea that a technology could be used by anyone, with little or no training. However, the term has become a cliché, and many products that claim to be user friendly are anything but easy to use. Transparency may be a better term, indicating that the technology does not get in the way of its use—the equipment and technical aspects of the service are transparent. This is more difficult to achieve than many assume. It requires considerable effort by designers, engineers, and human-factor specialists, followed by extensive testing of the product with consumers and changes in design based on the research findings.

1. *Complexity has become a greater obstacle over time.* One of the hurdles in achieving transparency is the increasing complexity of many new media technologies. Users often cannot figure out how to navigate through complex menus or work remote controls with a seemingly endless array of buttons. Furthermore, most people (especially men) have little tolerance for any form of written instructions. To some degree, these problems may be associated with the rapid dissemination of so many new electronic products. In the past, consumers were confronted with simpler technologies—for instance, tuning a radio or dialing a telephone—and most had years of experience (as children growing up) observing others use the device before being called on to make it work themselves. By contrast, digital television grew rapidly in the first decade of this century and brought into the previously simple world of television video on demand, interactive program guides, menus of services, and hundreds of extra channels. People had to learn how to use these new options within a short time, and the transition was not smooth.
2. *The skill level of the general public in using technology has improved over time but is not sufficient when technology is poorly designed.* What is the skill level of the general public in using technology, and what strategies are available if target adopters lack all the skills needed to use a device? The good news is that the skill levels of an average person are much higher than was the case 20 or 30 years ago. Groups introducing new media services back then encountered many people who did not understand the concept of hitting an "enter"

button or pressing buttons to control information on a screen.[20] School and work environments have introduced millions of people to computers and helped to develop technology skills that can be applied in the household. In addition, automated teller machines (ATMs) and automated information kiosks at airports or shopping malls have helped in training the mass public to use computer-based technologies. The bad news is that most people still lack advanced degrees in engineering, which some organizations appear to take for granted when designing new media devices and services. The first generation of DVD recorders is a good example—poor design made them very difficult to use.

3. *Good design takes time.* Often there is a tradeoff between the time and effort put into the design phase for new media and transparency to a user. Companies pay one way or the other. Putting in the necessary effort to achieve transparency has a cost in personnel and time. Taking shortcuts in the design process can lead to more calls to customer service later as well as disgruntled customers.

Targeting Early Adopters

Who are the candidate early adopter for a new media technology or service?

1. *Technophiles, households with home offices, and households with two working spouses are strong candidates to be early adopters.* A review of adoption trends for earlier technologies suggests that three important groups of consumer early adopters exist. The first is technophiles, who feel compelled to have the latest electronic gadgets and hot-rod delivery systems. Traditionally, most members of this group have been male and middle-aged and have had high incomes. More recently, many younger people, both males and females, have joined the ranks of early adopters for technologies such as next-generation mobile phones. A second group consists of households with home offices and a need for many of the new technologies. Third, households with two working spouses and children often have the financial resources and need to acquire many new media services. Many parents believe that their investment in some information technology, especially computers, and some services, such as broadband access to the Web, will help prepare their children to do better at school and to find better jobs in the future. Children also have shown a strong interest in computers, mobile phones, and the Web, although this interest may result as much from entertainment considerations and a desire to stay in touch with friends as from an interest in education.

2. *Businesses and education groups are target early adopters.* Business and education are important target groups that may lead to consumer adoption of new media services. In the past, many technologies first entered businesses and schools, creating habits and appetites that people eventually brought home. The telephone and mobile phones, for example, were predominantly business services at first and then entered households of businesspeople who wanted the same services at home. Similarly, many people developed an appetite for personal computers and the Web in business or education settings and then brought those technologies home.
3. *Plan ahead for second and third waves of adopters.* In targeting early adopters, it is important to plan ahead for the second and third wave of adopters and not to assume that later adopters will be just like the first group in terms of demographic characteristics or uses of the product. For example, later adopters of DVRs were not as fanatical about this technology as the first wave of adopters; the second wave of cable television adopters (who lived in cities and wanted more choice and better reception) were very different from the first wave (who lived in rural areas and were happy to have any access to TV signals).
4. *Be flexible.* Since it is hard to plan far ahead, it is important to be flexible in product development, content creation, and marketing so you can adapt to the changing environment. An early example of poor planning and holding onto an early adopter group as the model for those to follow was the phonograph. Thomas Edison invented it as a device that could both record and play back. The early adopters were businesspeople who used it for taking dictation and for later playback to secretaries, who would type up the contents. When Edison began to offer the phonograph to the general public, he believed that the recording feature was very important and had available relatively little prerecorded content such as songs. A rival, the Victor Talking Machine Company, emerged with a playback-only phonograph and extensive prerecorded songs. Stuck in his concept of business use for the phonograph based on the early adopters, Edison lost the battle.[21] A similar case can be made about IBM and the PC. IBM dominated the market when the PC was a tool for businesses and used for spreadsheets and word processing. However, the company lacked the vision to foresee the landscape of applications after the PC became a consumer staple and was used widely for entertainment.

Motivations and Desires

Why do consumers adopt new technologies and services? What are their motives and desires?

1. *Strong need is a motivator.* One important motivation to adopt new technology and services is a strong need: a consumer has an existing unmet need in his or her life; a new service meets the need at an acceptable cost; the consumer adopts it. There are many examples of the adoption of new technology based on need: even in the 1980s, when home satellite dishes cost between $2,000 and $3,000, they were adopted by 20–25 percent of households in western states such as Montana and Idaho, where there were few local broadcast signals or cable systems. These people had a strong need.
2. *Latent needs can sometimes be identified.* In the absence of a strong need, those marketing a new service can sometimes identify a latent need—that is, one that consumers do not recognize until it is explained through marketing or demonstrations or until they see friends using it. For example, ample evidence from the first decade of mobile phone use showed that millions of people, not just business executives and emergency workers, had a latent need to make and receive phone calls in many locations where no landline service was available (see chapter 10). Further, many new media, including the DVR, have created a demand by providing a very appealing service that consumers want after experiencing it.
3. *Insatiable appetites drive behavior.* Another motivator is an insatiable appetite for some content or service. Many people cannot get enough of some content, such as movies, soap operas, or sports. Consumers with insatiable appetites often add the new technology or service to the old rather than substitute the new for the old. Many sports fans were early adopters of sports video over the Web. They did not stop watching sports on television but added new sports content, such as games not carried on their local cable system, to their viewing habits.
4. *Inconvenience and pain are motivators.* Inconvenience is a notable motivation for adoption and change. Many models of change are based on positive motivations, but painful experience with an existing service can provide an incentive to adopt a new one. In planning advanced media services, it is useful to ask where consumers are experiencing inconvenience or bad service that might be relieved by a high-capacity communication networks and new communication devices. Painful experience can lead to an erosion or churn in an existing service and an opportunity for a new service. For example, the inconvenience of going to video rental shops with limited inventories led many people to adopt video rentals delivered by mail, at a kiosk, or over the Web.
5. *Supplier pressure can lead to adoption and change but can also backfire.* Suppliers of services may have sufficient control over markets to force consumers to change behavior. For example, a bank that dominates a market might in-

crease the price of all services provided by tellers and thereby motivate consumers to make greater use of ATMs. Software suppliers that dominate a market have also been able to force change. However, in a competitive media environment, it is not clear if such a strategy would work. For example, a cable operator could require customers to adopt a new service, but they might switch to a satellite or a telephone supplier of video services.

6. *Motivations and desires can change over time.* As a service is adopted more widely, the mix of users and their wants can change. For example, the wants of Internet users changed when it became a mass market service. While the early users of the Internet included mostly well-educated information seekers, it then became a mass market service with users from mixed education backgrounds, members of younger and older age groups, and people looking for entertainment as well as information.

Content

Who controls content creation for a new technology?

1. *Entrepreneurs or existing players can lead in content creation.* Sometimes a new group of entrepreneurs leads content development, as with early personal computer software, much of the early content on the Web, and much video content when broadband was introduced. In other instances, existing players control content for the new technology, as in the cases of CDs, DVDs, and high-definition DVDs, which were produced by the same industry that created record albums, audiocassettes, movies, and television.
2. *Different groups bring different strengths and weaknesses.* Entrepreneurs are more likely to bring creativity to the process and to generate new ideas; existing players are more likely to bring financial resources, organizational relationships, and marketing skills to help ensure that the technology gets a reasonable opportunity in the marketplace. Each group has strengths and weaknesses that are likely to affect the adoption process. In addition, amateurs and entrepreneurs can get the process started, only to be replaced or bought out by larger organizations.
3. *User-generated content is not free or carefree.* In some cases, content is created by users, as with a mobile phone call or text message. User-generated content has no cost to create—users pay for the right to create the content that they consume. However, costs are incurred in developing the device and, users must acquire software to generate content. Further, the management of user-generated content is not without problems. In the case of e-mail, person-to-person messaging opened up the door to spam. In the case of on-

line forums and chat rooms, civil exchanges can be overpowered by crazies or used by predators to lure the unsuspecting. Developers of these services have to find ways to manage user-generated content without impinging on the rights of end users or becoming so heavy-handed with rules that users are driven away.

The Trojan Horse Strategy

Existing technology platforms and infrastructures can be helpful in the uptake of certain new services by making potential users effortlessly aware of them and letting people try them with little if any risk or cost. This is a Trojan Horse strategy. Harold Innis has noted that popular books in eighteenth-century England developed on a platform for the distribution of patent medicines.[22] Peddlers who went from town to town selling patent medicines began to carry and sell books as well. Many other examples of this strategy can be found: games and ring tones were added to existing mobile phone service; automated voice services (audiotex) were added to the telephone network; the sale of products on the Web built on top of a base established by e-mail and information services; text-based information services (stock quotes and sports scores) were added to satellite radio; and video games have been added to many cable systems. In each case, it was easy for people to see or hear the service and decide if they wanted it.

The Trojan Horse strategy eliminates the need to develop a new platform or infrastructure for a service, though there may be a need to develop application software. It also reduces marketing costs, to some degree. At the same time, there is no guarantee of acceptance by end users.

Stunning Innovations

The Holy Grail in new media adoption is stunning innovation—a device or service that not only meets a need but dazzles people through its creativity, user interface design, and appealing content. It is a worthy but rarely achieved goal. It is more common to introduce a technology or service with modest enhancements over incumbents, better marketing of a similar product, or a confluence of services that collectively has appeal.

Apple's iPod, introduced in 2001, is an example of a stunning innovation. How does one plan such a device? Understanding needs in the marketplace, social trends, and principles of adoption can help bring a new media device several steps along the road to wide acceptance, but chance invariably plays a role. In the case of the iPod, the product appealed to values of convenience and control while on the move. There was a great deal of available content, both legal and illegal. It allowed people to customize their content by organizing it in several ways. The user interface was well designed and elegantly simple. Apple introduced the iPod at a high price but then provided lower-price models to appeal to second and third waves of adopters, who likely would not have paid for the expensive model. The later models were designed explicitly to be worn like clothing, adding to their appeal as fashion statements, and the white earbuds made a statement that the user owned a product everyone was talking about. Apple continued to innovate with new applications for the iPod, such as video. However, even superlative design and strong functionality need an element of good fortune, in the form of favorable reviews, photos of famous personalities carrying iPods, and so on, to achieve such a high level of status and become an icon for cool technology.

Strategies for Assessing the Possibility of Failure and the Opportunity of Finding Success in the Ashes of Failure

Failure is more common than success with new media as well as other products. There are strategies to assess the chances of failure, identify end users' willingness to adopt a product that might fail, and capitalize on earlier failures that might have a second, successful life.

1. *Assess the risk of failure.* It is possible to assess the risk of failure by identifying the key elements that are likely to influence success or failure and making judgments about where the new media product or service stands in relation to them. One can consider, for example, how much time is needed to establish a base of acceptance in the marketplace and whether the company or group supporting the new technology or service is likely to provide sufficient time before pulling the plug; how difficult it will be to compete with entrenched incumbents; whether there is a target early adopter group with a clear or latent need; and so on. This assessment can aid a decision about whether to introduce the new media product or service or what additional work is required before introducing it.
2. *Assess end user willingness to adopt a product that might fail.* Innovators have a high tolerance for the possibility that a new media product might fail. The reward of being the first to own a product comes with that risk. Later adopters' tolerance for possible failure is influenced by a few factors, such as expected length of ownership and the impact on use if the product is removed from the marketplace. If a product has a short life—for example, a mobile phone—it does not matter so much if a user is stuck with useless features for the short period of time until the phone would be replaced anyway. If it has a long expected length of ownership—for example, a high-definition

DVD player—then getting stuck with a player for which there are no DVDs (should the player be withdrawn from the market and content suppliers no longer produce DVDs for it) is more consequential. If the product has a long expected life and can be used without loss of functionality, the downside of its being withdrawn from the market is also lower. In the case of an MP-3 player, for example, the risk from failure is low if a user can continue to download music and later transfer the music to another player; it is high if the user can no longer download music when the model is withdrawn or if the user subsequently loses the ability to transfer songs to another player because of digital rights restrictions.

3. *Comb the ashes of failure for near misses.* Many new media products—early subscription television, online services, and VCRs, for example—failed, only to succeed when reintroduced later. In some cases, the product was introduced too early; in other cases, the product lacked one or more critical elements necessary for success. With this history in mind, recent failures can be assessed for near misses that might succeed if reintroduced at the right time and with all the elements necessary for success in place.

// TWO //

The Fragility of Forecasting

'Tis easy to see, hard to foresee
—*Poor Richard's Almanack*

Generally, when dealing with the weather a few days ahead, the monthly demand for electricity a few years ahead, or the size of national populations two or three decades ahead, professional forecasters can justifiably lay claim to increasingly impressive results. Weather forecasts are considerably more accurate than they were a few decades ago, and population forecasts have proven to be reasonably accurate. There are exceptions, of course, and they can occur even when professional forecasters deal with well-known products or events and have many data points at their disposal. Exceptions do not, however, diminish the overall trend toward greater accuracy.

One may be tempted to believe that forecasting methodology has been improving across the board, and provided that the necessary financial and intellectual resources are devoted to it, forecasting the demand for a new media product or service could be equally impressive. This belief, however, would ignore the fact that if it is still too early to know whether the product will succeed or fail, forecasting its future demand is a very different—and far more difficult—type of undertaking.

The forecasts considered in this chapter are estimates of the level of demand for a new media product at some point or points in the future. (Except where otherwise indicated, the term *product* will be used in this chapter to include intangible services as well as tangible products.) Forecasts are made before the product has established itself in the marketplace—in many cases, even before it has been launched. There are three categories of forecasts: (1) forecasts before a concept has been turned into a concrete design; (2) forecasts in the immediate prelaunch phase, after it has been turned into a concrete design; and (3) forecasts after launch but before takeoff.

Forecasts sometimes take the form of an estimate for only one period, but they usually provide estimates of the demand for each of a range of periods and are presented as graphs or as time series—estimated figures for each of a succession of periods. (For example, a forecast might estimate the sale of high-definition TV sets [HDTVs] in 2012 or the cumulative penetration of HDTVs in households from 2006 to 2012.) An alternative is to forecast an upper bound—a ceiling—on sales or uptake rather than actual sales or uptake, but such forecasts are much less common. Organizations have various good reasons to feel that they need such forecasts, but they may not be able to satisfy this need.

One of the prerequisites for a soundly based forecast of the demand for a new product is an understanding of what it will be used for. How can one forecast the growth of a new media product when one doesn't know how it will be used? Obtaining such an understanding is often more difficult than it might seem. If Alexander Graham Bell had commissioned a forecast of the demand for his new invention, the telephone, he would probably not have done particularly well: he would have told the forecasters that it would be used for relaying concerts and church sermons and for important conversations by elite businesspeople. Along the same lines, Western Union initially dismissed the telephone, turning down the opportunity to buy its patents for $100,000.[1] Should one be confident that today's corporate world would do any better? In the late 1970s, about a century after Bell, the British Post Office, soon to be followed by its French counterpart, launched what came to be called videotex—a service that transmitted data over telephone lines for display on computers and, in its early days, television sets (see chapter 7). Both organizations saw videotex primarily as a service through which consumers would buy information in the form of screen-based text and graphics from a large array of different firms, each deciding for itself how it would price its information. Videotex had a messaging component, too, but it was treated as a relatively unimportant add-on when first launched. As things turned out, however, the person-to-person messaging component achieved moderate success; the one-to-many information access component was a failure (except in France, where the service enjoyed significant subsidy from the government). The providers of videotex made the same kind of conceptual mistake as Bell had made a hundred years earlier.

Videotex illustrates a common pattern: when ambitious new communication products are launched into the residential or business market, the question is often whether they can reach takeoff speed before they run out of runway. For applications that succeed, those that turn out to provide sufficient value (reach takeoff speed) sometimes differ substantially from those originally envisaged by marketers and their supporting casts of consultants and experts from academe. And by the time these applications are found, demand forecasts may be much less important.

Videotex was a radical and complex new service that required substantial change in users' behavior. What of less bold ventures? Many other anticipated uses for new media products or services also were too limited or too expansive in scope or were just plain wrong. Some groups thought that a major use for the radio would be to deliver speeches to the public; the transistor was seen initially as just a replacement for vacuum tubes in radios, though its range of applications turned out to be very much wider; the mobile phone was envisaged primarily as a tool for emergency workers; and no one who developed HDTV anticipated that its principal use in the first few years of rollout would be to display DVD movies.

While it is rather unlikely that those who introduce less radical products will confuse services that should be for user-generated content with services that should be for professionally created content, gross errors in forecasting the demand for new communication products are overwhelmingly the rule rather than the exception. When one examines the business context of forecasting efforts and the methods available to undertake them, it is not surprising that their track record in this field is as bad as it is. Significant early improvement appears unlikely; what is necessary is to make the best of a bad job.

The Core Forecasting Problem

The chapter will focus on forecasting the demand (in terms of revenues, number of units sold, number of adopters, or any other appropriate measure) for certain classes of new media products. New products are defined as ones which have not yet established themselves in the marketplace—as not yet having reached the take-off point in the diffusion curve defined by Everett Rogers as the point of critical mass.[2] (In this sense, videophones, first introduced in the 1960s, are new, but cellular telephones, introduced almost two decades later, are not.) We consider demand at the level of a market sector, not demand for individual products within a sector—the distinction is that between the demand for satellite radio as a whole and the demand for either XM Satellite Radio or for Sirius before their merger.

A distinction can be made between discretionary and nondiscretionary products. The former are those for which the prospective purchasers or users are individuals or families who have the discretion to make for themselves the decision to purchase or use a product—for example, a digital video recorder. For nondiscretionary items, the purchase decision is typically made by an organization; those who work for it—and, often, those who wish to do business with it—may not have this discretion. For example, a corporation may decide to adopt a particular software platform, requiring all workers as well as outside organizations that wish to do business with the corporation to adopt the same platform. Though many of the forecasting issues are the same, there are some differences in the methods available. We focus here on discretionary products.

A new product, in our sense, is either one that has not yet been launched, so there are no sales data to inform the forecast, or if launched already, one for which it is too soon for sales data to allow a good estimate of whether or when it will become established. The uncertainty about when, or even whether, the take-off point will be reached is the key characteristic distinguishing this problem from other demand forecasting problems. A corresponding mathematical formulation appears in the box. Although this is not the usual formulation, it provides the advantage of distinguishing the two types of uncertainty: when, if at all, demand for the product will take off, and if it does, what the demand will be at any time thereafter.

MATHEMATICAL FORMULATION OF FUTURE DEMAND

One possible formulation of the future demand generated by a new service is

$$D(m) = \sum_{n=1}^{\infty} d(m/n)p(n)$$

where $D(m)$ is the demand for the service at time period m,
$p(n)$ is the probability that the service takes off in time period n,
and $d(m/n)$ is the demand for the service in time period m, given that it takes off in time period n, for $m > 1$.

The time periods can be years or smaller intervals. *Take off* would be defined as the lowest level of demand at which one could be confident that the service would not be withdrawn because of subsequent lack of demand.

This formulation suggests a question about how those who directly provide subjective estimates of the demand in successive periods incorporate the possibility that the new product will not be a success. A highly simplified example illustrates an interesting point. Suppose that someone feels that the probability a new product will succeed is 0.8; that the forecaster's best guess is that, if the product succeeds, it will generate 100 units of demand in year N; if it does not, it will generate 0 units of demand in year N. Would the estimate of the demand in year N be 100 units or 80 units? If it were 100, the possibility that the product would fail would have been ignored. If, however, the estimate were 80 and the product were a success, then even in the event that the best guess of 100 units would have been exactly right, the estimate provided would have been 20 percent too low. More generally, those who provide subjective forecasts of the future demand for new products without separately estimating the probability of failure can be right on average only if they deflate their estimates to allow for the fact that the probability of failure is not zero. They would thereby underestimate the demand of those new products that succeeded.

From a practical standpoint, forecasting the demand for new media products is at its core so rough and ready that this effect is unlikely to matter. Nevertheless, the effect appears not to have received attention from authors who believe there is a scientific basis for such forecasting and seek to improve it.

In some cases, the object of interest is not the particular product but an upgrade of infrastructure or a new platform. An example of the former would be fiber-to-the-home (FTTH); videotex was and MP-3 players are examples of the latter. Here one must try to forecast the aggregate demand for all the new products or services that will be supported. As a result, the forecasting problem acquires two additional aspects. One is the risk of entirely overlooking new products that will succeed in the not-too-distant future. This is a matter not of developing too low a forecast for any particular product but of failing to realize that a viable service or application needs forecasting. An example was the failure to predict the success of a variety of new touch-tone services when rotary dialing was to be replaced. When an upgrade in infrastructure is justified primarily by greater efficiency in the provision of established services, such oversights may not matter. In the context of FTTH, however, where the cost of an upgrade may be $1,000 per household, or more than $100 billion across the whole United States, these oversights probably matter a great deal.

When considering an upgrade in the infrastructure, the other distinctive aspect of the problem is that even though a new service may establish itself, some other new technology may siphon demand away from the enhanced capability in the infrastructure. Bandwidth compression technology made it possible to offer some of the services touted by the promoters of FTTH in the late 1980s at rates up to 400 kilobits per second (within the compass of ISDN, the basic digital telephone offering of that time); such a mistake should have been easily avoided. For an upgraded infrastructure, it becomes necessary to forecast the demand not only for a new service but also for the portion of that demand that would be carried on the infrastructure in question but could not be carried on some lesser infrastructure.

An upgraded infrastructure is likely to support many new services, some of the less profitable of which may compete for attention and revenue with the principal services for which the system was upgraded. For example, in upgrading cable networks to digital transmission, cable operators sought to gain new revenue from video-on-demand (VOD) services. The digital networks supported not just VOD but many extra regular channels and HDTV programming. The latter compete with VOD for viewers' attention and can affect the revenue from VOD.

Track Record

Who Creates Forecasts?

Relatively few forecasts of the demand for new media products are created by academics or those working in research institutes and published in the open literature. In his valuable review of the research literature—such as it is—on telecommunications demand forecasting, Robert Fildes comments, "In particular there has been limited discussion comparing the usefulness (and accuracy) of alternative approaches when applied to the same problem."[3]

Many forecasts are prepared by what journalists often term "consulting firms" and are featured in market intelligence reports that are sold to whichever corporations choose to buy them. (Some are produced after a core group of purchasers has made commitments; others are produced on a speculative basis.) A seeming advantage they offer over in-house forecasts is that the outsiders are seen both as expert in forecasting and as more objective and hence more credible than those who have a direct stake in the market concerned. While the reports are not in the public domain, the forecasts they contain generally feature prominently in press releases sent to journalists covering the industry. Moreover, it is understood that purchasers and journalists can quote from the reports, so the forecasts generally become public information. However, the full reports are not generally available to journalists for scrutiny about assumptions and methodology, and many reporters lack the training to assess them as an academic might.

Other forecasts are prepared by appropriate departments for in-house use at large corporations or are prepared by outside consultants for the use of a single client. Naturally, many of these are initially treated as confidential. (An exception occurred in the days when forecasts had to be provided to regulators who needed to ensure that a monopoly would not cross-subsidize a new venture at the expense of existing captive customers.) They, too, often remain unpublished: if the new product is a success, it speaks for itself; if it is a failure, managers seek to bury the past and move on without adding further to the embarrassment.

Discussions of forecasts runs the risk of being disproportionately influenced by forecasts sold to multiple users, which tend to become public, at the expense of those prepared for single users, which tend to remain private. By necessity, most of the examples used in this chapter come from the former domain. However, our observations over the years—when acting as consultants to companies in the communication sector—as well as discussions with those employed in this sector have provided us with no evidence to believe that single-user forecasts are less prone to error than the multiuser variety.

How Accurate Have the Forecasts Been?

Forecasting has almost certainly become far more difficult in the past 20 years or so as fierce competition and turbulence have replaced the earlier tranquility of the new media field. However, forecasting the demand for new consumer communication and information products and services has always been problematic. The past century is littered with erroneous forecasts and predictions. Examples of underestimation have included the telephone, VCRs, answering machines, cellular telephones, personal computers, and the Web.[4]

While some forecasts have seriously underestimated the demand, most have overestimated it.[5] This finding is in line with the first half of a widely quoted observation, attributed to a variety of sources, that people generally overestimate the short-term impact of a technological change but underestimate its long-term impact. Table 2.1 shows six different forecasts from the early and mid-1980s for the household penetration of videotex in the United States in 1990. The median forecast predicted a penetration level of around 9 million households, but only about 1 million households subscribed to a videotex service by 1990. In other words, the forecasts had errors ranging between a factor of 7 and a factor of 20 or more. It may be more revealing to regard these forecasts for videotex as primarily qualitative rather than quantitative failures. All indicated that by 1990, videotex would be a success or on its way to becoming one. In fact, neither was the case.

Table 2.2 shows six late-1980s forecasts of the penetration of HDTV in households. As in the case of videotex, the forecasts show incredible range. Two strongly overestimated demand, while one slightly underestimated it. Presumably, all of the forecasts anticipated that people would buy HDTV sets to watch high-definition television. However, this was not the case in the early 2000s. In

TABLE 2.1. Market Projections for Penetration of Videotex in U.S. Households by 1990

Forecasting Group	Penetration (millions of households)
Advertising Age	6.6
AT&T	8.0
International Resource Development	9.8
IFTF	11.0
Strategic Inc.	4–12
Southham	20–25

Source: J. S. Thompson and Nolan Bowie, *Videotex and the Mass Audience* (Cambridge, MA: MIT Future of the Mass Audience Project, 1986).

TABLE 2.2. Forecasts for HDTV

Projected Cumulative Penetration of HDTV in U.S. Households		
Group Making Projections	Year	Projected Penetration (%)
NTIA	1997	1
	2002	25
	2008	94
Electronic Industry Association	1997	10
	2000	25
	2003	33
American Electronic Association	2000	1
	2003	6

Source: National Association of Broadcasters Newsletter, March 1989.

2003, 9 percent of U.S. households had sets capable of displaying HDTV, but most were used to watch DVD movies, not HDTV. HDTV signals were not yet widely available on cable or satellite, and few households chose to buy separate HDTV receivers and install HDTV antennas to pick up digital terrestrial television from local broadcasters.

Forecasts for similar products often err in assuming which features of the competitive products will have appeal or how marketplace conditions will influence adoption. Figure 2.1 shows a forecast made in 1980 for VCR and videodisc player sales. In 1980, many people assumed that the videodisc, which offered better picture quality, would eventually win out over VCRs. However, VCRs had already been in the marketplace for five years, and the price had dropped considerably below the price of videodisc players, which were just entering the marketplace. Further, VCRs could record, and movie studios had by this time released thousands of movies for distribution on videocassettes. Videodiscs were an unknown, struggling to license movies for rental or sale. In the end, that generation of videodiscs achieved a very small market share among movie aficionados who valued the slightly better picture quality.

In other cases, wildly optimistic forecasts of demand have proven even more embarrassing—actual penetration of the product was zero. In the 1960s, AT&T forecast that one million Picturephones would be in use by 1980 and two million by 1985.[6] However, picture telephones failed in the marketplace, achieving virtually no penetration. Similarly, Link Resources forecast in 1983 that 1.8 million U.S. households would subscribe to direct broadcast satellite services (DBS) by 1985.[7] However, DBS proved too costly to launch, and the service had no subscribers in 1985. In 1995, a telecommunications consulting group forecast that 50 to 60 percent of U.S. households would have enhanced "screen phones" by 2005. In reality, screen phones, which were intended as an alternative to a PC for accessing online information, never took off and had zero penetration of

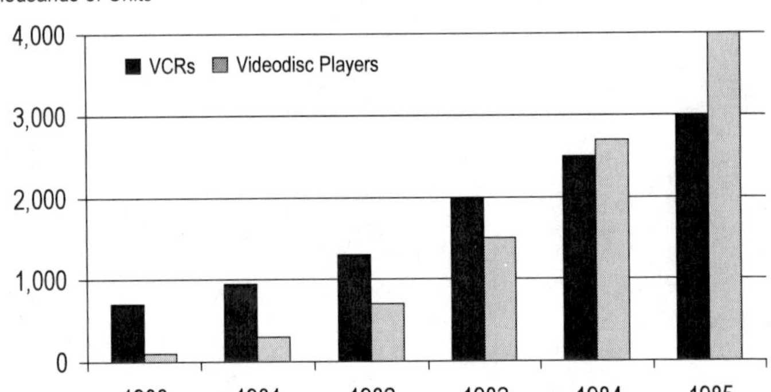

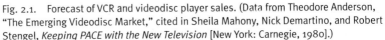

Fig. 2.1. Forecast of VCR and videodisc player sales. (Data from Theodore Anderson, "The Emerging Videodisc Market," cited in Sheila Mahony, Nick Demartino, and Robert Stengel, *Keeping PACE with the New Television* [New York: Carnegie, 1980].)

households in 2005. In 1997, Jupiter Communications forecast that smart cards (a more advanced form of credit card) would account for 10 percent of online transactions by the end of 1998; in reality, smart cards were slow to develop and accounted for almost no transactions in 1998.[8]

Context

When a corporation is considering whether to launch a new product or planning to do so, a forecast of its demand would seem to be essential to rational decision making. Estimating the return on investment in a new product, for example, requires a forecast of its future revenues and hence of its future demand. Or if a new service will require new infrastructure, a decision on the capacity of the infrastructure will have to be made ahead of the launch, and the necessary capacity will depend on demand. A sad illustration of the need for forecasts can be found in the satellite-based mobile telephony services Iridium, Globalstar, and ICO. In 1998, Wall Street analysts forecast that 30 million people would be using satellite phones by 2006.[9] Reality differed greatly:

> The failure of the mobile-phone satellites is legendary: aside from their huge costs and complexity, they underestimated the speed at which terrestrial competition, in the form of wireless networks, would take off. By the time Iridium came to market, most of the customers it was hoping for were well served by ordinary mobile phones. . . .
>
> This highlights a big problem with satellites: the long wait between design and profitability. Manufacturers must "lock down" the technology at

least three years before launch; but many satellites do not make money until 10–12 years after they go into orbit. So satellite firms must make a bet on a market as much as 15 years in the future. For new services with untested demand, the risk that the market will shift dramatically between design and orbit—or never emerge at all—is huge.[10]

In addition to the vendors of new products, potential investors—possible partners or venture capitalists—use forecasts, as do those who need to assess the future social impact of new technologies. Journalists, too, can be regarded as users of forecasts since they like to include forecasts in articles about new technologies.

The Failure to Account for the Possibility of Failure

Users of forecasts must realize that the majority of new communications products fail. The same holds true in other, long-established, and better-understood markets. According to Clayton M. Christensen et al., of the 30,000 new consumer products launched each year, more than 90 percent fail.[11] It would be surprising if a higher success rate were found in the much less well understood markets for new media. Table 2.3 presents a short list of new media failures.

We are not aware of any published forecasts that predicted the failure of a new media product but a simple line of reasoning illustrates why failure is likely. An estimate of the probability that a new product will attain a specified level of demand by a certain date is less complex than most forecasts (which usually deal with a range of time in the future, not just a single date). Suppose that corporations considering major investments in bringing new products to market could estimate these particular probabilities with a high level of confidence. Above what threshold of probability would proceeding become rational? The level clearly would vary from one situation to another, but it often might

TABLE 2.3. New Media Failures

Broadcast subscription TV	Videotex
Divx	MDS
8-track cartridge	Cable game channels (1980s)
Quadraphonic sound	Smart screen telephones
CD-I	3-D TV
Videodisc	Teletext (in the United States)
Videophone	Iridium satellite phone system
Fax newspapers	Fiber-to-the-home (1990s)
Car phonographs	Interactive TV (1980s–1990s)

BINARY PREDICTIONS OF SUCCESS VERSUS FAILURE

The question of whether a new product will succeed or fail lies at the heart of the forecasting problem. A demand forecast will inevitably be useless if those who made it assumed that the product would succeed but it turned out to fail (or vice versa). A. Michael Noll has proposed an approach to this binary prediction problem.[1] In his formulation, a new business venture or a new product must succeed in each of five areas: technology, finance and economics, policy and regulation, management and business, and consumers and their needs. For example, new products will fail if their technology does not work well enough; if they are not profitable; if the regulatory environment changes in such a way as to impose severe constraints on demand; if the companies concerned lack expertise to run the associated business well enough; or if consumers do not want to buy the products at the price at which they are offered.

As obvious as these factors are, planners might have avoided many of the new media fiascos of the past if they had given sufficient consideration to the complete set of them. Noll proposes a highly disciplined multifaceted assessment of possible new products that should be undertaken before—probably long before—the stage of needing a demand forecast is reached. In addition, considerable expertise in each area is required to assess a new product thoroughly. One certainly cannot expect to find all the necessary expertise within, say, a group of forecasting and market research analysts. If one uses expert groups to produce a forecast and follows J. Scott Armstrong's advice about decomposing the problem, the five factors suggest one way to structure the process.

1. A. Michael Noll, *The Evolution of Media* (Lanham, MD: Rowman and Littlefield Publishers, 2006), 165–70.

be quite low. Provided that a corporation has deep enough pockets to afford some failures, what matters is the ratio of the value of a success to the cost of a failure. If this ratio is, say, 10 to 1, then it could be rational to proceed with any project that had little more than a 10 percent probability of success. Moreover, a corporation may need to weigh the risk that delay associated with an attempt to improve its assessment of the probability would enable a competitor—maybe from a different industry sector—to beat it to market in such a way as to reduce its probability of success or eventual market share. This risk clearly is considerably greater in today's much more competitive environment than in the fairly recent past.

This analysis represents a considerable oversimplification for a variety of reasons: it ignores both the fact that there would be degrees of possible success and the fact that it might be necessary to select from a set of candidate projects each of which has a probability of success above the appropriate threshold. Nevertheless, the conclusion that it may well be rational to bring new products to market even if their chances of success are closer to 0 than to 100 percent is valid. No need to tell this to a venture capitalist or to a professional gambler! In an advanced economy, particularly in the United States, a relative lack of failures would be a sign of excessive timidity and thus a matter for concern.

Bias

Bias may be attributable to the fact that a dramatically high forecast produced on spec rather than commissioned will advertise itself. For some, the name of the game is getting the forecasting firm's name prominently into as many newspaper articles as possible and preferably into the headlines, and thereby generating numerous telephone inquiries that will lead to the sale of consulting services.[12]

A serious risk of bias comes from the fact that forecasts accurately reflecting low probabilities of success would be decidedly unwelcome to certain of their users—in particular, to the subset of users from whose budgets they are bought. (Indeed, a sponsoring organization may suppress results from a study that yields a conservative forecast. We are aware of a number of cases in which this phenomenon occurred.) A forecast is not just a tool for making decisions about a product; it may also be a useful tool for promoting that product. As noted in chapter 1, new products are more likely to succeed if others—in some cases, prospective suppliers of content, in some cases prospective purchasers—judge that they will succeed. In addition, at an earlier stage in the process, those who want to bring new products to market must secure the necessary investment funds, whether from boards of directors or from outsiders. For this purpose, realistic forecasts may well be interpreted as indicating that promoters lack confidence in their projects, especially in an atmosphere of pervasive hype surrounding the prospects of new products.

Whether they will be produced within the corporation concerned or by outside consulting firms, forecasts are generally ordered or purchased by the promoters of new products rather than by boards of directors or outside investors who might wish to strike a safer balance between bullishness and realism. Bias is also present in the government environment, where there also appears to be an inclination to support studies that will yield optimistic forecasts. In the United States, a member of Congress or a state legislator may have taken a position favoring the deployment of certain technologies, committee staff may see future job prospects in the industry, and, equally important, optimistic forecasts imply increased revenues from taxes on the industries concerned.

LOOKING IN THE SHADOWS

When an exciting new service is widely heralded as being just around the corner, it may well be worth looking not just at what is in the spotlight but also at what is in the surrounding shadows. They may be obscuring a much less dramatic new service that offers much of the value of the brightly illuminated one but at a much more attractive cost. And the more modest offering may make the running in the marketplace, sometimes for a decade or much more.

TABLE. New Services: Under the Spotlights or in the Shadows?

Time Period[a]	Region	Under the Spotlight	In the Shadows
Early 1970s for 30+ years	North America mainly; also United Kingdom and elsewhere	Videoconferencing	Audio conferencing
Mid 1970s for 10+ years	Western Europe mainly	Videotex (online information)	Teletext
Late 1970s for 20+ years	United States	Interactive television	Pay cable channels, Pay-per-view TV and video rentals
End of 1980s for 15+ years	North America	Residential broadband networks (fiber-to-the-home)	DSL and cable modem technologies
Late 1990s for 5+ years	United States and elsewhere	Online subscriptions to electronic magazines and newspapers	Buying printed publications, for example, books, online with regular postal delivery
Second half of 1990s for 5+ years	Europe mainly	WAP for mobile phones	SMS

[a]Starting approximately when the spotlight was turned on and covering the period during which the service in the shadows continued to grow rapidly.

Of the services listed in the table as having been under the spotlight, all those that entered the marketplace were disappointments. Yet all their far less technologically ambitious counterparts enjoyed at least moderate success. This situation suggests that those championing the former were probably right about the market being ready to accept services of the kind they envisaged (the services met a real need). But these champions may have underestimated the technological hurdles standing in the way of getting an easy-to-use version of their service into the market fairly soon. For forecasters, the lesson is clear: look in the shadows.

Moreover, government studies tend to request forecasting data that no legitimate forecasting organization could possibly provide. A particular absurdity was one federal agency's late-1980s request for a forecast of penetration levels for all present and future information/entertainment services by race, income level, and other demographic characteristics of households—25 years into the future!

Those who produce forecasts can be assumed to know on which side their bread is buttered. If there were proven techniques for forecasting that did not require a great deal of judgment, structural biases might not matter so much; it would then be possible in principle to examine any forecast and determine whether it had been "properly" produced. But such techniques do not exist (and even if they did, a comparison with the more codified field of accounting would not be encouraging in light of its scandals around the turn of this century).

Self-serving bias toward overly optimistic forecasts is built into the way decisions about new media products are made. Corrective mechanisms might appear if boards of directors or venture capitalists commissioned independent forecasts or if journalists more often treated forecasts with a questioning attitude rather than as convenient copy. Conversely, the fact that the time horizons of these forecasts are generally years—often many years—into the future means that embarrassment or financial loss resulting from inaccuracy contributes little as a possible corrective mechanism. By the time that any inaccuracies are evident, the individuals responsible may well have moved on to other jobs or retired, and probably few others will remember the name of the consulting firm from which the forecasts came.

Notwithstanding the built-in biases favoring hype, gross errors in forecasting are not universally excessively optimistic. Some very costly failures have occurred when forecasters did not predict that particular products would be highly successful. In the early 1980s, AT&T commissioned a forecast from McKinsey and Company, a highly respected management consulting firm. The forecast suggested that the total worldwide market for mobile phones in 2000 would be 900,000 subscribers. (In reality, the United States had 106 million mobile phone subscribers in the United States by 2000.) AT&T subsequently pulled out of the mobile phone market. In 1992, it reentered the market by buying one-third of McCaw's cellular holdings for $3.8 billion; in 1993 it paid $12.6 billion for the remainder.[13] Such failures rightly suggest that much more is wrong than bias alone. In the case of the mobile phone forecast, the analysts apparently focused too narrowly on the mobile phone as a tool for emergency calls and lacked the vision to foresee that it might become a ubiquitous device for communicating with others about nearly anything from nearly anywhere.

Assumptions

Another weakness in the field is the pervasive neglect of the assumptions on which forecasts are based. In some cases, the assumptions are never stated; in other instances, they are only weakly alluded to. Even when they are made explicit in the initial statement of any forecast, they tend to be somewhat boring and to turn a pithy statement or graphic into something far more unwieldy. That is probably the main reason why they so often and so soon fall by the wayside. But since forecasts extend years into the future, assumptions about associated markets and technologies, about the economy, and about society in general can be crucial.

Many of the assumptions are of the form that no significant changes will occur in this or that external factor. The example of how cellular telephony destroyed the potential market for satellite telephony offers a good illustration of the associated perils. The problem with assumptions that other things will be equal often is not that they fall by the wayside but rather that they are not made explicit.

Some assumptions have rested on false premises or comparisons that should have received more careful scrutiny before they were built into forecasts. For example, in the early days of online services (see chapter 7), some providers reasoned that if many customers were willing to pay $100 per hour for an online information service, a mass market would consider $20 per hour a bargain. This idea seems ludicrous in hindsight, but many forecasts were built on this kind of assumption. The problem was that the many customers who were willing to pay $100 per hour for online information were businesses with very specific information needs for which they would pay a great deal, but the price comparison had little meaning for consumers. A more recent example is VOD. Many analysts assumed that the movie studios would readily license their content to VOD on the same basis and timescale that they licensed movies to Blockbuster and other video rental houses. Why would they not pursue this additional revenue stream? However, some studios feared that the new service might cannibalize the $20 billion in yearly revenue from DVD sales and rentals without replacing the revenue lost from this distribution path with equal or greater revenue from VOD.

Other assumptions presume a neutrality of attitudes—about a specific company, for example—when there may actually be hostility or concern. Microsoft has made a number of forays into the market for set-top boxes (for television), seemingly assuming existing industry groups consider the company a neutral or positive organization. However, it encountered much suspicion based on concerns that it might try to use its new platform to build a monopoly, just as it did in the personal computer industry. The company's attempt to enter the market for operating systems for advanced mobile phones encountered a similar reaction, and players in that industry formed the Symbian alliance to counter Microsoft.

Language and Definition

Imprecision in the use of language is more of a problem in forecasting than one might expect. A classic example was an early 1970s forecast in which a leading expert predicted that the cost of long-distance telephony would fall by a factor of ten by the end of the decade. He was referring to the cost of the trunk portion of the transmission. Before long, however, his prediction was applied to the price of end-to-end service. Since the latter had to cover the costs of the local portion of the transmission and the costs of switching, neither of which was falling at such a rapid rate, the prediction was transformed into nonsense. However, this failure to use language with sufficient precision did not detract from the popularity of the forecast for a few years.

Other problems of language are less obvious. For example, slippery definitions commonly plague forecasting studies. When videotex first appeared in North America, its supporters were quick to differentiate it from existing online services such as Compuserve. Videotex is different, backers said: its page format is much more user-friendly; it supports color and graphics; and its tree-and-branch organization makes searching easy. A great deal of money was spent promoting the new concept, and its name became a valuable property in its own right. Not for the first time, however, a newcomer failed to live up to the hype. Supporters then found it convenient to broaden the definition so that preexisting services—not formatted into pages, without color and graphics, not structured in tree-and-branch form—could be encompassed and a more respectable penetration claimed. Not surprisingly, those associated with the more rudimentary predecessor services did not complain. Why should they object to the sex appeal conferred by the new term? In similar fashion, in some quarters in the late 1970s, the term *videoconferencing* grew to encompass the combination of audioconferencing and freeze-frame television (see chapter 6). (Early in the decade, AT&T apparently decided that all that could be salvaged from its Picturephone Service was its name, so it confusingly christened its new public studio videoconferencing service Picturephone Meeting Service despite the fact the technology, the concept, and their applications differed completely from those of the picture telephone.)

The importance of care in defining exactly what is being forecast cannot be overstated. Sony introduced its Betamax VCR in 1975. After a promising start,

VCRs using that standard lost the market to those on the VHS standard, introduced two years later. An optimistic 1975 forecast for VCRs could have proved either fairly accurate or wildly inaccurate, depending on whether it was meant to apply to VCRs based on Sony's standard or VCRs in general.

Forecasting Methods

Many forecasts are based on indications by a sample of the public that they would buy a product or use a service. In this case, the critical issues are whether respondents have sufficient experience with or knowledge of the product to make an informed response and whether the verbal response is a reliable indicator of future purchasing behavior.

In the case of products that are well known to the public, the issue of how to pose the question is straightforward—e.g., "Do you plan to buy a new car in the next six months?" While respondents may overestimate or underestimate the likelihood that they will buy a car in the next six months, at least they understand the question and can provide reasonably informed responses. The issue is much more complex when people have no experience with a product and may not have any understanding about what the product is or what it can do, as is the case with many new information and communication products.

In response to this problem, researchers have employed a number of techniques. One of the most common is to use a standard telephone survey and try to describe the new product or service over the telephone. This technique is the least expensive way to approach the problem—and probably the weakest. It tends to inflate positive responses, since verbal descriptions can emphasize positive attributes, and respondents have no experience with the product that would help them to understand potential negative attributes. They may also mistake the new product for an existing one. This problem occurred in early surveys about intent to purchase high-definition TV sets. Some respondents thought they were being asked merely if they intended to buy a new TV set with a good picture. Of course they did!

A second technique is to intercept individuals in a mall setting and bring them into a room or recruit a large group into a theater setting and show them still photographs, drawings, or a simulation of the service. This approach is used when the product itself is not yet ready or if it would be very expensive to bring the technology into the research setting. The same problem arises here: respondents do not really experience the product or service, and verbal descriptions that accompany the drawings or simulation tend to emphasize positive attributes. With little chance to understand potential negative attributes, respondents tend to report high interest. A major multiclient proprietary study in the early 1980s used a simulated home banking and shopping service in a theater setting. The results were extremely positive, as were the forecasts derived from the study. They indicated that a majority of consumers would readily subscribe to electronic home banking and shopping services. A number of large corporations used the results to develop and launch these services. However, when they were introduced, the general public showed very little interest.

A somewhat better technique is to allow a sample of the public to try the service or product in a laboratory or field setting. Here, people can experience the product for 20 or 30 minutes or longer and provide more informed responses about potential interest. While this method is clearly superior to using responses based on verbal descriptions, it is subject to a novelty effect that can last for several weeks: when people first start using a product, they often respond positively based on its novelty and use it more than they will subsequently (i.e., after several weeks of experience with it). One way to overcome the novelty effect is through a field trial, in which the product is placed in dozens or hundreds of homes and usage is tracked over a long enough period of time for the novelty effect to have worn off; once it has done so, indications of users' willingness to pay for the product are more meaningful. This approach, described in the appendix to chapter 4, is time-consuming and expensive, however. In a competitive market, many companies hesitate to postpone the launch of a new media product for six months or longer (as well as incur costs that can run into millions of dollars) to gain a better understanding of potential demand.

It is generally accepted that even when respondents have seen or tried a new product, market research studies of their intentions to purchase it have not had great success. People's answers to questions about whether they would buy the product provide very unreliable indicators of future behavior.

Those who produce forecasts of demand for new products have an even harder task than those who undertake market research studies of these items; the former must provide quantitative estimates of what demand will be at a specific time or times in the future. What tools are available to them?

Where the One-Eyed Man Is King

The Delphi Method is one of the best-known approaches to forecasting the demand for new communication products. The technique seeks primarily to derive a consensus forecast from a group of experts.[14] In an iterative process, members of the group independently and anonymously provide subjective forecasts; the aggregate results are fed back to each participant, sometimes together with an indication of how his or her forecast deviated from the average. Each then independently provides a revised forecast, perhaps with some justification for its difference from the previous aggregate forecast. The new group forecast is fed back, perhaps with some of the anonymous justifications, and so on. After three to five iterations, the process usually converges in the sense that progressively smaller differences from the average have diminished to a level at which a consensus can be declared. Some observers would argue that, in essence, the technique is less a forecasting technique than a technique for bringing a group to a consensus.[15] Variations include allowing members of the group to educate one another by meeting for group discussion between iterations (this is sometimes termed the Modified Delphi Technique) and weighting initial inputs to reflect participants' varying degrees of expertise or confidence.

The Delphi Method and its variants have proved very popular as a means of forecasting demand for new media products, and these methods do have some value. Interaction among the participants in the modified version can certainly produce insights that may be of practical value to marketers. The techniques bring some discipline to guesswork. And they have a certain credibility: How can one do better than to rely on acknowledged experts in the field? But is this credibility merited? Though evidence indicates that group predictions are less inaccurate than those of individuals,[16] little evidence shows that experts' guesses about the future are better than anyone else's. Indeed, there is some reason to expect that experts' guesses may be worse if, as may well be the case, they are likely to be biased by personal interest in the success of the technology in question. And although the question is less relevant than it has been in the past, one can also ask how a person can be an expert in something that is radically new. Where should one have looked for experts in residential picture telephony in the 1960s or videotex in the 1970s? Expertise in the technology would surely have been of little value. Maybe one should have turned to experts in human behavior. But what kind of behavior, and from what disciplinary perspective? There was and is an enormous variety of specialties from which to choose. It is now possible to find experts with decades of research experience relating to the marketing of new media products. But it may not have been easy to know where to look if one had been creating a Delphi panel in the early 1990s to forecast the demand for personal video recorders or in the early 2000s for VOD. (The box on binary predictions suggests the kinds of expertise that may be relevant in the type of assessment of a new product that should be undertaken before any forecasting process is started.)

In his definitive work on long-range forecasting, J. Scott Armstrong has commented on the use of experts:

TABLE 2.4. 1994 Delphi Study's Forecasts of Media Penetration in 2005

	Forecast (%)	Actual (in the United States) (%)
Video CD player (DVD)	15.1	70
CD-I	12.2	0
CD-rom	20.5	65
Virtual reality system	5.5	0
VOD	16.8	24
Digital terrestrial broadcast	17.3	<2
Fiber-to-the-home	12.2	<1

Source: Digital Media Forum, *Digital Technology Timeline,* 1994.

> Expertise beyond a minimal level in the subject that is being forecast is of little value in forecasting change. . . . *Do not hire the best expert you can—or even close to the best. Hire the cheapest expert.*
>
> . . . [T]heir place is in saying how things are (estimating current status), rather than in predicting how things will be (forecasting change). The estimation of current status does, of course, play an important role in forecasting. (Expertise in *forecasting methods* is also valuable.)[17]

His conclusions rested on a wide range of studies and he indicated that they applied to the use of experts in Delphi studies as well as in other frameworks.

We are aware of no evidence to confirm the accuracy of Delphi forecasts of the demand for new media products. Table 2.4 shows the results of a 1994 Delphi research project that tried to forecast the adoption of several new media in 2005. The participants came from several countries in Europe, North America, and Asia (although the results were not broken down by country). For comparative purposes, we provide the actual 2005 penetration figures for the United States.

The Bass Model

The most sophisticated method of forecasting the demand for new products was created by Frank Bass and those who have built on his work.[18] (Since we will now explain why this sophistication should not blind those with little experience in mathematical models to the method's substantial limitations if used in making the kind of forecasts considered here, less technically minded readers may wish to skip this subsection.) In line with Everett Rogers's theory (see chapter 1), Bass developed a mathematical model of the diffusion of new products that assumes that potential adopters are influenced by one of two types of communication channels. One group is influenced only by mass media (ex-

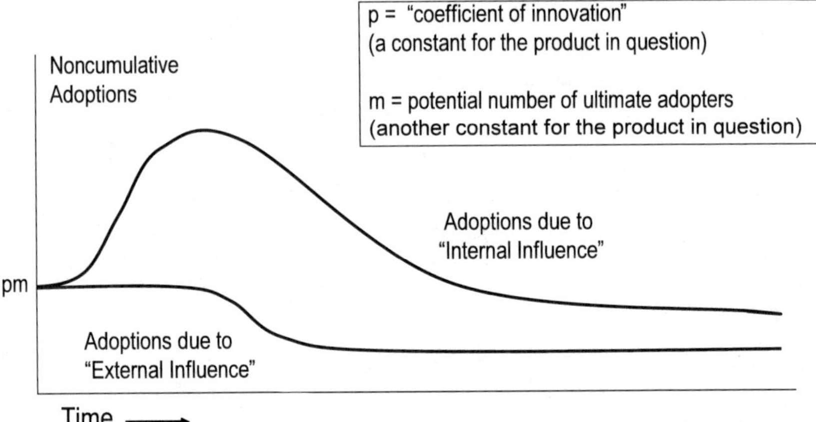

Fig. 2.2. Factors affecting adoption in the Bass model. (Data from Vijay Mahajan, Eitan Muller, and Frank Bass, "New Product Diffusion Models in Marketing: A Review and Direction for Research," *Journal of Marketing* 54 [January 1990]: 1–26.)

ternal influence). Though their decisions to adopt occur continuously during the process of diffusion, they are concentrated in the earlier periods. The other group is influenced only by interpersonal word of mouth (internal influence). Members of this group increasingly decide to adopt during the first half of the diffusion process and then decline (see figure 2.2).

The result is an S-shaped diffusion curve characterized by a formula with three parameters, which Everett Rogers, a supporter of the approach, describes as

> "a coefficient of mass media influence,"
> "a coefficient of interpersonal influence,"
> "and an index of market potential, which is estimated by data from the first few time periods of diffusion of a new product."

Rogers summarizes the "assumptions necessary for the basic simplicity of the original work":

1. That the market potential, m, of a new product remains constant over time.
2. That the diffusion of the new product is independent of other innovations.
3. That the nature of the innovation does not change over time.
4. That the diffusion process is not influenced by marketing strategies, such as changing a product's price, advertising it more heavily, and so forth.

5. That supply restrictions do not limit the rate of diffusion of a new product.[19]

With the possible exception of the last assumption, it is most unlikely that any of these would fit the cases of interest to us. Consider, for example, the assumption that the market potential of a new product remains constant over time. In 1982, the market potential for the personal computer would have reflected the fact that it was then used primarily for spreadsheets and would have changed subsequently to reflect a succession of new uses such as for word processing, for accessing the Web, and for entertainment. Or consider the omission of marketing variables such as price. Regarding diffusion models in general, Robert Fildes remarks, "The consistent failure to estimate marketing effects illustrates the problem [of limited data on potentially important (and often unmeasured) variables] as no economic model of adoption justifies their omission."[20] However, as described in the valuable review of diffusion models by Vijay Mahajan, Eitan Muller, and Frank Bass, others have shown how—at the cost of making it more complex—the original model may be refined and extended to relax these and other assumptions.[21] The model's weakness for forecasting demand for a new product that has not yet established itself in the marketplace can be seen in the estimation of its parameters rather than in its assumptions.

Discussing statistical methods for estimating the parameters from sales data, Mahajan, Muller, and Bass state, "Parameter estimation for diffusion models is primarily of historical interest; by the time sufficient observations have developed for reliable estimation, it is too late to use the estimates for forecasting purposes." They cite studies that "suggest that stable and robust parameter estimates for the Bass model are obtained only if the data under consideration include the peak of the non-cumulative adoption curve" (which is roughly halfway through the period of rapid growth after the curve takes off—that is, when the product is no longer new in our sense of the term). They also state, however, "If no data are available, parameter estimates can be obtained by using either management judgments or the diffusion history of analogous products." They also refer to some proposed methods for deriving estimates of parameters from judgments made by managers.[22]

Forecasts will be no better than the judgment about what product to use as an analogy or more detailed management estimates relating to the curve's parameters. Implicitly, moreover, either type of judgment almost certainly rests on the implicit—and frequently incorrect—belief that the new product in question will be a success. As a consequence, this family of models should not inspire confidence when used for forecasting the demand for products that have not yet established themselves in the marketplace.

The Seductive S-Curve

Other approaches to forecasting are simpler. The starting point for some is the assumption that, through time, demand will follow an S-shaped curve—a safe cumulative assumption provided that the product will be a success. It starts slowly, at some point develops rapid momentum, and eventually flattens out as the saturation level is reached. A typical way of proceeding is to estimate the saturation level, to estimate when it will be reached, maybe to estimate when the takeoff point will occur, and then to fit an S-shaped curve to these estimates, perhaps borrowing the particular S-shape from some past product that shares attributes with the one being forecast.

This approach avoids two ways of failing: having an unrealistically shaped curve for the progression of demand through time, which is a most unlikely mistake whatever method is used, and having an unrealistically high level for demand at saturation. But other—easier—ways of failing remain open. In particular, there may be little basis for estimating when, if ever, the curve will start to rise sharply; the service may never come near its projected saturation level; and even if it does, there may be no basis for estimating how long it will take to get there. At its weakest, this kind of approach assumes the success of the product and uses the S-shaped curve as a framework for a set of guesses. Strengthening this method would require explicit consideration of the probability that the product will succeed and some quantitative justification for estimates of time to takeoff, time to saturation, and level of saturation. There are no credible techniques to fill these gaps.

Gilt by Association

Another seductive and widely used approach to forecasting involves deriving a forecast for the total demand in an established market that will contain the new service among other existing services and then multiplying this large number by an estimate of the market share of the new service. So, demand for videotex was seen as a percentage of consumers' expenditures on information gathering (note the misconception of how videotex would provide value to its users); demand for teleconferencing was seen as a percentage of the projected number of in-person and electronic business meetings; VOD was considered as a percentage of expenditures on cable television and video rentals/purchases. Forecasting the already established base market is not the problem. A reasonable base of understanding and data exists, meaning that one is unlikely to go seriously astray. The problem lies in obtaining a static estimate, let alone a dynamic forecast, of the market share of the new product.

This approach to demand forecasting would almost certainly have yielded erroneously positive forecasts for 3-D movies in the 1960s, residential picture telephony in the 1970s, and videotex in the 1980s. It would also have underestimated the demand for MP-3 players, including iPods, since the base would have been existing portable music players, and for mobile phones in developing countries, since the base would have been existing landlines.

Some forecasters appear to avoid the problem by offering seemingly conservative forecasts. They estimate a small fraction for market share, thus appearing to be highly cautious. But a small fraction applied to a large base can yield a number that looks quite respectable. For example, if by 1996, only 10 percent of revenue from cable television and videocassette rentals and sales in the United States had moved over to DBS services, $4 billion in revenue would have resulted—quite impressive. However, the possibility that the fraction might be zero, thus yielding a forecast of zero demand for the newcomer, must also be taken into account.

In the 1970s, a collaborative project of several European telecommunications administrations attempted a scientific approach to estimating the share of a larger base market when forecasting future demand for teleconferencing.[23] The research team disaggregated business meetings into different types and used the results of controlled laboratory experiments on media effectiveness to derive estimates of the fraction of meetings for which users should in the future substitute different forms of teleconferencing for each type. The fractions were derived from models of user choice—in this case, normative models of the rational economic man or woman—informed by the results of an impressive program of psychological research. The model was intended to provide a forecast of the demand for each form of teleconferencing if potential users were to choose rationally. It could not produce forecasts of what the demand would actually be since it was too early to develop and test models of the processes by which potential users of teleconferencing would actually make their choices. Moreover, as chapter 6 explains, assumptions about how potential users should make rational choices were substantially flawed at that time.

Bottoms Up

Rather than work downward from a larger market to the one of interest, other analysts attempt to proceed in the opposite direction. They start with the individual using or purchasing unit (an individual or a family) and, with widely different degrees of sophistication, build a model of this unit's choice behavior in a market in which the new service is present.[24] For different values of its parameters, the model represents the behavior of different kinds of individuals or families that will be present in the marketplace. The model may be expressed mathematically or may take the form of a computer simulation. Either way, aggregating the individual decisions to obtain estimates for the market as a whole is methodologically straightforward, although extensive survey data may be necessary to obtain estimates of how many purchasing/using units of each kind exist. Further, considerable uncertainty may arise about estimates of the values of certain variables (e.g., the future price of competing products). Here, too, however, the main problem lies in the model of choice behavior.

Such a model cannot be properly tested if one is dealing with a new service. Nevertheless, using historical data, one can and certainly should test the generic model to see how well it would have forecast demand for comparable new products and services in the past, of course including failures as well as successes. Such models also are likely to require forecasts of other variables, such as disposable income, interest rates, or price levels. Difficulty in accurately forecasting these economic measures is well known and does not lend confidence to this technique.

The construction of a valid model of this kind clearly requires an understanding, at an appropriate level, of how the user will derive value from the product in question, an area in which many failures have occurred.

Prediction Markets

Will prediction markets be the "next big thing" in forecasting the sales of new media products and services? A prediction market is a specially created market for trading assets

> whose final cash value is tied to a particular event (e.g., will the next US president be a Republican?) or parameter (e.g., total sales next quarter). The current market prices can then be interpreted as predictions of the probability of the event or the expected value of the parameter. Prediction markets are thus structured as betting exchanges, without any risk for the bookmaker.
>
> People who buy low and sell high are rewarded for improving the market prediction, while those who buy high and sell low are punished for degrading the market prediction. Evidence so far suggests that prediction markets are at least as accurate as other institutions predicting the same events with a similar pool of participants. Many prediction markets are open to the public.[25]

Devotees of this method of forecasting have suggested its application to much more unlikely topics than the sales of new media products. One of the more creative plans was that the U.S. Department of Defense should operate a "Policy Analysis Market." In the summer of 2003, however, the public outcry provoked by the proposal that topics for this market could include future terrorist attacks soon caused the department to cancel the plan.

One variation is the "corporate prediction market," in which corporate employees receive "virtual trading accounts and virtual money [to] buy and sell 'shares' in such things as project schedules or next quarter's sales." Hewlett-Packard has experimented with applying the method to sales forecasting; Intel, Microsoft, and Google have also tried it for various purposes. In 2005, Yahoo, in partnership with O'Reilly & Associates, an organizer of technology conferences, launched the "Tech Buzz Game," described as "a fantasy prediction market for high-tech products, concepts and trends."[26]

If a new media product is about to be or recently has been launched, and if one wishes to forecast whether it will reach a particular level of sales within a year or two, it would be possible to formulate the issue with sufficient precision to make a prediction market applicable. It will be interesting to see whether this approach is used in such situations; if it is, it is very much to be hoped that it will be evaluated relative to more conventional methods. Since it may be less prone to bias, particularly if it is open rather than, say, restricted to corporate employees, it is conceivable that it will perform reasonably well relative to other approaches to forecasting—but that is not saying much.

If, conversely, one wished to look further into the future, forecasting the sales of the same product when it is still at the concept stage, formulating the issue appropriately would be very much harder. The costs of mistaken forecasts will, unfortunately, generally be much higher in this situation, since this is when winners may be missed or large but fruitless investments may be made. Also, it will unfortunately but inevitably take longer for evidence to accumulate regarding the effectiveness of this approach for forecasting further into the future. At least in this field, however, lack of evidence that a forecasting technique works has not inhibited its use (especially when the stakes are high).

Making Good Use of Early Postlaunch Information

A forecaster can, of course, do better when early sales data for the new media service are available because it has already been launched, even though it has not (yet) taken off. Nigel Meade provides an intriguing and instructive treatment of such forecasting problems that involves estimating the probabilities that the available data sets (sales) could have been generated by each of four different forms of diffusion curve and then using the sum of forecasts individually yielded by each of these curves.[27] The forecast formed from the weighted sum of the four component forecasts has been shown to be more accurate than the forecast provided by the best of the component forecasts.

The Leading Edge Method is used in business settings, where it has enjoyed some success. The technique develops forecasts based on the experience of those pioneering early corporate users of new systems that have established reputations as successful trendsetters in the use of new technologies. It may be adaptable to products for the residential market. It might also be useful in connection with field trials, which make users' experiences with a new product available for research before the product has become established. However, the users involved in trials generally will not be the types of people who have established reputations as trendsetters.

For new residential products, certain types of users may provide a useful early experience base—e.g., male teenagers, consumers of adult entertainment, and other early-adopter groups. At the same time, care must be exercised in applying what is learned from these groups to other segments of the population. Similarly, caution is necessary in applying what is learned from a group in one culture to a comparable group in another. For example, when text messaging (SMS) became popular among teenagers in Japan well before it did among teenagers in the United States, how safe would it have been for the former's usage patterns to provide the basis for forecasting adoption in the United States?

Boundary Markers

One family of techniques, of which the Historical Analogy Method and Income and Expenditure Analysis are key members, can be useful after a service has started to establish itself. Care is needed, however, because they assume the market success of the product in question. Consequently, for products that have not reached this point, these techniques can only provide an upper bound to a forecast.

The Historical Analogy Method is based on time series data on the early sales growth of past communications products. It provides a means of making projections using only the first few years sales data. The technique was developed by Roger Hough at the Stanford Research Institute around 1969 for use in the National Aeronautics and Space Administration's forecasting of the demand for new telecommunications services that might be relevant to its future programs. He used sets of time series data of the annual sales of a number of new "information-transfer" products and services, starting from the year of their introduction. He focused on the average annual growth rate from the year of introduction through a particular number of years later. He noted that (in the

United States) this number always remained at or above 200 percent in the first and/or second year before decreasing over time.[28]

Table 2.5 shows some of the figures he derived for the United States and Canada. For the two products that can be compared, the growth rates were lower in Canada. Such rates clearly must be expected to vary across countries.

Income and Expenditure Analysis is based on constancies or trends in the proportion of a household budget that is spent on certain forms of consumption—e.g., entertainment and information.[29] It is, therefore, a more disciplined variant of the method described earlier in which demand for a new product or service is estimated as a fraction of the total demand in a larger market. Unless used to provide an upper bound, this method is subject to the same underlying problem of estimating what value (other than zero) the fraction should take. In this sense, it is not really a forecasting technique.

Other regularities, too, can be employed to obtain upper bounds. For example, spending patterns for communication information and/or entertainment services can be translated into a percentage of weekly household income, as in chapter 1. However, while useful in understanding historical trends and helping to rule out unrealistically high forecasts, this form of analysis cannot help in estimating whether or when a new product or service will take off. Like the study of political history, it can inform an understanding of what may happen but cannot predict it.

TABLE 2.5. Growth Rates for Selected New Products and Services in the United States and Canada

	Average Annual Growth Rate (%)				
	First Year	First 2 Years	First 5 Years	First 10 Years	First 20 Years
Unites States					
Telephone	200	200	80	50	28
B&W TV	75	370	320	190	58
Color TV	260	310	133	88	55
Radio	567	356	157	77	37
CB radio	496	309	102	a	a
Cable TV	114	115	90	51	35
Pay TV	263	279	182	a	a
VCRs	144	126	85	60	a
Canada					
Telephone	90	73	52	34	21
B&W TV	67	213	184	98	45

Source: Roger Hough, *A Study to Forecast the Demand for Television Services Over the Next Ten Years* (Ottawa: Department of Communications, 1980).

[a]Too soon after launch for data to be available when the table was compiled.

Making the Best of a Bad Job

Progress in improving the methodological tools available for the kind of forecasting considered here is likely to be both difficult and very slow at best. Nevertheless, a focus on related nontechnical issues could substantially reduce the risks that forecasts will lead people astray. These include being an informed consumer, integration of forecasting and decision making, and reduction of bias.

The main reason for lack of optimism on the technical front is that forecasts of new media products will continue to rely primarily on judgment, although complicated mathematical formulas or complex computer models may sometimes obscure this fact. Another reason is the role of sheer luck combined with positive feedback in the success of product launches, as Brian Arthur observes.[30] (How, for example, will reviewers treat it? Will talk show hosts showcase it? Will celebrities use it in a public forum?) Those to whom the forecasts are served up need only ask themselves a few simple questions to appreciate the inevitable subjectivity of the process: for example, how did the forecasters deal with the probability that the product would not reach its takeoff point, or what potentially significant external factors were submerged under assumptions—probably implicit—of ceteris paribus?

Becoming an Informed Consumer

Some users of forecasts—that is, those who receive them direct from the forecasters—are better placed than others to be informed consumers. These users may be the managers who purchase the forecasts from an outside source, the managers who commission them from an in-house department, or specialized journalists who quote them in articles. These users should already know—or should be sure to ascertain—the forecasters' qualifications and track record. They should not need to request that any forecast be accompanied by clear statements both of the methodology used and of the underlying assumptions. When either of these statements is omitted, users should downgrade the credibility of what has been provided, even if they insist that the omission be rectified.

These opportunities are not enjoyed by those who do not order forecasts unless they are journalists in a position to withhold publicity. Beyond never trusting press release forecasts, what can they do? They would be wise to consider carefully information provided regarding source, methodology, and assumptions—or, too often, to consider the implications of omission of such information—before deciding how much, if any, weight to give a forecast. When writing about some new technology or some proposed service, journalists like to include forecasts to give concrete (or seemingly concrete) indications of its potential. It is as though citing the source along with the forecast is enough: the quality of the forecast is assumed to be the responsibility solely of the source and not of the journalist. But surely this is too lazy a practice. Many readers will not be as well placed as journalists who have been following the communication industries for years to appreciate just how fragile forecasts are. The *Wall Street Journal* has done a commendable job in creating a new beat, "The Numbers Guy," a journalist who scrutinizes forecasts and other data served up by organizations that otherwise would pass unchecked.

Integrating Forecasting and Decision Making

For corporate planning regarding new products, some researchers have suggested the value of employing more than one methodology.[31] We strongly agree. Multiple perspectives can provide a range in forecasts rather than a single estimate and can highlight any differences in the assumptions that underlie each forecast. Planning must not be based on the approach that says, "We will make (or obtain) the best forecast possible, then we will make the best plan we can in light of it." It is far more productive to recognize from the start that any single forecast can very easily turn out to be seriously in error and to plan accordingly.

The use of scenarios can be a good way to construct a long-term plan. A scenario provides an internally consistent picture of a possible future based on a particular set of broad assumptions. If a family of alternative scenarios is constructed, one can explore how well the plan that created the need for a forecast would work for each member of the family.[32]

If a forecast appears necessary, the first thing to do is to search for ways to reduce the need rather than consider ways to meet it. A key means to this end is to build in as much flexibility as possible to adapt very quickly in the light of what emerges following the launch of a product and to minimize the costs of its possible failure. We were once contracted to conduct research on the likely characteristics of demand for an electronic messaging service to be offered on a proprietary videotex platform soon to be introduced in the United States (see chapter 7). The research was commissioned to help the company decide on the capacity required in certain computer-related subsystems of the platform. The results were intended to contribute to forecasting the demand for the messaging service, which, in turn, would be used to estimate the necessary capacity. Realizing how prone to error any such forecast a few years into the future would be, we emphasized the importance of designing the system so that capacity could be added within a time frame consistent with what could be expected from short-term forecasting of demand after the service had been introduced.

Setting the need for a forecast in the context of the decisions to which it will be relevant should indicate the uncertainties on which focusing will be most useful. It could, for example, be much more important to estimate the probability that sales will reach their takeoff point within four years of a product's launch than to estimate the level in each of the first ten years. In principle, the more precisely one can specify what needs to be estimated, the better the estimate is likely to be.

Within a corporation considering or planning the launch of a new media product, forecasting must not be divorced from decision making. Much less progress is likely to be made in improving forecasting methodology than in the design of relevant decision options and the design of mechanisms for speedy gathering of information from the field.

Reducing Bias

Boards of directors, investors, and others who must assess proposals in which demand forecasts are significant should certainly consider the extent to which projects have been planned to minimize reliance on the accuracy of the associated forecasts. Difficult as it may be in a business climate of bravado and hype, those responsible for investment decisions should beware of the easy assumption that if the authors of a proposal explicitly address the possibility that a forecast is wrong, they are betraying a lack of the confidence necessary to make a new product a success. Responsible parties could also consider whether to commission either independent forecasts or expert critiques of forecasts presented to them.

Such actions may help counter self-serving biases toward underestimation of the probability that a product will fail in the marketplace. Other means of reducing bias also exist. Corporations that are regular purchasers of multiclient forecasts could use simple performance indicators to track their accuracy, as could journalists who specialize in the communications industries. Another possibility would be for a corporation to commission forecasts simultaneously for a set of several essentially unrelated products. If, as a set, the resulting forecasts suggested that the associated probabilities of failure were appreciably lower than those observed historically, the companies would have a strong case for concluding that the forecasts in the set had a strong bias toward optimism and away from realism.

It appears unrealistic, however, to expect change in the established pattern in which forecasts produced within the private sector—the vast majority—are hardly ever released in full to the press or the academic community. Instead, a press release is prepared with major findings from the study, while the study itself, the methodology employed, and the assumptions made are not subject to the scientific scrutiny that a university or government study would receive. As a result, weak or even fraudulent research may pass under the guise of a press release and be published in major newspapers and trade magazines.

When Prelaunch Forecasts Are Needed for Decision Making: Some Practical Guidelines

By now, it is abundantly clear that we have very little confidence in forecasts of the demand for new media products before they have established themselves in the market. Nevertheless, we can offer some guidelines to those who have to make the best of a bad job. While they inevitably fall far short of providing a strategy for success, we are confident that ignoring them will likely make a difficult situation even worse—probably a good deal worse.

1. *Follow good practice in obtaining judgmental forecasts.* If the product in question has not yet been launched, sales data will be unavailable, and one or more judgmental methods will have to be used. The two most frequently employed approaches are the Delphi Method and group meetings intended to result in an agreed forecast; the former seems likely to produce the better results.

Whatever method is used, good practice will very probably involve the following:[33]

- Decomposition—dividing the forecasting problem into subproblems, solving them separately, and combining these individual solutions to obtain an overall solution.
- Appropriate structuring of group meetings if they are used to generate forecasts.
- Appropriate selection of experts if expert opinion is used to generate forecasts. Here, the major danger to be avoided is bias. One should particularly avoid experts who would be affected by the success of the product being forecast. Nor should one expect experts inside an organization for which the forecast is being produced to be unbiased. Beyond a minimal level, degree of expertise is unlikely to improve accuracy.
- Critical examination of the assumptions underlying any forecast. This includes using "what if" questions to challenge assumptions, which may well be implicit, along the lines of "other things being equal."
- Combining forecasts obtained by different methods or from different sources. For example, if expert judgment is used, different forecasts may be produced by using different groups of experts or by posing questions in different forms. This is not a matter of selecting what one hopes is the single-best candidate from two or more forecasts obtained by different means; rather, it involves combining these different forecasts appropriately. There is good evidence that the combined forecast will outperform the best of its component forecasts.[34]

2. *Make an explicit forecast of the probability that the product will fail after it has been introduced into the marketplace.* This could be seen as repetition of the advice about decomposition. (The forecasting problem can be divided into two: what is the probability of takeoff being reached by a particular point in time, and conditional on that answer, what will the sales be at some particular point thereafter?) Even so, the advice is more than important enough to bear repetition.

3. *Retain a focus on the decision-making context.* Why is the forecast necessary? What exactly needs to be forecast? What are the possible costs of error in the forecast? How can the possible adverse consequences of error be minimized (possibly by increasing flexibility of downstream decision options and increasing the speed of gathering and analyzing market data)?

Follow accepted good practice in using forecasts for decision making, including the following:

- Obtaining different forecasts and considering the possible reasons for variation between them (see "Combining Forecasts").
- Assessing the uncertainty in the forecasts.
- Conducting sensitivity analysis—varying the assumptions on which a forecast using any one method is based and examining how the decision seemingly implied by the forecast would work out in practice.
- Considering the applicability of criteria such as robustness as alternatives to optimality when developing a multistage plan. (When plans are conceptualized as a series of decisions to be made at different points in the future, the robustness of any decision is a measure of the extent to which it leaves open later decisions that would be well suited to any of a range of situations that may develop after the decision in question has been implemented.)[35]

4. *Capture the potentially useful by-products of the forecasting process.* The process of forecasting is likely to produce insights of potential value to those responsible for marketing: for example, regarding contingencies that may arise and options for addressing them or consumer groups that should be targeted at an early stage and ways of reaching them. Indeed such by-products may turn out to be more useful than the forecast itself. They need to be captured.

5. *Conduct the forecasting and associated decision making in a way that will provide information about how to improve the processes.* If it is probable that the company will again be involved in prelaunch forecasting of the demand for new products, it should organize these processes to learn in light of how events turn out. At a minimum, processes should be documented, and that documentation should be retained in spite of possible embarrassment if results are disappointing—in which case the documentation becomes even more important.

// THREE //

Implementation

"If you build it, will they come?"

Implementation, which is where the rubber hits the road for new media projects, suffers from an image problem. It is widely considered to be a rather dull, largely technical process that, when successful, stretches between approval of the funding for an exciting concept and the concrete realization of a new service with actual, satisfied users. Yet on the basis of more than 25 years experience in a wide variety of new media start-up services—sometimes conducting research on their implementation, sometimes involved in other capacities—we have found the reality to differ greatly from this image. It usually involves far more than selection and installation of equipment, along with an as-needed sprinkling of changes in procedure and a little training. Rather, it is often a complex, broadly defined, process with multiple phases encompassing social, technical, and organizational components that, in addition to installation of a technical system, include managing relationships with partners, dealing with end users, marketing, interacting with equipment suppliers or manufacturers, overcoming obstacles, managing costs, and much more. As such, it presents significant challenges, failures are frequent, and it can often provide the research community as well as media professionals with valuable opportunities for learning at a time when the media concerned are not at all well understood.

While a project management literature treats implementation of information technology (IT) infrastructure and services, issues that are distinctive to the implementation of new media technologies and services have received relatively little attention in academic or industry circles.[1] In part, this gap may reflect a reluctance on the part of companies and public service agencies to report on the many problems encountered in implementing new media services. If the implementation succeeded, it did so because of a brilliant vision; if it failed, bury the evidence! This is a shame: implementation projects that have been dismissed as failures as well as those that succeeded have often provided us with valuable pointers to the future of new media. We have also encountered many unsung heroes.

This chapter is directed toward a broader audience than just practitioners directly involved in the process. If those responsible for funding implementation do not understand the types of challenges that typically arise, their expectations will be unrealistic. If those who conduct research, write, or teach about new media do not understand the major challenges, they may draw incorrect conclusions from a project that fails, perhaps seeing the concept of a particular new medium or service as having failed, whereas the true reason for failure lay at the level of implementation rather than in the concept. Furthermore, as we discussed in chapter 1, innovations often go undergo reinvention; this process may be facilitated during implementation.

A comprehensive treatment of the implementation process would require much more space than is available here. Rather, we discuss the major topics that arise, emphasizing aspects that are distinctive to today's new media and their users. The projects with which this chapter is concerned cover a wide range in each of three characteristics:

technology,

users, and

purpose.

The service being implemented may be based on any of the rapidly proliferating new media technologies, or it may be an innovative service based on a mature technology. An example of the latter was a mid-1970s trial telemedicine service whose considerable success was based on radical redesign of service delivery along with use of the simple telephone (see "The Value of Simplicity: Lessons from Telemedicine"). We are not concerned with technologies whose implementation has become routine in the settings considered.

Users may be a closed community formed by those working in a defined organization or set of related organizations, as when a new service is introduced for internal communication. Users may come from a combination of two different kinds of community: a closed community of service providers within an organization and an open community of members of the general public who are their clients, as when a new media service is introduced into processes by which the clients are served. Or users may form an open community: members of the general public who are the intended consumers of, say, a new interactive television service.

Intended users also differ in their degree of discretion in deciding whether to use a new media service. Although discretion is associated with whether the user community is closed, open, or mixed, members of the general public do not always have the most discretion and employees within an organization do not always have the least. For example, members of the general public may be unable to avoid interacting with a user-hostile interactive digital response system when telephoning a corporation, while managers may be well be able to avoid using a new videoconferencing system installed within an organization.

At an obvious level, the purpose of an implementation project is to reach the point at which the proposed service is working as intended for enough users at an acceptable cost. The question also arises of why the service is being introduced. It may be a pilot, field, or market trial; a demonstration project; or the rollout of a new service to the public. This aspect, too, should be regarded as a part of the purpose of a project that affects how it should be implemented.

The next section deals with planning an implementation project. It covers the importance of identifying and addressing possible conflicts among the interests of different stakeholders, together with the sometimes associated matter of resistance to change as well as more obvious issues such as estimating cost and time components. Implementation of new media is necessarily concerned with what users need at a time when their relevant needs may not be clear enough, so the section that follows is concerned with needs, including the process of needs assessment. We then turn to the intended users of the innovations. Here, somewhat greater emphasis is placed on the challenges of implementation within organizations, such as turf issues, staff turnover and training, product champions, and budget cycles, but many of the challenges in introducing new services for the general public are also discussed, including the technology skill levels of consumers and difficulties in providing training for end users who are not working within an organization but sitting at home and seeking an entertainment experience. The final section examines a set of issues relating to equipment, such as the location of equipment that is to serve a group of users and its reliability, as well as matters of users' comfort. These might appear to be a set of obvious and simple issues to resolve, but our research has found them to be surprisingly problematic in many instances.

While the chapter is divided into sections on "Planning," "Users," "Needs" and "Equipment," these compartments are anything but watertight. Most of the considerations raised in the final three sections should be considered at the planning stage. Most of the matters discussed under "Planning," "Needs," and even "Equipment" relate directly to users.

Planning

It may seem unnecessary to suggest raising at the start the simple question of who's in charge. Experience suggests otherwise, however, at least for the many large media conglomerates in which two, three, or ten people may have responsibility for "new media." In such organizations, people can often compete

CHANGING IMPLEMENTATION STRATEGY

A cable company began to implement a broadband Internet service using professional installers who drove to each house and manually installed the service. The pace of installations was slower than officials hoped, and the cost was high. The company wanted to implement a new self-installation strategy but did not know if customers could handle the process, which at the time involved opening up the personal computer, inserting a hardware component, installing software, and running cable within the household. The company conducted research with existing cable subscribers with a wide range of technical skills. Participants were brought into a simulated home office at the company's facility, observed as they went through the entire installation process, and subsequently interviewed.

The company learned a great deal. Installing the hardware proved easier than installing the software, which was a surprise. Women (who were more likely to read and follow written instructions) were more successful than men. Very few people watched a demonstration video contained in the installation kit or read any of the manuals. Nearly all used the quick-start guide as their main source of help. Subscribers fell into three categories: those who could install broadband with ease; those who could install it but needed moderate or significant help from the technical support help line; and those who could not do it no matter how much help was provided.

The company changed its implementation strategy accordingly, eliminating the video and reworking the quick-start guide in light of the fact that it would be the primary source of information. Salespeople received a list of questions to ask subscribers who wanted broadband: based on their answers, those who had little chance of successful self-installation were steered toward professional installation. The company also decided to provide more telephone technical support, reckoning that doing so was cheaper than providing professional installers for the group with moderate technical skills.

The pace of broadband installations increased sharply, overall costs for installations were reduced, and the self-installation program was deemed a success.

for control of a project, with all those responsible trying to put their stamp on the plan.

An implementation plan identifies where one wants to go and how one intends to get there. A good plan will also describe who will accompany one (partners), how long it will take, what it will cost, and what one expects to happen (outcomes) after one gets there. Planning should be a rigorous and disciplined process, built on a broad vision of what the project seeks to accomplish.

In any but the simplest projects, there are two straightforward reasons why there is unlikely to be a single implementation plan, laid out before the process starts and implemented as is. First, it is normal for unanticipated delays or difficulties to arise, requiring plans to be revised in light of events. Second, the full information necessary for detailed planning of some aspects may not be available until implementation is well under way; one of many possible examples occurs when locations for equipment are to be decided jointly with users, whose participation in the planning does not start until after implementation has commenced.

This means that a plan should build in flexibility so that the project can adapt to the unanticipated. It is also important to monitor the implementation process and change the plan as needed.

One of the distinctive features of new media projects is the way that technophiles—i.e., people who love the latest gadgets—take to them like wasps to honey. These technophiles bring enthusiasm and often strong technical skills, but many technophiles cannot distinguish features and services that people want from those that make little sense other than to boost the total number of features offered. If a technology can offer 33 features, why settle for 8, even if users want only 8 and the others will both get in the way of transparent usage and increase costs? It is important to seek out technical people who are not only competent but also understand the needs of end users and can speak in plain language to the implementation team. Whether utilizing internal resources or outsourcing the project implementation, it makes a great deal of sense to meet directly with the technology team and assess their skill levels, attitudes about features in the product or service, and ability to communicate with a wide range of managers and end users.

Research Objectives, Demonstration Objectives, and Funding Purposes

Some issues need to be thought through at the outset of planning the implementation process. One is agreement on and formulation of the project's objectives. Alongside the points usually emphasized in the wider project-planning literature, others can arise from the fact that new media implementation projects may include research or demonstration objectives.

Some new media projects evidence a surprising failure to agree at the outset (and then to remember) what the implementation team is conducting—i.e., a trial, a demonstration project, or the rollout of a service. Is there to be a pilot phase, or is the product or service going directly to full implementation? Disconnects at times arise between the implementation team and senior management. If they do not agree, proper planning can become difficult or impossible, and end users and journalists who follow the industry can develop false expectations. This was one of the problems with Time Warner's Full Service Network (see chapter 8). The team implementing the interactive television service thought that it was a trial, whereas senior management told the press that it was the start of a national rollout.

In field trials in particular, planners need to be aware of the possibility of conflicts between research objectives and service objectives after the project is under way (see chapter 4).

As in other kinds of implementation projects, one needs to consider the purpose of any document containing an implementation plan. The document as a whole may really be a proposal to raise money. For a university or nonprofit agency, the document may be a proposal to a funding agency. For a business, the document may be a proposal to corporate management or outside investors for support for a new venture. Plans included within a proposal for funding must be taken with a grain of salt. Proposals are written to sell projects and often ignore obstacles and known problems. Time and budget constraints may, therefore, prevent entirely predictable stumbling blocks from being overcome unless sufficient resources are hidden under other budget headings. The gamesmanship of proposal writing makes a negative contribution to dealing with the real problems an implementation team will face in developing and launching a service. To plan well, a team must identify what may go wrong and then take steps to reduce the corresponding risks and cater to the problems if they do nevertheless occur.

While implementation plans included in or accompanying business plans may have weaknesses, there is another side to the story for nonprofit organizations, especially in the fairly frequent cases when the implementation of a new media service is funded by an external source. It is much less usual for nonprofit organizations than for corporations to produce business plans. However, many project managers of new media ventures in nonprofit organizations told us that a formal business plan can be very helpful even to nonprofits. The process of developing it focuses attention on costs, revenues, target audiences, marketing, and other vital issues that affect noncommercial as well as commercial ventures.

Outside funding of new media projects in nonprofit organizations generally has a time limit, after which the organization is expected to pay for the service from its regular budget. From Day 1, the planning process should address the sustainability of the service after the start-up funding ends. One should generally avoid high-end services that can be supported by an initial grant but would be beyond the means of the user organization after the grant period. User organizations need to be aware of costs early on and to know when grants will run out. If they come to perceive a new service as free, they are less likely to retain it later when they would have to pay for it.

Few authors write about an ethical aspect of funding that can arise in field trials and demonstration projects. While it would definitely be a mistake to take success for granted when embarking on an implementation project in a closed or mixed-user community, it would also be a mistake to overlook the possibility that one will enjoy success—and along with it a far-from-welcome problem. The user community will very probably have been cajoled into making a significant investment of time and effort to adjust—maybe in connection with associated changes in organization and procedure, maybe in learning how to use new equipment well—and will be enjoying the benefits of this investment when the funding, which was sufficient to get the new service up and running for long enough to serve the project's research or demonstration objectives, runs out. If the new service must be withdrawn because there is no longer money to support its technology component, it surely amounts to breaking faith with the user community.

There are examples of transitions from project funds to regular budgets or other forms of financial support for services that have proved successful in field trials and demonstration projects; unfortunately, there are also examples where seemingly worthwhile services have had to be withdrawn for lack of continuing funding. What seems to distinguish the implementation of the former from that of the latter is that in the former, the need for the transition was identified and planned for from the outset.

Conflicts of Interest and Resistance to Change

When new communication technologies are to be introduced into an organization, one of the issues that needs to be thought through when planning the implementation process and kept under review thereafter is the possibility of conflicts between the interests of an organization and certain groups or individuals within or closely associated with it.

In a closed or mixed-user community, some stakeholders can easily perceive the success of a new media service as likely to disadvantage them. Even if they do not perceive this danger in advance, they may discover it later. Net benefits overall need not mean net benefits for all. In some cases, it is—or should be—hard to miss the possibility. For example, a telecommunication service that allows meetings at a distance and thereby reduces travel may benefit the organization concerned but not employees who like to travel or who feel that too much valuable in-person contact would be lost in a teleconference meeting. Other examples arise when a new service increases scrutiny of job performance. A new use of telecommunications to support distance education may make a teacher more open to evaluation by others. In some cases we have studied, nurses were apprehensive that a new telemedicine system would lead to more frequent checking of their work by physicians. More generally, by offering an additional means of communication, a new media system brings with it the possibility of reducing the autonomy of those who may have derived some benefit from traditional barriers to communication. Associated with actual or perceived loss in autonomy may be an actual or perceived drop in status.

We have encountered an interesting variation of this phenomenon when those who enjoy more power in a system are at the losing end. Organizations often come to operate in ways that suit the convenience of those who are at the top of their hierarchies more than those who are lower down; this development may be accepted on the grounds of efficiency, since the time of the former costs the organization more. In health care systems, the convenience of doctors may take precedence over that of nurses (and patients); in health care systems in prisons, the convenience of personnel can be expected to take precedence over that of prisoners; and in educational organizations, the convenience of teachers may be favored over that of students (though probably not over that of senior administrators). As a result, when service delivery is reorganized around the use of a new media service, some of the previous privileges of position may be at risk. In our research on implementation problems in field trials and demonstration projects of new telecommunications services in educational organizations, health care systems, and prisons, we have found that students, patients, and prisoners were more likely to be satisfied with the innovation than were teachers, physicians, and prison personnel.

Real and perceived conflicts between an organization's interests and those of some of its stakeholders may exacerbate the widespread but natural phenomenon of resistance to change and can even result in the emergence of saboteurs. It can therefore be quite helpful to identify and consider those risks early on.

Product champions—energetic change agents who strongly support and promote a new media innovation—can provide a powerful force in overcoming resistance to change.[2] For new media ventures within organizations, these champions may be senior managers who back the innovation and make sure that the right people within the organization provide whatever support is needed and that personnel use it. Senior managers can also take the necessary steps to remove or work around obstacles. Product champions are often people who see successful implementation of the innovations in question as advancing their careers; in a new media start-up, they are often high-energy salespersons who can inspire staff and promote the product effectively in the marketplace. It is difficult to create or train product champions. They have to be found within an organization or recruited from the outside.

If product champions can boost the chances for successful implementation of a new media product or service, saboteurs can throw a monkey wrench into the process. When implementation is within an organization, saboteurs may be disgruntled employees who do not want others in the organization to succeed, members of a group that is angry because funding did not go to a project they advocated, or workers who had resources diverted from their groups to the new project. Political rivalries within an organization can also breed saboteurs. Unless a successful appeal can be made to their altruism or they are co-opted, bought off, or kicked out, trouble will arise. Saboteurs can drain energy, time, and life out of new media innovations.

Opposition to a particular project can also arise from those who are not intended directly to use the technology. Within an organization, for example, opposition may result from associated organizational change that reduces the status of some department. Losing parties can also come from outside the system in question, at least as it is defined by those planning a project. For example, a local college may lose students to distance learning courses to the point that the college's viability is threatened, thus creating a problem for future local students wishing to enroll in other courses for which there is no distance learning option. Should those responsible for implementation of new distance learning programs consider this issue? We believe they should—and not only because local colleges sometimes turn out to have powerful political allies.

Time and Money

When dealing with new media, levels of uncertainty are likely to be relatively high. How well will a new media service and its technology work? How can the service best be used, or how should content for it be designed? What hidden problems may emerge? Will intended users be prepared to make the necessary adjustments in their established habits and procedures? These uncertainties can make for additional difficulty in estimating the time and budget required for implementation.

There are no standard periods for implementing new media services, but many project managers have reported that implementation took appreciably longer than they expected. Indeed, time appears to be a more precious commodity than money: fewer reported insufficient funding for implementation. Common sources of delays have included environmental impact studies, gaining regulatory approval, and partners who did not meet deadlines. As is to be expected, having insufficient time was much more likely to be a problem when organizational innovation was involved.

When implementation occurs within an organization, rapid technological change can create difficulties. A new technology may be surpassed before the implementation of a service based on it is completed. It may well be necessary to follow technology trends carefully and be prepared to shift technologies or adapt to new ones that come along, which can take up additional time. In consumer markets, the existence of competitors may result in considerable time pressure, causing organizations to "get it out the door" or "open for business" before a system or service is fully debugged. Such actions can lead to unsatisfactory initial experiences for users. Time constraints can also set off a chain reaction, as when a shortage of time leads an organization to eliminate a pilot stage in a project, which in turn leads the service to be launched with defects that could have been identified and remedied in a more controlled pilot setting.

A recurring issue that can affect both timescale and cost is whether to use internal or external resources to manage technology or create content. For example, should a text-based Web group that wants to add a video service to its site build the necessary capability internally or utilize an outside production group? There is no single answer. It depends primarily on the organization's capabilities and the relative costs of the two approaches. One way to resolve these questions is to examine what other Web sites have done and how well it worked. If using an external resource, it is important to do more than a cursory check on its reputation for reliability. Some observers suggest maintaining a backup external resource in case a primary provider cannot meet project requirements or deadlines.[3]

Some costs can be anticipated and accurately built into the project budget—e.g., new equipment and regular staff. Other costs sometimes are hidden or escalate quickly beyond the budget. In organizational settings, the unanticipated or higher-than-expected costs that occur frequently include training end users, retrofitting old equipment, internal wiring in buildings, ongoing equipment maintenance, and network connection costs. There are accepted approaches to dealing with these issues—if not always resolving them completely. In the case of retrofitting old equipment, it is important to decide which equipment is worth the cost of upgrading; if the cost of an upgrade begins to approach the cost of new equipment, it is clearly not worth retrofitting. One needs to be aware that the cost of internal wiring in buildings and ongoing maintenance can be higher than expected. Network connection costs can also be significant. The high demand for training end users can cause costs to escalate unexpectedly.

When new media products and services are introduced into consumer settings, the unanticipated or higher-than-expected costs that occur frequently are acquiring or creating content, gaining regulatory approval, replacing faulty parts, and providing warranty service for products that have been mishandled. Satellite radio is an example where content costs escalated sharply for the service providers; telephone companies such as Verizon and AT&T experienced very high costs in winning regulatory approval to provide television services; a number of digital cameras had to be recalled as a result of faulty batteries; and MP-3 player manufacturers experienced high service costs when the units were mishandled by consumers and required service under warranty.

Boring practicalities receive almost no attention in the literature. Nevertheless, these examples of factors causing unanticipated or higher-than-expected costs in organizational and consumer settings occur fairly frequently. For how much longer will they remain unanticipated? Implementation is often difficult; it may be too much to expect to avoid all mistakes. But it is better to make new mistakes than to repeat the old ones.

Market Issues at the Planning Stage

Planning must be based on a sound understanding of outside forces and organizations that can shape a new media product or service and their likely impact on implementation. In the case of satellite radio, the early service was shaped in part by radio manufacturers and the features they were willing to build into the first generation of radios. For high-definition DVDs, the early product was shaped by movie studios that licensed their content for each format and manufacturers that received licenses and built players. For manufacturers of portable music devices such as MP-3 players or mobile phones that store and play music, the iPod, the dominant product in the marketplace, shaped nearly all competitors since they would be measured against it in product reviews and consumers' minds.

New media innovations within organizations are shaped by many factors, such as available personnel to implement the innovation and budget cycles. The planning process can be used to identify and develop a strategy to deal with many of these factors. One of the many contextual elements specific to different markets is the planning of a new media service for the primary and secondary school markets in the United States. In this context, it is essential to understand relevant budget cycles. It often takes a year from a purchase decision to the actual purchase.

In consumer markets, the cost of making the first-generation product often exceeds what most end users would be willing to pay. In some cases, it is possible to identify innovators and early adopters who are willing to pay a high introductory price so that a second generation of the product and economies of scale in manufacturing can bring the price down to an acceptable level (as discussed in chapter 1). In other cases, there may not be a large enough group of people who are willing to pay a high price and sustain the product until the price can be reduced. Here, the organizations introducing the new media product commonly have to consider subsidizing it. Satellite radio providers Sirius and XM subsidized the first generation of their radios; Sony subsidized the first generation PS3 game consoles, as did Microsoft with its Xbox game console. From a planning perspective, the goal is to sell enough of the product to be viewed in the market as a success while containing the loss as a result of the subsidy. Some organizations limit the number of units introduced in the marketplace to control the loss and try to create buzz that the product "sold out" and cannot meet the demand from consumers, as Sony's PS3 did.[4]

Needs

Observers have often commented that a new media product or service failed because it did not meet a "real need." This assessment is generally understood as a stronger statement: there was no real need it could have met. Such statements may make nice epitaphs, but it is not particularly easy to turn them into practical advice for the living. In part, this seems to result from confused thinking about the concept of need.

Needs for new media products and services of the kinds that concern us here are often relative rather than absolute. They can be created by providing people with something that they subsequently are not prepared to do without. They can also be created by removing alternative means to desired ends. In this sense, perceived needs or wants matter; real need is not a useful construct.

The term *need* can also be used to denote a logical necessity: to speak with someone from one's car, one needs to use a mobile phone. A new media service with certain characteristics may be logically necessary to some new activity—for example, to watch favorite television shows whenever I want, I need a device such as a personal/digital video recorder (PVR or DVR) that can record and store them for schedule-free viewing. The new activity may or may not become a perceived need. Conversely, it can become a habit into which people fall because the new technology is available to them—e.g., many have become addicted to Blackberries though their actual need for portable e-mail is not strong; many others say they could not live without their PVRs, though these users had little apparent need for such devices before trying them. Or an activity may be perceived as an opportunity seemingly presented by a new use of technology, rather than a need.

Sometimes it is necessary to consider needs at two levels. An example from the early 1970s involved a projected interactive cable television service to provide in-home courses on parenting and other topics. At one level, the question arose as to whether such in-home courses were needed in the community; at a lower level, the question arose whether, if such courses were needed, an interactive cable television service was needed to provide them. In the case of two-level needs, it is important to consider the possibility that some other approach will be more cost-effective in meeting the higher-level need (see "Looking in the Shadows" in chapter 2).

Needs may range from strong to weak. The strength of a need can have a major impact on a new media project, particularly when technical problems exist.

In one situation, users who experienced few technical problems reported that they were a major deterrent to use of the equipment. However, users in another situation that had many technical problems reported that they did not deter use. These seemingly contradictory reports are explained by the fact that the second group was widely separated physically and had no adequate option other than using a teleconferencing system that had a number of bugs. The strength of their need affected their willingness to live with technical problems.

Need is often treated as something static and unambiguous. However, needs change over time, and some needs are surrogates for others—e.g., the desire to make money or advance one's career. It is useful to understand when a seeming communication need is a surrogate for something else. This knowledge may suggest an alternative approach to a particular problem. One should also not assume that members of an organization always want to meet any of its "obvious needs." For example, an organization might have an obvious need to earn more revenue. However, because a particular new media service would allow the organization to do more business and earn more revenue, it does not follow that the organization's employees would necessarily desire that new service. If they perceive the new business to entail extra work for them with no extra compensation, some of them may oppose or reject it.

It is commonly assumed that better communication is both a need and a want for an organization. This often proves not to be the case, however. For example, a teleconferencing service may encourage more meetings than are necessary or bring people into encounters under the wrong circumstances. Even if an "objective" need for such communication exists, users may not want it. Put simply, "What's in it for me?" They may not want to do their jobs better, or they may oppose any change in their current pattern of work. Similarly, a planner may assume that people will value more communication, saving time and saving money. Not always. Many new media services for consumers involve spending a lot of money for something that takes up time for no extrinsic purpose and discourages people from communicating with others—e.g., video games.

New media technologies and services often are purchased to meet one need but are used to meet another. Many parents purchase mobile phones for their teenage children so that the teens and parents can reach each other in case of emergencies, to arrange pickups after school, and to coordinate other activities. However, the teen primarily uses the mobile phone for social networking with friends.[5] Nor can perceived needs be taken at face value. In the past, potential users of a teleconferencing service often expressed a need for full-motion video. Yet experience led many of these users to be satisfied with an audioconferencing service supplemented by still images and graphics distributed via the Web. In sum, analysis of assumptions about need is a decidedly necessary but demanding activity. When considering need, it is a useful mental exercise to complete the phrase "need in order to . . ."

One alternative is to appeal to fear rather than need. Fear can be a powerful motivator, but strategies based on it can backfire. As the year 2000 approached, many information technology companies instilled fear of Y2K (remember that?), the idea that at the turn of the century, computer programs that were not designed to turn their internal calendars to the new century would crash and disaster would follow. Banks would lose track of billions in currency, airplanes would go out of control, company databases would be erased, and so on. Fear led many corporations to invest heavily to overhaul their computer systems. When disaster failed to strike those that were less prepared, many of those same corporations became cynical about information technology companies and for the next several years hesitated to invest in system changes where genuine needs for greater security existed.

The Substitution Paradigm

Much current thinking about new media technologies and services is based on a substitution paradigm. In organizational applications such as corporate Web sites for in-house use, the service may be perceived as a substitute for corporate brochures, training manuals, and other documents. In consumer applications such as PVRs, the technology may be perceived as a substitute for VCRs. There is good reason to challenge this thinking. In the case of corporate Web sites, the information provided often duplicates that in printed documents, which continue to be needed even if they circulate less widely. The site is likely to increase rather than reduce overall costs, especially if it utilizes advanced features such as video clips.[6] If designed well, a corporate Web site will stimulate new thinking and provide a central location for corporate information that would not be possible for printed documents. PVRs foster a new style of television viewing that differs substantially from that of households with VCRs. (In the 1990s, when VCRs were widely used, only one in four VCR households recorded any programs at all; most used them to watch rented movies.) Most television programs are time-shifted or watched in a time-delayed buffer so that a viewer can fast-forward through commercials. New communication technologies offer a relaxation of constraints: they make it possible to undertake new activities or to undertake old activities in a wider range of situations. Thinking based only on the substitution paradigm focuses on a technology's enabling users to perform existing activities better or at lower cost; it is likely to miss the potential benefits of uses other than substitution and to overestimate the degree of direct substitution that will occur. How well would the need for photocopiers have been understood if people had seen them only as substitutes for carbon paper?

How well would the need for personal computers have been understood if organizations had seen them only as a substitute for adding machines?

The substitution paradigm has been used extensively and often successfully in marketing new media services, though little evidence supports the contention that significant cost savings accrue when communication technology is used to replace print. In addition to the limitations in the argument for substitution already noted, at an organizational level, substitution often requires that funds shift from one budget to another, which can be problematic and provoke turf wars.

Needs Assessment

A needs assessment may precede implementation, as when a company is conducting research to determine whether a particular product or service is worth developing. Alternatively, such an assessment may be part of the implementation process, as when a decision has been made to conduct a field trial or a demonstration project and a needs assessment is conducted to determine the most suitable sites and applications. On the surface, the term suggests that it provides a way of avoiding the criticism that some new technology or service is a solution in search of a problem: *needs pull* sounds much better than *technology push*. But that is only on the surface. A needs assessments rarely starts with a blank technological slate. It is an empirical process for systematically identifying and investigating possible needs for a particular technology or family of technologies. Since its starting point is generally a limited range of possible ways (sometimes only one way) to meet any needs that are identified, it is, after all, very much a process in which a solution or limited range of solutions is looking for a problem.

This fundamental weakness of needs assessments, coupled with our remarks in chapter 1 that many successful new media were introduced into the market in the absence of an apparent need, cause us to have reservations about the methodology. Nevertheless, any systematic, empirical process that focuses on the possible relationship between potential users and a proposed technology or service can certainly be useful, provided one bears its limitations in mind.

A case can at times be made for conducting a needs assessment before new media technologies and services are created, when one of the assessment's roles may be to filter out schemes that would not be worth pursuing. At a later stage, there is a greater likelihood of unintended bias, as when it is part of the process of product development—often to justify funding for the project. Bias is less likely if a needs assessment includes sufficient consideration both of users' other needs—maybe higher priority needs that do not involve the technologies in question—and of the possibilities of meeting any needs that are found with other, more cost-effective solutions. Such possibilities too often are overlooked.

Sometimes one of the purposes of a needs assessment is to identify organizational units in which to conduct a demonstration project or to start the rollout of a new service. In such cases, one must beware of the fact that where the need for the improvement in effectiveness that the new service might bring seems to be highest, successful implementation may be the hardest. This is the case when, for example, current effectiveness is low because management is weak, morale is low, or turnover is high. Ironically, implementation may be easiest where the need is lowest: unto him that hath shall be given.

Realistically, needs assessments are a necessary evil as part of the process of new media product development—often to justify funding for the project. A needs assessment certainly is substantially better than nothing in filtering out

FILTERING OUT BAD IDEAS—THE CASE OF E-COM

One use of a needs assessment is to filter out bad ideas. There are many examples of truly bad ideas for new media services that should never have seen the light of day. One is E-Com, an electronic computer-originated mail service launched by the U.S. Postal Service (USPS) in 1982. E-Com allowed companies, which had to be "certified" by the USPS, to send documents electronically to one of 25 post offices that were equipped to receive the transmission. There, the document was printed out, put in an envelope, sent through the regular mail system to the local post office near the addressee, and physically delivered. At the time, terminal-to-terminal electronic mail existed, and fax machines were common in many offices. Though it could provide service in some situations in which regular e-mail or fax transmission was infeasible, E-Com was decidedly inferior. Moreover, for users of bulk mail, such as credit card companies or insurance providers, the slight saving in time of delivery meant little compared to the much higher cost (26 cents to deliver a one-page letter). For the USPS, providing the service was very expensive—the USPS lost money on every piece of E-Com mail. A simple needs assessment would have shown how end users viewed E-Com in the context of what regular e-mail or a fax offered; an inquiry among direct marketers would have shown that saving one day in delivery time was not worth the added expense. However, the USPS was not focused on end users or customers. It was trying to position itself in the emerging electronic mail market. Regulations restricted it from creating a true electronic mail service, so it found a differentiator that fit within its regulatory restrictions but made little sense in the marketplace. With few customers and bleeding money, the USPS shut down E-Com three years later.

schemes that would not be worth pursuing and in providing information useful in the planning of those that would.

Users

The end users of new media technologies or services are a surprisingly neglected group. In the whirlwind of activities to fund, develop, and launch new media, it is easy to take the intended users for granted, to think only of the average user without appreciating that the heterogeneity of users may matter, to treat users simply as inanimate and predictable components in an organization; or to consider them merely as buyers. Moreover, when potential buyers are studied, market research is likely to focus primarily on demographics—i.e., age, gender, race, income, and other social categories. However, a much wider range of variables is associated with the successful implementation of new media. Even the study of demographics should take time into account. The demographic characteristics of early adopters may differ markedly from those who purchase or use new media later (see chapter 1).

There is a difference between purchase and use. Some new media are purchased, used a few times, and then left to gather dust in closets. The distinction may not matter—a company may need to be concerned only about sales if, for example, its product is a novelty watch that has a built-in FM radio. In other cases, however, successful implementation requires that the new media product or service continue to be used over time—for example, a satellite radio, an MP-3 player, or a video mobile phone. Continuing use matters because it will generate revenue (e.g., monthly or per-use fees), content will be sold that plays on the device (e.g., songs for an MP-3 player), or the organization's mission is associated with continuing use (e.g., with telemedicine applications).

A focus on the user reminds us that innovations in which people operate or interact with new media are always social as well as technological. Among the many neglected issues is skill level in using technology. The broad public in developed countries generally has much greater skills in using technology than was the case 20 or 30 years ago. The ubiquitous presence of ATMs, personal computers, and even TV remote controls has taught most of the public basic skills in interacting with technology. The same can be said for many people in developing countries as a consequence of the widespread adoption and use of mobile phone technology.

Large differences exist in skill levels, however, and some people's skills are quite low, raising a few questions for those implementing new technologies or services. How much skill do intended users need? What are their present skill levels? Could better design of the product or service reduce the required skills? A related question is whether there is an opportunity to train users? In the absence of direct training, the available tools are user manuals, quick-start guides, online tutorials, and customer-support help lines. Few people read user manuals, and those with weak skills are not likely to use online tutorials. This leaves quick-start guides, which may not be sufficient, and telephone help lines, which are expensive to operate.

TAKE NOTHING FOR GRANTED

A telecommunication company was implementing a video-on-demand service that would display on regular television sets. Because the service involved a purchase, a password feature was added for security. The company tested the prototype with a broad range of potential users, giving them a mock password (1234) for the testing. One of the test participants, a male in his late fifties, entered the password and the screen displayed four asterisks, a convention familiar to anyone who has used an ATM machine or a password-protected Web site. On seeing the four asterisks, however, he said, "I guess I did something wrong." During follow-up questioning, he revealed that he had never used an ATM machine, a personal computer, or the Web—but he did watch a lot of television.

Much closer to the other end of the scale are users in organizational settings, who, although they have a good deal of experience in using computers, are less knowledgeable than they think they are. Patience and diplomacy may be necessary in responding to their "helpful" suggestions. Listening to their suggestions is useful; following all of them without careful scrutiny can be a formula for disaster.

The issue of user training illustrates a divide between open and closed settings. In the former, a new media product or service is made available to the general public; in the latter, implementation takes place in an organization such as a company, a school, or the military, where users can be trained and usage can be controlled to some or a large degree.

User Issues in Organizations

Our discussion of planning has already introduced the subject of resistance to change, which has been well documented as it applies to users of new media.[7] Exceptional leadership and people skills may be required to overcome this resistance.

Resistance to change can take many forms. The group for which a new service is intended may refuse to use it or may do so only when forced. Intended users may complain that the equipment does not work although it actually works well or engage in negative viral marketing—bad-mouthing the project to others in the organization. (Many people assume incorrectly that viral marketing is always good.) There are several reasons for resistance. Some people may have had bad experiences with technology in the past—it did not work well or did not meet their needs—and fear that the new service will also be disappointing. Others may perceive the new service as disruptive and simply do not want to change the way they currently do things. In a number of cases, we have seen resistance occur because people had to change their schedules. Many professionals—teachers, doctors, and lawyers, among others—function under heavy workloads that constrain their time. It is difficult for them to find the time to learn about new technology services, receive training, and integrate the services into their work environment. Resistance is almost certainly higher when people perceive a new media service as initially requiring too much time relative to the time that subsequently will be saved. Schedule issues can also arise when a new technology anticipates real-time communication among people in different time zones and members of one group must adjust their schedules.

The problems of resistance to change are mitigated to some degree if the workers concerned can be required to use the system, if they can treat or serve more people and thereby make more money by using the system, or if the technology relieves them of unwanted travel assignments.

Two different types of training are often required for new media systems and services: training to use the technology and training for new organizational roles associated with the introduction of the technology. Training in the use of technology will depend on the system and users' existing skills. In projects we have studied, technology training often worked best when it was in two phases: an initial wave of training to develop basic skills and a second wave a few months later to develop more advanced skills and answer questions that emerged as a result of their using the technology. It is important to recognize the limits of training and to avoid going beyond the point at which professionals should operate the equipment or complement regular users in performing certain technical tasks.

A few additional lessons stand out from our research about training within organizations. First, even if a system is very easy to operate, there is often a value in allowing intended users to try it out on a demonstration basis, when mistakes do not matter, before using it *for real*. Second, whether instructions are written or presented in person, they work better if offered on a colleague-to-colleague basis rather than being handed down by specialists. A third and related lesson is that peer training seems to work well in a variety of projects. Some projects have adopted a "train the trainers" approach in which an initial group of users is trained in using the technology, and they in turn become peer trainers for others. The advantages of peer training are that a peer shares a common language with other users, there is less concern about looking foolish in the presence of a peer, and most users have ready access to peers for subsequent assistance.

The chances for successful organization-wide implementation are enhanced when the initial groups that use the service have a high chance of success, thereby fostering positive word of mouth. Choosing candidate groups for early implementation may be based on perceived need, enthusiasm within the group, and knowledge gained through the training process. Training can be used to identify both people who are likely to experience early success and other people who will require more time and support.

When staff members need to be recruited to manage and operate a new media service within an organization, it is important to define their roles clearly before hiring them. Staff should also understand and be comfortable with the project goals. In many situations, these employees will have to interact both with technical people and those who know absolutely nothing about technology. In such projects, they need to be able to function comfortably in both worlds. Technical staff members need to be skilled in explaining technical issues in plain language for nontechnical colleagues and end users. A positive attribute of new media projects within organizations is that they often have high status, which helps to attract skilled staff. In an organization that will continue to implement new media services, the other side of the coin is that staff then acquire skills which are in high demand and may be recruited away to other companies or other groups within the organization. For this reason, it is important to ensure where possible that key staff can advance their careers within the new media project group.

Many nonprofit organizations that undertake new media projects have special staffing requirements. A strong need often exists for staff members who are skilled community organizers, since much work involves coalition building and marketing to other nonprofit organizations. A straightforward but often overlooked need is for someone who knows how to obtain purchase orders and generally navigate the bureaucracy, which can be daunting in large nonprofit organizations such as universities. Nonprofit organizations with limited funding can rely on students and community volunteers for some tasks, but such people typically have a high turnover.

In some user groups, we have observed problems with turnover and low morale. We have studied a number of new media services that were set up to provide previously unavailable services for organizations in remote rural areas. High turnover commonly occurs among personnel working in such areas as a consequence of professional isolation, social isolation, low pay, or other factors. Some user organizations estimate turnover rates to help plan how often a new training or promotion phase will be required. High turnover can also lead to problems if subsequent user groups do not support the application as the first group did or if they have problems with the system that were not present earlier. One telemedicine application had high turnover among a group of doctors using an interactive video system. The later users included many foreign-born doctors who had difficulty being understood over the video link and ultimately rejected the system.

Low morale within an intended user group can also prove to be a serious problem. In some cases we have observed, groups felt that new media services were taking money away from other projects that, they felt, were more needed; in other cases, low morale made intended users generally negative about any changes in the way they worked.

SOCIAL AND CAREER ASPIRATIONS OF NEW MEDIA USERS: THE CASE OF TELECOMMUTING

Telecommuters are people who are employed by organizations but spend one or more days a week working from home or a satellite office. The number of telecommuters in the United States has grown steadily over the past decade, reaching approximately ten million by the mid-2000s.[1] The scope for telecommuting has been greatly enlarged by advances in technology and telecommunication networks—in particular, by broadband, powerful personal computers, and improved corporate IT systems. Most telecommuters like the flexibility it brings in their schedules and the reductions in the cost and hassle of travel to work. Employers like telecommuting because it generally lowers their costs—for example, they need less office space—and because it sometimes helps them recruit or retain specialist staff.[2]

A minority of telecommuters do not like it, and many of these return to regular office work because they miss social contact with fellow workers, fear that they will find career advancement more difficult if they are seen less at the office, need technical support that is not available in the home, or cannot fight the temptation to goof off. Communication technology and corporate policy can help to solve or reduce some of these objections. Instant messaging, e-mail, and the telephone can provide some social contact; audioconferences or Web conferences can link telecommuters to meetings at the office; technical support can be provided over virtual links that let technicians literally take over personal computers from remote locations; and company policy can explicitly provide equal career advancement opportunities for telecommuters.

---

1. Sue Shellenbarger, "When Working at Home Doesn't Work: How Companies Comfort Telecommuters," *Wall Street Journal*, August 24, 2006, D1.

2. Mitchell Moss and John Carey, "Telecommuting for Individuals and Organizations," *Journal of Urban Technology* 2, no. 1 (1994): 17–30.

In many organizational applications of new media the goal is an information exchange between experts and those in need of the information they can provide. This can raise some subtle but important issues. First, in some cases, there can be different perceptions about whether the flow of advice should be one-way or two-way. We saw one example of this in a service in which a group of research doctors were consulting with a group of practitioner doctors. The research doctors viewed themselves as experts who were providing advice to the practioners. The practitioner doctors, however, felt that they were the equals of the research doctors and could provide advice as well as receive it. It is also worth noting that information exchanges on the Web often blur the distinction between expert and novice. The Web as a medium fosters a sense of equality and a—sometimes dangerous—perception that all opinions are valuable. Second, in some community settings, people assume that all expertise needs to be imported from outside, but important latent resources or relevant expertise may exist within the community. Such resources may be more acceptable than outside experts, and utilizing those resources may strengthen the community.

User Issues Arising Both in Consumer Applications and within Organizations

Many user issues such as security, privacy, and the initial experience of the technology or service arise both in applications for consumers and within organizations. Security of information about users is a large and growing problem. Unfortunately, many of the measures undertaken to increase security get in the way of a good user experience. The issue is highlighted by "password hell." At the workplace and on consumer Web sites, more and more new services require passwords. We know many people who have more than 50 passwords. At some universities, each student or faculty member must have 10 or more passwords just to use the university's Web site. Many corporate networks are even more onerous, requiring multiple passwords and mandating that users change them every month. As a further protection, systems require long passwords that mix letters, numbers, and symbols. In the real world, we have observed that many workers, often in open cubicles, write down all their passwords on post-it notes and stick them onto their computer monitors in plain sight for all to see.

Many consumers avoid sites with strong password restrictions. One research study of a new Web site for a credit card company had particularly strong password requirements. Users were brought into a laboratory and asked to create a password and navigate through the site. After hearing the password requirements, one person after another said, "I'll never use this site." The company's director of security, who was observing the users' behavior from an adjacent room, responded, "Well, people are just going to have to change their behavior."

Users' privacy involves a complex set of issues. Many people (for example, those who worry how information collected about their visits to Web sites will be used) view privacy as a major concern, while others (for example, those who display intimate videos of themselves on Web sites such as YouTube or Facebook) do not. New media can threaten privacy, as in the case of ubiquitous mobile phone cameras, camcorders, and surveillance cameras in public locations, or provide privacy, as in the case of Japanese teenagers who use text messaging at home to have private communication with friends. (Telephone conversations can be overheard by parents.) We have encountered some privacy concerns in organizations that use video teleconferencing systems. These concerns often are related to whether people out of the view of the camera can see and hear what is being said or to whether a video recording is being made. Such concerns may be justified or unjustified. Where they are unjustified, they may be alleviated if the system and its procedures are explained to users. One criminal justice application used a two-way video system for arraignments. The person being arraigned was in one location, while the public defender and judge were in another. The public defender's office demanded a means of private communication with clients, outside the earshot of the judge and police. Meeting this requirement (with a telephone call that others could not overhear) was essential for the acceptance of the new service even though the private telephone links were rarely used. User privacy needs to be addressed in implementing new media services, but it has not been an insurmountable obstacle in the applications we have studied.

We have touched on the importance of having a user's initial encounter with a new media service be a positive experience. Disappointed users are unlikely to return or to recommend services to others. At a later stage, within the context of successful prior experience, occasional difficulties are less serious. Yet problems are most likely at the start: technical malfunctions are more probable; users are more likely to make mistakes; and there is less understanding of how to manage or work around problems. The lessons are clear. It is not wise to release a new media service that has significant technical problems; more technical support is needed at the launch of the service, when bugs are more likely; and, in many cases, it is helpful to release beta versions of services to groups of technically proficient users, who often enjoy playing with the latest technology, identifying bugs, and making recommendations about how to improve it. Some new media technologies or services can be introduced in stages, ensuring that the first stage provides a positive experience before later components are added and thus buying time to develop them properly.

THE SMART CARD TRIAL IN MANHATTAN—NOT READY FOR PRIME TIME

A smart card can provide a faster and more secure alternative to a credit or debit card. Smart cards each have an embedded computer chip that incorporates its own processing capability and can store very much more data than a magnetic stripe. One of their many uses is as a *stored value* device. In this case, funds are downloaded to the chip's memory from a customer's bank account, and when a payment is made via a special reader, the memory is updated to store details of the transaction and the credit balance remaining. During such a transaction, there is no need for a telecommunications connection between the reader and a central computer, as there is when a credit card relies on a magnetic stripe. Smart cards are in much wider use in Europe and Asia than in the United States. One contributing factor to the slow development of smart cards in the United States was a major trial conducted on Manhattan's Upper West Side during the late 1990s.[1]

Large local banks issued thousands of smart cards, and 650 merchants participated. The goal was to replace credit cards and cash for a range of transactions, including the purchase of small items such as newspapers. Since transactions would not have to be authorized by computers over telephone links, the smart card was expected to be faster—good for the merchant and good for the customer. But the service was slower than either a credit card or a cash transaction; card readers were placed out of the way in stores; and consumers told friends that the smart cards did not work well. Such early experiences gave both merchants and customers negative impressions of smart cards, and the failed trial cast a pall over smart cards in the U.S. market for years.

1. Patrick Lambert, "Smart Cards: From Manhattan to the Web," *Business Week Online,* June 22, 1998.

The implementation process, through product design and training, needs to address how users interact with the new media technology or service. Two of the issues that arise here are social conventions and the user interface. Social conventions are the unwritten rules about how people interact with others face-to-face or through technology. They tell us to say "Thank you" if someone holds a door open for us or "Hello" when answering a landline telephone. Social conventions may change over time or vary by culture or region, and, central to our discussion, they are linked to specific media. In an organizational setting, it is sometimes possible to develop and teach social conventions through training sessions. Consumer applications generally develop their own social conventions over time, a process that can be a problem during the implementation stage. When the Web was first introduced to the public, social conventions in user forums were inconsistent. In the early days of e-mail, there were no emoticons such as :) to indicate wry comments. And, SMS abbreviations such as *cu* (see you later) took time to develop. In the short term, when there are few or inconsistent social conventions, users sometimes misinterpret what others intended to communicate. During the early years of e-mail and online bulletin boards, people would often angrily flame about messages they had misinterpreted.

The user interface is a principal component of new media design that affects how people interact with technology and with other people through technology. The user interface includes the design of the hardware (size, shape, number and location of buttons, and so forth) and the design of on-screen navigation features. In a rational world, the design of a new media product or service would precede implementation. In our experience, however, many new media products are rushed to market with incomplete or bad designs that must be changed during the implementation phase. Generally, insufficient time and attention are given to the user interface before and during implementation. Another problem can arise when the designers want to make radical changes from what users have experienced with other products and services. It is necessary to balance new design features that may enhance the new media product or service with a design that is consistent with major navigation features that users already know from experience with other services.

Designing an effective user interface takes time. We know of one company that assigned 12 people to the task of designing a remote control. It took six months, but they got it right, and the product was launched to rave reviews. We know of a publishing group that assigned 10 people to the task of designing a Web site that could handle complex transactions. They required 18 months, testing the product with end users in three waves and adjusting the design based on what they learned, but they got it right and the service worked flawlessly as soon as it was launched.

When pressed for time and forced to roll out a weak or incomplete user interface, the chances for successful implementation are reduced. Even when the user interface appears to be adequate, it is important to get user feedback during the implementation phase and make adjustments. Most applications do not get the user interface completely right by the start of implementation.

Equipment Issues

Many technical issues are associated with the implementation of new media equipment—for example, reliability and the speed with which necessary repairs can be made. Social and psychological issues associated with equipment, such as feeling comfortable using it or how location can influence people's use of it, have received less attention. We will treat both. Differences also exist between equipment issues in organizations and in households.

Nuts-and-Bolts Equipment Issues

Matching equipment characteristics to user needs and situational constraints requires considerable attention. We have observed many mismatches: a remotely controlled zoom lens was too slow for a crisis situation in a hospital setting; the wrong microphones were selected for a situation in which there was much background noise; a Web site used advanced software and high-end graphics for an education application directed toward schools with older computers that could not display the content; and an application used video monitors that were too small for users with poor eyesight. Knowledge about the user group and the situation where equipment will be placed must inform the criteria for selecting equipment. One constraint is a policy in many organizations, especially government and publicly funded institutions, of accepting the lowest bid for equipment. It is foolhardy to choose equipment exclusively based on the lowest bid. While cost is obviously an important criterion, it is only one element that should be employed in the decision-making process.

In general, it is better to purchase off-the-shelf equipment, which is cheaper and more readily available than custom or untried equipment, as long as it meets the application's needs. Installation and repair of equipment are so important that the quality and availability of those services should be part of the criteria for selecting equipment. Equipment frequently needs to be changed after projects are under way for a variety of reasons: the original choice was not appropriately matched to the needs of users, was too costly to operate, or did not perform as specified by the manufacturer. Anticipating at least the chance that this might occur, the project team needs to build flexibility into the budget and the implementation timetable.

A related issue is whether to choose a high-tech or low-tech solution. In general, high-tech solutions provide more options, are often easier to use, and are more attractive to groups such as young adults who like bells and whistles. However, they are generally more expensive and can bring reliability problems with them. Low-tech solutions are typically less expensive, are more reliable, and provide a familiarity that is attractive to many adults. However, low-tech solutions sometimes involve older equipment that needs more frequent repair, and the technology may become obsolete.

In order to choose sensibly between a high-tech and a low-tech solution, it is important to ask what are our technical skills and resources and whether our group can manage the technology and repairs or will we rely on a vendor. In general, it is wise to match the demands of the technology with the technological skills within the organization concerned. Bleeding-edge technology (the latest and most advanced) should probably be limited to groups with significant technological and financial resources. For others, it may be better to stay a few steps behind the cutting edge while trying to avoid technology that will become obsolete overnight. It is important to monitor technological change and distinguish what is significant and relevant from what is marketing hyperbole.

THE VALUE OF SIMPLICITY: LESSONS FROM TELEMEDICINE

Telemedicine seems to be reinvented every five years, though its origins can be traced to the nineteenth century, when some doctors diagnosed ailments by asking a series of questions via telegraph. The lessons about what does or does not work well in telemedicine have been repeatedly learned, forgotten, and relearned. In recent years, telemedicine applications have surged, in part because of the aging of the population and a need to monitor people at home. Some applications are decidedly high-end, such as operations performed by robots controlled by surgeons hundreds of miles (or more) away. Some of the most notable successes in telemedicine are, however, strikingly simple, cheap, and effective: e.g., nurses who follow up patients' visits to clinics with phone calls to make sure the patients are following instructions.[1] Such programs reflect lessons learned three decades ago in the Boston Nursing Home Project.[2] In that project, individual members of a team of nurse practitioners made routine visits to senior citizens living in nursing homes at intervals determined by the individual patients' general state of health. The nurses detected many conditions before they had deteriorated to the point that the patients would have had to make uncomfortable and expensive trips to hospital emergency rooms. On some occasions, nurse practitioners needed to decide whether patients should be referred to health care facilities or whether to administer tests or treatments. When physicians needed to be involved in this decision making, they could often be reached immediately by phone; where helpful, the results of simple, on-the-spot diagnostic tests (e.g., using portable EKG equipment) could be communicated to the physician over the telephone. The system's effectiveness and overall cost were significantly superior to those of a control group of nursing home residents whose health care was provided in the conventional manner.

---

1. Elena Cherney, "New Ways to Monitor Patients at Home," *Wall Street Journal,* April 18, 2006, D1.

2. Martin Elton and John Carey, *Implementing Interactive Telecommunication Services* (New York: New York University, Alternate Media Center, 1977).

What are the weaknesses or flaws in a technology that is being considered for use in a new media project? Some of them are hidden by the manufacturer and may not show up until a project is launched. They can often be detected through testing or by talking to people who have already installed the technology. The weakness may be deadly for the intended tasks or it may be something that is not crucial to successful use. Voice recognition technology, for example, works for some applications but is not ready yet for free-flowing speech from an unknown person calling an automated service center.

Users generally expect a high degree of reliability from equipment. When they do not get such reliability, their reactions vary in relation to their expectations (e.g., physicians are less tolerant of equipment breakdowns); the degree of their need (if the new media technology is the only way to get a vital service, problems are more likely to be tolerated); whether use is voluntary; and other positive aspects of the experience (e.g., whether they enjoy using the system). To safeguard against unreliable equipment, it is useful to build redundancy into the technical system. In this way, alternative or backup equipment can be used rather than losing service entirely or continuing with bad equipment

WHEN EQUIPMENT IS NOT THE PROBLEM

A cable television company decided to implement an advanced two-way PDA system for its installers in the field. Installers had previously used two-way radios or mobile phones to call the dispatcher for information about subsequent assignments. The new system had many advantages, such as a large information display and significant data storage, as well as e-mail and an instant messaging capability for communication with the dispatcher and other installers. The company conducted a pilot test of the new system with a few dozen installers. They initially complained about the equipment and the system, and some installers wanted to return to the old way of doing things, which they preferred. An investigation showed that while there were some equipment problems, they were minor. Direct observation of how the installers and the dispatchers used the new system pointed to the real culprit. Under the previous system, users had developed social conventions, including simple pleasantries at the beginning and end of conversations—e.g., "Thanks," "Talk to you later," "How ya doing?" However, they had not yet developed a new set of social conventions for use with the new system. Furthermore, it was difficult to enter text using the device's tiny keyboard—a strong disincentive to adding any language that was not strictly necessary. It became clear that the main problem was social, not technical. The solution was to add a component to training sessions that taught them the contemporary shorthand of text messaging and acknowledged the importance of simple social pleasantries.

until repairs can be made. In some cases where no immediate fix or alternative is available, it helps to identify how or where equipment is unreliable. One company we studied began to use an advanced mobile phone for field workers but had problems with gaps in coverage areas, resulting in many complaints. When the company provided workers with maps detailing areas where coverage was poor, unreliability became more predictable and complaints were reduced.

Many managers of new media projects have told us that the installation of equipment presented more problems than they expected. Relatively few individuals in large companies (and even fewer, of course, in small companies or nonprofit organizations) are highly experienced in installing advanced new media systems. Installation nearly always involves debugging. Often, insufficient time and personnel are budgeted for this task. Debugging consists of at least two phases. The first phase involves those problems that the installers or technical staff uncover. The second phase involves those problems that are discovered only when users get their hands on the equipment.

We have heard many nightmare stories from projects that depended on installation assistance from a faraway company. A potential installer who will not be available to come back many times for repairs and debugging should not be regarded as adequate. Project managers who have reported satisfaction with how equipment works have a common element: a first-rate technician on-site or available on a regular basis.

Location, Location, Location

The location of equipment can have a significant impact on usage of technology in organizations. There are at least five issues associated with it. The first is the physical distance between a user and where the technology is located. Proximity encourages usage. It does not appear that any precise distance can be assigned across situations or technologies beyond which individuals will not use a system. When users report that equipment is "too far away," it is a matter of that person's perception more than a measurable distance. Selection of locations for equipment is often a matter of accepting what is available. It is unlikely that good space is ready and waiting to be used in most existing office buildings, hospitals, schools, and so on. In one case, the space for the new media system was not secure. To prevent theft, the organization locked the equipment in a closet and provided the key to a supervisor. Finding that person and arranging to unlock the closet was a significant nuisance and negatively affected the service. Difficulties in finding nearby and easily accessible locations for new media equipment have arisen in many of the projects we have studied.

Turf is a second issue. In most organizations, different groups have different areas of a building assigned to them—a floor or a row of cubicles that they consider their turf. Locating equipment on the home turf of intended users encourages them to make greater use of it. A third issue is the normal traffic patterns of intended users. Locating equipment where people normally travel in their everyday routines affects perceived ease of access and encourages usage. A related issue is the existence of perceived barriers such as stairways, elevators, and security checkpoints. We have heard people say, "If I have to take the elevator downstairs, walk to another building, go through security, then walk upstairs, there is no way I'm going to use it," even though the journey might take only a few minutes. Users also expect that technology will be portable and therefore available wherever they wants it. In some cases (e.g., teleconferencing equipment), equipment must be placed on movable carts. In other instances (e.g., Blackberries, PDAs, and advanced mobile phones), each person must receive a unit of the technology and carry it with them.

It is useful to determine the social definition of the space where equipment will be located and whether the definition is compatible with the usage intended. For example, are executives expected to use a modern Web conferencing system with whiteboards and other new gadgets in what was previously a storage room? This may pose less of a problem if the room will be altered significantly for the new application. Also, some groups (e.g., students) are more malleable than others (e.g., bankers). If a space is used by multiple user groups, who are they, and will they have an impact on others who would not want to be associated with them and their applications by sharing the space? Dedicated space is clearly better. Problems may also arise from proximity to undesirable spaces. For example, outside noise and smells drifting in from an adjoining cafeteria have negatively affected some applications.

If a new media service links groups in separate physical spaces, as in audio-, video-, or Web conferencing, are they compatible? We know of one case where videoconferencing linked two groups of doctors, one in a university setting and one in a rural setting. Each group behaved appropriately for the space it was in, but this led to problems. The rural doctors dressed and acted casually, while the university doctors dressed and acted more formally. The rural doctors thought the university doctors were snobbish, and the university doctors thought the rural doctors were boorish. Had either group visited the other, they would likely have adapted to the other's social space and been more compatible.

The Web provides an opportunity and a challenge to create a virtual space that users enter into, leaving the social space they are in, at least psychologically. Avatars (iconic representations of a person in the virtual space) can further reinforce the entry into another space. Video games are all about virtual space, and many people derive great enjoyment when entering these fantasy worlds to battle demons, take part in adventures, or build virtual communities. We have seen fewer examples to date of successful virtual space applications for more down-to-earth tasks in organization such as education business or health care. However, virtual worlds have received renewed attention. Many observers advocate the use of virtual worlds in a broader range of settings, and much research is under way to measure their effectiveness and impacts.[8]

Comfort

Users need to be comfortable in both a physical and a psychological sense. Physical elements that affect comfort include the design of chairs, glare from lights, and cramped space. These factors can affect perceptions about the system or service as a whole. Many issues related to physical comfort are easy to identify. If members of the implementation team find the lighting or chairs uncomfortable, users probably will too. The difficulties that have arisen generally resulted not from a lack of concern about physical comfort but from the project team's inability to do enough to correct the problem—for example, a cramped room may be the only available space. It is a different matter with ergonomic issues such as the angle of a computer monitor or the height of a chair at a workstation. We have been surprised by the number of business, university, and library computer environments that have terrible ergonomics: for example, users may have to look up at an angle to see the monitor and then down sharply to see the keyboard, or chairs may be too low for a desk, forcing people to type with their forearms raised above their elbows. Many implementation teams apparently do not notice that something is wrong, and users often notice only that after a few hours at a workstation, their backs and necks ache or their wrists are painful. Simple guides about appropriate ergonomics for computer use are readily available.

Seemingly minor psychological elements in a new media environment can also affect users' attitudes toward a system. When using a two-way video teleconference system, some users worry that outsiders who are not part of the teleconference can see them. Potential embarrassment is another concern, especially when a person is using a system for the first time, since few people want to look foolish in front of others. The social definition of the space, discussed earlier, can also influence psychological comfort. Does it match the tasks to be performed? For example, a room with open access and people passing by is not psychologically appropriate for tasks that require privacy or a high level of security.

Consumers and Equipment

Many of the equipment issues that pertain to organizations affect consumer applications of new media as well, but people at home or in mobile settings have some unique requirements. Many of these are known and can be incorporated into product development and planning. Others will be discovered only after the new media product or service is introduced—another argument for building flexibility into the implementation phase so that changes can be made. Our treatment of consumer issues emphasizes the U.S. environment, with a caveat that household environments in other countries often differ markedly.

U.S. homes vary from small studio apartments to very large houses. In smaller apartments and homes, space for equipment is an important issue. On the one hand, the miniaturization of equipment (e.g., laptops replacing desktop PCs) and the combination of multiple devices into one box (e.g., a personal video recorder inside a cable box) have helped to alleviate space problems. On the other hand, large-screen HDTVs and larger computer monitors have increased space problems in some households. Open floor architecture, where walls do not divide a space into separate rooms, presents a challenge for new media with sound, which will leak into other areas unless listeners use headphones. If two or more devices are playing at the same time, the sounds mix. Some people tolerate such mixing, while others find it distracting.

Wireless networks have provided a solution to wiring problems. The combination of a laptop, broadband Internet access, and a wireless network is a powerful tool for accessing information and entertainment. The wires needed to connect different items of equipment or to recharge portable devices still present two problems. One is that they can take up space—for example, many households set aside space on a counter or a desk as a recharging station for multiple devices. The other problem is that some people find wires ugly. We have studied households where one spouse resisted a new media technology unless a partition or custom cabinet would be built to hide wires.

The social definition of a space and turf apply to households as well. Some spaces are work areas where people may resist technologies that are purely for entertainment. However, many homes mix work and entertainment in the same space. Turf issues arise when some household members are not welcome in certain rooms—e.g., teenagers generally do not want adults to spend time, let alone hang out, in their rooms; a home office may be off-limits to all but the people who work there. Equipment that is placed in these off-limits spaces is not likely to be used by multiple household members. A useful question to ask of a new media technology is: will it be a personal unit used by one person or a multiple user device? Many new media technologies—TVs, telephones, and home computers—have evolved from multiple-user to single-user devices.

Households, in turn, adopted multiple units of the technology to serve individuals rather than the family.

As noted, design and implementation of products are interrelated, as demonstrated by issues such as the reliability of equipment in households, which is surprisingly complex. Shouldn't all technology be as reliable as possible? It depends. Who will use the equipment, and how are they likely to handle it? A 15-year-old male might be expected to treat a product more harshly than a 40-year-old female. What is a product's expected life cycle? TVs are expected to have a long life cycle; mobile phones a short one. It may be argued that mobile phones are replaced frequently because they break easily. This is partly true, but they are also replaced because new features are released at a rapid rate, and many people want to get the latest. Reliability affects price. Many parts in a new media product come with a rating, which may be expressed as an expected lifetime in months or years or as amount of use. For example, an earphone jack has a rating for how many times the earphone can be plugged in. A 50-cent jack may have a rating of 300 uses; a $3 jack may have a rating of 5,000 uses. The implementation team must estimate how often the jack is likely to be used (higher for an MP-3 player, lower for a laptop). Designing a product may involve 30 to 50 such decisions, each of which affects cost and overall reliability. Poor reliability can have many negative effects, among them bad word of mouth, negative reviews, and costly recalls.

It is generally not possible to train consumers in the use of a new media product. Our research indicates that quick-start guides and calls to customer service are the most widely used instructional aids. Alternatives exist in some cases. If the new media technology or service is installed (e.g., by a cable or telephone company), the installer can provide some training. However, installers are often under time pressure and may skip training or give it short shrift, and the person who needs training may not be home when installation takes place. Trainers sometimes emerge naturally: a member of the family is technically proficient and trains others; or, a neighbor or coworker drops by to help. The need for training is affected by a technology's complexity and design. Resisting all the bells and whistles that are possible in a device and spending time on a transparent user interface can reduce the amount of learning necessary to use the technology.

One way to provide support for consumers is through customer service. Customer service calls tend to be front-loaded—i.e., most calls come in the first 30 days after a new media technology or service is acquired. Such calls can be very expensive, and many companies try to divert calls from live staff to automated telephone response systems and to offer relevant information online. Some compromise by providing live online help, which is cheaper than telephone calls to customer service but still provides contact with a real person who can respond to users' specific questions. Automated response systems and online help can answer many questions and may be reasonable parts of the solution. Many companies, however, go to extremes, making it very difficult for users to contact live customer service representatives. This option often is not on the menu of a voice response system, and customers must try to figure out how to break through the wall of canned responses. Indeed, third-party Web sites have been created to help consumers learn the secret codes that provide access to live people at customer calling centers. From an implementation perspective, it is important to find the right balance between saving on customer service costs and making users angry.

Equipment standards affect consumers in several ways. A lack of standards—for example, two or more incompatible technologies providing the same service—can confuse people and make them reluctant to adopt the technology until a unified standard is created or a winner emerges among the competing standards, as was the case for the two high-definition DVD standards. Standards issues arise not only with the core technology but also with components built into a device. Here, a lack of standards can increase costs in ways small and large. Many mobile phones have a jack for an earpiece that is not compatible with the standard plug for earphones. Anyone who wishes to use such a mobile phone for audio or video must purchase an adapter or a second set of earphones, adding cost and decreasing convenience. Why don't companies standardize parts? Many see nonstandardized parts as a revenue generator; others are motivated to use proprietary technology so that consumers become locked into the service provider. Very few batteries and battery chargers for mobile phones, digital cameras, MP-3 players, and other portable devices, for example, have compatible batteries or chargers. People traveling must carry two, three, or more chargers to provide for all their portable media.

// FOUR //

User Research

In telecommunications research, too much emphasis has been placed on technology and not enough on human behaviour and organizational dynamics.

—*Alex Reid*

This chapter discusses research that seeks to understand users at the individual rather than societal level. Such research may be conducted either at the level of a particular service or type of service (e.g., e-mail) or at the level of a medium (e.g., asynchronous computer-mediated text communication). It may focus on actual users of services that are already available or on potential users of services that are as yet available only on a limited basis or that are still to be developed. Using the term in its broad sense, we will refer to such research as *user research*. The term is also frequently used to refer to the much smaller field of activity centered on "usability" testing—for example, testing a prototype Web site to find out if real-world users understand what is offered and can navigate comfortably within it.

While user research is just one of many different types of research—pure and applied, quantitative and qualitative, from a wide variety of disciplines—that have been undertaken to investigate new media, it is the most relevant to the issues with which this book is concerned. Moreover, the understanding this research seeks to provide is essential to the analysis of a variety of important issues at the intersection of new media and such fields as mass media, public policy, health care, and many others. While some user research is pure research (in the sense that its objective is to develop theory rather than to contribute to decision making or the development of policy), much is applied research. Before many new media services became established, applied user research was typically directed to such questions as

For what purposes might it make sense for different kinds of people to use a particular service?

How would this service's effectiveness for specific purposes compare with that of established ways of pursuing those purposes?

How acceptable would the service be to different types of people for different purposes?

If intended to serve a specific function, how well does it serve that function; if intended to entertain, how entertaining do potential users find it?

How should the service be used to best effect?

How should associated equipment and content be designed?

How should the service be priced and promoted?

What effects would use of the service likely have on people's perceptions, attitudes, or relationships with one another?

What would be the probable side effects of using the service?

Now that the use of new media is widespread, corresponding questions are also asked about actual rather than potential services.

Although differences exist between pure research that seeks implications for theory and applied research that seeks implications for action, whether a particular study was undertaken as one or the other usually matters little, if at all, to readers who encounter it in the open (i.e., nonproprietary) literature. What matters are the actual findings and the rigor with which they were obtained; the latter can be assessed in the customary fashion. (Often, of course, proprietary research undertaken within a corporation or by a private consulting firm is not published.) Leaving aside market research, the same range of research methods has been used in each type of research (though field trials, since they require very large budgets, have naturally tended to be undertaken as applied research).

From the 1930s until the late 1960s, user research on new media was limited to—one could say bottled up within—educational research and ergonomics. The former goes back to the 1930s and was principally concerned with the relative effectiveness of different media for teaching, rarely finding much difference in effectiveness between use of the face-to-face mode and the media of radio, television, and later teleconferencing.[1] The latter, also termed *human factors*, was pioneered at Bell Laboratories in the 1940s and focused mainly on the design of the telephone handset.[2] (It is of little consequence here that the early ergonomics should probably not be regarded as relating to new media inasmuch as the telephone was well established by the 1940s.)

From the late 1960s to the mid-1970s, the field expanded rapidly, driven mainly by interest in whether and how emerging communication systems could be put to worthwhile use. In the United States, the United Kingdom, and Canada, government agencies played an important role in jump-starting research, often initiating it rather than responding to unsolicited proposals. Although the telecommunications industry spent considerable amounts on research and

DIFFERENCES BETWEEN PURE AND APPLIED USER RESEARCH ON NEW MEDIA

The key difference between pure and applied research on new media lies in context rather than methodology. In pure research, context is provided mainly by the current state of theory. In applied research, a key part of the context is the existence of clients with decisions to make. In consequence, applied research is often not worth undertaking if findings are unlikely to be obtained in time or are unlikely to affect decisions; conversely, other uncertainties may be worth addressing even when applicable methodologies are relatively weak.

Important differences exist in the two value systems. While significant findings of pure research are very likely to be published, such is not the case for applied research unless it is funded by public agencies or foundations: the published results of successful research undertaken or commissioned by a firm could well help competitors. However, unpublished research lacks the quality controls offered by peer review prior to publication or open review thereafter.

Another unfortunate aspect of keeping research results confidential is that they may well perish, particularly in the case of in-house reports of research on the early lives of new systems and services. After the immediate needs that led to the research have passed, the reports are generally regarded as having little if any value. Corporations are reorganized or taken over, researchers move on, and in-house reports are lost or thrown out. In some cases, companies have been unable to locate internal research reports just a few years old that contain valuable information. And research findings or data that would have no future commercial value to the company concerned (or its competitors) might well have a value within the wider research community.

The lack of communication between pure and applied researchers can be striking. For example, to the best our knowledge, one annual convention of the International Communication Association included not a single researcher from the media industry, though the gathering took place in midtown Manhattan, within spitting distance of a dozen of the largest media companies in the world. The situation is only slightly better at media industry conferences and conventions, where only a small group of academics may attend.

development for the new technologies, it was slow at first to recognize the contribution that user research might make. Until the arrival of the Picturephone, the huge monopolies that dominated telecommunications services perceived little need for marketing and hence for understanding users; they had moved from a rationing mentality ("You can have a telephone in any color, provided it is black") to a *Field of Dreams* mentality ("Build it and they will come"). The industry was shaken out of this complacency for two reasons: (1) the unexpected difficulties encountered in selling the Picturephone in the United States and a few years later in selling videoconferencing on both sides of the Atlantic and (2) companies' desire to have a presence in the rapidly growing field of user research on their technologies. Table 4.1 shows some of the major publicly funded research programs and projects initiated between 1969 and 1975 in the United States, the United Kingdom, and Canada.

TABLE 4.1. Substantial User Research Programs on New Media Initiated between 1970 and 1975 (in the United States, the United Kingdom, and Canada)

Main Technological Focus	Prospective Users	Main Funder(s)	Primary Reason for Funding
Teleconferencing	(1) Civil servants (2) Private sector managers and professionals	(1) UK Civil Service Department (2) British Post Office	(1) Need to find out how teleconferencing could facilitate dispersal from London (2) To explore the potential market
Teleconferencing	Civil servants	Canadian Department of Communications	To explore the potential enhancement of civil service efficiency
Teleconferencing	Members of a proposed "New Rural Society"	U.S. Department of Housing and Urban Development	To explore possible shifts of living and work out of cities
Telecommunications with a heavy emphasis on two-way television	Physicians, nurses, patients	U.S. Department of Health, Education, and Welfare, National Library of Medicine, Veterans Administration. U.S. National Science Foundation	Desire to explore how telecommunications could improve the delivery of health care
Two-way cable television	City residents and city governments	U.S. National Science Foundation	Proactive exploration of the social value of the technology in anticipation of future FCC rule-making
Potential contribution of Picturephone in the criminal justice system	Judges, court personnel, defendants, lawyers, probation officers	(1) AT&T (2) U.S. Law Enforcement Assistance Administration	(1) Part of a program to explore potential market for the technology (2) To facilitate improvement of the criminal justice system

Looking back, one can distinguish three eras of user research. The first was dominated by work in the fields of education and of ergonomics. The second, starting at the end of the 1960s, was given over mainly to work on emerging media, which, with a few exceptions, did not become established as soon as proponents had expected. It was a time of research on potential services more than on actual services. In hindsight, it can be seen as the calm before the storm.

In the third era, which started in the 1990s and was ushered in by the Internet and the online services that rode on it, the research scene has changed beyond all recognition. Drawing in many researchers from other fields as it continues to expand rapidly, it exhibits some of the same characteristics of vigor and unruliness as the Internet itself.[3] But while failure to accept conventional ways of doing things has lain behind much of the success of Internet innovators, thumbing one's nose at the principles underlying sound research would hold little promise.

In our view, it is too early for confident assessment of the value of the user research undertaken in the first decade or so of its present era. For this reason, our comments on differences between the second and third eras of user research will be somewhat brief. Most of the chapter focuses on the quarter century of research that started around 1970, with an emphasis on interesting lessons this research provides about methods rather than on findings. Much of the associated research literature is not freely available (in either sense) on the Web. Those who want to delve more deeply may need to rely on libraries for books or for their subscriptions to online journal archives.

The Emergence of a New Field of Research: The Late 1960s to the 1990s

As table 4.1 suggests, in the late 1960s and the early 1970s, government agencies' practical concerns created a demand for user studies of new media. The 1973 oil crisis added to this demand, since telecommunications were seen as a way to reduce transportation and associated reliance on foreign sources of energy. At an international level, the cold war provided incentives for Western governments to develop advanced technologies, and competition among Western countries spurred the development of new telecommunication services. As a consequence of these domestic and international pressures, government agencies in Washington, London, Ottawa, and beyond began to believe that some emerging forms of telecommunication could play an important part in helping solve some of the problems that fell within the agencies' areas of responsibility. The need to explore this potential created a situation in which funds sought researchers as much as researchers sought funds.

Since the relevant technologies were for the most part interactive rather than one-way, mass communication theory and research were not well positioned to make a significant contribution. With the important exception of Everett Rogers and a few others, scholars of mass communication were strikingly absent from the field until the explosive growth of the Internet commanded their attention about 25 years later. User research might have grown within or branched out from the field of ergonomics, but despite some early studies on videoconferencing by celebrated ergonomist Alphonse Chapanis,[4] it did not do so, possibly because of the difference between focusing on people using a particular piece of equipment in a particular setting and focusing on people communicating at a distance via particular media. It is understandable that there was no significant contribution from research on the relative effectiveness of media for teaching and from those who conducted such research. The latter's well-established research paradigm involved controlled experiments in which subjects were taught the same content via different media in natural environments, with effectiveness measured by, for example, test scores. It is vastly easier to use this approach with teachers and their students than, for instance, with health care professionals and their patients, salespeople and their customers, judges and defendants, or civil servants and other civil servants or the public. The educational setting offers an ample supply of subjects, readily available and accepted measures of outcomes, and little risk to subjects' performance and well-being.

Outside the field of education, researchers from a very wide variety of disciplines examined new communication media and technologies, generally working in interdisciplinary teams. Most research projects fell into one or more of the following categories:

1. Studies of the perceptions, attitudes and intentions of potential users.
2. Controlled experiments in a laboratory environment.
3. Field trials and demonstration projects.
4. Controlled experiments in natural environments.

Different approaches had different strengths and weaknesses in providing indications of the future use and usefulness of new media in particular settings (i.e., for the specific purposes of certain types of users in certain situations). For some research questions, certain approaches could not be applied: for example, it was not possible to investigate two-way cable television by means of a controlled experiment with one group of towns having a two-way cable system and a control group of towns not having it—installing the necessary infrastructure in the treatment group would have been too expensive.

Studies of Perceptions, Attitudes, and Intentions

The simplest way of investigating the possible use of a new communications technology is to describe or demonstrate it to possible users or let them try it out and then use questionnaires, interviews, or focus groups to find out what they think. This approach is associated more with the market research field than with noncommercial research. Unfortunately, however, whether the studies were conducted by market research professionals or by others, responses usually provided seriously misleading indications of future use: even though participants were often positive about a technology, they—or others like them—typically failed to use it when given the chance to do so subsequently. Various possible explanations exist for this phenomenon: people can be dazzled initially by the glamour of a new technology; they may not be good at predicting how they will behave in unfamiliar situations; they may not take costs sufficiently into account; and they may not anticipate the technical glitches that will subsequently dampen their enthusiasm. Whatever the underlying causes, such studies commonly failed.

As far as focus groups are concerned, there really was no good reason for hoping otherwise. Although they have their place in, for example, helping to raise research questions or providing information that may be useful to designers of equipment or content, focus groups, not surprisingly, were of no value in indicating the kind and number of people who would use a new technology. Focus groups may be biased by moderators, any group may be dominated by one or two participants, and because participants within any group influence one another, it cannot be assumed that comments by different participants are independent. In consequence, there is no basis for assuming that the output is statistically representative of what would be found in the population that the focus groups may have been intended to represent.[5]

Controlled Experiments in a Laboratory Environment

At the level of specific tasks that require communication either between people or between people and machines, controlled experiments in the laboratory are very well suited to the rigorous comparison of new and established media or technologies—for example, performance of a task undertaken using a videoconference may be compared with performance of the same task undertaken in a face-to-face meeting. Highly developed methodology is available for making comparisons in terms of the effectiveness with which the tasks were performed and of various other measures, such as subjects' perceptions of effectiveness or their views about the outcomes. Creating a suitable technological test bed in a laboratory is very much simpler, faster, and cheaper than installing a service in the field for an experiment or trial. When a program of laboratory experiments is undertaken, the program can be adjusted as the research team proceeds, since team members may decide on the specific objectives of a subsequent experiment in light of the theoretical implications of findings earlier in the program.

In the first half of the 1970s and primarily through a program of laboratory experiments, the Communications Studies Group (CSG) at University College London played a pioneering role in shaping research on users of new media

THE COMMUNICATIONS STUDIES GROUP

A 1969 planning grant from the United Kingdom's Civil Service Department (CSD) led to the creation of the Communications Studies Group (CSG) at University College London under the sponsorship of the CSD and the British Post Office. The recipient of the grant and the director of the research group that emerged from it was Alex Reid, and the CSG's primary goal was conducting research on the possible use of teleconferencing to replace a portion of the face-to-face meetings in business and government. The CSD's interest in telecommunications stemmed from its need to know how telecommunications might ameliorate some of the "communications damage" that could result from the further dispersal of civil service work away from London, a topic on which it was conducting a major, multiyear study. The British Post Office's interest followed from its then status as the monopoly supplier of telecommunications services in the United Kingdom and, as such, from its development of picture telephony and videoconferencing, among other technologies. In less than three years, the CSG had grown to more than 15 research staff and was being funded by more than 10 government agencies, foundations, and corporations in the United Kingdom, the United States, and Canada.

The CSG conducted a variety of studies—surveys of the types of business meetings in which people engaged, mathematical modeling, and cost studies—but became best known for its psychological studies (directed by Brian Champness), especially its program of laboratory experiments that explored differences in outcome when using audio, video and face-to-face communication for different tasks. Most of the more than 30 controlled experiments involved communication between pairs of subjects, though a few extended to small groups. Reid obtained permission to build a set of laboratories in the Civil Service Training College, which provided him with access to a constant supply of middle-ranking civil servants as volunteers for the experiments.

It should be noted that, while one of the authors was associated with the CSG, its international reputation was well established before he joined it, the credit being due to Reid, Champness, and their colleagues.

and influencing scholarly studies over the next quarter century. Broadly speaking, the CSG experiments indicated that for many tasks—for example, information exchange and certain types of problem solving—performance would not be significantly affected by the choice among the three media. This finding implied that a substantial proportion of business meetings that occurred face-to-face could be conducted effectively by some form of teleconferencing. When differences were found among the media—for example, in tasks involving conflict and bargaining—perception of the other and coalition formation were sometimes affected. On the whole, however, video communication came closer to audio communication than to a face-to-face meeting. As would be expected, in some asymmetrical cases, audio communication worked best for one of the parties—for example, for civil servants defending positions in which they personally did not believe.

Actual experience in the teleconferencing field over the following 35 years—with the considerable success of audioconferencing and the lackluster diffusion of videoconferencing (see chapter 6)—was in line with the CSG's conclusions. But broad generalizations do not do justice to the value of their detailed findings to the theoretician.[6] Applied research made a significant contribution to the agenda for pure research: according to Ederyn Williams, the CSG's and similar findings have identified "many media differences . . . though not as many as might be expected from a reading of the nonverbal communication literature. However, a unitary theoretical explanation for these differences has yet to emerge."[7]

With more modest objectives, laboratory experiments may also be helpful as a preliminary step in a field trial. They were used, for example, to explore issues relating to the design of pages in a teletext system introduced in a field trial at the start of the 1980s (see chapter 4 appendix). For this purpose, it was straightforward to simulate the teletext system using a computer.

This kind of use is a reminder of an important point made by Edmund Carpenter in his classic essay, "The New Languages."[8] He and Marshall McLuhan had conducted a carefully designed controlled experiment comparing the teaching effectiveness of television and radio with the effectiveness of older media. They found—or so it seemed—that television was the most effective (for students and subjects of the kinds used in the experiment). However, in an exaggerated pursuit of rigor, they constrained the use of each medium in an attempt to ensure that the words used in each treatment were identical: the radio treatment was simply the sound portion of the television treatment, and the print treatment was the transcript. Consequently, they had the results of a comparison of the effectiveness of different media when none of them was used to best advantage. When they repeated the experiment with the form of the teaching presentation tailored to each of the media, radio was the most effective and television came second. The wider implication is that it can be a mistake in laboratory-based research to insist that the experimental treatment (for example, a message to the subject) must be exactly the same and that only the medium be varied.

An associated difficulty has been little discussed in the research literature on media introduced since the mid-1960s (indeed, Carpenter's essay rarely seems to have been cited in this literature): experiments on the use of new media may provide misleading results if the media are not used in at least a reasonably appropriate way. A variety of aspects may need to be considered here: how content is presented, how interfaces are designed, and how equipment is laid out, among others. But if a medium or technology is really new, how can one know when sufficient understanding exists of how to use it well? Though it may be impossible to provide a useful answer to this question with any confidence, it would appear sensible to have it in mind when conducting or reviewing empirical research in the field. It may be relevant not only in connection with qualitatively new media but also when substantial improvements have occurred in the associated technologies—when exploring the added value of high-definition video for certain purposes other than television programming, for example.

For one important reason, the value of controlled experiments has been even higher than might have been expected: the evaluation of new media has frequently produced surprises both in controlled experiments and in other research. Such results raise the issue of drawing conclusions that would be valid in the real world from results obtained in an artificial environment. Here, two lines of thinking need to be distinguished. The popular line regards the laboratory as an inevitably unrealistic microcosm but hopes that the results will be sufficiently indicative of what would happen in the real world. The scientific line, in contrast, holds the principle that such experiments allow the rigorous testing of hypotheses drawn from theory; if the hypotheses fail the test, the theory needs to be adjusted in light of the findings. Theory sound enough to provide correct predictions of what would happen in the messiness of the real world should enable acceptably accurate predictions of what would happen in the much simpler environment of the laboratory. When such is not the case, the theory must be flawed. The scientific perspective, therefore, allows strong conclusions to be drawn from surprising results in the laboratory: for example, "The results from the laboratory showed that there is something wrong with our understanding of the use of this particular technology or medium, so assumptions based on the same understanding about what would happen in the real world are also likely to be wrong." This statement also holds if common sense rather than theory provided the shared basis for both the hypotheses and the real-world predictions.

SOME SURPRISES

Past empirical research on the relative strengths of different media for particular communication purposes has sometimes produced surprises. This chapter discusses David Conrath et al.'s findings regarding physicians' use of two-way video[1] and Carpenter's findings that radio was more effective than TV in certain settings,[2] and chapter 6 discusses some unexpected findings regarding the relative effectiveness of audioconferencing, videoconferencing, and in-person meetings.

Other surprises have related to acceptability rather than effectiveness. For example, in one experiment, blind typists significantly preferred audio to Braille feedback when making corrections.[3] In a field trial in the mid-1970s, British investigators were surprised by the high level of acceptability of a computerized telephone information service; its convenience apparently more than compensated for defects in the quality of its synthesized speech.[4] Rather more surprising were the results of a trial by an American telephone company in the 1970s: consumers preferred to dial in credit card numbers to make long-distance calls from pay phones rather than speak the numbers to an operator; dialing them in was perceived as faster, although it actually was slower.

More recent surprises have included many consumers' willingness to pay for radio (over 18 million U.S. satellite radio subscribers); millions of mobile telephone users' preference for texting over e-mail and even over voice messages; the acceptability of two-way video for psychotherapy sessions; the finding that improving the audio quality of a TV signal creates the perception that video resolution is better; and why some people cannot see a difference between regular definition TV and HDTV. Particularly surprising, even if it is now just accepted wisdom, is the observation that people will pay for books, magazines, and newspapers in hard-copy form but not in electronic form to be read on their computer monitors (electronic downloads to mobile devices have broken the barrier).

---

1. David W. Conrath, William G. Bloor, Earl V. Dunn, and Barbara Tranquada, "A Clinical Evaluation of Four Alternative Telemedicine Systems," *Behavioral Science* 22, no. 1 (1977): 12–21.

2. Edmund Carpenter, "The New Languages," in Edmund Carpenter and Marshall McLuhan, eds., *Explorations in Communication* (Boston: Beacon Press, 1960), 162–79.

3. R. S. Hirsch, "Procedures of the Human Factors Center at San Jose," *IBM Systems Journal* 20, no. 2 (1984): 123–71.

4. I. H. Witten and P. H. C. Madams. "Telephone Enquiry Service: A Man-Machine System Using Synthetic Speech," *International Journal of Man-Machine Study* 9, no. 4 (1977): 449–64.

Although the selection or development of outcome measures for the standardized tasks used in controlled experiments is often conceptually straightforward—how long it takes to retrieve required information, how accurately radiological diagnoses are made, how well instructional objectives are met, and the like—it is often necessary to think beyond a one-dimensional measures ranging from bad to good. The use of one medium may differ from the use of another in several dimensions—for example, how well a task is performed, the time taken to complete it, and the parties' estimations of how well it has been accomplished—being more desirable in some dimensions and less in others. Another situation in which there are effects on outcomes that cannot be placed on a single scale arises when there is conflict between the parties involved: what is better for one party may be worse for the other, as when the party with the stronger case prevails more often in the audio-only mode than in two-way video.[9]

Valuable as experiments employing standardized tasks and outcome measures have proved in research on new media, usually they are possible only in the artificial environment of the laboratory. This limits their usefulness in exploring a variety of issues. In laboratory experiments, the task is taken out of the context in which it arises naturally, potentially affecting subjects' motivation to perform the task or their confidence in how well they did so. Such experiments are rarely applicable to the study of other than immediate outcomes. Moreover, the framework provided by tasks may be inapplicable, as in the use of interactive television for entertainment purposes. And laboratory experiments are not well suited to questions regarding when, how, and with what effects a particular system would be used if it were available in a natural setting. Trials and experiments in the field do not face these obstacles.

Another limitation of some laboratory studies is the use of available subjects—that is, college students—to compare media. Might the results of a laboratory study differ if another demographic group were used as subjects? Would such differences matter? If the end users of an intended service will be students or if the findings will be applied primarily to students, such discrepancies may not matter. If, however, the intended user group includes a significant proportion of senior citizens, for example, their skills, likes, and dislikes may differ in important ways from those of students.

Field Trials

In considering past research in this field, distinctions among the terms *field trials*, *market trials*, and *demonstration projects* are of little significance. Customary use of language would suggest that uncertainties regarding how useful an innovation will prove should be lower in demonstrations than in trials, but such does not appear to have been the case in practice. Market trials are private sector initiatives, while field trials are generally funded by public sector agencies. As a result, the former often include pricing issues among their foci, while the latter do not, and results from the former are much less likely to be publicly available unless they are subsequently thought to be useful for marketing or public relations purposes. Nevertheless, the commonalities among the three types of activity are much more important than their differences.

In all three, an innovation involving the use of communication technology was introduced into a natural setting in which it was expected to be valued, and a combination of straightforward research methods was used to explore how well it worked in practice and the effects of its use. The fact that the setting was natural did not, however, mean that the field trial would be realistic in all respects: for example, similar funding mechanisms would generally not be available for the application elsewhere; a site particularly favorable for the innovation might have been chosen for the trial; implementation might have a much higher level of support than could be expected at subsequent sites; and the people concerned would generally have known they were participating in a trial.

The assumption that the innovation would be valued was crucial: if the service in question was discretionary (those concerned could choose not to use it), little worthwhile learning would result if they did not chose to participate. Very often, however, preexisting options remained available, an unavoidable circumstance in the case of market trials and an understandable circumstance in many other field trials, since the innovation had not yet proved itself. As a result, use of the trial services was generally discretionary and disappointingly low. Hence the amount of learning of the kind that had been hoped for, was also disappointing.

For some research teams, the field trial had been preceded by other projects in an ongoing program; for others, it stood alone. Loosely speaking, the distinction was between treating the trial as part of a larger research process and treating the research process as part of a trial. Projects of the latter kind tended to fare poorly, which is hardly surprising.

If an innovation failed in a trial because it had not been well enough implemented, it was very hard to draw any conclusions about the potential value or lack thereof of the underlying concept. Services did not fail in field trials because the technology was too expensive; funds had already been made available. They did not fail because outdated regulations needed to be changed. Observers sometimes concluded that a service featured in a field trial had failed because "it did not meet a real need," with the implication that no real need existed. Such a conclusion was unwarranted if it was likely that the service simply had not been implemented in a way that provided a good enough chance of success.

Implementation turned out to be much more difficult than expected for a variety of reasons (see chapter 3). In many cases, the process involved organizational change, collaboration among different organizations, and/or the installation and maintenance of immature technical systems. When researchers rather than experienced managers were in charge of implementation, the associated management challenges were not of a kind that the project leaders would necessarily welcome, be experienced in meeting, and have budgeted for.

Underlying these challenges was the importance of service objectives relative to research objectives. The service had to perform well if utilization was to be meaningful, but this objective could conflict with research objectives, and not only because funds and time were limited. Conflict could arise, for example, if experience during a trial with a quasi-experimental design suggested that changes should be made to the technology or service in question; these changes in "the treatment" could make drawing conclusions about its effects more difficult. A different kind of problem lay in the fact that users sometimes needed to invest significant time and psychic energy to take advantage of a new service. Would it have been ethical to ask them to make such investments without making them aware that, however valuable the service proved, it might well have to be withdrawn when the research funds ran out?[10]

Planners of trials seem to have assumed that summative evaluation (informing external clients how well an innovation worked in practice) and formative evaluation (conducted to assist internal clients in the successful implementation of the innovation) were distinct activities and that only the former had lasting value. This assumption is open to challenge on both theoretical and practical grounds. On theoretical grounds, it would be challenged by proponents of action research, which has recently started to be applied in the field of new media.[11] In addition, followers of operations research as it was originally developed in the middle third of the twentieth century rather than as it is practiced today might well observe that in its older form it could have provided credible evaluation as well as have minimized conflicts between research and service objectives. (Operations research was originally developed in World War II as a process in which teams of scientists from different disciplines supported military decision making.[12] Today, it can be regarded as a specialty within management science, which emphasizes the use of mathematical models.) On practical grounds, one might comment that what usually matters most in a field trial is that the service in question should be used (an exception being if it is like a fire extinguisher, for use only in an emergency); otherwise, little useful research can be conducted. The complexity that is often involved in the implementation of new media means both that future use should not be taken for granted and that much of value to external clients may be learned from formative research.

After research (or demonstration) funding came to an end, the continued operation of those trial services that had attracted a sufficient level of worthwhile use and whose future running costs would not have been unexpectedly high might have been expected. It might also have been expected that success would have led relatively quickly to the initiation of somewhat similar services at other sites. In fact, however, survival, let alone transfer, was decidedly problematic. The fates of four acknowledged successes from the mid-1970s to the mid-1980s are instructive. Although the city of Phoenix was more than willing to pay to keep the Picturephone system in operation following the criminal justice system trial, AT&T withdrew the system after concluding that the overall market for Picturephone would be too small for economic viability and that the cost of maintaining the experimental system would be prohibitive (see chapter 6). Warner Cable installed its interactive cable television system, Qube, in Pittsburgh, Cincinnati, Milwaukee, and Dallas after the moderate success of a market trial in Columbus, Ohio. Nevertheless, a few years later it started renegotiating its franchises and phasing Qube out in all these cities on the grounds that it was not commercially viable (see chapter 8). With funding mainly from community arts grants and local commercial sponsorship, the two-way cable television system for senior citizens, installed in a field trial in Reading, Pennsylvania, continued in operation after National Science Foundation funding came to an end, albeit with considerably less ambitious use of its two-way capability. However, the application never transferred to other cities, primarily, it would appear, because funding such a service was not regarded as being of a sufficiently high priority and the organizational costs of developing and maintaining such a system are high. For two reasons, the highly successful Boston Nursing Homes Telemedicine project (a controlled experiment in the field rather than a field trial, which is briefly described in the following section) almost expired when the experiment ended: budgetary inflexibility meant that federal monies could not be used to fund it even though the project would save the federal government more than it would cost, and it was almost impossible to find a hospital-based physician who would agree to be on call 24 hours a day. At the last minute, the state of Massachusetts stepped in with the necessary funding, and a suitable physician was found.

One of the lessons regarding public sector trials was the importance of preparing from the start of the project for possible success and transition to more secure funding (as had been done for the Reading project). A second lesson was that lower cost and readily available technology often trumps its more sophisticated and costly cousins, as in Reading and the Boston nursing home project. Unfortunately, it is often harder to obtain government and foundation funding for projects with simple off-the-shelf equipment and easier to gain funding for state-of-the-art yet untested systems.

A wide variety of methods were used to gather data about users and uses in this period. General concerns included the use of unobtrusive methods and the avoidance of intrusions on privacy. Most of the methods were well

ETHNOGRAPHIC RESEARCH

Ethnography is a form of qualitative research that emerged from anthropology in the late nineteenth and early twentieth centuries. Anthropologists used it to study distant cultures, visiting with and often living with native groups for months and sometimes years. These participant observers took detailed notes about customs, behavior, and cultural values. Many anthropologists used photography, audio, and film to record behavior and complement their written notes. Since the cultures under study were typically not well understood, anthropologists concentrated on very basic behaviors and customs, such as what people ate, how they dressed, the structure of their language, and the organization of ceremonies such as weddings and funerals.

By the mid-twentieth century, some researchers began to use ethnographic research methodology to study everyday behavior in developed countries. Erving Goffman was a key figure in this transition to the study of everyday life using ethnography.[1] Beginning in the 1970s, scholars began to use ethnography to study media behavior. Europe took the lead, but researchers in the United States and Asia also adopted ethnography. By the twenty-first century, ethnography was widely if not universally accepted by many academics and commercial researchers and was used by Intel and NBC, among many other companies.

Ethnographers observe behavior in homes, businesses, and public places, conduct in-depth interviews, and identify patterns that reflect broader cultural values, new ways of communicating, and consumer attitudes. These observations and interviews are often recorded and subsequently presented along with written reports. Many ethnographers have studied behavior associated with mobile telephones across a broad range of cultures.[2]

Ethnography should be considered a complement to quantitative research methods. Both have strengths and weaknesses, but they mitigate each other's weaknesses. Much of our research utilizing ethnography has been complemented by a survey or other quantitative measurements. In some cases, especially when there is little knowledge about behavior involving a new media technology, it is beneficial to start a research program with ethnography and follow it with a survey. Ethnography helps to discover patterns, and the survey can quantify how many and what types of people are using the technology in these ways. In other cases, ethnography is a useful tool to put qualitative flesh on the quantitative bones of a survey.

---

1. Erving Goffman, *The Presentation of Self in Everyday Life* (New York: Doubleday Anchor Books, 1959).

2. Laura Forlano, "Wireless Time, Space Freedom: Japanese Youth and Mobile Media" (paper presented at the University of Pennsylvania Digital Media Conference, October 2003); Lee Humphreys, "Mobile Sociality and Spatial Practice: A Qualitative Field Study" (PhD diss., Annenberg School for Communication, Philadelphia, 2007).

established—questionnaires, interviews, logs—and need not detain us here, though ethnographic methods also began to be used. Where a trial service was computer-based—for example, computer conferencing—a considerable amount of data was generated automatically; in other cases, it was necessary to prevent record keeping from becoming too much of a burden. Where a service was not interactive—for example, teletext—planners could consider installing a meter into terminal devices to capture usage data. All of these projects were conducted before the era of institutional research boards—and their stringent privacy requirements—at universities. The boards might have killed some of these research projects. How, for example, could one have protected the privacy of senior citizens in the Reading project when programs were transmitted to all cable subscribers in the city?

Controlled Experiments in a Natural Environment

For the new media of interest in the 1970s and 1980s—principally, Picturephone and two-way television in business, government and health care, interactive cable television, computer conferencing, and videotex—it would generally have been impossible or far too expensive to meet the methodological requirements of controlled experiments in the field (in particular, treatment and control groups containing sufficient numbers of independent experimental units, no risk of contamination between the two groups, and a treatment that would be held constant for the duration of the experiment). However, two early telemedicine projects made good use of this approach.

In the early 1970s, the Boston Nursing Home Telemedicine Project, conducted by Roger Mark, who was at the same time a practicing internist and a member of the electrical engineering faculty at the Massachusetts Institute of Technology, showed that it was possible simultaneously to improve the quality of care provided to nursing home patients and to reduce the cost of the care with a telemedicine approach based on a team of nurse practitioners supervised by a hospital-based physician and using decidedly modest communication technology (principally telephones and Polaroid cameras). In a rigorously designed experiment, patients in the treatment group were drawn from 13 nursing homes, those in the control group from 11 others.[13]

Also in the early 1970s, David Conrath and Earl Dunn, a management scientist and a physician, respectively, carried out a multistage research program on telemedicine in Canada. The first stage was an observational study focusing on the extent to which primary care physicians used different senses when examining patients; finding the importance of the sense of touch, they concluded that nurses should be with patients when physicians were engaged in remote diagnosis. In the second stage, the researchers conducted a controlled experiment comparing four modalities to link physicians to patients and nurses—color television, black and white television, still-frame black and white television along with a hands-free telephone, and a hands-free telephone alone. Patients who came to a clinic seeking medical attention were invited to take part in a trial of telediagnosis as well as to receive an examination and, as appropriate, treatment by a physician in the usual way. More than a thousand patients accepted the invitation, enabling comparisons between the physicians' diagnoses and decisions made via telecommunication links with those in person.[14] The researchers found no statistically significant differences in diagnostic accuracy, proportion of supporting investigations requested (e.g., laboratory tests and X-rays), time taken for the diagnostic consultations, and effectiveness of patient management across the four communication modes, though patients slightly preferred the more sensory-rich modes of communication. Conrath and Dunn then designed a third stage: a telemedicine field trial in which hospital-based physicians used still-frame black-and-white television and hands-free telephones for communication with distant nurses and patients. The trial took place at six sites in the Sioux Lookout Zone in northwestern Ontario and at two hospitals in Toronto.[15]

A Time of Rapid Transition: The 1990s Onward

The explosive growth of the Internet and Web-based services caused dramatic change in the user research scene during the 1990s. Previously, most user research had been directed toward answering questions about services that were not yet in widespread use—if they were in use at all. Subsequently, however, those seeking understanding for its own sake faced an abundance of opportunities to study how new media were actually being used. At the same time, naturally, rapid growth occurred in private sector and public sector demand for research that would contribute to decision making. Also playing their parts in driving the expansion of research activity were other new media services—in particular, wireless telephony, which was also growing explosively.

Changes in the industries involved with new media and in the associated infrastructures created a very different research environment. And as a result of the Internet, new types of data become available and new research methods were developed.

The Environment for Applied Research: The Need for Speed

By the 1990s, regulatory changes, together with versatile and rapidly improving new infrastructures, had caused fierce competition to replace slow-moving monopoly as a characteristic of nearly all markets for new media and created a need to bring new services to market much more quickly than in the past. At the same time, it became possible to a much greater extent than in the past to launch new media services without the heavy cost of installing new or improved infrastructure, whether locally or nationally. For many new services, expensive new terminal devices were unnecessary. Some new services could be provided via the Web, making them immediately available to subsets of users with adequate local connections and sufficiently up-to-date computers. For others, would-be users had only to buy relatively inexpensive new terminal equipment. Associated services could be launched or test-marketed without the long lead times and heavy infrastructure costs that had been associated with, for example, Picturephone in the late 1960s or two-way cable television services in the 1970s. Further, rapid turnover in some categories of equipment—e.g., mobile phones—eased the process by which new generations of equipment and associated new services were brought into homes and businesses.

Mobile telephony somewhat resembles the Internet in stimulating and enabling the need for speed, though expensive upgrading of infrastructure is also required. Although cable television companies still receive some protection from their status as local monopolies, their market is increasingly open to competition from landline telephone companies (and satellite television companies), so they too face the need to introduce new services quickly on their new two-way digital infrastructures.

The introduction of other new services requires substantial investments in new infrastructure. From a carrier's perspective, the whole point of a set of new services may be that they cannot be accommodated to an acceptable standard using existing infrastructure: making them available would require an expensive upgrade. The claimed demand for such services played a large part in carriers' arguments for the substantial investment in infrastructure that would be required for both integrated broadband networks around 1990 and 3G cellular services about ten years later. Even in such cases, a need for speed exists if another new infrastructure may compete with the proposed one. 3G cellular services, for example, faced potential competition from an infrastructure combining WiFi and 2.5G.

User research is often undertaken to improve people's ability to predict or to answer "what-if" questions. When doing so, there is the risk of failing to take properly into account relevant changes that will occur in related areas. With the greater interconnectedness typified by convergence of technologies and services (think of the Web, though convergence encompasses much more) and the increasing pace of innovation, the number of relevant related areas increases and assumptions of ceteris paribus become riskier. Chapter 2 brought up the example of corporations investing in satellite-based mobile telephony but failing to allow for the explosive growth of much less expensive terrestrial mobile telephony. This case, however, was relatively simple: underestimating the success of a competitive technology that already existed. Other cases may be far less straightforward. For example, telephone companies investing in fiber-optic networks to or near the home need to be concerned about change in people's television viewing habits.

Within the private sector, the need for speed has created a motivation to "get it out there" as quickly as possible and hope all goes well, without waiting for the results of research on whether and how to get it out there—for example, computer software is often launched both with many flaws and with uncertainties about demand. Companies bet that demand will exist and hope that they will have time to fix flaws and offer downloadable patches to users before the level of pain reaches a threshold where people abandon the product. Much less of a case can be made for the applied research that might have been undertaken in the more sedate era of a few decades ago. Either no research or a different kind of research with a faster turnaround is undertaken.

On their domestic fronts, governments do not face competition in the way that companies do, so it might be thought that they would lack a similar perception of the need for speed. To a lesser degree, however, governments seem to share this perception, whether they are providing new systems on behalf of their citizens or developing new public policy. As an example of the former, it would seem—at least with the benefit of hindsight—that various e-government initiatives around the turn of the century, including e-voting in the United States, might well have profited from more prior research. The hype that surrounded these initiatives may have provided an incentive for unwarranted speed.

Even in the slower-moving era of the 1970s, the manager of the relevant program at the U.S. National Science Foundation described the daunting difficulties inherent in undertaking user research to guide important public policy decisions, particularly the incompatibility between the timescale within which policy decisions needed to be made and the generally longer timescale needed for the design, funding, and execution of sound research programs.[16] As technological change speeded up, that incompatibility became more severe.

In today's environment, in which rapid technological change and fierce competition combine to put pressure on companies to release new media technologies and services as quickly as possible, can research be conducted at a faster pace but remain sound? And, are certain types of research more or less useful in the new environment? Some types, such as field trials, clearly require considerable time and are not suitable to highly time-sensitive research. Similarly, when research requires careful deliberations about the questions to be asked, as in much policy research, it is unwise to save time by cutting corners. However, we have been involved in a number of corporate research projects where the pace was very rapid indeed. Some of these involved usability research about new electronic products. The research questions were known, and participants were recruited beforehand. The engineering team delivered a prototype product on a Friday, intensive usability testing was conducted over the weekend, and the results were communicated to the engineering team on the following Monday morning. They then reworked the software and delivered a revised prototype on Friday, and the process was repeated. (Usability testing is often iterative—one tests, revises, and tests again two, three, or even more times, depending on the product, the complexity of the design and the problems encountered.) After another week of revisions, the final specifications were sent to a company in Asia for manufacturing.

We are also familiar with media companies that have established large "panels" of people—sometimes 20,000 or more—who agree to test new services, watch special programming, or give opinions about potential new services. Such an approach can provide very rapid feedback—e.g., several thousand responses in 48 hours.

"Firehouse research" is another form of research in a hurry. If an unexpected event occurs and waiting to conduct research about it with a typical timetable might miss important knowledge as memories fade, can the research be deployed very rapidly? The first example of firehouse research with which we are familiar followed Orson Welles's radio broadcast of *War of the Worlds* in the late 1930s. Using a documentary news format, the drama caused panic, as many listeners thought that the earth (more specifically, New Jersey) was being invaded by Martians. CBS, which broadcast the drama, was very concerned about reactions and potential penalties from government agencies, so the company's head of research, Frank Stanton, immediately commissioned Princeton University researcher Hadley Cantril to investigate what had happened. Cantril rapidly deployed a research team, and produced the classic study, *The Invasion from Mars: A Study in the Psychology of Panic.*[17] Other events that have triggered firehouse research are the use of mobile phones and pagers on 9/11,[18] fax communications about the events surrounding the repression of demonstrators in Tiananmen Square, and the use of mobile phones to help topple the president of the Philippines (see chapter 10). Firehouse research has many limitations, but it is sometimes acceptable to learn what one can and accept weaknesses in the research design rather than miss the opportunity to study important events while or immediately after they occur.

New Types of Data and Research Methods

From their introduction at the start of the 1970s, computer conferencing services offered their operators data of unprecedented richness about how individuals were using the services, since a record of every interaction with the computer hosting the service was created and stored. All online services—but especially Web sites—have this natural capability. Even when sites do not solicit information that would identify users—e.g., for registration or in electronic commerce—individuals (more accurately, the groups of people sharing a browser) can be tracked through multiple visits to the site by means of cookies.

Numerous e-commerce firms use analyses of data generated by users' online activities to optimize marketing offers and their designs; other Web site operators, too, use such data to optimize the content conveyed on their Web pages. The data and the results obtained in these studies are generally proprietary. Although one would not expect employees of firms in competitive markets to publish results of such research, reports from which information identifying the firm and its specific market has been omitted are likely to trickle out. When outsiders—for example, consulting firms and consultants from the academic world—are important partners, publication of a sanitized version is generally in their interests.

Organizations for whom such research is conducted may know or be in a position to know the identities of the individuals whose behavior at particular sites has been studied. Clearly this poses risks to individuals' privacy. These risks are greater if individuals' actions are to be tracked across Web sites oper-

THE PROBLEM OF MAKING WEB SEARCH DATA ANONYMOUS

A situation in 2006 involving the release to the research community of proprietary data on people's Internet searches illustrates how problems can arise. In 2006, AOL published three months of search records for 658,000 Americans. The records were intended for the research use of academics and technologists, and the company thought it had made the records anonymous: the specific searches were not linked to user names or IP addresses; instead, searches by individual users were grouped together by means of randomly assigned numerical identifiers. Nevertheless, "New York Times reporters matched some user numbers with the correct individuals. Others identified sensitive and occasionally disturbing personal information in the AOL search data, including user searches for 'how to kill your wife,' 'anti psychotic drugs,' and 'aftermath of incest.' In response, several privacy groups filed complaints with the Federal Trade Commission."[1]

1. Electronic Privacy Information Center, *Privacy and Human Rights Report 2006: An International Survey of Privacy Laws and Developments* (Washington, DC: Electronic Privacy Information Center, 2007); Electronic Privacy Information Center, "Search Engine Privacy," http://epic.org/privacy/search_engine, undated (accessed November 2008).

ated by different organizations or if individuals' actions on one site are to be linked to information about them held in other databases.

The Web can also provide a very convenient platform for experimental research designed to optimize the content and form of the communication it carries. The possibility of providing different versions of a Web page to different users makes it possible to design ongoing experiments that compare the effectiveness of a message with that of one or more variations on it. Along with practical guidelines for applying this approach, R. Kohavi et al. provide two examples in which this process has produced useful surprises.[19] One involved the comparison of nine different designs for an e-commerce checkout page; the other compared alternative designs for a page on which users could rate articles provided in response to the use of Microsoft Office's "help" function. Kohavi and colleagues also provide a brief discussion of the limitations of the method—for example, it identifies effects without identifying their causes and can measure only short-term effects—and briefly discuss how to compensate for these limitations.

This kind of research method is far from new. In the 1960s, for example, it was applied to compare commercials carried on cable television systems. The theory on which it is based goes back at least to the work of eminent cybernetician Stafford Beer in the middle of the past century. Its relevance at this time lies in the fact that both the Web and interactive television provide such inviting platforms.

Some less radical changes in data collection methods are also apparent. One is the growing use of the Web for long-accepted research activities such as focus groups and surveys. If the latter were used only as substitutes for conventional surveys, their statistical weaknesses—relating to self-selected samples, for example—would probably have doomed them. However, their offsetting advantages—very rapid turnaround, modest cost, and ability in many instances to generate very large samples—mean that the alternative would often be no survey or one that produced results much later than desirable. In some cases, participants in Web surveys are recruited ahead of time and stand ready to respond to research questions. These panels are often very large and can provide a rapid turnaround. The problem of self-selection can be mitigated in a few ways. Some research groups use random-digit telephone calls to recruit the panel. Others filter the panel (i.e., select a subset of responses by using specific criteria) to try to obtain a sample that represents the general population (for example, asking people if they are early, middle, or late adoptors of new technology and selecting a sample that matches the general population on this attribute). The use of Web surveys and panels has also become more acceptable, with the limitations noted, because of a growing problem in telephone surveys—poor response rates (the percentage of people called who can be reached and agree to participate in the survey). As response rates for telephone surveys have declined, the chances of achieving a truly random sample that is representative of the general population have been reduced.

The use of Web surveys is a double-edged sword on many counts. It is now much simpler to conduct surveys on the Web, using a variety of very well designed software packages and Web services that make it very easy and cheap to create questions, send out links to the survey, and tabulate results. Almost anyone can create and administer a survey. But without professional training, many people and companies create very bad surveys with biased questions. It is easy to understand how a marketing group within an electronics firm might unknowingly ask about a new media technology in such a way that people would be encouraged to say that they would like to have it.

Better measurement of the fragmenting linear and interactive television audiences has been made possible by the continuing improvement of meters designed for this purpose. These meters automatically keep records of what is being viewed. Earlier systems of measurement, still employed by some researchers, involved telephoning people and asking what they had watched the previous day or week or asking household members to keep a record of what they had watched. These earlier systems were subject to errors in memory and lack of knowledge if the person answering the telephone or filling out the diary provided inaccurate information about the viewing patterns of others in the household. Like computer conferencing in earlier periods and Web usage measurement, digital cable and satellite systems and DVR systems can track every button pushed by a household. Putting aside for the moment the question of privacy, these systems can provide much more information about how new media services are being used.

Although very much overshadowed by changes in the research scene associated with the use of automatically generated computerized records, a trend at the opposite, qualitative end of the range is notable: ethnographic methods were very rarely used in the 1970s but have since gained much greater acceptance in corporate research on new media as well as in academic research in the field.

Challenges

On the surface, the present might seem like a golden age for user research on new media. For those conducting pure research, so much is new, there is so much to be found out, and fairly straightforward methods can be used to seek it. What did different types of people do when offered a new kind of service or a new feature in an existing service? What effects did certain experiences of new media have on different types of users? And so on. But of course, discovering why people acted as they did or why the experiences had the effects they did may well be far harder.

Those conducting applied research have access to a vast wealth of automatically generated data and new techniques to gather other data that are not generated automatically. The range of software with which to conduct analyses continues to expand, and powerful new options continue to become available. The Web can provide a platform for experimentation and for simulation. For all researchers, the combination of powerful search engines, the Web, and specialized databases greatly eases the otherwise impossible task of keeping up with research activity that has been expanding so rapidly.

While the explosive growth of the Web has created a cornucopia of opportunities for conducting original research (which differs greatly from conducting research originally) and while other new media have created additional opportunities, major challenges exist in obtaining as much value as could be desired from the research that is done. These challenges will be all too familiar to readers with research experience, but others may not appreciate these challenges as clearly.

Scholars regard research primarily if not solely as a means to advance theory (and the authors believe there is much truth in the cliché that nothing is as practical as good theory). Especially when the media environment is changing so rapidly, findings from diverse studies about how, say, particular types of users behaved in a particular situation may have little if any value unless either they inform theory now or the right variables pertaining to the situation were measured so that they can inform theory in the future. At a more fundamental level, assuming that the answers to research questions are valid, they are much more useful if they were good questions. As Sheizaf Rafaeli wrote in 2001 about the Internet as an area of research,

> I wish to propose some *constructs* to guide our thinking and study. These constructs, I hope, should shed some light on what can be investigated, and suggest manners to do so. Constructs can suggest what should be asked. . . .
>
> I propose focusing on several defining qualities of *communication* on the Net: multimedia, synchronicity, hypertextuality, packet switching, interactivity, logs and records, simulation and immersion, and the value of information.[20]

For applied researchers, the main challenge in the short term is likely to arise from the reduced timescales on which decisions need to be made. When possible, it may be better to minimize errors by decreasing emphasis on using research in advance of decision making and by increasing emphasis on making decisions that are likely to be approximately right and can be adjusted quickly in light of fast turnaround research on what happens subsequently in the field.

A longer-term challenge, especially for in-house researchers, arises from the fact that the cumulative value of a corporation's or government agency's research studies is likely to go far beyond their value relative to the decisions they were intended to inform. This potential is unlikely to be realized unless those in a position to act on it take it seriously. In this respect, our personal experience in the less pressured decades at the end of the last century was not encouraging: remarkably often, far from any synthesis being conducted, there was no corporate memory of earlier research: the people had gone and the research reports had been tossed. It will not be enough for the knowledge management systems that started to become fashionable in the mid-1990s to succeed as far as the retention and location of knowledge is concerned: synthesis will be necessary, too.

APPENDIX: Teletext in the United States: Design and Implementation of a User Research Project

This sketch of a research program on teletext conducted between 1979 and 1982 illustrates the problem of using field trials in policy research; the value, when the unanticipated occurs, of the flexibility offered by a loosely coupled multicomponent research program; the complementary roles of laboratory experiments and field trials; and the value of using multiple methods in gathering data on user behavior.[21]

Background. By the late 1970s, teletext was successfully established in Europe, and international rivalry existed among the competing national teletext standards of the United Kingdom, France, and Canada. In the United States, where all of the three standards were being promoted vigorously, the air was thick with competing technical and economics claims, but little else appeared to be happening. The situation caused concern at the Corporation for Public Broadcasting (CPB) and the National Telecommunications and Information Administration (NTIA) in Washington, where officials believed that teletext was of particular relevance to the Public Broadcasting System (PBS).

Planning study. In 1979, the Alternate Media Center at New York University undertook a planning study to identify the public policy issues related to a public broadcasting teletext service and to make recommendations as to whether and how a field trial should take place.

Research program. The National Science Foundation and the CPB eventually funded a research program, with additional support provided by the NTIA and the U.S. Department of Health, Education, and Welfare. The research program confronted a number of challenges. Because the teletext field trial would be costly, funding would have to be obtained from four different agencies, each of which had somewhat different expectations for the project. In particular, a conflict existed between some agencies' desire for scientifically rigorous research and others' goal of a successful demonstration of the new technology. Various technological hurdles also needed to be overcome, including the scarcity of teletext decoders that could be used with the U.S. television standard and significant reception problems that would affect field testing in general and systematic sampling in particular. Further, the PBS station where the service was to be based (WETA in Washington, D.C.) had very little experience in the type of work required for teletext, which is akin to a small newspaper or a radio news service. The project needed (and developed) public information providers such as federal agencies, local libraries, and community service agencies, but these organizations were experiencing budget cutbacks that reduced the effort they could put into the project.

The overall plan called for the project to be split into two phases. The first would have two components: a pilot field trial (involving 40 households and 10 public sites) and laboratory studies. The division into two phases was an attempt to deal with funding problems, to iron out technological problems before large-scale field research began, and to explore general research issues before formulating specific hypotheses that could be tested during the second phase.

Laboratory studies. The laboratory studies, which were intended to start after the pilot field trial was under way, sought to investigate a series of general issues that appeared both practically significant and suitable for testing in the laboratory: for example, how long people would be prepared to wait for a page of information to appear before irritation set in. Some of these issues had been identified prior to the start of the project, while planners anticipated that others would be identified during the pilot.

The most important product of the laboratory studies was methodological: a set of scales that could be reduced to three major factors that accounted for 60 percent of the variance in users' reactions to teletext pages. As a cross-check on validity, one of the experiments was repeated some months later using the same page designs in the homes of users taking part in the pilot. Results were reassuring.

Engineering tests and problems. Teletext is more vulnerable to reception problems than is regular television; furthermore, the project was to use a UHF channel with above-average reception problems. Engineering tests had difficulty identifying suitable locations, but three neighborhoods eventually were chosen from which a sample of homes would be selected. Since the trial service would be carried on the local PBS station, the research team accepted the possible demographic bias of using its membership list as a sampling frame and selected the 40 matched pairs of households needed for the treatment and control groups. However, reception ultimately was much more sensitive to location than had been assumed, causing further delay and expense.

The control group was abandoned (it was raided for additional subjects). The consequent damage to the research design was not serious, since the pilot incorporated a control group primarily because the research team wanted to check the procedural problems and costs of incorporating a control group in the following phase.

Research data on use of the trial service. The research instruments used for the household subjects included a series of face-to-face interviews, diary records kept by users, and purpose-designed meters that recorded each page request by time of day. The research instruments used at the public sites included the meters, a one-time written survey of user reactions, and nearly 200 hours of ethnographic observation of user behavior at and around the teletext terminals.

The multiplicity of different instruments provided useful information on a wide variety of specific topics. Meter readings, for example, tracked the novelty effect within households and determined whether subjects switched to teletext during commercial breaks. Comparison of diary records with meter readings illustrated the systematic biases in the use of diaries. The ethnographic study provided firsthand observations of usage behavior.

Change of plan. The trial service started in June 1981. Six months later, a combination of considerations demonstrated that a major change of plan was required. Public research funds had become very tight, and evidence was mounting that the pilot service was more seriously underfunded than its designers had realized. On the positive side, more progress was being made in the research than had been anticipated. The research team decided, therefore, not to proceed to the planned second phase but to extend the pilot by a few months. In the end, the project generated a great deal of useful research findings, even if the journey to get there had some twists and turns. It demonstrated the value of building flexibility into a research project and using multiple research components. The project also illustrated the complementary roles of laboratory experiments and field trials and the difficulty (but not impossibility) of working with multiple funders.

// PART 2 // · Case Studies

// FIVE //

How New Media Affect Television Viewing

Television viewing is not context-free: in particular, it is affected by the technologies used to access programs, the social spaces where it occurs, the values and interests of those who are watching, and the forms of content that are available.[1] Driven by the needs of advertisers, commercial research about television viewing has emphasized what programs people watch and the size and composition of audiences. This information is important for advertisers and contributes to a broad understanding of the television experience, but by itself, it provides a rather superficial understanding of the subject.[2] Academic research, especially in recent decades, has emphasized the potential social impacts of content on audiences: for example, whether television content reinforces racial and gender stereotypes. While valuable, this research too provides an incomplete picture of television viewing. Some scholars have examined television in its broader context and the ways in which it functions in everyday life: Harold Mendelsohn, Leo Bogart, and Lynn Spigel have looked at everyday uses of television in the United States;[3] David Morley, Roger Silverstone, and Shaun Moores have studied the broad context of television viewing in the United Kingdom.[4] This chapter follows their tradition, focusing on U.S. experiences to clarify some components in a broader picture of television's functions in everyday life.

Technology is one factor that can contribute to a more comprehensive assessment of television viewing. What role does technology, especially new media technologies, play in the television viewing process? How does technology affect the behavior of viewers, where TV viewing occurs, and the content created? In turn, how do other factors in the broad TV viewing context influence what new media technologies are developed and which succeed or fail?

As a technology is adopted, it often leads to lasting changes in user behavior: for example, the remote control led to more changing of channels.[5] In response, behavioral changes can lead to the creation of new forms of programming. In the case of the remote control, increased channel changing led to changes in the design and placement of commercials, greater segmentation of content within programs, and the placement of icons in the corners of screens to flag channel names for high-speed channel surfers. Changes in programming and behavior may then create opportunities for new generations of technology that take advantage of the new environment. The cycles of interactions among technology, behavior, and programs can continue over many years or decades. At the beginning of the process, few observers can anticipate the longer-term effects of technological change.

Scholars have shown much interest in the impact of the current generation of new television technologies such as high-definition television (HDTV), digital video recorders (DVRs), portable video viewers such as advanced mobile phones and MP-3 players, and digital cable TV systems that support video on demand (VOD) and interactive program guides. Do they fundamentally affect how people access, watch, and are influenced by television? Will they lead to new forms of programming and threaten existing programs and business

RELATIONSHIPS BETWEEN NEW MEDIA TECHNOLOGIES AND SERVICES

Some new media technologies are independent of any new services but can nonetheless affect TV viewing behavior: for example, the remote control did not provide a new service as such but led to more channel changing and a different TV viewing experience for many people. In other cases, new technologies and new services are closely linked: for example, DVRs, which were designed to enable users to capture programs for later viewing, fast-forward through content, and provide instant replays. A third variation occurs when new technologies such as advanced digital cable systems provide platforms for the development of new services, such as VOD or interactive program guides.

New media technologies may also be distinguished by who controls services and content. Some are under the control of the user, not requiring content created specifically for them. For example, DVRs are under users' control and do not require separate content from program providers (except for the channel guide needed for scheduling what programs will be recorded), although some producers offer content specifically for DVRs. In other cases, the technology has little value by itself without content. For example, HDTV sets require either HDTV programming or DVDs if viewers are to gain additional value.

In addition, a new media service may require a series of incremental advances in associated technology before it becomes enjoyable. Television over the Web can be accessed via dial-up connections, but it is a far better experience with broadband and better still with faster personal computers, video servers near end users, advanced compression technology, and other technological enhancements that have been introduced over time.

models? To understand their role in television viewing and their potential impacts, it is useful first to establish a baseline for how television has been used in the past and to examine the role of earlier new technologies in changing television viewing. Television viewing patterns were not static over the medium's first 60 years. New technologies contributed to many of the changes that occurred.

This baseline is based on an examination of what happened when black and white television sets were introduced in late 1946, after a series of experiments and false starts in the 1920s and 1930s. The first new technology to affect TV viewing was TV itself.

Television Enters the Scene

People old enough to recall when television first entered their homes in the late 1940s or early 1950s can recount strange tales of viewers so mesmerized by this new technology that they watched test patterns broadcast before or after the regular programming day. When programs were on the air, not only did the family watch television as a group but, on any given evening, friends and seemingly half the neighborhood might drop by to watch the magic box.[6] Others, whose families could not afford a TV (costing six weeks' salary for an average household in the late 1940s) and who had already worn out their welcome at the homes of neighbors, may recall hanging out in neighborhood taverns or department stores to catch a glimpse of television. Early U.S. press accounts of television indicate that much viewing occurred in public places, including bars that wanted to attract customers and department stores that wanted to sell TVs to consumers. TVs were also located in many other public spaces that simply wanted to draw people. Watching TV in public locations built an appetite for the new medium and encouraged word-of-mouth discussion that led to its adoption in homes.

Photographs of people watching television when it was first introduced in the United States show them sitting relatively close to the screen—two to five feet away. The screens were small (typically measuring between 12 and 15 inches for household sets from the late 1940s through the early 1950s) and images were fuzzy. Each household had only one set, and a very limited number of channels were available, so little channel changing occurred. In spite of the high prices, television penetration grew very rapidly: more than half of U.S. households owned a TV by the mid-1950s, as shown in figure 5.1.[7]

Many early TV sets were built into fancy furniture and often combined with a radio and phonograph. One early RCA model was marketed as a five-in-one television console. In addition to a TV, it included an AM/FM radio, a shortwave

TAVERN TELEVISION

In his classic study of early television, Leo Bogart divided the first several years of television into three phases.[1] The first he called the tavern phase to indicate the importance of local taverns in giving ordinary people a taste of television. To attract customers, local taverns paid the high price of TV sets (more than $1,000 for 15 × 20-inch sets designed for public settings). The strategy succeeded. Tavern owners reported a 500 percent increase in customers when major sporting events were broadcast.[2] Three million people watched the seventh game of the 1947 World Series between the New York Yankees and the Brooklyn Dodgers, with 90 percent of those viewers in public places, mostly bars. The following year, 99.7 percent of all TVs were turned on during the heavyweight championship bout between Joe Louis and Jersey Joe Walcott, with an average of 12 people watching per set, indicating that taverns provided a large share of the audience.[3]

Newspaper articles reported that some people arrived at taverns an hour before the start of major sporting events to secure prime seats. Even when no sporting events were being shown, bars filled with customers who wanted to watch TV. Some columnists lamented the loss of vibrant conversation in taverns, as customers sat in silence watching the screen; others characterized television as "the best thing to happen to the neighborhood bar since free lunch."[4] State legislatures even debated whether to charge taverns a cabaret tax because they were taking so many customers away from nightclubs that paid such taxes.

1. Leo Bogart, *The Age of Television,* 3rd ed. (New York: Frederick Unger Publishing, 1972).

2. James Von Schilling, *The Magic Window: American Television, 1939–1953* (New York: Haworth Press, 2003).

3. "The News of Radio: 354,000 Television Sets in Use, Gallup Poll Shows," *New York Times,* June 30, 1948, 50.

4. Richard Maney, "Barroom Lament," *New York Times,* June 13, 1948, 6.

radio, a phonograph with automatic record changer, and a record storage compartment. Such features may have helped justify high prices ($750 in the case of the five-in-one RCA TV). Advertising for early TV sets often showed people in formal evening gowns or tuxedos in party settings, another indicator that earlier adopters came from high-income households. Many magazine articles of the time depicted television as a "window on the world." It later came to be characterized as a home theater.

The TV was generally placed in the living room, where it sometimes displaced a piano, and furniture was organized around the set, making it the cen-

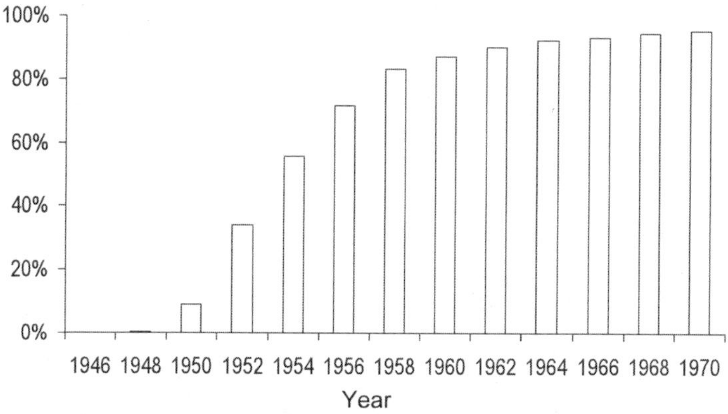

Fig. 5.1. Percentage of U.S. households with TV: 1946–70. (Data from Christopher Sterling and Timothy Haight, *The Mass Media: Aspen Institute Guide to Communication Industry Trends* [New York: Praeger Publishers, 1978].)

tral focus of the room. It was a high-status, luxury item. Advertising for babysitters frequently announced the presence of a TV in the hope of attracting good sitters.

By the early 1950s, some TVs had begun to migrate into other rooms, and manufacturers responded accordingly. One enterprising manufacturer combined a TV set with a stove, hoping to entice women who spent a lot of time in the kitchen and wanted to watch TV at the same time (early multitasking). It was not successful, but small, regular TV sets eventually made their way into millions of kitchens.

In her remarkable study of early television, *Make Room for TV*, Spigel has observed how viewing, listening, and reading habits affected content and schedules.[8] Many of the first program formats were borrowed directly from popular radio programs with established audiences. In addition, early daytime shows for women borrowed formats and names from print magazines. As viewing habits formed, networks responded with schedules intended to steer the audience from one program to another. NBC, for example, developed a lead-in strategy—people who liked one show were led naturally into a following show with a similar appeal. Spigel also notes that commentaries about early television were filled with both awe and gloom. Observers predicted that television would not only bring families together but tear them apart. Children could be positively influenced if television kept them off the streets and out of trouble, but they could also become addicted and have their eyes "glued to the tube."

New TV Technologies from the Mid-1950s to the 1990s

1950s and 1960s

During the 1950s, television viewing stabilized for a while as family groups watched entire programs, usually together, selecting from the small number of choices available on a single, living room set with over-the-air reception. To change channels, someone had to get up, walk over to the set, and turn a dial—a clear disincentive. Changes in technology, however, soon led to changes in viewing behavior.

By the 1950s, TVs in fancy pieces of furniture began to be replaced by those in plain metal shells—simple console sets. The change may have been part of an attempt to bring down the price of sets for the mass public, which was beginning to buy them. During this time, another curious sociological phenomenon emerged. Contemporary photographs show that some families began to place photographs of family members or memorabilia such as Little League trophies on top of sets. This development probably reflected the increasing time people were spending with television and its acceptance as part of the family. By the late 1950s, when color was introduced, many sets were once again encased within furniture, repeating the earlier pattern: as color technology drove the price of sets back up to six weeks' salary for an average household, wooden cabinets may have helped to justify the price. Figure 5.2 shows the growth of color TV.

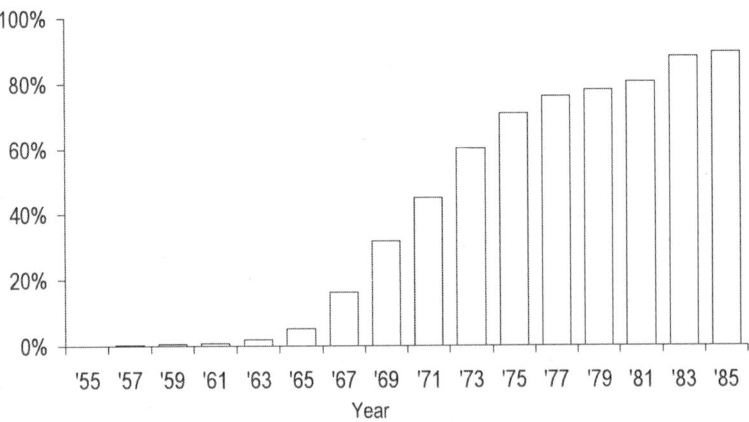

Fig. 5.2. Percentage of U.S. households with color TV, 1955–1985. (Data from Christopher Sterling and Timothy Haight, *The Mass Media: Aspen Institute Guide to Communication Industry Trends* [New York: Praeger Publishers, 1978]; and U.S. Census Bureau, *Statistical Abstract of the United States* [Washington, DC: U.S. Department of Commerce, multiple years].)

When color sets began to enter homes in the late 1950s and 1960s, television was reinvigorated, and people watched more programs. Color did more than make programs more appealing; it affected content as well. The major networks began to produce more programs in color and to emphasize color in scenes as well as in promotional advertising. Some scholars argue that viewing color television even influenced political views. Erik Barnouw points out that the Vietnam War was not only the first television war but also the first war in color. Blood was red, not muddy gray.[9]

1970s and 1980s

Television continued to serve as a significant medium for group viewing through the 1960s and into the 1970s. Although the number of channels available to the average household grew from two or three in the early 1950s to five or six in the early 1970s, relatively little channel changing took place, and the three broadcast networks accounted for 70 to 90 percent of U.S. viewing. However, the seeds of change in viewing patterns were sown. First, the average screen size had increased from 15 inches to 17, 19, and then 21 inches by the 1970s, allowing people to sit farther back from the set. Second, many households acquired multiple TVs. In 1955, only 3 percent of U.S. households had more than one TV, a number that increased to 43 percent in 1975 and more than 70 percent by the mid-1990s, as shown in figure 5.3.

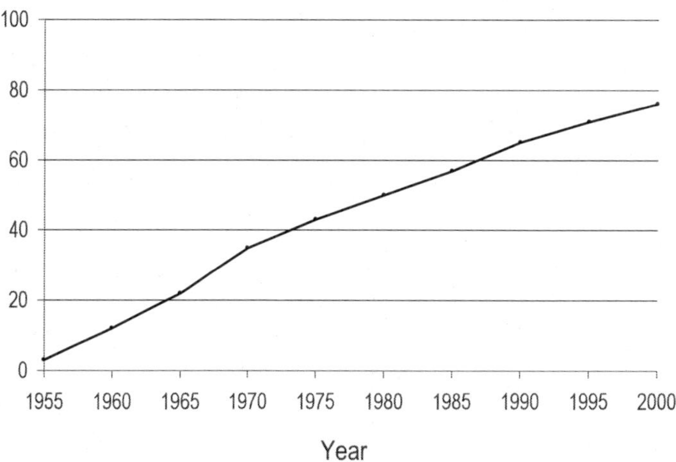

Fig. 5.3. Percentage of U.S. households with multiple TVs, 1955–2000. (Data from U.S. Census Bureau, Statistical *Abstract of the United States* [Washington, DC: U.S. Department of Commerce, multiple years].)

In the 1970s and early 1980s, cable television systems were introduced into many large U.S. cities. Cable television had previously been a simple service—often built and installed by owners of appliance stores who wanted to sell television sets—that received a few distant broadcast stations and retransmitted them into homes in rural areas. Now, channels—e.g., HBO and Superstation WTBS—appeared specifically for cable systems, increasing the number of channels available to viewers to 41 for the average household in 1995. Was this development planned by the industry? Not at all. It was initiated by entrepreneurs (Charles Dolan in the case of HBO and Ted Turner in the case of WTBS) who saw the opportunity made possible by advances in technology: satellite distribution of television signals was crucial to the development of HBO and superstations, despite the cable industry's initial reluctance to purchase the satellite dishes necessary to receive the signals.

The new generation of cable television increased the time people spent watching television[10] and demonstrated that subscribers were willing to pay not only for more channels and better reception but even for specific cable-only channels. Pay television had already been tried several times—for example, Zenith's Phonevision system in 1951 and subscription television in 1964—but had failed each time. With viewers now prepared to pay for content on cable, a major shift in the business model for television had begun: payment for programs shifted toward viewers and away from advertisers. The shift occurred slowly at first but continued for the next three decades. The new model also included more specialized channels, providing content exclusively for children, teenagers, sports fans, and other groups. The additional channels were made possible by the increased capacity of cable systems and by multiple TVs in households, allowing family members to watch different content in different rooms.

Among the most significant technological innovations introduced during this period was the remote control. While remotes were available in the 1950s, they did not enter a significant number of households until the 1970s, as shown in figure 5.4. They then spread rapidly and were in nearly every household by 1990. The remote control became an instrument of power. Whoever controlled it controlled the TV—usually Dad. With multiple sets, remote controls, and a larger number of channels available, television viewing became more personalized, and channel changing became more common. An individual could now separate from other household members and watch programs with more specialized appeal, such as sports, from a bedroom, den, or basement "TV room." Some people, mostly males, spent much of their TV viewing "channel surfing," watching a few seconds or minutes of many different programs in succession. At a fundamental level, the remote control created more active viewers.

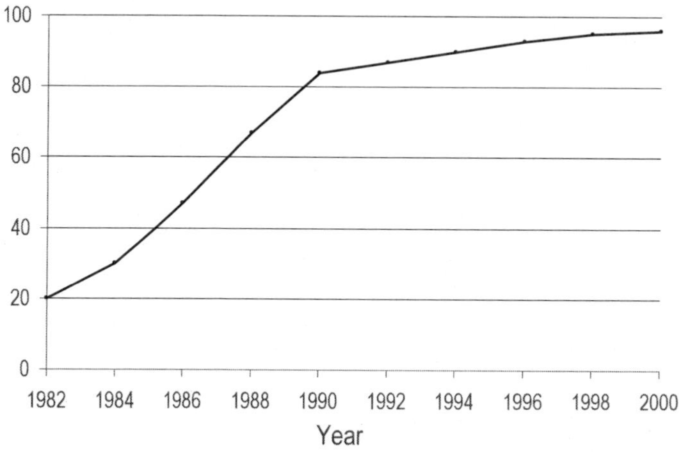

Fig. 5.4. Percentage of U.S. TV households with a remote, 1982–2000. (Data from James Walker and Robert Bellamy, *The Remote Control in the New Age of Television* [Westport, CT: Praeger Publishers, 1993]; and *Television Ownership Survey* [Westfield, NJ: Statistical Research, multiple years].)

These changes in viewing behavior were evolutionary, not revolutionary, occurring gradually. Group television viewing did not disappear but simply became one of many viewing patterns. Further, group viewing itself continued evolving. Families spending the evening in front of a TV in the living room formed just one type of group viewing. Families also watched in the kitchen or while eating in the dining room, and smaller groups gathered elsewhere—e.g., groups of children watching from the floor in a den or bedroom.[11] In addition, the number of channels people watched grew much more slowly than the number available to them. Even though the average household had 41 available channels in 1995, members watched only 10 of those channels in any given week. As the number of channels received grew dramatically over the next decade, the number of channels viewed grew only moderately.

During the 1970s and 1980s, the use of TVs changed in another significant way, as they also became display monitors for VCR and video game content. Each television became connected to multiple boxes, and multiple remotes occupied coffee tables, couches, and floors. One impact was the movement of family photos from atop the TV to the side to make way for the various boxes. Remotes also became a problem as well as a helpful tool for viewers. They were sometimes lost in the pile of equipment associated with TVs. Viewers encountered problems with the different modes for the TV set (TV, Video, Auxiliary Device, and so forth) and with selecting the proper remote to control which box or function.

THE REMOTE CONTROL

The first remote control for television sets was Zenith's Lazy Bones in 1950. It was connected to the set by a cable, and users complained about people tripping over the cord. In 1955, Zenith developed a wireless remote, the Flash-o-Matic, and in 1956, it introduced Space Command, a remote control that used ultrasound to connect to the TV (each of these early remotes had a name). The infrared technology used in nearly all remotes today was introduced in the 1980s. The early remotes were quite expensive, adding as much as 30 percent to the price of a set. They were accepted slowly at first, mostly for luxury color TVs.

Some patterns of remote use include zapping (avoiding commercials or other undesired content), zipping (avoiding content by fast-forwarding through recorded programs), and grazing or channel surfing (sampling many channels briefly). The remote has also become a tool for much DVR behavior.

Much disagreement exists about exactly how often people use the remote to avoid commercials. Many switch to other channels when a series of commercials begins. However, some researchers have found that people tend to overreport how often they zap commercials.[1] Others have pointed out that before remotes came onto the scene (and after), many people avoided commercials by talking, reading, or getting drinks.[2]

The use of the remote control has led to many changes in programming and advertising. Program producers responded to more active viewer behavior by creating shorter segments within long-form programs, such as drama, and developing formats comprised entirely of short segments, such as much of MTV's programming. Formats for CNBC and Bloomberg mix commercials and content on the same screen in response to remote control behavior. If content is provided when a commercial plays on part of the screen, it gives viewers less incentive to change channels.

The tendency of some viewers to hit the remote at the end of shows, when programmers used to run a series of commercials, has led many channels to utilize "hot switches," in which one program ends and another begins with no commercial break. The advertising industry has responded to remote control behavior by creating commercials that were more targeted and shorter. They have also inserted program content within a series (or pod) of commercials to entice viewers to stop for the content and stay for the next commercials (podbusting).

---

1. W. Russell Neuman, *The Future of the Mass Audience* (New York: Cambridge University Press, 1991).

2. A. Abernathy and H. Rotfield, "Zipping through TV Ads Is Old Tradition—but Viewers are Getting Better at It," *Marketing News,* January 7, 1991, 6–14.

VIDEO GAMES

Video games displaying on TVs were introduced in the early 1970s. They were an outgrowth both of experiments in computer science during the 1950s and 1960s and of games in arcades (pinball and later video games). Atari's 1974 Pong video game helped to popularize video games at home. The home video game console improved every few years as the technology evolved from 8- to 16-, 32-, and 64-bit central processing units (CPUs), and graphic designers honed their skills. Video was eventually incorporated into video games, and the graphics began to approach the level of computer-animated scenes in motion pictures.

The home TV provides just one way that people experience video games. Alternatives include arcade video games, personal computer software games, online games, digital cable games, mobile phone games, and portable game units. However, home video games have had enormous success. More than 40 percent of U.S. households have one or more video game consoles. Most players of television video games are young males, though one in four is female and one in five is older than 35.

Video games displayed on television, with content that is in some ways quite distinct from television programs, compete directly for television viewing time. Unlike television, video games are highly interactive and generally have no time limitations—play can last for hours. In other ways, they are merging with television and movie content. Many video games are based on sports and movies. Furthermore, advertising has been introduced into them.

Some households have a TV set dedicated to video games, which reduces competition between watching television programs and playing video games. People in the household can split up and do one or the other. Some do both: it is not uncommon to find a teenager in his bedroom or a den with two TV sets on, playing a video game on one and taking in television programs on the other. A question for the long term is whether those playing video games on TVs will develop habits and appetites that affect the types of content produced as regular programming—in particular, favoring more interactive content.

After two false starts in the early part of the 1970s, the VCR was launched in the middle of the decade and had entered millions of homes by the mid-1980s.[12] VCRs initially changed viewing patterns by allowing people to "time shift," or record programs and watch them later. Time shifting was the dominant use of VCRs for several years. In the early 1980s, the average household with a VCR recorded five hours of television per week,[13] with women doing most of the time shifting. In 1979, only 22 percent of VCR households rented or bought prerecorded cassettes. Rental cassettes were not widely available during this period and purchased tapes were very expensive—typically between $50 and $80 each.[14] Approximately 40 percent of the videos rented or purchased had R- or X-rated content.[15]

Time shifting increased television's overall audience, allowing people to watch programs they otherwise would have missed and giving them more control over when they watched programs. It increased the convenience of television and led to more active viewing behavior.[16] Early VCR users reported that they frequently zipped past commercials in recorded programs, leading to speculation that VCRs presented a major threat to the business model of advertiser-based television. However, the threat never materialized, since the people who zipped past commercials on time-shifted programs were watching content (and some commercials) that they would probably not have watched at all without the VCR.

After the early 1980s, the amount of time shifting declined, and the number of rentals increased. In 1982, just under half of households rented videocassettes; by 1986, that number had jumped to 90 percent.[17] As prices declined, households also began to purchase videocassettes and build collections of tapes, helping to shift the primary users of videocassettes to young people. By the late 1980s, children under 18 watched twice as much VCR content as adults did, and a "home video culture" began to emerge.[18] Some families collected and displayed videocassettes prominently, much as other households displayed book collections. Eventually, however, time shifting declined to a point where only one in five households did any recording at all,[19] and some research indicated that as many as half of recorded cassettes were never watched.[20]

The VCR is instructive because its use changed significantly over time, moving from recorded content primarily to rentals and some recorded content to rentals and sales with a modest amount of recorded content. VCRs provided control, convenience, and greater enjoyment of television viewing and, at least at first, encouraged more active viewing behavior. In the long term, the most important effect of the VCR may be that it began the process of freeing viewers from time constraints resulting from the interaction between the television schedule and when people could watch television.

The VCR also introduced complexity into a world of TV viewing that had previously been very simple, as many people struggled to figure out how to set the VCR to record programs or to understand the many added features built into it. It created a conflict between marketing and use of television technology. Features such as freeze-frames, slow motion, and recording multiple events helped to sell VCRs, but these features were rarely used and confused many people.

TABLE 5.1. New Television Technologies and Their Impacts, 1946–90

New Technology or Change in Existing TV Sets	Impact
Larger TV sets	Allow people to sit farther from set for more enjoyable group viewing; eventually transform TV into a multimedia entertainment center
TV as furniture	Softens the blow of high price for early B&W and color TVs; enhances TV as luxury item; replaces piano as center of living room in many households
Remote control	Increases channel changing during commercials and surfing through channels; becomes an instrument of power in control over TV set
Color sets	Reinvigorate TV; enhance appeal of programs including many scenes in color; may have influenced reactions to Vietnam war
More channels	Support niche programs; increase competition for major networks; segment audiences by categories of interest
Multiple sets in households	Make TV more pervasive in households; support viewing alone; segment audiences according to where they are watching
VCR	Introduces time-shift viewing; turns set into a display monitor; frees people from TV schedule; makes viewing more efficient through fast-forwarding of recorded content; provides new competition for TV programs through rented and purchased movies
Video games on TV	Compete with TV programs for people's time; stimulate multitasking; develop people's appetite for interacting with content; turn set into a display monitor
C-band satellite dishes	Allow people in rural areas to receive more channels; increase TV viewing in households that own a satellite dish

Table 5.1 summarizes many of the impacts of new technologies on television viewing from the late 1940s through 1990.

1990s

By the 1990s, television viewing encompassed a complex and elaborate set of behaviors. Traditional viewing remained the dominant use of television, but people also used TVs to display many different video services (particularly, videocassettes, camcorder tapes, video games, and later in the decade DVDs) in many different rooms, with different mixes of viewers. The average U.S. household had the TV on for seven hours a day. It was both watched and listened to—many people listened to it as they got dressed, prepared dinner, or did house-

FAILURES AND DISAPPOINTMENTS

Many new television technologies or changes in existing sets failed during this period. The outright failures included Telefirst, over-the-air pay TV, interactive television, teletext (in the United States), and videotex on a TV. Among the technologies that found only small groups of users were videodiscs, stereo TV, picture-in-picture, MDS (wireless cable), second audio programs (SAP) in its first decade of use, the text channel on Line 21 Closed Captioning, and the first generation of DVD recorders. The failures offer many lessons. In the case of stereo television, the industry did little to promote it and very few programs utilized it in their production. In the case of SAP and the text channel on Line 21 Closed Captioning, the services were hidden in layers of menus, and many people never found them. Early DVD recorders were difficult to use, encountered competiton from legacy VCRs which already recorded shows, and had to displace DVRs that had come to the market earlier and performed more or less the same function.

work. In these ways, television took on some of the functions served by radio in earlier decades. It filled the house with sound and pictures, shaping the environment in which people lived. TVs were also multitasking devices, as many people opened mail, read newspapers, talked on the telephone, and so on while watching or listening to it.

The size of TVs continued to grow in the 1990s. The average main TV set was 27 inches, and one in four households had a TV of 30 inches or larger. The "home entertainment center" emerged as well. Approximately one in six households had a very large size screen (40 inches or larger) with stereo speakers and multiple boxes attached. Households with home entertainment centers frequently had six, seven, or even eight remote controls on a table in front of a large-screen TV. It both dominated and defined the room.

While the screen size for the main household TV increased during the 1990s, other household sets varied greatly in size depending on the room where they were placed and how they were used. Smaller sets were located in kitchens, bedrooms, and even garages. These TVs often were placed inside other furniture, such as armoires, that dictated screen size as well as its orientation within a room—it could be seen from some parts of the room and heard from others, depending on where a person stood or sat.[21]

Direct broadcast satellite service (DBS) was introduced in the United States in the 1990s, following a limited rollout of large C-band and of Ku-band satellite dishes in the 1980s and early 1990s. DBS grew very rapidly as a service for rural areas unserved by cable and then as a direct competitor to cable in major markets. By the mid-1990s, DBS offered all-digital service, forcing cable operators to upgrade their systems to compete. Digital technology would be the crucial foundation for many of the new TV technologies rolled out in 2000 and later, and these technologies, in turn, had a major impact on television viewing behavior.

Digital versatile disks (DVDs) more commonly called digital video disks, were introduced in the United States in 1997 and were adopted very rapidly. Within eight years, they had entered three-quarters of U.S. households; by the mid 2000s, more than half of U.S. households had two or more DVD players, including not only DVD consoles but also DVD drives in desktop and laptop computers, portable DVD players, and video game consoles that can play DVDs. DVDs were adopted so quickly because manufacturers sharply reduced the price of players from about $700 to $300 within the first two years and because the motion picture industry made many movies available relatively quickly. DVDs were also smaller than videocassettes, offered higher quality, and included extra scenes (for example, funny outtakes) that appealed to many people. They surpassed videocassettes in sales within five years and led in rentals within six. The absence of a recording capability did not limit acceptance because relatively few households did any recording; those households that wanted to record already had VCRs and, later, DVRs.

DVDs had a strong impact on television viewing. They competed with regular television, especially on weekends, when people had more time for watching two-hour movies. Many households built large collections of DVDs, giving them immediate access to many movies and later television shows. The popularity of television programs on DVD surprised many observers, demonstrating once again that people were willing to pay for convenience and control over television viewing. In some households, people also use DVDs to create a background environment for other activities: for example, playing a favorite movie or television program that they have watched many times before while reading or doing housework. People have commented that even though they are not watching the DVD, it creates a pleasant mood for the other activities.

In the 1990s, TVs also reemerged as significant devices in public locations—offices, building lobbies, and airport waiting areas. Television watching in public locations was not the main means of viewing, as it had been for some people in the late 1940s and early 1950s, but a complement to viewing at home. TVs in public locations signaled just how dependent people had become on television; they wanted it outside as well as inside the home. On September 11, 2001, a majority of Americans first learned about the terrorist attack from television, many of them at workplaces or schools.[22]

One way to perceive the changes in television viewing from 1950 to the end of the 1990s, is to think of the television set in 1950 as a magic window on the world, with families gathered round.[23] By the 1990s, television had become part of the environment surrounding people wherever they were, both inside and outside their homes. People consumed TV constantly, but for different purposes, depending on time of day and location.

New Television Media: 2000 Onward

How are people using all of today's new media for television—high-definition television, digital video recorders, electronic program guides, video on demand, and Web video? A review of available studies as well as extensive interviews paint a picture that is both fascinating and more complex than a simple count of who has which new technologies, how often each is used, and what is watched.

For the most part, the technologies currently on the scene fall into two groups: digital television and broadband-delivered Web television. Digital television includes HDTV, VOD, electronic program guides (EPGs), digital video recorders, the now familiar DVDs, and newer high-definition DVDs. Broadband-delivered Web television provides videos that are streamed (watched as they are transmitted) or downloaded (stored and watched later) using broadband Internet connections. This group also includes wired and wireless domestic broadband networks for sending Web video to other computers or TV sets in the home as well as new generations of display devices for Web video, such as advanced mobile phones that can access television content in mobile locations and next-generation MP-3 players that can download and store video.

One of the most important characteristics of the current media environment is not technological but social. It is the expectation that media and content should be available on demand almost anywhere. John Pavlik observes that people, especially the younger generation, have pervasive access to a broad range of media and have developed expectations that they should be able to get what they want, when they want it, and where they want it.[24] This idea holds true for television as well as mobile phones, e-mail, and information from the Web. People also experience television on a wider range of display devices, many of which are not TV sets (e.g., laptop computers and portable media players), with screens varying in size from the more than 60 inches of some HDTV sets to the 2 inches of some MP-3 players. Television is thus no longer a single medium but includes many different media with the common element of video, just as books, magazines, and newspapers are different media with the common element of print.

Television is increasingly digital, recorded and transmitted in the 0s and 1s of computer code and hence supporting many new features, such as on-demand video retrieved from a server whenever it is requested. Fewer than 12 percent of households receive television exclusively from over-the-air broadcasts. However, very few households with digital TVs have purchased antennas for over-the-air digital reception. The transition to over-the-air digital transmission has therefore had little impact on television viewing behavior except to drive some households to cable or satellite subscriptions because they could not receive adequate digital signals. Over-the-air digital transmission promised to provide a broadcast station with four or five additional channels at some times of day and an HDTV channel at others, thus allowing broadcasters to compete with cable for viewers with special interests. Acquisition of the necessary digital antennas by the public has, however, been very slow.

Cable television, satellite television, and the Web are a different story. Satellite television is entirely digital, cable TV has been converting subscribers to digital service at a rapid pace, and broadband Web video is entirely digital. When asked, most consumers do not understand the nuances of digital television, noting only that it has "better pictures" and allows many new services. They experience rapid change in services and the technologies that provide them as well as some confusion over the range of options. Viewers' experience of television underwent moderate changes during the medium's first 50 years, with a handful of devices such as remote controls and VCRs leading to behavioral changes. From 2000 on, much more extensive change has occurred.

HDTV

In the late 1990s and early 2000s, HDTV sets were slow to enter U.S. households as a result of disputes over standards, high early prices, and poor marketing.[25] The television industry's interest in HDTV varied, in part because some officials were unable to see the business case for a new standard. Would advertisers pay more for commercials in HDTV? If not, why invest millions of dollars upgrading to it?

The years 2004–7 provided a breakthrough period, as prices dropped, sales increased sharply, and consumers became aware of the medium. Prior to this, and unlike when black and white or color TV was introduced, there were few displays of HDTV sets with full high-definition programming in electronics stores or at other public locations. Showrooms often displayed regular programming on HDTV sets, which did little to help sell them. Many surveys showed high false positives when consumers were asked if they had high-definition TV sets. Not having seen HDTV sets or knowing what they were, many responded affirmatively merely because they believed the pictures on their regular TVs looked very good.

Almost in spite of the electronics industry and its retailers, consumers slowly learned about and began to acquire HDTV sets, although much early use involved playing DVDs, since HDTV content was in short supply. Households with HDTV report that it restores the luster of television and makes it a central focus of whatever room it is in. This phenomenon is a consequence both of HDTV's sharper images and the size of the sets. Most people buy HDTV sets that are larger than their previous TVs. Observations of HDTV viewers show that they appear to do less multitasking than when watching regular television, since HDTV holds their attention so strongly. In turning on their HDTV sets, most viewers go first to channels that carry HDTV (which are generally grouped together). Only if they cannot find an appealing high-definition program do they then go to regular channels. HDTV sets have also brought back "TV parties," with friends invited to watch major sporting events or simply have a dinner party with high-resolution content playing in the background.[26] As in the early days of black and white television, this is probably a short-term development.

Viewers of HDTV report that shows with high production values look much better in high definition and that shows produced with low budgets generally look worse than on regular television. Viewers also comment that certain types of visuals—generally, bright colors and physical movement such as from a helicopter passing over a city—work very well in HDTV and are more likely to attract people. For this reason, sports are a big draw for many HDTV households. However, relatively few of the early HDTV programs were produced to take advantage of the wider format and sharper resolution. Moreover, although most HDTV sets have very good sound capability, and some households have added high-end home theater systems to their sets, people indicate in interviews that the sound in HDTV productions varies from spectacular to terrible, and as in the case of low production values, poor quality audio sounds worse on HDTV sets. About two decades ago, Russ Neuman demonstrated that sound quality affects people's perceptions of a screen's visual resolution—improving the quality of the audio alone makes the visual resolution appear higher,[27] which makes the industry's error in not paying attention to HDTV sound even more egregious. Prior to 2007, very few commercials were transmitted in HDTV. Like the electronics industry, the advertising community was late to realize the new technology's appeal for viewers.

DVRs

We discuss two types of digital video recorders (DVRs) here: stand-alone boxes such as Tivo, and DVR technology built into a cable or satellite box. Both allow viewers to record programming easily and watch at their convenience. They also allow people to create their own instant replays—for example, to review the last several seconds of a play during a football game—and to start watching "live" programming after it has started. Many DVR owners call the latter "building a buffer," taking advantage of the time delay to fast-forward through commercials or boring scenes.

For five years, DVRs entered homes very slowly, beginning to accelerate in 2004 when cable and satellite companies began to put DVR technology into digital set-top boxes. One of the early problems was that many people did not understand what DVRs did, and some promotional materials made them seem like high-end VCRs. While word of mouth about DVRs was very positive, such publicity has much more effect after adoption reaches a certain threshold: five thousand people spreading their enthusiasm for a new product is not as valuable as five million people doing so.

In many households, DVRs are controlled by one person, who manages what will be recorded for everyone in the household, a pattern similar to that previously found in many households using VCRs to record programs. Some recorded programs are watched and erased within a week; others are stored for months, either because they are forgotten or because they are favorites and stored like a collection of DVDs. A combination of long-term storage and automatic recording of favorite series whenever they are transmitted (a feature called "Season Pass" on Tivo recorders) can quickly fill a hard drive, as many people—even those with the highest-capacity DVR units—report.

DVRs have been associated with *time-shift television*, a term developed to describe how some people used VCRs. A better term may be *schedule-free television*. DVRs allow people to watch any program without worrying about when it is transmitted. Users' experience is that the technology goes out and gathers programs on any channel and at any time, making them available for viewing whenever convenient. The TV schedule becomes almost irrelevant. Moreover, schedule-related concepts such as prime time have less meaning in a DVR environment.

Another way to characterize the change from pre-DVR to post-DVR use of television is to divide viewing into two categories: open-ended and controlled. Open-ended viewing involves going through a channel lineup to find programs available at a given time. Controlled viewing involves watching something under one's own control, free of time or channel constraints. In the past, most television viewing was open-ended, and a smaller share (prerecorded videocassettes or DVDs) was controlled. With many DVR households, the balance shifts, and more TV viewing is controlled.

DVR users report that television becomes a more enjoyable experience because they watch more of the programs they like rather than settle for what is on at any given time (evoking the "200 channels and nothing to watch" syndrome). They feel more in control of the television experience, strengthening their perceptions of higher-quality experiences. Viewers also believe that time spent watching television is used more efficiently, since they can watch the programs they want in less time. For example, a DVR user can watch three half-hour programs in one hour by skipping past commercials, boring scenes, and opening credits. Those who appear to benefit most from DVRs are those who have limited time to watch television and whose schedules are inflexible. They report that the full 24-hour schedule is now available to them even though they may be able to watch television for only 1 hour a night. This also appears to confer a modest benefit on programs that are not in prime time and therefore unavailable to the largest audiences. However, published reports on DVR usage indicate that people tend to record the same shows that are the most popular with regular television viewers.

Many side effects are associated with DVR usage. One is that owners channel surf less, since they have already found what they want from the full week's schedule. They are also less likely to multitask (for example, to read while watching television) or listen to television as background to another activity, such as housecleaning. Group viewing appears to occur slightly more frequently in DVR homes, since the technology is typically on only one TV yet many household members want its benefits. The impact on commercials has been discussed at great length: DVR users watch fewer commercials. Some important nuances exist, however. Many people report that they have stopped watching commercials completely, but follow-up discussions indicate that people still watch some commercials—for example, promotions for movies and television programs, funny or favorite commercials, and commercials with visuals that catch viewers' eyes as they fast-forward. Indeed, it is reported that during the Super Bowl (the traditional occasion when U.S. advertising agencies launch striking new commercials), a common use of DVRs' instant replay feature is for watching commercials a second time. Even when fast-forwarding through commercials, users see clear images for a few seconds; by contrast, those who channel surf can entirely avoid commercials. Some advertisers have begun to put still images, which can be seen clearly in fast-forward mode, on a part of the screen. Nevertheless, some analysts believe that DVRs will have a significant impact on advertiser-based business models for television, though this effect may be mitigated because most DVR users watch more TV than people without DVRs and channel surf less during commercials.

DVRs are essentially computers. They have hard drives, operating software, and sophisticated user interfaces; users interact with them as with computers. DVRs thus can (and sometimes do) crash and send error messages. They also require periodic software updates. People have come to expect such problems with personal computers but not with television.

VOD

VOD allows viewers to access specific content at any time. The selected program or movie is transmitted to a TV for which a person has the same controls as for a DVD player—play, stop, reverse, fast-forward. Some VOD programming has a usage charge, generally for a 24-hour rental; some is included in a monthly subscription package of programs; and some is free, with or without advertisements. Content includes movies, regular television programs, special interest programs, classified advertising, and games. Since it is stored on a server, there is no schedule, and programs can be of any length. Nor is there any theoretical limit to the amount of content stored. If the provider has enough storage capacity, there could be 10,000 movies or 10 seasons of a situation comedy. VOD is a major offering in digital cable services, and many observers believe that it provides cable with a competitive advantage over satellite services. However, it grew slowly during the first few years of its availability.

Consumers like the concept, but some found the reality of early services disappointing. VOD has not been able to offer the latest movies, since major studios release them first to rental shops. Availability of VOD television programs has been slowed in some cases by contract negotiations with program providers. Subscription video-on-demand (SVOD), such as HBO on Demand, which allows viewers to watch any movie offered by HBO in a given month any time they wish, has been received positively.[28] SVOD inherently meets viewer expectations about content that will be available, since it does not promise to deliver any programming other than that which is on the pay movie channel's regular schedule for the month. A key long-term question is whether VOD providers will emphasize paid content without commercials or free content with commercials. Some evidence suggests that consumers find the latter more attractive.

Observations of VOD viewing behavior reveal some of the challenges. One is the menu for available content. Some people say it is difficult to find programs when navigating through several layers of menus. Others avoid menus and may not see what is available. In response, many cable systems have put an "entrance" to VOD services on regular channels. Another obstacle is the delay in accessing VOD menus on some cable systems. Even though viewers may have to wait only a few seconds to see the menu, some move on rather than wait.

VOD is a work in progress, with significant potential benefits for viewers. Beyond solving early technical glitches and obtaining more first-run movies, two core issues that must be resolved concern the user interface[29] and the appeal of micro-niche content. First, VOD requires a user interface for viewers to access programs, just as computer users require user interfaces, but what is the optimal design for a television user interface? This is much more challenging than it appears at first because of the resolution of most TV sets, viewers' expectations and habits, and the limitations of remote controls in navigating through menus. Second, over the past few decades, television programming has changed from content with mass appeal to a combination of mass and niche content. VOD offers the opportunity to focus content on even narrower (micro-niche) interests. It remains unclear, however, what people are prepared to pay for different degrees of specialization and hence what levels can be supported by viable business models.

Web Television

To understand how people are using video on the Web, it is important to know how faster access through broadband cable, DSL, and optical fiber lines has changed Web usage in households. Broadband has enabled many people to use the Web in ways similar to television, easing the transition to watching video on the Web. Typically, personal computers with broadband connections are on whenever anyone is at home, as is common with TV sets, and people use them for much longer sessions than they used dial-up computers. In some cases, people sit at their computers in easy chairs instead office chairs, perhaps because they spend so long there. Also, many users decorate the area on top of or next to the monitor with stuffed animals or family photographs, much as they decorated TVs in the 1960s and 1970s. Moreover, some people, especially children, use the Web in groups. For example, two or three children may sit together at a computer while using an entertainment site. In addition, since wireless networks have facilitated the location of computers in all rooms and not just home offices, as in the past; computer monitors and laptops are now found in living rooms, bedrooms, and other rooms that were previously the domain of TVs. The TV and the computer are often used together. Moreover, broadband supports a range of entertainment, not just information and e-mail. Many people use computers equipped with DVD drives as "second TV sets" to play DVD movies. As the use of computers for entertainment increases, it is easier to make the leap to video over the Web.

The amount of video watched over the Web increased dramatically between 2003 and 2009. At first, most of the programming was short—news clips, sports highlights, or brief amateur videos—but as more people adopted broadband and more content became available, many began to watch full-length television programs. What types of video content does a Web user encounter? A review of content models reveals that there are at least seven categories. The first may be called sampling or provision of short excerpts from longer television programs or films, often to encourage Web users to watch them on cable or purchase them as DVDs. A second, related category involves providing promotional trailers for television programs or films. Typically, these are the same trailers that appear on television, in movie theaters, or on DVDs. Third, traditional third-party advertising appears on some Web sites—e.g., a video commercial for a soft drink company appearing on a general entertainment Web site.

A fourth category includes full-length television programs and films as video streams or downloads. Amateur video, as is found on sites such as YouTube, is a fifth category. These are particularly popular with younger audiences and range from short clips for mobile phones to video blogs to mashups (which mix professional and amateur content, often for satirical purposes). The sixth category, two-screen TV, includes video content on the Web that complements regular television programming. In this case, the distribution of content for a program utilizes two channels, regular television and the Web, which may provide some scenes that were not in the broadcast channel. (Two-screen TV fits within a large subset of user behavior that involves simultaneous use of the Web and television. Most of this simultaneous activity consists of unrelated television and Web usage: for example, someone may watch a sports program on television while surfing the Web for news content.) Finally, parallel broadcasting is the transmission of the same content on the Web as on a cable or broadcast channel at the same time or in a similar time frame—for example, video coverage of a major concert.

A unique variation on two-screen TV was launched by CBS during its coverage of the NCAA basketball tournament in 2009. CBS carried every game online and broadcast selected games to markets where they expected higher interest in those teams. However, if a game was a blowout, they would switch the broadcast to another, more competitive game, telling fans that they could watch the other game online.

At least five types of video streaming and downloading service providers exist: original producers and distributors of video for the Web; content aggregators, who specialize in video streaming (e.g., YouTube or Hulu); video search engines and portals, such as Google and Yahoo; social networking sites, such as MySpace and Facebook, that let people post videos; and video distributors, such as cable or broadcast networks, that offer some video on their Web sites. The sources of content include traditional television groups (NBC or ESPN, for example), underground video producers, and amateurs who create programs such as video blogs. The experience of watching Web video has improved markedly, but it is not as consistent as for video received over cable or satellite TV. Some content is poor quality (e.g., content created with mobile phone cameras) but acceptable in small windows. Increasingly, however, content is of reasonable to excellent quality.

Video file sharing of television programs and even movies is widespread, especially among young people, in spite of efforts to stop it. Gali Einav found that video file sharing is very common among college students for reasons of convenience, control, and immediacy.[30] Very few students were concerned about the legality of sharing copyrighted material, regarding it as a form of sampling content to determine if they wanted to buy it.

From a viewer's perspective, Web TV promises access to an in-depth inventory of video content across a broad range of categories, all of it on demand and much of it interactive. A specific program might be free with advertising or available for a fee without commercials. A movie might be offered in different price ranges depending on when it is rented or on its level of resolution. Such is the potential flexibility of the Web as a video distribution channel.[31]

Video for mobile devices, such as for storage on iPods or streamed to mobile phones, is another important category, discussed in chapter 10.

Implications for the Future

The new television technologies have led to several common changes in consumers' experience of television and their viewing behavior. Overall, these technologies have provided more control over viewing, created more active viewers, reduced dependence on schedules, and increased the time people spend with video programming. That viewing is more active does not necessarily mean it is more active for all viewers all the time: degrees of activity vary by time of day, age, gender, and personality. In addition, increased activity does not diminish the relaxation function of television. Some people find increased activity to be relaxing. Increased time with video programming does not necessarily mean more time with traditional broadcast or cable TV programs, since many people now spread their television viewing across more delivery systems such as DVDs, the Web, and on-demand content. Traditional television viewing on TV sets remains a major component of the average person's day but it is not as dominant a force as in previous decades.

Some of the new technologies—e.g., HDTV and DVRs—have increased the amount of group viewing. This, however, may be an artifact of the fact that a household has only one HDTV set or one DVR that everyone wants to share. As households acquire second and third units, they may return to more personalized consumption of television.

Changes in television technologies and viewer behavior have a number of implications for consumers, content producers, and media organizations. One important consequence of the new television environment is complexity. Users used to take for granted the easy operation of a television set: turn it on, change channels, set the volume, sit back, and watch. In the new environment, TVs are computers with multiple modes, inputs and outputs, and complex remote controls for operating numerous functions. Some viewers, especially older people with little or no computer experience, have trouble operating these TVs and finding programs that may be a few steps down in a series of menus.

The future will offer no escape from television sets with user interfaces, but what forms will they take? What, for example, is the best way to organize and access television channels in a digital cable or satellite environment? Current options include a traditional linear channel lineup accessed by up/down arrows on a remote or direct entry, an on-screen menu, and special keys on a remote control. The linear channel lineup becomes problematic with hundreds of channels/services; special keys on a remote are problematic in an environment where households have several remotes, each with dozens of keys; and menus require submenus and raise the possibility that some viewers will become lost while trying to find channels. The design challenge is significant.

Will television schedules disappear, except for live events? Possibly, but the timing is unclear. DVRs, VOD, and Web TV effectively take away the television schedule and make programs available at any time. If these technologies become widely accepted in the marketplace, television schedules could become history. Someday, a broadcast network or cable channel might announce, "We have 235 programs available this month, watch them when you want, where you want, and on any display device you want."

As television schedules become less important, storage and networking of television programs become more important. Storage of television programs began with the videocassette. VCRs were also rudimentary forerunners of home networks, linking stored content with the TV. Today, DVDs, DVRs, computer hard drives, and servers at cable systems or Websites provide additional storage devices for programming. Networks linking stored television content and display devices include wired and wireless home networks, cable systems, broadband, and 3G networks for mobile phones. Many more such systems are emerging or under development—for example, devices that forward video content received at a person's home to virtually anywhere (sometimes called place shifting).[32] Both the time and location of television viewing are much more flexible than in the past.

Given consumers' very positive reactions to DVRs and the dramatic changes in viewing behavior evidenced by some of those households, the question has arisen whether DVRs will destroy the business model of commercial television, in which advertisers pay for programs because people watch the advertising placed in them. The answer hinges on whether the mainstream users of DVRs built into cable and satellite boxes will change their viewing habits as much as the earlier adopters of stand-alone Tivo boxes.

Mainstream DVR users are not as extreme in using the technology as the earlier adopters. A study by Horowitz and Associates for ABC/ESPN in which a large group of households received DVRs found that many people did not use them very much or found only modest value in their core features. This parallels earlier research about VCR households, which found that over time, the use of VCRs to record TV programs diminished.[33] Interviews also suggest that second-generation DVR households are not changing their viewing behavior as dramatically as the earlier adopters. Added to this, both groups watch more TV because of DVRs. The jury is still out on the long-term impact of DVRs: while they do not appear to represent the end of commercial television as we know it, even a moderate loss of eyeballs watching commercials could affect business practices.

What is the future of advertising in traditional television, Web TV, and television watched through DVRs? If many people change channels during commercials and fast-forward through them on a DVR, advertising and television may respond in any of several ways: (1) the viewer may pay for more content, and advertising will diminish; (2) sponsorships of programs, common in 1950s commercial television and used today on public television in the United States, will become more frequent; (3) product placement within programs may continue to increase; (4) more advertising may be digitally inserted as background within content; (5) a "newspaper model" of advertising may be employed on television, with content and advertisements appearing in different windows on the same screen; (6) icons or message flags may be inserted in commercials to signal DVR users about the type of commercial through which they were fast-forwarding; and, (7) prime shelf space in EPGs and interactive TV menus may become a valuable advertising venue. Advertisers have been slow to experiment with exactly how people fast-forward through commercials and why they watch some but not others. Experimentation may lead to a new style of commercial for the DVR environment. Regulation may also play an important role. For example, the U.S. regulatory environment is relatively lax compared to Europe on the issue of product placement, meaning that Europeans are less likely to see branded soda cans, candy, and cars in programming.[34]

Just as advertisers have been slow to adapt to the DVR environment, program producers have been as slow to adapt to the HDTV environment. A great deal of content is recorded and transmitted in HDTV, but the style of the programs has generally followed the style of traditional programming. HDTV viewers report that wide shots in sports programming work much better in HDTV because they can see details that are lost in traditional television. In addition, blemishes, wrinkles, and even sweat are visible in HDTV, making some actors and reporters look better or worse. In the long term, after HDTV sets are in a majority of homes, producers will have learned how to create programs that take advantage of the special features of HDTV. What is unclear is whether a new generation of actors, reporters, and politicians will advance to new heights of popularity because they come across well on HDTV, as happened after radio, black and white television, and later color television were introduced. We may look back at some point and realize that Barack Obama was the first HD U.S. president. As we gain more knowledge about the HDTV viewing experience, many surprises are likely to affect content. Robert Kubey and Mihalyi Csikszentmihalyi, for example, hypothesize that HDTV will increase eye movement and involve greater cognitive activity, much as in watching a movie in a theater.[35]

Web TV is the new kid on the block. A few years ago, many media analysts dismissed it because of the belief that Web technology could not adequately handle video and that people would not watch TV programs on computer monitors or laptops, much less on mobile phones or small-screen portable media players. However, households with broadband Internet access have accepted many forms of Web TV, and the technology continues to improve. Equally important, many viewers have come to accept the computer monitor or laptop as a second television set, much like a kitchen TV.

Audio provides another challenge. Much Web video viewing occurs in offices where audio could reveal that a person is not hard at work. Many workers have found ingenious methods to mask the fact that they are listening to their computer—for example, using one earbud on a side that cannot be seen by someone walking by a cubicle. Web video programmers may adopt the strategy of CNBC (which is often muted in office environments) of presenting key information visually and therefore not requiring audio. More generally, the challenge is to adapt content to meet the characteristics of the Web environment, with its different broadband speeds, screen sizes, and social contexts for viewing.

For a long while, television content providers such as the major networks perceived the Web as a competitor for people's time, and it is. However, content providers now believe that the Web offers an opportunity to distribute programming. Just as they feared cable and satellite but ultimately came to embrace them as new ways to deliver programs, the television industry has come to view the Web as yet another distribution opportunity. Beyond distributing regular programs and short excerpts from existing shows, it is unclear where program providers will obtain content to feed the voracious appetites of Web users. They could turn to Web users themselves to generate content in the form of games, chat, and other types of interactive television (see chapter 8). They could also repackage user-generated content, as some do now, in the form of even more *Funniest Pet Tricks* or newsmagazines based on video captured by ordinary people. New micro-niche programs are also possible, assuming that production costs remain manageable and revenue will support them. However, such programming presupposes that the trend of audience fragmentation will continue. As David Waterman observes, the efficiency of fragmentation was supposed to create a higher advertising cost per thousand viewers, but it simply has not materialized.[36]

Regardless of changes in technology, television's core functions of providing relaxation, entertainment, information, and escape[37] are unlikely to change. However, the ways in which these core functions are provided will change, thereby affecting both viewing behavior and content. As long as television technology continues to change—and there is no indication that it will slow down in the near future—viewing behavior and programming will continue to evolve.

// SIX //

Videophones and Teleconferencing

The ear is probably the most intelligent organ the body has.

—*Daniel Barenboim*

When AT&T introduced the Picturephone in the middle of the twentieth century, it was the start of another era for new media. Unfortunately, it was a false start. A prototype had been created in 1956; it was unveiled at the New York World's Fair in 1964; soon after, it was launched as a service for business subscribers; in 1970, it was introduced in Pittsburgh and Chicago as a service for residential subscribers, and AT&T forecast that 2 million units would be in use by the mid-1980s. However, it was withdrawn in 1973, having cost the corporation an estimated half a billion dollars (vastly more in today's dollars). Many successor videophones have been launched in North America and around the world, but video telephony is still not fully established in the marketplace. Over the succeeding four decades, Picturephone's spin-off, videoconferencing, fared distinctly better, but even it has done far less well than was widely expected. In the case of videophones and videoconferencing, the most important lessons—and the main reason that expectations proved unrealistic—relate to repeated failure to understand intended users and their needs.

This case study focuses on two-way, real-time, audio-only, and audiovisual media. The three main technologies are videophones, videoconferencing systems, and audioconferencing systems. (The term *teleconferencing* has sometimes been used to include computer conferencing, a very different medium [see chapter 7].) These technologies differ greatly in the speed with which they have moved along the adoption curve. A decade or so passed before audioconferencing became commonplace, but videoconferencing required two to three decades to achieve rather modest adoption, and videophones still have not been widely adopted after about five decades. If the most rapidly adopted of the three, audioconferencing, appears too ordinary to be interesting, bear in mind that it is indisputably by far the most successful and that the reasons for this phenomenon go a long way toward explaining the relative lack of success of the more glamorous members of its family.

With a few exceptions—for example, when it is used for formal presentations or for instruction—the content of this set of technologies is not created by media professionals for consumption by an audience; instead, it is generated by purposeful interaction among end users (creating, in modern parlance, user-generated content). In consequence, these technologies raise issues in which scholars in the field of mass communications, with a few exceptions, have shown little interest, perhaps because the theoretical constructs in the field are not easily applied to these media. Fortunately, however, the findings of others, together with the industry's half century of success and failure, have created a good understanding of the user issues involved, even though no established theory yet explains why, in many situations, the addition of a visual channel adds so little to the efficacy of a speech channel.

TERMINOLOGY: AUDIOCONFERENCING

An audioconferencing system gives three or more users at two or more locations the ability to hear and be heard by one another. Three-way calling and use of loudspeaking telephones are the simplest examples of this functionality, but much more sophisticated technology is necessary to provide good sound quality if there are more locations and/or larger groups at any location. The former requires a *bridge* to connect the telephone lines, each of which joins the bridge at a separate port.

Enhanced audioconferencing refers to the enhancement of basic audioconferencing by a parallel low-bandwidth system that usually provides for the transmission of graphics. Starting in the late 1990s, Web conferencing has provided a significant means of enhancing some kinds of audioconference.

Users and Providers of Audioconferencing

Some historians might argue that the first audioconferences were shared party lines in the late nineteenth and early twentieth centuries, but such lines provided inadvertent conference calls mostly as a result of eavesdropping. Conference calls as such date back about a century to an early 1900s three-way call between an insurance salesman, his client, and the salesman's boss, all of them in New York City, to close a sale. However, the use of the audioconferencing medium started to build momentum only at the beginning of the 1970s, a time of structural stability in the telecommunications industry when markets were dominated by AT&T and by its overseas counterparts, almost all state-owned monopolies. Their interests in new person-to-person services were limited to videophones and videoconferencing. The initiative and energy behind audioconferencing's early years came not from within the industry but from the user community, and even then not mainly from corporate users but from the public sector, including education.

In the United States, the indisputable leader in attracting interest to the medium was a team at the University of Wisconsin-Extension that was propelled into the field in the second half of the 1960s, when the state legislature mandated that the state university make continuing education available across the state through centers in close proximity to residents. This development solved the critical problem faced by working professionals such as nurses and teachers who needed to obtain training necessary for recertification. Audioconferencing appeared to offer the only affordable means of meeting the requirement. The team's successful pioneering work bore a strong evangelical tone and soon diffused to other centers of continuing education.[1] In the United Kingdom, the baton was carried by the government's Civil Service Department, which managed the domestic civil service, the country's largest user of telecommunications services. Within a few years, the United Kingdom's Open University was significantly involved as well. While it was best known for its use of television and radio, it designed its teaching with a sophisticated understanding of the importance of finding not the right medium for a particular course but the right mix of media to match each course's component activities. For widely dispersed students, a local teacher used conference calls to provide group tutorials, a valued feature of the British approach to university education. In Canada, early leadership came from the Department of Communications, stemming from its interest in effective use of telecommunications within government.

Initial Technical Problems

In the late 1960s, important technical challenges needed to be met. One related to the equipment available to enable groups, rather than just individuals, to participate at any location. The loudspeaking telephones of the time could provide adequate speech transmission for only about five people sitting within roughly three feet of the microphone. The conference telephones that accommodated larger groups were somewhat clumsy to use and decidedly vulnerable to poor room acoustics. Both kinds of devices suffered from the need to include mechanisms to stop positive feedback—i.e., the leakage of sound from a loudspeaker into a nearby microphone creating what is appropriately known as howlaround. In addition, to prevent an accumulation of background noise from obscuring the signal, only one microphone usually could be live at a time. The voice-switching mechanisms used for these purposes often clipped the opening syllable from speakers' remarks and made for awkward transitions among speakers.

The other main technological challenge arose from the need to interconnect multiple sites. What works well enough for an amateur electrician—merely connecting together the copper wires—would not have worked for conference calls. The signals arriving at the common point needed to be boosted to be heard adequately at their destinations, and differences in signal strength needed to be reduced to avoid disconcerting differences in the loudness of sound from different locations; these processes had to be carried out without injecting interference into the signals. Purpose-designed bridges accomplished this task, but in the late 1960s, the available bridges were very limited in both quality and functionality.

Neither bridges nor conference telephones existed that were adequate for the purposes of the distance learning system that the team at the University of Wisconsin needed to establish. The team commissioned its own equipment of both kinds and used it initially on a network of private telephone lines, which provided a better quality of transmission than the regular dial-up telephone network of the time.

By the mid- to late 1970s, about 25 U.S. corporations and research organizations (including the National Aeronautics and Space Administration) had permanently equipped teleconferencing rooms. Most were only for audioconferencing, and they were linked together by dedicated circuits. By the end of the decade, however, technology had improved to the point that many corporate conference calls took place over the dial-up network rather than over private networks. The market has subsequently continued to develop, and a continuing stream of improvements has occurred in the effectiveness, functionality, and value for money of the associated technologies. The replacement of analog by digital equipment in the dial-up network has also played a significant part in raising the overall quality of conference calls.

Other Early Problems

Other significant obstacles to widespread adoption of audioconferencing could not be overcome by improving the technology. One was the general lack of interest in the market shown by AT&T and its counterparts in other countries. This lack of interest both reinforced and was reinforced by a lack of understanding of how customers actually used audioconferencing. As a result, AT&T did not pursue possible technical improvements that could have reduced users' irritation with some aspects of the services, and they were unaware of the medium's enormous potential. Because bridges were relatively expensive, required specialized expertise, and for technical reasons had to be positioned at an optimal location inside the network (not on users' premises), it made economic sense for bridges to be owned and operated not by user organizations but by companies that provided interconnection on a fee-for-service basis. The Bell System had a long-established service—"the conference call operator"—but it was expensive to provide, offered poor value for money relative to what others were soon to offer, and was not promoted. Before the telecommunications industry became highly competitive following the breakup of AT&T in 1984, much easier pickings lay elsewhere. A related obstacle was created by the fact that until the 1990s, the quality of the dial-up network was such that technical problems were frequent: particular examples occurred when sound quality deteriorated or the connection to one or more of the locations was dropped. Ensuring that a conference call was technically satisfactory required an operator to monitor it, taking the appropriate action if the sound quality deteriorated or one of the parties was dropped. However, regulations to protect the privacy of telephone users prevented Bell System operators—but not those of other telecommunications companies—from monitoring telephone calls. As a result, even if the Bell System had wanted to, it could not have provided a high-quality service.

A third obstacle was the heritage of the Bell System as a monopoly that perceived no need for aggressive marketing of its services or for user-friendly sales language. So, for example, some brochures directed toward potential users described teleconferencing as a "tariffed service," a description that conveyed little information to lay users. AT&T also set up barriers for end users and third parties who wanted to attach equipment to the network, a holdover from the days when the Bell System was an end-to-end monopoly that owned both the network and all attached equipment.

The fourth and certainly not the least important of the obstacles was the novelty of the medium. Strange as it may seem now that conference calls have become commonplace, as recently as the late 1970s, prospective users typically underestimated by a large margin how well the medium would work in a wide variety of situations and were nervous about their ability to use it. They needed to have their hands held, a process that often involved advice for the chair ahead of an audioconference, the reassurance that a skilled operator could immediately jump in if necessary during it, and sometimes the facilitation of questions and comments from locations the chair could not see. In particular executives, who were used to high levels of control needed extensive hand-holding; the lack of the visual communication channel was prone to cause them anxiety. In addition, they did not want to look stupid when problems arose—problems such as fire engines passing a location with an open window or a presenter who was difficult to hear because he put his speakerphone's microphone in his desk drawer to get it out of the way. In such cases, only the conference operator could immediately identify the site causing the problem and take the necessary corrective action. Other aspects, like how to phrase a voice vote to make sure that people really were agreeing, required a little coaching, but such advice resembled what people learned in public speaking courses. As one of the nascent industry's most successful leaders put it at the time, "high touch" was more important than high tech. He commented on those days,

> I recall that most of our early clients were very frustrated with their conference calls. I decided that their frustration levels were so high they would remain deaf to suggestions of any other applications until I fixed their most pressing communication problems. The "high touch" approach helped create a bond between the operator and the person most likely to be in the line of fire when a conference call didn't work—the administrative assistant and/or secretary. Once we fixed the most critical problem, it was much easier to suggest other applications or changes to the way they handled their calls.[2]

Examples of applications he subsequently suggested included a routine of quarterly conference calls and use of the medium for press conferences. Several other service bureaus—companies started to provide the interconnection service—also strongly emphasized providing user support via their operators, thereby playing a crucial role in opening up the market. The contrast with AT&T is again notable: even if the company had not been restricted from monitoring calls, human operators would not have represented one of the strengths of the Bell System's operating companies or of its overseas counterparts. Nor, as organizations, were giant telephone companies suited to nurturing a fledgling "high touch" business.

Some may question whether audioconferencing made use of a new medium or represented for most users simply a new application of the long-established telephone. The answer depends, of course, on exactly how one defines a *medium*. Though an interesting theoretical question, it does not need to be answered to address the issues with which this chapter—or this book as a whole—is concerned. What matters here is that for the vast majority of its users, it clearly differed sufficiently from the regular telephone that they reacted to it as though it were a new medium.

Some Variations on a Theme

Conference calls are not used exclusively by those working in corporations or public sector organizations. Sometimes they link members of the corporate world with interested parties outside it; sometimes they are used entirely within the community. In both cases, some of the calls have a very large number of participants.

GAB services were essentially conference call services for recreational purposes. They allowed any members of the community to call in and join conference calls on a wide variety of topics. (The term GAB is a play on words, both an acronym for group access bridging and slang for talk.) They were first introduced in Argentina in the early 1970s and spread via the United Kingdom to the United States by the early 1980s. In the United States, they generally used the 976 service, in which a local call was billed at a premium rate, typically about 35 cents per minute. Use grew very rapidly, and the services generated easy profits for the telephone companies that offered them. The number of participants on a call was sometimes very high, which led to the development of a new generation of bridges with hundreds of ports, rather than up to 96, which had been the previous limit. However, concerns arose about the lack of barriers to prevent children from calling into discussions considered inappropriate for them or from running up enormous telephone bills; the resulting regulation effectively stifled the U.S. market for more than a decade. The services later returned in the form of today's "chat lines" (audio services, not to be confused with text chat services).

Very large conference calls with more than 100 participating locations sometimes occur in the context of multilevel marketing. The largest call thought to have ever taken place involved Tupperware and linked about 300 locations. Some of the largest of today's calls include well over 100 participants in church services. The calls provide those who are unable to travel to church with an easy and relatively inexpensive means of joining in group worship. Michael Luo has described a variation on this theme:[3] four nights a week, a one-hour conference call links immigrants to the United States from China's Fujian province, who use their mobile phones and free "night-and-weekend minutes" to join in Bible study and prayer conducted in Mandarin and led by the minister of a Fujianese Protestant church in Manhattan. Most of these participants are isolated and lonely illegal immigrants working for low wages in Chinese restaurants scattered across the country.

Until 2000, corporations often held conference calls to discuss their quarterly earnings figures and related matters with invited securities market professionals. However, the U.S. Securities and Exchange Commission concluded that participants had an unfair advantage because they were slightly ahead of others in receiving information that could affect stock prices, and it issued Reg FD (Fair Disclosure), which required that all such calls be open to any individual who wanted to participate. The initial result was very large and hence unwieldy and expensive conference calls, but a hybrid approach subsequently emerged: financial analysts and members of the press (or the favored among them) were invited into a regular conference call; the content of this call was simultaneously made available to anyone else who wanted to hear it as streaming audio on the Web. In addition to saving money, this strategy eliminated the possibility that unfamiliar members of the general public could surprise company officials with unwelcome comments or questions, another risk of a conference call open to anyone.

The idea of having two classes of participant—an inner circle with a two-way connection and an outer circle with only a one-way connection—has been implemented in a variety of videoconferencing situations as well, including the Reading two-way cable television project (see chapter 8). A creative variation in the audio realm was started in the 1980s. Ahead of important football games, radio sports reporters were invited to take part in a regular weekly conference call with coaches of the Big 8 Conference football teams. The sports reporters recorded the event, then wrote down the questions that they had asked and edited out all but the coaches' responses. Local outlets created "actualities," in which local reporters read the questions and then played the tape of the coach's answer, giving the impression that small stations had increased clout and substantially improving the ratings for their news broadcasts. The number of small stations paying access fees to participate in these calls grew rapidly.

From Operators to Automation

In addition to their crucial role in making audioconferencing user-friendly and providing low-key instruction, operators performed other tasks. An important one was to connect participants to the bridge. For some years, this process meant calling out to each location in turn (hoping the line would be free and someone would answer), exchanging a few words, and connecting the line to the bridge. When many locations were involved, the process took a long time to complete. Calling out was gradually replaced by calling in, but it remained necessary for an operator to check that the callers were authorized participants and then connect them to the bridge. Over the years, as automation increased, participants became able to use preassigned PIN numbers to enter the bridge without the intervention of an operator. By the end of the 1990s, operators had become unnecessary for the majority of calls. Users had long since ceased needing their hands held. With PIN numbers for security, users could enter bridges by themselves; they very rarely encountered technical problems. Organizations and individuals had contracts with service bureaus that provided bridging services on demand, eliminating the need for prior reservations, and users could use telephone keypads to control various functions—for example, turning sound volume up and down or muting the microphone at their location.

Increasing automation occasionally caused problems for users. In some embarrassing cases, unauthorized people (sometimes financial journalists) eavesdropped on conferences because, for example, PINs were not changed after an employee had been dismissed. And the increasing use of mobile phones created difficulties when participants in a conference call did not appreciate the importance of avoiding noisy environments. But such problems could be avoided by the disciplined adoption of sensible procedures. For service bureaus, automa-

FROM AUTOMATION TO COMMODITIZATION

Automation brought a very rapid transition in the bulk of the business from operator-handled to user-handled calls. In 1997, about half of all calls were operator-handled; five years later, customer-handled calls had grown to more than 90 percent of the market in North America and other industrialized countries.

It became impossible to distinguish one automated conference call bureau's service from another's. Automated conference calls became a commodity, to be bought on the basis of price alone. A cutthroat price war broke out, first in the United States and within two to three years in most of the rest of the industrialized world. Prices plummeted. In 2000 the average price of all calls (automated and operator-assisted) through North American service bureaus was about 24 cents per connected location per minute; by 2005, this number had fallen to 8 cents. Some large corporations negotiated prices of less than two cents per connection per minute for their automated calls, including the long-distance charges for the toll-free lines used.

Service bureaus are still necessary to provide operator-handled service for a minority of calls, but their role in what has become the commodity end of the business is a historical anomaly in the evolution of the public telephone network. Human operators originally were essential to conference calls, but they are no longer necessary for about 95 percent of today's business. Automated conference calls are essentially a network operation—like call-forwarding, for example—that ought to be most efficiently handled as just one of the many features in the networks of the various companies that provide telephone service. Conference calls can also be handled by users' computers. Skype has been moving ahead rapidly in this area, as have Microsoft, Cisco, and other major players. For three decades, service bureaus played an essential role in the emergence of a modest but extremely useful and heavily used medium. While their era appears to be ending, audioconferencing itself is certainly not going away.

tion immediately lowered labor costs, thereby providing higher margins and, as volume continued to soar, considerably increased profits. A happy picture? No, a vivid example of hubris.

The Conference Call Industry

U.S. service bureaus initially were small independent companies, happily tolerated by the telephone company giants for whom they generated long-distance traffic. The bureaus were responsible for the widespread adoption of audioconferencing except in the specialized field of education. Business boomed, and in the early 1990s, some were bought up by telephone company giants, who finally entered the market. Consolidation of the industry started in the late 1990s. By 2006, it was dominated by West/Intercall, MCI, AT&T, and a few other large players formed from the amalgamation of what had once been much smaller service bureaus. The industry's total global revenues in the mid-2000s were estimated as somewhat over $2.5 billion a year. Growth has remained at a consistently high level for two decades.

Visual and Other Enhancements for Audioconferencing

Although the diffusion of audioconferencing has been highly successful for more than three decades, this was not the case in one area associated with it: the provision of various relatively low-cost nonspeech enhancements that could operate over regular telephone connections. Systems were developed and marketed for each of the following purposes:

- automatically identifying the individual speaking at another location;
- indicating to the chair that someone from another location wished to speak;
- controlling slide projectors at other locations;
- transmitting still video images to the other locations (e.g., slow-scan television);
- transmitting writing or drawing in real time to monitors at other locations (e.g., electronic blackboards);
- sharing computer applications among locations.

Except for occasional modest successes with the use of various visual adjuncts in audioconferencing sessions over the telephone network for the purposes of education and training, these enhancements have failed. On the surface, this development is surprising: any of them would have enabled users to overcome an obvious limitation of the speech-only medium at a relatively moderate cost. The reasons seem likely to stem from the fact that their use would have substantially interfered with two distinctive advantages of audioconferencing: its convenience and its flexibility.

Web conferencing, introduced in the mid-1990s, opened a new chapter in enhancements to audioconferencing.[4] It enables

computer applications to be shared among locations;

a Web page to be shared among all locations and modified in real time by participants at any of them;

those at all locations to view a PowerPoint presentation or a video file and discuss what they are seeing;

the distribution of documents before or during a meeting via e-mail;

back-channel communication between two or more people in the meeting via instant messaging.

It can be used in either a passive mode (viewing a presentation) or an interactive mode (contributing to a Web page). Services come in "meet-me" or assisted versions and in a wide range of pricing options, including free.

Web conferencing services differ from earlier enhancements to audioconferencing in three respects. First, they provide an integrated package of enhancements on a familiar platform (the Web), while each of the earlier enhancements, operating over the telephone network, generally required a distinct system. Second, the ubiquity of the Web and the large number of Web conferencing service providers (more than 60 companies in the mid-2000s) have made it far easier for the services to receive wide exposure. Third, unlike most of the earlier enhancements, Web conferencing requires only personal rather than shared terminals, making it easy to try out and generally much less inconvenient and inflexible than earlier visual adjuncts.

Users and Providers of Videoconferencing

In the mid-1960s, videoconferencing took place ad hoc between groups of people at two points. But the only transmission plant available was analog, with the result that a videoconference required about a thousand times the transmission capacity of a comparable telephone call. Significant costs were also associated with physical facilities: color cameras that required extra lighting and hence extra cooling that often exceeded a building's existing capabilities; a large com-

TERMINOLOGY: VIDEOPHONES AND VIDEOCONFERENCING

Videophones are desktop, tabletop, or handheld (in this case, third-generation mobile phone) devices, generally intended for the use of only one person at each location. They allow users to hear and be heard by and see and be seen by users at one or more other locations. In the past, they were generally stand-alone, purpose-designed devices. However, the necessary functionality can also be provided by personal computers equipped with cameras, microphones, and speakers. In this chapter, computers functioning in this way are considered videophones.

Videoconferencing systems also allow users to hear and be heard by and see and be seen by others; unlike videophones, they are designed for groups of people at any of two or more locations, not just a single user or two. They are often permanently installed in conference rooms, though some can be moved among rooms on carts and set up as needed. They generally use higher-capacity transmission and larger screens than do videophones and provide better audio. In addition, they are likely to have features such as additional cameras for showing documents as well as a control system to allow someone at each location to control the outgoing video signal (e.g., switching between a view of participants to an image from a document camera).

As the terms are commonly used, there is no clear distinction between *video telephony* and *videoconferencing*. Suitable videophones can, for example, be used by some participants in a videoconference.

The term *videoconference* has sometimes been used to cover two other types of event, but it is not used for either here. In one, a television signal is conveyed unidirectionally from one location to a number of others (sometimes with a parallel audioconferencing system enabling interaction among the locations). This is essentially closed-circuit television. Transmission used to occur by satellite but now generally takes place by video streaming. It has proved useful and cost-effective for such purposes as training and for conveying messages from CEOs to corporate employees, with the number of receiving locations ranging from a handful to a hundred or more. It has previously been described by more specific terms, particularly *ad hoc videoconferencing* and *point-to-multipoint videoconferencing*. The term *videoconferencing system* has also been used rather misleadingly to refer to audioconferencing systems that provide the additional capability to exchange still video images among sites.

mitment of floor space; sometimes large and expensive satellite transmitters and dishes; and a new group of support personnel. Videoconferencing was a decidedly expensive proposition.

A four-city service operated by the German post office—Fernsehgespräch—in the mid-1930s was probably the first public videoconferencing service,[5] though the concept (the telephonoscope) was envisaged in the late 1870s in both Europe and the United States.[6] At the start of the 1970s, AT&T introduced a trial service linking together public conference rooms in a few major cities. The British Post Office, the forerunner of British Telecom, did likewise with its Confravision service and was followed by a few other telephone administrations in Europe and later in other parts of the world. Users could reserve a pair of rooms (and the link between them) and pay according to the duration of the time reserved. These trials did not produce promising results. The main challenge was perceived as being a significant reduction in the costs of transmission (in the United States, a videoconference meeting between New York and San Francisco cost approximately $2,000 per hour), which was achieved by digital compression. A variety of other problems existed but were not well perceived at the time.

Digital Transmission and Compression

At the start of the 1980s, very substantial reductions in the transmission costs of videoconferencing were achieved with the introduction of codecs to transmit signals over digital circuits. Codecs translated signals between the analog versions then used by cameras (as well as monitors, microphones, and loudspeakers) and corresponding digital versions and then processed the digital versions (in real time) so that they would require much less transmission capacity. With lower degrees of digital compression, the loss in picture quality was imperceptible; with higher degrees, transmission costs dropped, but the savings had to be weighed against noticeable degradation of picture quality.

Highly impressive improvements in codecs have been made during the past 25 years. The most important have occurred on three fronts: squeezing the digital signals so that they require even less transmission capacity (lower data rates), offering better picture quality at these lower data rates, and becoming much cheaper. (With improved audio systems and cameras no longer requiring high light levels, special treatment of conference rooms became unnecessary, too.) Since about the mid-1990s, it has been possible to install a functional corporate videoconferencing system for under $10,000 per location, though it is easy to spend much more. The corresponding cost in the early 1980s was about 100 times higher.

The use of codecs and digital transmission initially did not provide a complete solution. During their first decade of use, serious problems arose in interconnecting private videoconferencing systems. One problem was that three competing manufacturers made incompatible codecs. Another was that digital transmission networks available from competing long-distance carriers

(AT&T, MCI, and others) did not interconnect. While third-party companies offered gateway services to solve interconnection problems, these services added to both the cost and the effort required to set up videoconferences. Since user organizations naturally ensured that their different videoconferencing rooms used compatible codecs and were on the same carrier's digital network, interconnection problems arose only when there was a need for videoconferencing between different organizations. Since the demand for interorganizational videoconferencing in the absence of these problems is not known, it is not clear how much they held the field back. Nevertheless, the awkwardness of interconnecting video users stood in stark contrast to the ease of interconnecting audio users via the telephone network.

The problems were resolved with two developments at the start of the 1990s. One was the design and adoption by a working party of the International Telecommunications Union of global standards for codecs operating over digital networks. The other was the deployment of ISDN, a public, dial-up digital network to which any location could be connected, just as with the regular (analog) public network. Videoconferencing could operate over ISDN, generally using the equivalent of between two and six digital telephone lines in parallel, with toll charges between two and six times what they were for a regular dialed telephone call. Most user organizations soon installed new standards-compliant codecs and connected to the ISDN network.

To judge from the subsequent increase in the sales of codecs, these two developments substantially enlarged the videoconferencing market, in part because of a reduction in uncertainty (the risk of buying a codec that subsequently turned out to be of the wrong type) and in part because the increased reach and lower costs of ISDN foreshadowed an apparently better return on the investment in videoconferencing. That the standard was welcomed in the field was illustrated by the outcry when Intel began to develop a chip for videoconferencing that would not comply with the standard. The company quickly abandoned the idea in the face of complaints from suppliers and users alike.

Public Videoconferencing Services

By the early 1980s, essentially all videoconferencing was digital. By then, two different approaches were being followed. One was based on the use of public conference rooms that could be rented by any user organization. At first, generally only two locations were linked, though the ability to add a third and a fourth soon became usual. In the United States, AT&T offered its 12-city Picturephone Meeting Service. This videoconferencing system was not, however, based on AT&T's Picturephone but used entirely different technology; the name was probably the only useful asset AT&T was able to salvage from the debacle of its by then deceased videophone. A few other organizations—Sprint, Kinko's, GTE, and some hotel chains—later began to compete with AT&T in the United States.

None of the public conference room services had particular success in any country, and today they represent a very small portion of the overall videoconferencing market. They suffered from significant drawbacks. One was the need for users to leave their offices and travel to the unfamiliar turf of a public facility. The most disagreeable and wasteful parts of long distance travel—with which the industry thought it was competing—were often the local ends, and videoconferencing did not eliminate such needs. Another disadvantage was the fact that the lead time necessary for reservations reduced flexibility. For example, some international services in Europe in the mid-1970s required users to make bookings about a week in advance. Where speed was important, travel was much preferable.

Private Videoconferencing Systems

After digital transmission was introduced, the other approach featured user organizations' installation of private systems on their own premises at various locations. Two of the first systems, dating from the early 1980s, were at Bank of America and Citicorp. Each of the early installations required an investment of close to a million dollars per location for equipment and the adaptation of the conference room (particularly for acoustic and cooling treatment). Other costs were also involved, primarily for transmission and technical staff.

SATELLITE BUSINESS SYSTEMS

A particularly ambitious and high-profile videoconferencing service was launched in the early 1980s by Satellite Business Systems (SBS), a jointly owned subsidiary set up for the purpose by IBM, Comsat, and Aetna in 1975. The company launched its first satellite in 1980. Its main line of business was the installation of videoconferencing rooms on users' premises and the leasing of satellite transmission capacity for their interconnection. SBS was a pioneer in using satellites for business applications and took advantage of new Ku-band technology that significantly reduced the size of satellite dishes on users' premises. However, satellite transmission also introduced a slight delay in exchanges between people at different locations, and the service required companies to significantly alter their methods of business communication. The videoconferencing service was discontinued after a few very disappointing years, and in 1987, the SBS satellites were sold off to MCI to be used for other purposes.

Given the high fixed costs of installing videoconferencing systems, it is not surprising that the number of in-house facilities grew very slowly at first. Moreover, their utilization generally fell well below expectations.

Outside the Office: Need Can Overcome Lack of Transparency

The more corporate videoconferencing encountered disappointing results, the more professionals in the field emphasized the need for systems to be "transparent," by which they meant that using them should be as easy and intuitive as possible. Even though we regard this advice as sound, several of the videoconferencing systems installed between the mid-1970s and the mid-1990s were not at all transparent but nonetheless had great success. Significantly, none of these examples involved office communications or was successfully adopted elsewhere; however, taken together, they and other examples suggest that when the perceived need is high enough, transparency does not matter.

By the 1980s, Boeing was using 12 videoconferencing rooms, ranging from 3 to 38 miles apart, to link together work groups developing its 757 aircraft scattered around the Seattle area. The system was jerry-rigged, untidy, far from transparent—and highly successful. "In fact, at one point, the project was thirty days ahead of schedule and the company attributed this time saving to the teleconferencing system."[7] Contrary to the received wisdom of the time, the distances involved were fairly short, and the main benefit was speeding up work processes rather than achieving savings from substitution for travel. The system's ad hoc nature, with a low level of automation since it used human operators, made it very easy for those concerned to adapt its features as they went along.

The two-way cable television system implemented in the mid-1970s in Reading, Pennsylvania (see chapter 8) was both highly successful and very far from transparent. So was another two-way cable television system of the period, which connected elementary schools in Irvine, California. Both of these two-way cable systems were essentially videoconferencing systems linking together several sites at a time. In Reading, the users were senior citizens, while Irvine's system connected children, teachers, and guests. In comparison with managers and other corporate employees, both senior citizens and schoolchildren likely would place a decidedly higher value on becoming proficient in the use of the technology and a lower cost—if any—on the time spent in the process.

Around 1990, off-the-shelf corporate videoconferencing technology was put together to provide a connection via ISDN between a therapist in San Francisco and the home of a young autistic child in Sacramento, California. The family wanted to try a recently developed experimental treatment that required many hours a day of home-based treatment by two or more members of a team trained on the job and supervised, several times a week, by a specialist. The nearest specialist was in San Francisco; the family was unable to move, and the treatment needed to be started soon if it was to be effective. A variety of technical problems had to be overcome in assembling and operating the technology, one reason being that videoconferencing systems are designed to meet the needs of users who are fairly static, whereas this child, like others her age, moved around a good deal. The therapist visited the family in person once a month and used the videoconferencing system three times a week. The system's video and audio quality were far from impressive in relation to what would be ideal in such situations, but they were good enough for the purpose, and a clinical assessment about a year later found that the child was free of all symptoms of autism.[8]

Considerable good fortune was involved in this project: the experimental treatment was the right one for the child, the therapist concerned was both committed and flexible, and a volunteer from the videoconferencing field provided inspiring leadership, persisting until the equipment worked not well but well enough. Nevertheless, the project offers a dramatic example of what can be done with video technology that is awkward and performs indifferently provided the need is high enough.

Design Issues

A videoconferencing facility is very different from a broadcast television studio, in part because it has to be highly automated to avoid expensive labor costs and in part because the mentality of broadcast television would be detrimental to videoconferencing. A prime determinant of participants' satisfaction with a videoconference facility usually is the extent to which it enables seamless communication between locations and effortless transitions between people shots and images from graphics cameras or computers. Free-flowing interaction matters more than the polish associated with a television studio.

Within a videoconferencing room, many basic design decisions are important: camera locations (associated with the problem of achieving eye contact), camera height (level with participants or pointing up or down, thus conveying different impressions of relative status), and camera angle and image size (it can be awkward when one person is shown in close-up while the other is shown in a wide-angle view). The recent transition to high-definition videoconferencing has helped to overcome a problem with earlier systems: if the image from a remote site contained more than two heads, the resolution was insufficient to show facial expressions clearly.

In multipoint videoconferences, a system can simultaneously show people at two or three other locations. If more locations are involved, one of the signals can be automatically selected—almost certainly the one from the site where someone is speaking—and transmitted to all the others. But in this case, what image is shown at the speaker's site? No single rule will be best in all cases. Finally, although the selection of camera shots is almost always automated (triggered by information about which microphone is live), a manual override provision is necessary—to switch to output from a computer, a video player, or a camera focused on a whiteboard; to switch between the image of the speaker and a group shot from the speaker's location; or to allow the chair to look at one of the sites even though the current speaker is elsewhere. The control system for manual selection of cameras must be designed to minimize the chances of distracting those who are not yet experienced in its use. Audio signals are far easier in these respects: provided that only one person speaks at a time, they can simply be added together. The equivalent for video images would be to superimpose them on top of one another, which would destroy them.

As these basic issues show, two-way video is a much harder medium to work with than the two-way audio medium, as professional designers and installers have known from the start. In response, they have frequently concentrated too much on the video and not enough on the audio. Imperfections in sound have a far more damaging effect on a videoconference than imperfections in images. The need to pay sufficient attention to the audio side of videoconferencing is a lesson that different people learned the hard way many times over in the first two decades of videoconferencing.

Disappointment

Videoconferencing systems are now widely available both in the corporate world and beyond. The associated transmission costs are now low and are continuing to drop as large organizations are changing the transmission method used on their private networks to the same method (IP) used on the public Internet. Nevertheless, no disagreement exists within the industry that usage for regular business meetings is far below the levels that have continually been anticipated in the past. One industry watcher offers an educated guess that the average amount of audioconferencing activity per white collar worker in North America may well be 500 to 1,000 times greater than the amount of videoconferencing activity. While the amount of videoconferencing has increased following major disruptions to air travel—for example, the events of 9/11,[9] the SARS outbreak, and the terrorist plot thwarted in Britain in the summer of 2006[10]—these surges have to date proven short-lived.

Further improvements in videoconferencing technology do not seem likely to change this disappointing picture substantially in the short term. Periodic attempts have been made to achieve a breakthrough by designing systems that provide more lifelike images of participants, including high-definition and life-sized images. Under contract to DARPA (an applied research agency of the U.S. Department of Defense), the Media Lab at the Massachusetts Institute of Technology even developed an experimental system in the 1970s for simulating three-dimensional videoconferences.[11]

Soon after the turn of the century, a new generation of high-end videoconferencing systems began to employ high-definition cameras and monitors. These systems soon made significant inroads into the sales of regular-definition equipment. An even more recent generation, "Telepresence," aims to provide the illusion that participants are seated across the table from one another in the same room. Costing upward of one million dollars at each site, these systems have so far found few buyers.[12] The fundamental issues associated with videoconferencing apply to the latest systems as well as to less lifelike systems.

Four decades of experience suggests that for some purposes, the incremental value of the visual channel is so high that it will be used even if the system is not well designed for the purpose, but these opportunities do not generally arise in business meetings. For most business purposes, videoconferencing will not enjoy high demand, however inexpensive and well designed the system, because its incremental value relative to audioconferencing (with or without a Web component) is too low to compensate for the inconvenience involved. There is likely to be a middle ground in which the incremental value of video is high enough to outweigh its inconvenience relative to audio; here, good design could well make an important difference. This middle ground, however, is much more likely to be in the realms of telemedicine, education, and the law than in business.

Videophones

AT&T's Picturephone Service was launched in the mid-1960s with public booths in Chicago, New York City, and Washington, DC; in 1970, local-exchange service was introduced in Pittsburgh and, one year later, Chicago. The well-designed terminal used three regular telephone lines for transmission, operated in black and white, and provided about half the resolution of a broadcast television image (nonetheless, a good image). The underlying concept was that of a regular telephone that let one see the person with whom one was talking, so it was optimized to show the human face (rather than text, which it displayed particularly poorly), and like the regular telephone, the terminal was a single unit. Though the concept was obvious enough and does not appear to have been questioned in the literature, competing design concepts were at least as plausible.

In the early 1970s, Swedish manufacturer L. M. Ericsson conducted field trials of a very different videophone for the business market. Its technical design was optimized to show objects and documents, and it could operate to show either moving images or, with transmission stepped down, to transmit a series of still images over a regular telephone line. In addition, the overall design was modular: the speech unit was the company's regular speakerphone, which plugged into the core video unit; with the use of an optional accessory for navigating the page, the screen could also be used for reading remote microfiches (a medium much more used in Scandinavia than elsewhere); and alternative video inputs could be provided (for example, from a ceiling-mounted camera for potential telemedicine applications). Another distinctive feature of L. M. Ericsson's thinking was that video telephony would initially be used over very short distances—for example, to provide visual connectivity within a corporate campus. Only later would these islands of demand be linked together. Though the technology enjoyed some success in trials, the company concluded a market launch was not worthwhile. The Swedish concept may well have been better attuned to the reality of its potential business users. It is interesting that two such radically different designs of such a seemingly obvious product could have emerged.

At the end of the 1960s, videophones were also under development by NTT in Japan and by the British Post Office. Neither effort led to the launch of a commercial service.

AT&T made a most impressive effort to explore the market for visual communications. Well-funded field trials of the use of Picturephone were conducted both in health care settings and in the criminal justice system. In the most prominent of the former, however, at the Garfield/Bethany hospital system in Chicago, Picturephone was used primarily for hotline communication and was removed the day that the government-funded trial came to an end.[13] It was more successful in a field trial funded jointly by AT&T and the U.S. Law Enforcement and Assistance Agency, in Phoenix, Arizona, where a network was set up linking court facilities, offices of probation officers, the jail, the jail annex, and the public defender's office.[14] The most heavily used link was between the jail annex and the public defender's office. The evaluation component of the trial showed no reduction in in-person meetings between lawyers from the public defender's staff and prisoners in the jail annex; instead, the system increased the total amount of communication between the two. The system served other purposes, too, and the city, fully prepared to use its own budget for the purpose, was eager to have the system continue operating when the trial ended. By then, however, AT&T had firmly concluded that Picturephone was not commercially viable; a niche market in the criminal justice system, let alone one in a single city, would not provide a sufficiently large base for an affordable offering.

The Phoenix trial suggested three generalizations, however, which subsequent experience showed to be correct: visual communication services could be useful over short, intra-urban distances; at an aggregate level, they were not necessarily a substitute for travel; and, in the near future, visual services might have useful applications within the criminal justice system. These findings bring up a topic raised in chapter 4: What does it mean to describe a field trial as a failure? Within the context of research, a trial is a success if its contribution to knowledge is worthwhile in terms of the cost of the trial, even if the benefits its use provides are too low relative to the estimated future costs of its production, operation, and so on. Furthermore, in the limited context of the Phoenix criminal justice system, Picturephone appears to have been a success; the problem was that it needed to be a success outside the criminal justice system, too.

Most commentators ascribe the failure of Picturephone—and contemporaneous videophones such as Stromberg-Carlson's Vistaphone and GTE's Pictel[15]—to either or both of two factors. One is that it proved too expensive, an insuperable difficulty given the technology available at the time. But cheaper successor videophones failed as well. The other is expressed in comments along the lines that possible residential buyers were put off by the thought that others might see them when, say, they had just emerged from the shower. That problem could be solved with a privacy button that shut off the video, but some users worried that the person on the other end would wonder why the videophone was set in privacy mode. A full post mortem would probably have ascribed the demise of the Picturephone to multiple organ failure.[16]

In the mid-1990s, MCI started marketing a videophone; sales were disappointingly low. In 1992, AT&T reentered the arena with its $1,500 per terminal Videophone 2500, described as the first color videophone; again, sales did not meet expectations. Subsequent videophone launches have met with the same fate. For many of Picturephone's successors, public relations firms and sometimes also the press acted as though the product was being introduced for the first time. For example, a 1989 *New York Times* article stated that the recently launched Phonavision was the first videophone available for use by the general public.[17]

In principle, the environment for videophones improved considerably when ISDN was deployed in the United States and standards for codecs were introduced in the early 1990s. The digital standard accommodated transmission rates as low as 64 kbps, which was the basic building block of ISDN used for regular (digital) telephone calls. These two developments seemed to promise to overcome the twin problems of incompatibility of terminals and expensive transmission. These speeds created a fairly acceptable combination of picture quality (as long as users remained fairly stationary) and sound quality, provided that manufacturers did not make the initially too common mistake of compromising the audio by devoting too high a portion of the limited transmission capacity to the video. Nevertheless, in practice, the developments (as with the subsequent introduction of a standard for a videophone over the regular analog network) appeared to make little difference to the progress of video telephony—or, rather, the lack of progress.

The next significant development came from the Internet. For some years, people have been able to create low-end videophone capability using the combination of a computer, a broadband Internet connection, and a webcam (costing in the range of $50 to $100), microphone, and speakers (the last three of which are often built into computers). The other necessary component is an instant messaging (IM) system or some other Internet communications service (for example, Skype); most of these are free, but they are not compatible: the same system must be used at each location. There are also some purpose-designed Internet communication services that charge a monthly fee but offer somewhat higher video quality.

The picture quality and sound quality of such systems are markedly inferior to AT&T's original Picturephone, which had a $5 \times 5^{1/2}$ inch screen and a remarkable 250 lines of resolution. They involve the possible inconvenience of users at each location being on-line. There are compatibility problems. And it is not always possible, let alone easy, to use the systems from behind a firewall. Nonetheless, there was no shortage of new entrants to this market in the mid-2000s.

With the introduction of third-generation mobile phone systems starting in Japan in 2001, some handsets have provided videophone capability. By the mid-2000s, however, this was not a functionality that appeared to be causing users to upgrade to third-generation mobile phones. Unlike the camera capability of contemporary mobile phones, the videophone option does not appear to be widely used. Among other problems, mobile phones with a videophone mode place a heavy drain on the battery if it is left on continuously, and it is difficult to have the microphone near enough to the mouth to provide good audio at the same time that the camera is far enough from the face.

Today, videophones are widely available in a variety of forms for use over the regular dial-up telephone network, ISDN, the Internet, or cellular networks. By historic standards, their cost is very low—in the case of the Internet variety, vanishingly low. However, except for a very few limited applications, their significance for general-purpose communications is also very low.

Comparison of the Media

Videoconferencing: The Need to Weigh Convenience and Flexibility against More Fundamental Factors

In the real world, when using technology to communicate with others, people do not experience media in their pure forms. Their experience depends on the particular systems being used. No system is perfect; each is constrained by, among other things, what is technologically feasible and what is regarded as affordable. The fact that video is closer than audio to in-person communication is only one of many factors that determine user acceptance and behavior. A variety of practical factors relating to equipment also matter a great deal and probably go a long way toward explaining the success of audioconferencing and the disappointing performance of videoconferencing. Nor is the fact that video is more expensive the main reason for its poor performance, though it may play an indirect part by, for example, forcing people to leave their offices to go to a conference room to use it.

When comparing these two types of teleconferencing, their flexibility and the convenience they offer users differ enormously. Table 6.1 summarizes the

TABLE 6.1. Comparison of Audioconferencing and Videoconferencing in Terms of Flexibility and Convenience

Factor Affecting Flexibility or Convenience	Audio	Video
Lead time	Needs only to be as long as is needed to confirm a time with the intended participants	Needs to take into account reservation of the conference rooms at all locations
Constraints on location of participants	They need only to be able to use a regular or mobile telephone in a space that is not too noisy.	They generally need to be in a suitable conference room at one of their organization's offices.
Constraints on time of day of conference	Depend only on individual participants	May need to be when office buildings are open and support staff available
Constraints on number of active participants per location	Essentially none (provided the conference telephones are of suitable quality)	Depend on design of room. Often a limit of 8 to 12.
Constraints on number of locations	Essentially none	Depend on design of particular system. More than 2–4 locations may incur the need for prior arrangement with, and the additional expense of, a service bureau.
Constraints on behavior of participants during conference	Few. Multitasking cannot be detected at other locations.	Must remain seated at on-camera location. Multitasking is likely to be unacceptable.
Need for prior investment to have been made	Essentially none	Necessary equipment and connection to a digital network must have been purchased and installed.

general situation in this regard, clearly showing the superiority of audio. To assume that video must be better because it provides a visual channel would be akin to assuming that a truck is better than a sports car because it has a more powerful engine.

The comparison would have favored audio even more before videoconferencing standards emerged and the accessibility of suitable transmission networks improved. With continuing technological progress, some of video's relative disadvantages are likely to be reduced or perhaps eliminated. For example, as codecs are increasingly incorporated into computers, it will be possible to participate in a videoconference from any place that broadband access is available. But some of audio's relative advantages will never disappear because they are intrinsic to the medium. In the absence of a visual channel, users have much more freedom of behavior: they can move around, for example. And even with the development of intelligent cameras that follow video users if they move around, good manners will still generally prevent users from catching up with their e-mail or doing the other things in which users of audio rightly or wrongly engage during teleconference meetings.

The multitasking that audio allows is sometimes constructive, as when one is retrieving needed papers or reworking spreadsheet numbers to make a discussion more effective without having to worry about going in and out of the video frame. Sometimes, however, multitasking is counterproductive to the purpose at hand, as when a participant in a teleconference is engaged in some unrelated task while half listening to the discussion. In this case, conflict arises between the objectives ascribed to a teleconference and those of the separate individuals participating in it. In some situations, the positions of the different parties conflict, with the result that audioconferencing might be better for one and videoconferencing for the other(s). For example, research suggests that the party with an objectively weaker case is more likely to prevail in videoconferences rather than audioconferences, whereas those arguing positions in which they do not really believe do better in audioconferences than in videoconferences.[18] And as is to be expected, those whose personality inhibits them from speaking up in in-person meetings tend to participate more in audio-only meetings.

Some situations clearly favor video. Such situations include formal presentations followed by discussion among groups at up to four locations and trials where testimony is to be provided by a witness who is not in the courtroom (e.g., a victim in a case of alleged child molestation). Anecdotal evidence confirms that video is likely to be useful in situations in which participants do not share the same mother tongue. Videoconferencing has also gained acceptance for interviews of job candidates, though research suggests that by eliminating certain visual information—for example, candidates' appearances or ethnic backgrounds—the sound-only medium would sometimes lead to better decisions.

A more subtle situation occurred at a large overseas subsidiary of a U.S. multinational corporation located ten time zones away from headquarters. According to a human resources manager,

> Many of our teams have some of their members based here, but others based at sites—often more than one site—in the States. When a virtual team has just been formed, people generally don't know one another and there can be a certain amount of jargon, which any members who are new to the company are unlikely to understand. At times like this, we tend to use videoconferencing, but as soon as the team is up and running, we prefer audio. Using audio is much more considerate to our employees here, especially those who have families. When we use video, people usually have to be in the office late in the evening so as to overlap the working day in America. But if it's a conference call, they can join in from home.

The controlled experiments described in chapter 4 lead to the conclusion that for many business purposes, the audio medium may be as effective in accomplishing the purposes at hand as the in-person and video alternatives. While video is certainly superior to audio in some situations, audio may often be good enough.[19] Whether a videoconferencing system would be superior to an audioconferencing system on particular occasions may well depend on such mundane factors as the convenience and flexibility of the available real-world systems. In these respects, audioconferencing has an enormous advantage.

Audioconferencing has also enjoyed a major advantage in "trialability," one of the factors that Everett Rogers has indicated enhances diffusion.[20] The investment in equipment that needs to be made prior to trying it out for some purpose is very low—maybe zero. Users need no technicians on hand to set up equipment, and the costs of using it are generally insignificant. In addition, audioconferencing engenders modest expectations, reducing the risk of embarrassment if some new use does not work out well. One should never underestimate the insight and creativity that lead users to discover successful applications of communication technology that had not previously occurred to professionals. Users have found it much easier to explore possible applications of audioconferencing than of its video relatives. Though not to quite the same degree, Web conferencing also has a high level of trialability.

The Commonsense View of Teleconferencing

The commonsense view of teleconferencing rests on the following assumptions:

> *A Questionable Perspective on Teleconferencing*
>
> It is primarily a potential substitute for in-person meetings, to be used, in particular, when there is a need or desire to save the time and money that would be required for travel.
>
> It is most valuable in replacing long-distance travel.
>
> Except with regard to cost, videoconferencing is more effective than audioconferencing.

This perspective has provided a tempting and sometimes successful way of marketing videoconferencing, but it is incorrect or at least dangerously incomplete. It has led researchers to incorrect generalizations from their research; it has led analysts to underestimate the value of teleconferencing to their organizations; it has led marketers to pursue ineffective marketing strategies; and it previously led the telecommunications industry to underestimate the potential of less costly forms of teleconferencing that were nevertheless high in flexibility and convenience. This simplistic, commonsense view of teleconferencing is not a straw man: it was the predominant view and it was damaging. What is more, it remains widely held.

A more thoughtful use of common sense could and should have led to a more realistic and useful framework for thinking about teleconferencing. This framework is not as simple, but neither is the real world.

Though teleconferencing can save time and money spent in business travel, it can also improve an organization's performance in other ways that may be at least as important. In the famous story of *The Hound of the Baskervilles*, the fact that a dog had not barked during the night, though it should have done so, was the key clue allowing Sherlock Holmes to solve the case: what is not there is often as important as what is. Some potentially useful in-person meetings do not take place because their anticipated value is not worth the inconvenience of travel, because the lead time to arrange them is insufficient, or because people's calendars are in conflict. Teleconferencing has an easy role in substituting for these "nonmeetings." Users soon found this role even though it had escaped the attention of marketers and researchers.

It is a short step from those meetings that do not happen but should to in-person meetings that take place in a way that is overly constrained by the need to travel: meetings that cannot be arranged soon enough, meetings at which key people cannot be present, and so on. This type of meeting, too, provides low-hanging fruit for teleconferencing.

In many large organizations that introduced videoconferencing during the 1980s, telecommunications analysts conducted studies in which they went through logs of videoconferences, calculating for each use how much a conventional meeting would have cost in travel and in some cases in person hours and then estimating the savings attributable to videoconferencing (the return on the investment). Of even more dubious value were comparable prospective studies in organizations considering investing in videoconferencing, in which records of travel to business meetings were used to estimate future savings.

In a simple situation in which it is reasonable to consider a single meeting or teleconference in isolation rather than as part of a sequence of interconnected communication events, four related decisions made in advance likely determine effectiveness:

Mode: in-person meeting, videoconference, audioconference, or nothing.

Duration: how long it will last.

Participants: who will take part.

Timing: when the meeting or teleconference will take place (if at all).

It defies common sense to assume that duration, participants, and timing will not be affected by the decision on mode. The effectiveness of a meeting or teleconference clearly often depends on these choices, and it may not take much for a teleconference to be more effective than an in-person meeting that takes place too late or without a key person, let alone one that does not take place at all.

Other convenient assumptions also need to be questioned. One is the either/or assumption: *either* an in-person meeting *or* an electronic one. Why not both? Consider, for example, a lengthy meeting to which a few representatives of a company travel in an attempt to negotiate a substantial sale. On some occasions, it may well make sense to ask others who do not make the trip to stand by in their offices, ready to take part in a videoconference that could be embedded in their colleagues' longer face-to-face meeting. Questions about specialized technical details may arise, or a more senior manager can approve some variation in a proposed contract.

As users become accustomed to new applications, they find a variety of creative ways to combine the new and the old. Although some of these innovations are very hard to predict, it should not be hard to predict others. (A different example of the either/or fallacy frequently arose in the early decades of telecommuting, when the assumption was made that, for any worker, telecommuting would occur either very close to 100 percent of the time or almost never. Many of today's telecommuters strike balances between telecommuting and travel to the office that are much less extreme.)

To this point, meetings—actual and potential, in-person and electronic—have been considered as though they were isolated events, suspended in time, which can be too much of a simplification of reality. Consider the routine meetings of a large committee with widely separated members. Maybe the meetings take place on a monthly basis and include twelve or more participants. The effectiveness of such meetings is often significantly determined by what happens both before and after them, not just by what happens during them. Agreeing on an agenda is the most obvious part of the preparation; ensuring that agreed actions are pursued is the most obvious part of the follow-up. Relying only on convoluted series of bilateral telephone conversations and/or e-mail messages often is not an efficient means of dealing with the need for preparation and follow-up. Some organizations use teleconferencing for this purpose. A large in-person meeting involving substantial travel consumes substantial resources. In some cases, the value of teleconferencing may lie not in reducing a large expenditure of time and money by substitution but in accepting that expenditure and using teleconferencing to derive greater value from it.

This illustration exhibits a dissimilarity in logical type between the teleconference and the in-person meeting. Teleconferences enhance rather than substitute for in-person meetings. (In telemedicine, this kind of relationship can be of particular significance. A key role of a system serving a remote community may be to reduce errors about whether and how urgently to travel—patient to physician or vice versa.)

Relationships extending through time may be relevant in other ways. In some contexts, whether a particular meeting takes place in conventional or electronic form may not really matter. More important is the right mix of these two modalities through time. If a series of in-person meetings is replaced by teleconferences, something important in the long-term relationships between parties may be lost. The best solution may be to replace some but not all.

For many years, the idea of teleconferencing as a substitute for business travel focused attention on long-distance business trips, which were generally the most expensive and disruptive. However, the amount of short-distance business travel (up to about an hour or so in each direction, say) is often higher than is perceived; many people make very many more short-distance work trips—from one suburb to another or between a suburb and a downtown location—than long-distance ones. And relative to the distance traveled, such trips can be particularly time-consuming and frustrating. From the 1970s on, a number of successful videoconferencing systems have linked people over relatively short distances.[21]

The assumption that audioconferencing will be less effective than videoconferencing in practice is definitely wrong. Again, people do not experience the media in their ideal form; they experience particular systems and facilities that may have a variety of drawbacks. An audioconferencing system often offers far more convenient and flexible possibilities. In addition, research has shown that for some purposes—maybe the shared purpose of all, maybe the separate purpose of one or a subset of the participants—audio can be more effective than video.

The main conclusion to be drawn from this discussion of commonsense assumptions is not that the industry and associated commentators and researchers were led astray by common sense. It is that they were led astray by the superficial use of common sense.

Uses of Videophones outside the World of Work

While videoconferencing has been used primarily in the world of work, videophones may be of as much or greater use for a variety of consumer purposes. It is possible that if videophones replaced regular videoconferencing systems in workplace settings, the greater convenience of a videophone on a person's desk would sometimes outweigh its inferior quality, but few indicators that they will become used in this way are evident.

When discussing the use of teleconferencing in the office, meetings, including teleconferences, are typically classified as involving information exchange, problem solving, negotiation, and so on or as being meetings of project teams, of sales force teams, of financial analysts with corporate officers, for training purposes, and so on. When considering use of videophones (and occasionally teleconferencing) outside the office, consideration of other variables is likely to be more helpful: for example, whether feelings are of particular importance, whether there is an element of performance (though this can be important in some work situations, too), and whether the purpose of the communication is just to have fun.

One type of situation in which the inclusion of a visual channel alongside a speech channel would be expected to be valuable is one in which emotions are relatively more significant, especially when speech may not convey a great deal of information. A natural application for consumer videophones is to enable grandmothers to keep in personal touch with very young grandchildren living far away, and this application indeed appears to be relatively popular.[22] A related application of videophones (and of videoconferencing systems) has been more general use by families whose members are separated in distant countries. For example, a storefront operation in New York charges $1.50 per minute for a video connection between Ecuadorian immigrants and their families back home.[23] And Elliot Gold describes the success of these technologies for communication between troops serving in Iraq and their families in the United States as well as by parents and teens separated by thousands of miles.[24]

In other situations when a high level of reassurance is desirable, videophones may prove to be of value. People have suggested adding videophone kiosks at large amusement parks so that parents can report missing children. Trials have been conducted in which videophone kiosks were available to low-income people seeking legal advice; in this context, videophones may be even more useful when a language barrier must be overcome. Videophones have also been used by interpreters providing service to hospital emergency rooms from a distance.

Some types of person-to-person communication—e.g., formal presentations and certain teaching situations—have a relatively important element of performance that may make videoconferencing preferable to audioconferencing. In the residential context, many of the interactive television trials launched by the cable television industry have included a home videophone capability (see chapter 8). When the more ambitious forms of interactive television return, videophones may be used not only for communication with other subscribers (and eventually, via broadband Internet connections, with a much larger set of individuals) but also for call-in programs and may achieve some popularity in local programming aimed at children or pet owners. Both MTV and Fox Broadcasting have experimented with this type of format.

Away from the office, an element of performance is also required in adult entertainment. Pornography almost always rears its head early in the emergence of new media; occasional reports tying it to the use of videophones, particularly those based on webcams, have come as no surprise.

Since it first became both feasible and fashionable in Japan in 2001, people—especially young people—have enjoyed using mobile phones to take photographs that can be transmitted as e-mail attachments. While it is virtually impossible to predict what will become fashionable, it does seem reasonable to expect that if the use of mobile phones as videophones catches on, it will be among young people having fun rather than for any more serious purpose (and of course, having fun is a serious business for many young people). However, intimate private communication with boyfriends or girlfriends falls into a different category. While videophones may be used initially in contacting and screening people located in one of the many social networking services, it is difficult to think of any much more user-hostile technology for a pair of young people who have already developed a relationship with one another and desire intimate communication. It probably would not be at all easy to locate the devices in a way that is both comfortable for the users and appropriate for the cameras, and even if this obstacle were overcome, eye contact would be problematic. It is far more comfortable to be curled up on a couch with an ordinary mobile phone or telephone. Moreover, others have noted, the sound-only medium is particularly well suited to much intimate communication, and the video medium may detract from it.[25]

The history of videophones illustrates several of the issues discussed in other chapters. A great deal of initial hype took place, and forecasts were wildly optimistic. Videophone units were stand-alone devices without a common standard, and interconnection was a barrier to achieving critical mass—Why buy a videophone if one could connect to few if any of the others with whom one might want to communicate? Given the nature of past videophone devices, killer applications would have been necessary. The closest the devices have come has probably been use within families, especially those with very young children, but this use has not been powerful enough. (Grandmothers are generally not seen as opinion leaders.) However, now that technology has moved on, videophones may be able, at least in theory, to diffuse in consumer markets by the accumulation of incrementally valued applications. Some third-generation mobile phones bought for reasons other than their videophone capability may require no additional investment to provide their owners an opportunity to experiment with this capability. Likewise, videophones based on computers with webcams and broadband connections are readily available from a number of manufacturers. And as noted earlier, trialability facilitates diffusion. Nevertheless, while the latter is desirable, relative advantage is essential and remains a major question mark.[26]

Closing Thoughts

The three types of communication technology on which this chapter has focused have two obvious similarities. First, they are all designed for two-way, real-time communication. Second, although examples can be found of each being used in limited fashion in earlier decades, it is reasonable to treat all of them as having been introduced around 1970, when real muscle was put behind each. Nevertheless, striking differences exist in the speed and extent of their adoption, illustrating several of the points made in chapter 1.

Audioconferencing diffused rapidly and has become a commodity. It is cheap, highly automated, and ubiquitous. (Enhanced audio teleconferencing has achieved less impressive usage but seems to be in the process of establishing itself with the success of Web conferencing.) Videoconferencing could also be described as established at last, though at a very much lower level of usage. Videophones, however, have repeatedly failed in round after round of reentry and are still being marketed as a new medium. Many of the newer models work reasonably well and are much cheaper than earlier generations of the technology. A range of niche applications has been demonstrated, but they collectively represent the tiniest of markets.

If a market for videophones is to exist, it may come from a different direction—fun uses. Might some of the millions of IM users add an inexpensive webcam (the major IM providers support a video component) to chat about nothing, as they currently do? Could use of videophones become an extension of the playing of video games by competitors in different locations, enabling them to see their opponents, an application supported by Sony and Microsoft video game consoles? Might people with videophone-capable mobile phones use them not to see other people but to show them nearby friends? We would not place bets on any of these applications, but the videophone seems to be a technology that will not die.

The three types of technology showed how very different diffusion processes are consistent with Rogers's theory. Two of his constructs appear to help in explaining the differences. At least with benefit of hindsight, audioconferencing can be seen to have enjoyed a much greater relative advantage than videoconferencing as well as much higher trialability. As technology progressed and became cheaper, videophones have eventually found relative advantage in just a few small niches; only recently, with the combination of the Internet and webcams, has regarding them as having become reasonably trialable become possible. The three families of technology also differed greatly in the groups they attracted as innovators and early adopters.

All the forecasts of which we know greatly overestimated the uptake of videophones and videoconferencing. We are aware of only a few attempts to quantify the future market for audioconferencing—but they did not produce forecasts, since they sought only to determine the potential market without considering the time dimension. At a qualitative level, they were correct in indicating that the potential market was very large.[27]

The results of the laboratory-based psychological research described in chapter 4 strongly suggest why the relative advantage of videoconferencing was nowhere near as high relative to that of audioconferencing as the industry had assumed. In this chapter, however, we have suggested that the more mundane considerations of flexibility and convenience also play an important part in explaining why the assumption was incorrect.

Although this chapter has made little mention of the implementation process, readers may have noticed various implementation problems that arose in connection with videoconferencing. Some were mundane and specific to the technology of the time: for example, in the early days, cameras required high light levels, which generated heat and thus at times required upgrades to air-conditioning systems, increasing noise levels and requiring higher levels of sound insulation and thereby adding significantly to cost. Others were generic: in particular, connectivity problems as a result of lack of standards and of networks that did not interconnect. While the ubiquity of the Internet has greatly reduced connectivity problems, they have been replaced by other challenges, such as problems associated with firewalls and with upgrading virtual private networks to IP.

// SEVEN //

When Online Media Were New: The Missing Chapter

Where did the world of online services that we use every day come from? What were the initial services? How did content and applications evolve? Who were the early adopters? Did growth follow a smooth or rough path? Who made it happen? How long did it all take? Further, what general lessons can we learn about new media by examining the development of online services when they were new?

There is more than one version of the story about how online services emerged, each with its own set of heroes, villains, insights, and obstacles. The most widely told story attributes their germination to the U.S. Defense Department and projects it funded, beginning in the late 1960s, that led to the ARPANET computer network, which evolved into the Internet, the infrastructure that allowed the World Wide Web to emerge. Its heroes are well known: Vinton Cerf, Bob Kahn, and Tim Berners-Lee, among others. This chapter focuses on another path of development that is much less well known but provides an important part of the story. Although the technological concepts underlying it were very different and have gone the way of the dodo, this other path also evolved into the online universe that we inhabit today.

This part of the story includes developments in videotex, e-mail, computer conferencing, electronic banking, bulletin boards, and online terminals in public locations. It has its own set of heroes: Sam Fedida, Alex Reid, Harry Smith, Martin Nisenholtz, Murray Turoff, and Steve Case, among many others. It takes nothing away from the widely lauded contributions of Vinton Cerf and others. Rather, it highlights many applications that have been largely forgotten, partly because even those that succeeded were eventually superseded by their new, far more widely used equivalents on the Web. Nevertheless they contributed in a major way to understanding of user interfaces, advertising, content, shopping, online games, graphics, communications, and the needs and wants of ordinary people—key elements in the array of online services that emerged in the late 1990s and early 2000s. For many netizens who are even aware of them, the online services, including videotex, which preceded the Web, were a largely irrelevant prelude—a collection of rather expensive failures and a few rather humdrum successes. This view is incorrect: these earlier services made extremely important contributions to the Web's subsequent and amazingly rapid takeoff.

The Often-Told Story

In the often-told story, the early impetus for the development of computer networks is the Soviet Union's launching of the first satellite, Sputnik, in the late 1950s. Sputnik shocked the Western world, especially the United States, into a realization that it was not ahead, as most had thought, in developing real-world applications of scientific knowledge. Much investment by Western governments in applied science followed. One development was the creation of the Advanced Research Projects Agency (ARPA, now DARPA) in the U.S. Defense Department. The agency was charged with supporting research and development projects that went beyond purely military applications. In the late 1960s, ARPA funded the planning of ARPANET, a network that could link computers based on the new technology of packet switching. A widely held myth holds that ARPANET was created to protect military computers against a nuclear attack by the Soviet Union—that is, if one or more military computers (or transmission links) were knocked out, other computers (or transmission links) in the widely dispersed and redundant network could take over. The true motivation was much simpler: time-sharing.[1] In those days, computers were large, expensive mainframes, accessed from on-site terminals hard-wired to the mainframes or generally using stacks of punched cards or punched tape to receive input. Given the high cost and relative scarcity of these computers, developers thought that significant benefits would result if users could access a computer (the "host" computer) at one location from a computer or terminal elsewhere—for example, to use programs on the host to make calculations. Likewise, officials believed that greater overall efficiency would result if someone conducting research at one location could access a large database of scientific information at another, a phenomenon sometimes called distributed computing.

Following the networking of four computers in 1970, three other major developments can be identified. One occurred in the early 1970s with the development by Vinton Cerf, Bob Kahn, and their colleagues of the suite of protocols that came to be named TCP/IP (Transmission Control Protocol/Internet Protocol) that allowed computers with different operating systems to communicate with each other over packet-switched networks. The suite was released in 1978 and incorporated into ARPANET in 1983. Another key development due to Tim Berners-Lee and his colleagues at CERN (the European Organization for Nuclear Research) in Geneva, Switzerland, was the creation of the World Wide Web: a system of interlinked hypertext documents accessible via the Internet and the core component of the modern day Web. This was first demonstrated in 1991 and released by CERN for use by anyone in 1993. Finally, in 1993, a group working at the National Center for Supercomputing Applications at the University of Illinois–Urbana created the Mosaic browser, which eased access to Web sites. (Berners-Lee and colleagues had developed a browser in 1991.) Perhaps the most important collective contribution by the Illinois group was the development of a highly effective decentralized model for sharing information across computers, with no need for a single, large hub to store all information.

With a few minor exceptions, ARPANET was used initially by the military and Defense Department contractors, including groups at several major universities. Although user groups expanded, they never included the public or general businesses, and the network remained the exclusive province of sophisticated technologists—principally, computer scientists. Further, it was funded by the government—no one paid to use it—and no content (in a mass media sense), let alone advertising, was produced for it. In fact, advertising and marketing were so frowned upon that if someone created a forum entry that even hinted at promotion or marketing, they were likely to receive a barrage of angry e-mails. ARPANET was used for calculations, testing programs, accessing data, and soon thereafter electronic mail and information exchange forums called Usenets, which came to dominate usage. Person-to-person e-mail was not in the original ARPANET plan but was added a few years later. In fact, in the early days of ARPANET, many in the computer science community seemed to regard with scorn the use of computers for anything as mundane as text communication. NSFNET was created with funding from the National Science Foundation in the mid-1980s and replaced ARPANET in 1990. It is not clear when the word *Internet* was first employed, but by the early 1990s, the term was in widespread use for what was created from this internetworking of computer networks—the Internet was a network of networks.

This version of the emergence of online services is largely a story of outstanding technical achievements within a universe of sophisticated technologist users. Important as these advances were, however, they did not include much development of content, graphics, online games, shopping, searching, advertising, direct marketing, business models, or understanding the needs of nontechnologists who pay for the online services. Knowledge in these areas came from another set of applications.

The Other Path

Funded by the government and utilized largely by computer scientists, ARPANET and subsequently NSFNET were two among many online networks with a wide range of users and uses. The other networks fell into seven groups: database services for businesses, later offered to consumers; computer conferencing; electronic mail services; electronic banking; computer bulletin boards; online services for education groups and other nonprofit organizations; and videotex services that aggregated many different types of services. In the 1980s and early 1990s, videotex received much more attention in the popular press and academic journals (aside from computer science and information technology journals). A search for articles in 27 national and regional newspapers from 1980 to 1992 (in the ProQuest database) identified 493 articles with the keywords ARPANET, NSFNET, or *Internet* and 1,066 with the keyword *videotex*. Adding electronic banking or computer conferencing to the list of keywords would have yielded even more lopsided results.

These services (with the exception of AOL) have largely been forgotten, overtaken by the enormous success of the Web from the mid-1990s on. Why not leave them dead and buried? There are a few reasons. These services contributed significantly to the base of knowledge that so quickly made the Web successful. They contain many lessons about how new media succeed or fail. They can also inform us at a more theoretical level about why new technologies are adopted or rejected and how they interact with existing media habits. Further, these services were researched extensively.[2] The context for their development is informative as well, especially in the case of videotex. The latter involved government policies to support development for reasons of trade and international prestige; corporate investment for fear of being left out; existing technologies in homes to access new services; and the skill levels of the general public in using new media. Nonetheless, unearthing the pieces of the story and re-creating this lost empire that contributed so much to the online world in which we live today is akin to an archeological detective exercise.

Notes about the Period

To begin the story, it is necessary to understand the context in which these online services emerged. From the late 1970s through the 1980s, the context for developing online services differed greatly from today's environment. Very few North American or European households had computers, much less ones with modems that could communicate over the telephone network. The large mainframe computers and so-called minicomputers (still fairly large and expensive) prevalent in government, large universities, and major corporations were the domain of specialists, inaccessible to office workers and to most students. However, considerable interest existed in the potential of smaller computers for a variety of applications. Apple and several other companies introduced personal computers in the mid- to late 1970s, and with much fanfare, IBM introduced its PC in 1981 (at a cost equivalent to $4,000 in today's dollars). In 1982, the cover of *Time* magazine proclaimed the personal computer Machine of the Year. With a rapid heightening of interest in the potential of personal computers, they began to enter offices and then homes at a moderate pace.

The telephone companies were also part of the context. In almost all European countries, the telephone networks were owned and managed by the government (though a few had moved them to the monopoly ownership of newly formed state-owned corporations). In the United States, the Bell System (i.e., AT&T) owned and managed most of the public network. It was a large and very powerful monopoly but it faced pressure from the U.S. Justice Department to divest and break into smaller units. In 1984, to settle a federal antitrust suit, AT&T proposed divestiture, and the government agreed. AT&T became a long-distance company with the right to enter the computer business; seven regional Bell operating companies (RBOCs) were formed to own and manage the local telephone networks in seven regions of the United States; and a separate manufacturing unit was also spun off. Old and new, these telephone companies remained very powerful and saw electronic publishing as a potential source of new revenue, causing some publishing groups to fear the entry of these competitors into the field. In Europe, many of the telephone networks were underutilized, and videotex was viewed as a way to increase usage and revenue. In addition, governments more generally, as well as the telephone companies, viewed videotex as a catalyst for national economic development and leadership in international telecommunications circles.

Government policies also played an important role, and there was much debate about the potential impact of information technologies. Would videotex and related technologies have as much impact on economies as the telephone had earlier in the twentieth century? Videotex seemed attractive for three reasons: it could potentially drive economic development; an early entrant into this new field could come to dominate it and sell its technology to the rest of the world; and success in videotex would be a feather in the cap of the country that led the way and would bolster national pride.

The governments of France and Japan, longtime devotees of industrial policy, supported videotex development with grants for research and development. (The French government also provided a major subsidy so that free terminals could be made available to millions of households.) To a much smaller extent, the British, too, provided grants for research and development, such as the creation of education services on Prestel. In both the United States and Canada, where the telephone companies were in the private sector, governments followed similar approaches to foster domestic videotex industries. The Canadian government was particularly vigorous in support of its version of the technology (Telidon). In the United States, the government supported applications such as the Green Thumb videotex service for farmers and county videotex services to provide access to government records.

Officials in the publishing industries, especially newspapers, were quite uncertain about the potential for these new information technologies and feared that someone else (most obviously telephone companies) would take the lead, leaving publishing companies in the dust if not out of business. Some publishers saw opportunity in electronic publishing; others were motivated to enter it by fear. Companies disagreed about models for services. Was videotex a database service adapted for homes, a newspaper of the future, or a hybrid of many models? Should each videotex service stand alone, or should they be aggregated in a large mall of services?

All of this technology was new to consumers, who were not well prepared to adopt videotex or related services. They lacked computers, skill in using interactive terminals, and a willingness to pay high fees for unfamiliar services. Further, they were not in the habit of seeking out information—only 3 percent of U.S. households visited a library in a given year[3]—or of corresponding with others in writing (most first-class household-to-household mail consisted of greeting cards).

Major Developments in ARPANET and Videotex

Table 7.1 provides an overview of major developments in both the ARPANET path and what is here called the videotex path, which included the seven categories listed earlier. The two paths converged in the mid-1990s as the World Wide Web emerged.

One of the obstacles to the growth of online services in households was the low penetration of personal computers. By 1990, as figure 7.1 indicates, the United States had fewer than 2 million online subscribers. Furthermore, only 23 million households had personal computers. However, owning a computer was not sufficient to gain online access; computer owners also required modems to connect their computers to the telephone network. In 1990, only 15 percent of computers in households had a modem. In other words, approximately 3.5 percent of U.S. households had the equipment necessary to subscribe to an online service. This constraint was present in Europe, too.

We now turn to a review of early online media services and field (or market) trials, together with some of the lessons they provided for later Web applications and new media development generally. It is far from a comprehensive review and, aside from videotex, focuses on the U.S. experience. We hope that

TABLE 7.1. Major Developments in the Emergence of Online Services

Time Period	ARPANET ➞ WWW	Videotex ➞ WWW
Late 1960s	Funding for the planning of a computer network by U.S. Defense Department	Start of British Post Office's planning for its videotex service (called Viewdata)
1970	Four sites connected over ARPANET computer network	
1972	E-mail program for ARPANET created by Ray Tomlinson	
1973	Publishing of the design for TCP/IP, a protocol to allow computers to communicate with each other, developed by Vinton Cerf and Bob Kahn	Online access to news and data archives for businesses offered by Dow Jones News Retrieval and the New York Times Information Bank
	First international connection to ARPANET (England and Norway)	
1974		Viewdata (videotex) service (later to be called Prestel) demonstrated in the United Kingdom
1975	100 host computers on ARPANET	
1978		First personal computer bulletin board system developed in the United States
1979	Usenets—systems for exchanging views on topics (called Newsgroups) developed at Duke University	Prestel (videotex) service launched in the United Kingdom by British Telecom after lengthy field trial
		The Source and CompuServe videotex services launched in the United States
1981		Start of field trial of an electronic banking service by Chemical Bank in the United States
1982		Launch by Infomart of a videotex service in Canada using kiosks in public locations
		Launch of Minitel videotex service in France with millions of subsidized terminals for home use
1983	Start of use by ARPANET of TCP/IP protocol to link computers	Launch by AT&T and Knight Ridder Newspapers of major videotex trial in South Florida, with 750 content areas or services
		Formation by Ogilvy and Mather of first full service division at a major U.S. advertising agency devoted to online and other interactive media
		70 commercial e-mail providers in the United States, with 400,000 accounts
		Launch of CAPTAIN videotex service (including audio) in Japan

TABLE 7.1—*Continued*

Time Period	ARPANET ➤ WWW	Videotex ➤ WWW
1984	1,000 host computers on ARPANET	Launch by AT&T and Times Mirror of videotex trial in Southern California
1986	Creation of NSFNET, extending online access to many more universities	
1988		Launch by IBM and Sears Roebuck of Prodigy videotex service in selected cities, with flat rate pricing
1989		Just under 2 million users of public e-mail services and start of interconnection allowing users of one service to send e-mail to users of others
1990	Replacement of ARPANET by NSFNET	5,000 independent computer bulletin board systems in the United States
	Commercial access to the Internet begins	More than 1 million users of the French Minitel videotex service
1991	Release by CERN of hypertext markup language that creates the World Wide Web	
1993	Introduction of Mosaic browser, making Web surfing easier	AOL's introduction of a videotex service for Windows, marketed to people who are not computer savvy
1995	The Internet becomes "commercial."	8.5 million videotex subscribers in the United States. Subscriber access to the Web provided by major services—AOL, CompuServe, and Prodigy.

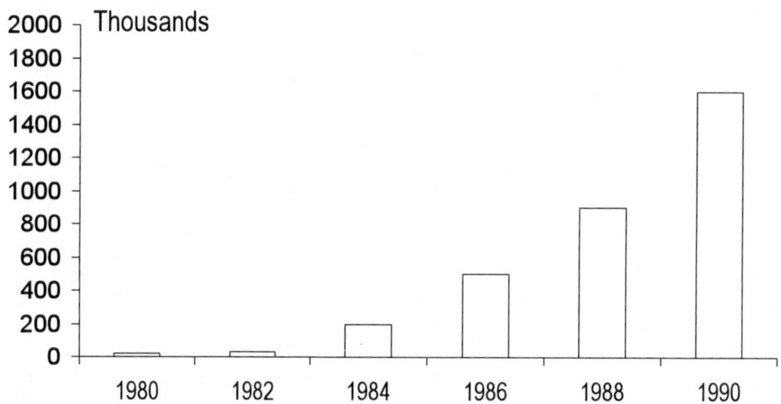

Fig. 7.1. Number of U.S. households subscribing to an online service, 1980–90. (Data from Gary Arlen, *Interactivity Report* [Bethesda, MD: Arlen Communications, multiple years].)

those who labored on dozens of additional services and trials in Asia, Europe, and North America will pardon the selectivity.

Prestel and Minitel

The development of videotex began in Britain during the late 1960s. The Post Office, the national provider of both postal and telecommunications services, had been banking on its equivalent of AT&T's Picturephone to provide a significant source of new network traffic and revenue in the face of an anticipated leveling off of telephone penetration. When U.S. experience demonstrated that this hope was forlorn, the Post Office pulled the Viewdata concept from the back burner. The idea was to provide homes and businesses with on-demand access to a centralized database. The service's architecture was designed by Sam Fedida, whom many consider the father of online services for the general public. As the term implies, Viewdata was intended to provide access to a broad range of information presented as pages of alphanumeric characters and very simple graphics. Communication was not part of the original planning, though the early service did allow users to transmit simple preformatted messages along the lines of "I will be late. Please expect me at [enter the time]." There was no reason to consider personal computers as access devices: very few households had them. The purpose-designed terminal initially developed as the access device was very expensive and was soon superseded: equipment was developed for purchase or lease by residential users that could access the service over a regular telephone line and display the information on a regular television set.

Prestel was intended as a service for homes and businesses through which anyone could provide information. Those who did, paid for storage of their information products on the central computer system; subject to a few limits, they could set a price for any of their pages retrieved by a user; they were credited with revenues from users' page charges minus a percentage retained by Prestel. The service was tested in three cities during 1978, then launched in London in the fall of 1979 under the direction of Alex Reid.

The service faced many difficulties on the consumer front. The residential terminal was expensive (renting at £8 to £10 per month), and while transmission speed was fast for the period, it still took several seconds for one page to "paint" on TV screens (which were also noticeably inferior to personal computer screens for reading text). Pricing was complex and expensive, with separate fees to buy or rent a terminal, connect to the Prestel computer (sometimes by a long-distance call), a time-sensitive usage charge, and a per-page charge varying by the provider (who set it) and type of information. Many household settings also provided obstacles. At the time, a substantial proportion of British homes had a single telephone located near the front door and hard-wired to a wall; the TV set was likely to be located in the sitting room, at a distance from the telephone. Installation thus presented problems. More importantly, Prestel tied up two key services: telephone and television. Given these obstacles, businesses accounted for approximately 90 percent of usage in the early 1980s, falling to 60 percent by the middle of the decade. Prestel may also have been hurt by teletext, a service that was much smaller in scale but was free. It used a portion of the broadcast television signal to send screens of text and graphics information to a TV set.

Early research identified a number of the challenges facing Prestel. Users wanted flat-rate pricing; they were unwilling to pay long-distance charges to reach its computer; the top ten information providers received more than half of all page views; tree-and-branch navigation (where users choose an item from a first level menu, then view a second and possibly a third or fourth menu before arriving at the desired page) was problematic for many; and people wanted to communicate with others through Prestel.[4]

The service responded to the challenges, but the process took time. Prestel added e-mail; created software so that users could access it with personal computers; introduced flat-rate pricing for consumers; added home banking, shopping, and other entertainment services; developed directories and indexes to help with navigation; provided a gateway to other online databases (a forerunner of the Web); introduced private service for companies (much like today's intranets); and initiated a range of education services.[5] By the mid-1980s, there were more than 1,000 "information providers" (a term that began with Prestel and was later changed to "service providers" as new kinds of service were added). The technology also placed more emphasis on marketing to businesses, which was by then perceived as offering greater opportunity. Although a few services were successful—most notably, one for smaller travel agents, who could use Prestel to book tickets—overall usage did not grow as fast as British Telecom (the Post Office's successor in relation to telecommunications, hence the owner of Prestel) hoped, and the service was phased out in the mid-1990s.

Prestel provided many lessons for later videotex services and for the development of Web services, though not all of these lessons were widely applied. It was clear that consumers would not buy or rent terminals that could access only videotex; computers were clearly preferable. People wanted to communicate and have fun more than they wanted access to large amounts of serious information. Much work was needed to improve navigation, and a flat-rate subscription to a service was much preferred to per-use charges.[6] Prestel certainly inspired others to test videotex. More than a dozen countries, including Germany's Bildschirmtext, used Prestel's technology to conduct trials.

TELETEXT

Teletext was developed in the United Kingdom in the early 1970s, at the same time as videotex. Especially when considered alongside the latter, it was one of the most modest of the new media. Nevertheless, teletext illustrates a few important points of wider applicability. Though a major success in much of Western Europe, it sank without a trace in North America during the first half of the 1980s.

Teletext provides an on-demand (well, almost) text and graphics information service via broadcast television. It employs unused space in the broadcast television signal to transmit numbered screens of information (pages) in continuous cycles; when a page requested via a viewer's remote control is broadcast, it is grabbed from the signal and displayed on the screen instead of the regular TV content. It can also be superimposed on regular content–e.g., as subtitles.

Teletext pages typically provide news headlines, sports results, weather forecasts, travel updates, and TV schedules. There is a trade-off between the size of its database on any channel (typically one to two hundred pages, each the equivalent of up to about two column inches of newsprint) and response time (typically five to ten seconds): greater depth requires more pages per cycle, but rapid response requires fewer.

When teletext was under development by engineers at both ITV (the United Kingdom's commercial television broadcasters) and, soon after, the BBC, Viewdata (videotex) was being created by the British Post Office. The three parties agreed to develop a shared standard for display of the text and graphical images, enabling economies of scale to be attained more rapidly in the display subsystems that the two types of service required. Although the French developed a competing standard (naturally!), and a few years later, the Japanese and Canadians developed more sophisticated standards, everywhere outside the United States there was a mandated national standard for teletext and a compatible de facto standard for videotex.

Teletext was able to skim the cream off the top of demand for information. It provided quick, easy, and free access to the small subset of information that was likely to be most popular. Why would people pay to access this material via videotex when it was free via teletext? However, it also helped videotex by getting people used to the idea of information retrieval and display via the television set and by helping bring down the cost of the display subsystem for videotex. Overall, the negative cream-skimming effect was probably stronger.

Videotex developments in Britain did not go unnoticed in France (where Jean-Jacques Servan-Schreiber's book on the challenge from America had recently had considerable impact).[7] The French were in the process of upgrading their telephone network and wanted applications that would boost its use. They were also seeking an alternative to the inefficient paper telephone directory. The hope of creating a technology that could be exported and thus could enhance France's image in the telecommunications technology community provided further incentive to develop a videotex service. The French Minitel service was rolled out in 1983. It utilized a small, stand-alone terminal with a nine-inch black and white screen that had the advantage of not requiring the television set. (The proper name of the service was Télétel, but it soon came to be known as Minitel, which was actually the name of its terminal.)

The French government subsidized millions of terminals, distributing the $167 device free of charge to households that agreed to forgo paper telephone directories. The government believed that providing free terminals would overcome the resistance to videotex encountered elsewhere. The online telephone directory was free; other services cost approximately $10 per hour. By early 1990, 5 million free terminals had been distributed to French homes. Businesses could rent terminals and many did. The ratio of home to business terminals was two-to-one in the early 1990s (very much higher than in Britain). Minitel used a centralized kiosk system for billing, an approach similar to that of Prestel. France Telecom, which managed Minitel, handled all the billing; charges were included in household telephone bills. Revenue was then distributed among service providers based on usage.

Many reports declared the service a huge success, largely as a result of the high penetration of terminals in homes—several million by the early 1990s—and the large number of services offered. Some observers, however, remained uncertain, claiming that no clear public accounting of total investment, operating costs, and revenues was ever provided. Though usage was generally low—less than three minutes per day in the early 1990s—it grew over time. As is typical, it was concentrated: 10 percent of terminals accounted for 50 percent of usage. The government said that the savings on printed directories more than paid for the subsidized terminals, but paper directories were not eliminated. People could choose Minitel or a paper directory, so the only savings were in printing and distributing paper directories that would otherwise have gone to Minitel homes.

Minitel usage mirrored that of Prestel in many ways. Communication services and professional applications were popular. There was a wide range of additional services, including news, banking, mail order, and booking travel. Particularly popular were *messageries roses* (sexually oriented chat areas). Their popularity created a public relations problem for Minitel: when France Telecom wanted to expand educational offerings, many educators and parents were concerned that teens would be exposed to pornography.

By the late 1990s, usage of Minitel started to decline as many users migrated to the Internet. The tide was held back for a while by the provision of software that allowed personal computers to access Minitel and by adapting Minitel terminals so that they could access Web content. Minitel clearly proved that government subsidies could drive terminals into homes and promote usage; the electronic telephone directory was an anchor service. However, this model was not directly replicated in other countries. (The U.S. government subsidized ARPANET and NSFNET but did not provide free terminals or subsidies for the general public.) Some observers have compared Minitel to the supersonic Concorde: an impressive technology that was widely admired but which required government subsidies throughout its useful life.

In the United States and other countries there was much interest in Prestel and Minitel; delegates from corporations and government agencies regularly visited Britain and France to observe and learn. Later in the chapter, we will treat a series of videotex trials and services in the United States built, in part, on the European models, but first we turn to two online services that preceded videotex.

Database Services

Online databases can be traced to the early 1960s.[8] They were made possible by the time-sharing of mainframe computers, greater storage capacity, and telecommunications networks that could provide economical connections between terminals in distant locations and host computers storing databases. Personal computers were not available at the time; most early terminals were adapted from devices designed for other purposes—for example, time-sharing terminals, communicating word processors, and teletypewriters. The earliest databases stored scientific information as well as journal articles and bibliographic information in science and medicine. They expanded to include law cases, journal articles in a wide range of fields, newspaper articles, stock market prices, financial records, encyclopedias, and airline guides, among much else. In some ways, these databases mirrored today's Web information services, but the means to access them and the way data were presented were different. Data were accessed through often complex logical combinations of search terms (Boolean searches), and information was typically presented as a series of records. Because of this complexity and high cost (typically $100 per hour), database searches at corporations or universities were conducted by librarians or other information specialists who understood the associated techniques and could minimize charges. A typical search by an information specialist cost $10–20. Over time, the search process was simplified, and many nonspecialists learned to conduct searches.

During the 1970s, a number of database companies were formed. Lockheed Corporation created Dialog (with access to 200 individual databases) in 1972; Lexis (a database of legal documents) was formed in 1973 and later expanded to include Nexis (a database of newspaper and magazine articles); the New York Times Information Bank and the Dow Jones News Retrieval were created in 1973. By the mid-1980s, there were more than 2,500 databases provided by more than 1,300 organizations and more than a million users, mostly in businesses, universities, and government.[9]

In the 1980s, a number of database operators decided to offer their service to consumers and small business by linking them to mainstream videotex services. These operators correctly anticipated consumer interest in locating old newspaper articles, current stock quotes, or airline schedules, all of which have now become common Web information services. However, these companies misjudged what consumers were able and willing to pay: if businesses were willing to pay $100 per hour to access this information, operators reasoned, wouldn't consumers view $12 per hour for (off-peak) evening access as a bargain? But consumers showed little interest at this price level. Nonetheless, online databases in this era created the initial designs for information services that later appeared on the Web.

Computer Conferencing

The development of computer conferencing was concentrated in the United States. Although the term has fallen out of favor (some prefer the more generic term *computer-mediated communication*—CMC), the constituent services it pioneered are very much present on today's Web as e-mail, forums, person-to-person and group chats, blogs, newsletters, and shared documents. Terminology differed in the early days of computer conferencing—e.g., today's chat was called synchronous conferencing, blogs were called electronic journals (though the latter were more formal than most of today's blogs), and shared documents were called notebooks—but the content was quite similar.

Computer conferencing grew out of a late-1960s initiative by the Office of Emergency Preparedness.[10] It then developed along a few paths, including services for research communities on ARPANET, proprietary services for businesses and university-based services on commercial time-share networks, and systems built into videotex services such as The Source (described below). Early systems included the EIES (the Electronic Information Exchange Service), developed at the New Jersey Institute of Technology; Forum (which evolved into

Planet), developed by the Institute for the Future; Confer, developed at the University of Michigan; and Participate, a service on The Source videotex service. The pioneers who developed computer conferencing included Murray Turoff and Starr Roxanne Hiltz at the New Jersey Institute of Technology and Jacques Vallée and Robert Johansen at the Institute for the Future.

The core concept was to harness the economical transmission of timeshare networks, along with the processing capability and storage of computers, for the purpose of person-to-person communication (using simple ASCII text without graphics). The idea of computer conferencing is now taken for granted but was far from obvious in the early 1970s. Indeed, many people could see no sensible connection between computers and communication. The software of a computer conferencing system was located at a particular host computer accessible on a time-share network. The basic organizational units were called conferences and could be restricted to named participants or open to all, however organizers chose. Typically (though there were other approaches), when users logged into a system they were authorized to join, they could select (from a menu) and enter any conference authorized for them or open to all. On entering, they would see and could select from a list of all messages they had not yet read—private messages, messages to all, or messages to any named subset of participants in which they were included. Fairly powerful search functions permitted users to retrieve past messages using combinations of straightforward criteria.

Computer conferencing's first users included academics, members of research organizations, corporate employees, and government workers, with professionals such as nurses, students, and some consumers joining in later. Computer conferencing was used principally for collaboration among dispersed experts, communication within teams, person-to-person e-mail, and distance learning. Today's online Web courses evolved, in part, from distance education services utilizing computer conferencing. Considerable experimentation also took place, and ad hoc fun applications were developed. One highly successful experiment on the EIES system was an interactive soap opera in which participants played roles in an ongoing story that they wrote collectively. It was the most read "conference" on EIES until that time.[11]

A great deal of research has been published about computer conferencing, much of it relevant to the development of Web services. Researchers have found that many people read the content in computer conferences but rarely or never posted any messages; they came to be called *lurkers*. E-mail was very popular; some people found it almost addictive. A number of systems allowed users to create anonymous pen names to hide their identity and develop alter egos, a feature that has subsequently become quite important on the Web. Computer conferencing also enabled people to mobilize quickly to take collective action.

In one famous incident, computer conferences were used to organize a protest movement against Lotus Marketplace after it announced plans to launch a "clipper chip" that contained the names, addresses, and spending habits of 120 million Americans,[12] foreshadowing the political role of blogs and forums on the Web.

Much research compared computer conferencing to audioconferencing, videoconferencing, and face-to-face communication for a variety of tasks.[13] In our view, however, computer conferencing is generally better seen as a complement to these other modalities rather than as an alternative (see chapter 6). This research also reached some general conclusions regarding the social psychology of group communications.[14] The fact that all communications were stored in a system's database provided researchers with a wealth of automatically generated data (even though private content was not available to them).

Early obstacles included high cost (EIES, for example, cost $75 per month per account plus per-hour connection charges as high as $6 to $8) and (since computer conferencing predated personal computers) the lack of terminals in many businesses, schools, and especially homes. Over time, however, prices fell and personal computers became the ubiquitous terminal of choice. Numerous behavioral obstacles also existed: difficult access to terminals and time-consuming log-on procedures discouraged many people from logging on frequently enough to prevent fast-flowing conferences from overwhelming them; some conferences became a disorganized muddle of many disconnected threads (with moderators playing a key role in countering trends toward entropy); others failed to attract enough input to reach a self-generating critical mass. Nevertheless, computer conferencing continued to evolve, becoming lost as a recognizable entity only as its functionality became woven into the fabric of Internet services.

ASCII and Graphical Videotex Services in the United States

The term *videotex* (sometimes with a final t but properly and most often without) generally referred to services transmitted over telephone lines, providing a broad variety of services, and intended for multiple groups of users, especially consumers. There are many ways to classify videotex services launched in the United States. We will divide them into two groups: ASCII videotex services, which used simple text with no graphics and were generally monochrome; and graphical videotex services, which had both color and graphics. The latter presented information in screen-size pages, using tree-and-branch menu systems for navigation. The former generally presented information as blocks of text of variable length through which the user had to scroll; navigation, which did not employ a tree-and-branch system, was reasonably efficient for the technically experienced but not user-friendly for others. Videotex companies and devotees initially rejected the idea that the new term should be applied to ASCII systems: they provided neither color nor graphics; they did not present output in easily understood page format; and their navigational features were not user-friendly. Within a few years, however, the graphical videotex community no longer objected to the dilution of the term, because the broader definition allowed them to claim a larger universe of users.

The best known ASCII videotex services were CompuServe and The Source. CompuServe (the service) began as a time-sharing service for mainframe computers in 1969. Usage primarily took place during the day. In 1979, CompuServe (the company) launched a videotex service for approximately ten dollars per hour to increase usage of the mainframes in the evening. The company offered the service in the daytime, too, but at a much higher price (more than twenty dollars per hour). The service consisted of news, games, e-mail, forums, and chat. It also contained a dating service and an auction component. Many early users were hobbyists who had purchased early personal computers and modems. (Hayes introduced a 300 bit per second modem in 1977 for $280.) Others used so-called dumb terminals to connect to the service, though these had little processing power or memory. Early users—90 percent male—came from a mix of businesses and households. The primary service (25 percent of all usage) was e-mail.[15] In 1980, H&R Block acquired CompuServe.

The Source was launched in 1979 by William von Meister and resembled CompuServe in design, applications, and user groups. The Source introduced private networks within the service, similar to today's intranets, allowed people to sell items, and provided keyword searches. Its popular forums included "Dial a Date," which resembled later Web dating services. The Source was purchased by Reader's Digest in 1980 and then acquired by a private venture capital group in the mid-1980s, by which time it had 60,000 subscribers. CompuServe acquired The Source in 1989 and absorbed its user base. By 1990, the combined service had nearly 600,000 subscribers. In the mid-1990s, CompuServe was one of three major videotex operators (along with AOL and Prodigy) that opened up its service to the Web. The early obstacles to rapid growth for both CompuServe and The Source were price, speed, and the scarcity of terminals in homes. Over time, pricing for both services was reduced, transmission speed increased, and the terminal problem was eased as millions of homes acquired personal computers.

Viewtron and Gateway were two prominent graphical videotex services in the early and mid-1980s. They used similar technologies, offered similar services, and met similar fates. Viewtron was a partnership between AT&T, which provided the technology, and newspaper publisher Knight Ridder, which managed the service and provided much of the content. There were also dozens of information providers. Viewtron began as a small trial in Coral Cables, Florida. It was then launched as a service for the public in southern Florida in the fall of 1983 and eventually made available on a national basis. When first launched, it employed the Sceptre terminal developed specifically for Viewtron by AT&T to access the service; content was displayed on television sets. The terminal cost $900, but the price was quickly reduced to $600, below its manufacturing cost. Alternatively, subscribers could rent the terminal. The service was relatively fast for that time (1,200 bits per second) and could display good graphics. Much work in graphics development preceded Viewtron, some for Viewtron and some for related services such as teletext.[16] As with Prestel, the service tied up both a telephone line and a TV set. Moreover, high-end graphics slowed it down significantly. Viewtron offered a robust range of services, including news, banking, travel, games, e-mail, chat, and forums. In the Gateway service, AT&T partnered with Times Mirror, another newspaper company, to launch a videotex service in southern California in 1984.

Both services became laboratories for advertising. One agency, Ogilvy and Mather, formed an interactive marketing group led by Martin Nisenholtz that created advertisements for multiple clients on both services. The group developed banner ads and advertising sites a decade before the World Wide Web emerged. The effort struggled with the technological limitations of slow modems—elaborate graphics took a long time to transmit—and began the process of graphics optimization, in which complex graphics are transmitted as simpler forms and smaller files.

Viewtron encountered strong resistance to buying or renting a terminal that had only one function—accessing its videotex service. At that time, personal computers were beginning to enter large numbers of households, so the project team scrambled and created software that allowed computers to access Viewtron. The company also reduced prices to subscribers and introduced a flat rate, thereby increasing the subscriber base, but not enough to sustain the service. Research revealed that consumers were more interested in communication than information—e-mail and chat were the most heavily used services, as had already been discovered in Europe. The Viewtron research offered some tantalizing clues about what would work in a future Web environment. For example, an eBay-style auction, Bidquick, was surprisingly popular, and a 1985 ad slogan captured what would become a core appeal of the Web—"What you want, when you want it."[17] By 1986, Viewtron had cost the two partners more than $50 million, and they decided to shut it down. Gateway followed a very similar path and was shut down in the same month.

These two services demonstrated the importance of using the personal computer as an access terminal and the value of communication in online services. Both started with an electronic newspaper supplemented by other services and finished with a communication and games service that included news and shopping. They also made significant advances in online advertising by mixing content and banner advertising on the same screen, a model that would later be imitated on the Web.

The Prodigy videotex service began as a trial in 1982. CBS Publishing and AT&T formed a partnership, Venture One, to test videotex technology, services, user behavior, and business models. The trial, which took place in Ridgewood, New Jersey, had two waves of 100 homes. It explicitly tested stand-alone terminals against computers, finding the latter the better alternative. The trial service, Reach, was not an electronic newspaper but an entertainment, communication, transaction, and information service. In the closed trial environment, the team experimented with many approaches away from press or industry scrutiny. Reach introduced a number of innovations: services for young children; Fast Track access to services (the equivalent of today's Favorites); information personalized for each user; information about best prices; local community information; and opinion polls. Reach also learned the importance of a subscriber help line.

Following the trial, AT&T dropped out, and, in 1984, CBS formed a partnership with IBM and Sears Roebuck called Trintex. After four years of planning, during which time CBS shifted its corporate strategy and dropped out, the partners launched Prodigy. Harry Smith managed the venture. His name is not well known in the various histories of online services, but his business model for Prodigy later became the core model for the Web as we know it—i.e., a service with low, flat-rate pricing supplemented by advertising and transaction revenue. Prodigy was created as a consumer service for households with personal computers; households that lacked modems could have them included in low-priced start-up kits.

Prodigy reintroduced many of the innovations that were identified in the New Jersey trial, including banner ads and customized information (e.g., personalized stock portfolios). It added keyword searches, paths (favorites), and jump (letting a user move quickly to another part of the service). It had a friendly graphical user interface (GUI) in 1988 and used caching (downloading and storing graphics on the user's computer) to reduce access time. The team also developed local access nodes, so users could reach Prodigy with a local phone call from most major markets. It opened an e-mail gateway to the Internet and in 1995 created its own Web browser, becoming the first of the large videotex services to offer Web access. It later pioneered broadband, with 1.3 million DSL subscribers by 2000.

Prodigy has received very little credit for these innovations. Though it reached a few million subscribers at its peak, it was far outpaced by its rival, AOL, and failed to turn a profit. The business model was correct for the long term but inadequate for the short term. Advertising revenue grew too slowly, and merchandisers came on board slowly and with little commitment. Prodigy also developed a large staff to create information, driving up operating costs, and when financial pressures rose, it abandoned the flat-rate pricing model (though returning to it later). The company was sold and resold before telecommunications giant SBC (now AT&T) absorbed it.

America Online (AOL) came late to the videotex arena and was, by some standards, unremarkable compared to rivals such as Prodigy. Yet it left its competitors in the dust and at one point had more than 30 million subscribers worldwide. In the mid-2000s, it lost considerable ground as subscribers migrated to broadband Internet service providers (ISPs), but it had previously been a remarkable success story. The company started in 1985 under the name Quantum Computer Services to provide online games and bulletin board systems (BBS) for personal computers. In 1989, it changed its name to America Online. Two years later, the same year that Steve Case became CEO, it launched a videotex service for computers running DOS (the operating system preceding Windows). In 1993, it launched videotex services for Windows computers and Macs. Case came from a marketing background, which strongly influenced the company's development. Just as millions of nontechies were buying computers, the company positioned itself as a service for people who were unfamiliar with them. It was simple to use and had content categories that appealed to the mass public. Emphasis was on communication services, not information; it provided an e-mail service for the masses. Early pricing was a flat $9.95 per month for up to five hours of usage and $2.95 per hour above that. Most subscribers never used the full five hours, so AOL made more money when subscribers used the service only a little but continued to subscribe.

AOL employed a simple but effective marketing strategy: the company mailed out tens of millions of diskettes with the software needed to access the service and a free trial offer. To manage costs, volunteers monitored forums, chat rooms, and conferences. The service expanded over time through dozens of acquisitions of both technology and content. When the Web arrived, AOL initially hesitated to make it available to subscribers but soon opened the doors to selected Web sites (a "walled garden" approach) and subsequently to the entire Web. The company also changed its pricing to a flat $19.95 per month for unlimited access. By 1996, AOL had five million U.S. subscribers. It was both a proprietary videotex service, with content and services it controlled, and the country's largest ISP. The company expanded internationally, acquiring millions of subscribers in Mexico and elsewhere. In 1998, AOL purchased CompuServe and absorbed its subscriber base. Then, at the height of the Internet bubble, the company used its enormous market capitalization to purchase one of the largest communication companies in the world, Time Warner. The merger was not advantageous for either company, but the history of AOL Time Warner in the first decade of the century is another, much longer story.

E-Mail

E-mail and electronic banking were core components in many general videotex services as well as stand-alone, proprietary services. People could subscribe to a service that focused primarily or exclusively on e-mail or electronic banking.

Some disagreement exists about the origins of e-mail. It really had no single inventor. Leaving aside the telegraph and teletype, the first electronic mail system using a computer was probably the MIT Mailbox, developed in 1965 by Noel Morris and Tom Van Vleck. The motivation to create electronic mail was to enable users of mainframe computers to communicate with the system operator. Electronic mail expanded to include other users of the mainframe, people using mainframes at other locations, and eventually everyone who had access to a computer. By the early 1970s, a literature about electronic mail existed.[18] Ray Tomlinson, whom some credit as the inventor of e-mail, made a significant contribution in writing a program for an e-mail service in the early 1970s and using the @ sign to connect the user and host name, a convention that later became the standard for all e-mail.

Our concern here is e-mail developed over multi-application computer networks, videotex systems, and stand-alone services. As opposed to public e-mail services, to which anyone could subscribe and then communicate with any other subscriber, stand-alone corporate e-mail services were installed primarily by businesses so that employees could communicate with one another. By 1983, North America had more than 70 commercial e-mail providers and many more corporate e-mail systems. The commercial providers had nearly a half million accounts; an estimated 750,000 office workers were using e-mail, too.

Some of the larger public e-mail services included Western Union Easy Link, ITT Dialcom, MCI Mail, and Sprint Telemail. Most charged by time on the service, typically 25 to 40 cents per minute of use. To keep costs manageable, they provided software that enabled a user to type outgoing messages and read incoming messages offline. The average e-mail message cost approximately 25 cents to send, nearly the same as a first-class letter. By the end of the 1980s, just under two million people used public e-mail services in the United States, and more than six million office workers used e-mail.

One of the serious limitations of early e-mail services was that they did not interconnect with each other: e.g., an MCI Mail subscriber could not communicate with a Sprint Telemail user. By the late 1980s, however, the different services began to connect with each other as well as with videotex services and NSFNET. Many etiquette and social convention issues also needed to be worked out over time. E-mail made it easy for rumors to spread quickly through a company; some users "flamed out" with an angry e-mail response to a message they misinterpreted; and many people sent e-mails to a large group that included recipients who did not need or want the message. Research about e-mail indicated that it substituted for some voice messages (there was little substitution for first-class mail), but its larger impact was to increase the amount of communication within organizations or among users. Junk e-mail was less prevalent than it is today, but some spam was being sent by the early 1980s. Public e-mail services eventually declined as people moved over to the Internet; corporate e-mail services moved to domains on the Internet.

Electronic Banking

Electronic banking was an extension of the computerization of banking in the 1960s and 1970s. Before computers, a person making a savings deposit at a bank would hand a passbook (about the size of a passport) to a teller along with the deposit. The teller would go to a filing cabinet, remove the card with the person's account record, and type the new account balance on the card and in the passbook. Mainframe computers replaced this system and became a central storage facility for bank records, but they were in a back office that customers never saw. Bank customers' first direct encounter with computer technology came with automated teller machines (ATMs), introduced in Britain by Barclays Bank in 1967 and in the United States by Chemical Bank in 1969. At first, the machines were costly and prone to breakdowns, and there were some significant customer acceptance issues, but, over time, ATMs became more reliable and widely accepted, migrating to many locations outside bank branches, including supermarkets, gasoline stations, and airports. It was a logical next step to think how banking might be brought directly into the home using computer technology.

Home banking trials began in the late 1970s in both the United States and Britain. (Prestel, for example, provided limited home banking.) Some banks chose to join one of the general videotex services; others set up proprietary home banking services. With low penetration of personal computers, banks also tried two other options. One was to display banking information sent over a telephone line on a TV set. This was unsuccessful, probably because of the perceived lack of security and privacy. The other option was a "screen phone" that could send and receive data, displaying it on a four-inch screen built into the telephone. Citibank called its enhanced telephone ET. The screen phone was simple to use but expensive—more than $500 to buy or $9.95 per month to rent. Banks had to wait for households to adopt personal computers, and home banking grew slowly.

Banks believed that electronic banking had many advantages. They were right about some but over-optimistic about others. For example, they thought that people would place a high value on controlling the float in an electronic payment (specifying when to pay a bill, thereby receiving interest on the money until the last moment before its transfer). Most people did not care; some found out that the money did not transfer precisely when specified, so they had to allow for a few days' buffer, reducing the value of the float. Banks also thought that people would welcome eliminating checks and saving on postage, but many U.S. customers liked checks or were too set in their ways to change. However, simple tasks like checking an account balance or transferring funds between accounts had a high appeal.

In addition to the low household penetration of computers, other early obstacles to rapid growth included the popularity of audiotex banking in the 1980s. Many banks set up automated telephone systems that people could use to inquire about balances or transfer funds between accounts, and millions of customers found audiotex banking sufficient for their needs. A second obstacle was gender. In the 1980s and early 1990s, 90 percent of those online were male, but in most U.S. homes, women managed the household finances and paid bills. The most important obstacle was price. Banks believed that electronic banking could become a profit center, so they charged a service fee of $10 to $15 per month. However, the households most likely to become early adopters of home banking were generally wealthy, had significant assets in their banking accounts, and paid nothing for bank services. People saw no reason to pay for electronic banking when the service saved the bank money by requiring fewer customer service representatives.

There was considerable progress in the user interface for electronic banking. Large banks—e.g., Citibank—undertook extensive consumer testing and simplified the process of home banking for ordinary people. They even established a group, Humanware, to design electronic banking services. Nevertheless proprietary electronic banking services grew only modestly through the mid-1990s. At that point, Citibank dropped its fee for home banking, and others followed. The pace of adoption then picked up significantly, and by 1998, more than seven million households were doing some form of banking online. Many banks watched activities on the Web but were not yet ready to offer electronic banking on it because of fears about security. Instead, these institutions set up modest Web sites with information but no banking services. Electronic banking on the Web emerged over the next few years as banks and their customers gained greater confidence in Web security. Larger banks led the way. The lessons from the proprietary electronic banking services were clear. People wanted security, simplicity, convenience, control of their accounts, and strong customer service—at no cost. Banks could earn profits from online services by reducing labor costs in back offices, selling new services, and charging transaction fees.

Noncommercial Online Services and Bulletin Board Systems

Throughout the early years of online media, nonprofit organizations played a prominent role in developing content and communication services. They employed a range of systems to deliver these services, including mainframe or minicomputers, existing videotex services, and small bulletin board systems (see below) on personal computers. Many applications were education-related, but others provided access to public records, help in learning how to use computers, specialized content such as health information, and community forums. Some of the many services were: Learning Link (local videotex services for school teachers and librarians operated by public broadcasting stations); SeniorNet (a group founded in 1985 that provides tutorials for seniors on how to use computers and online classes on many subjects); the Minnesota State Planning Department (access to public records); and Green Thumb (a U.S. Department of Agriculture trial that provided specialized information to farmers in Kentucky). Though it is hard to classify, The Well (The Whole Earth 'Lectronic Link) probably belongs in this category. It was founded in 1985 by Stewart Brand and Larry Brilliant as a for-profit and nonprofit partnership. The WELL began as a freewheeling online discussion service, running on its own computer, with topics that ranged from intellectual to radical to ridiculous. It attracted an avant-garde, counterculture following and later influenced much content development on the Web, as its members branched out and started Web services.[19]

Online services from nonprofits demonstrated that many groups previously lacking access to online media could benefit from them. These services also expanded the range of applications that people wanted (for example, access to government records) and provided important clues for the development of future Web services (for example, services that fostered communities of interest). There was a high turnover of these applications for reasons we discussed in chapter 3. Some were started with funding from an outside source and could not secure continued funding when the initial grant period ended, though others did obtain continuing funding from government, universities, or end users. Some aimed too high technologically and raised the financial hurdle for sustainability when end users had to pay for the service.

Bulletin board systems were poor people's computer conferencing. In most cases, they involved a single personal computer equipped with special software and a modem. The computer's owner kept it on 24 hours per day and let others dial in to read and post messages. Most were free, though some charged

$5–$10 per month. They were typically dedicated to a single topic and related subtopics. Many provided discussion about particular brands of computer, but the range of topics was very wide and included religion, hobbies, sports, pornography, and education. Most were operated by individuals, but schools, social organizations, and businesses also operated them. School districts in Brooklyn, New York, for example, operated a network of 20 BBS, and a commercial dating service, Dial Your Match operated 120 BBS around the United States.

BBS were a craze in the late 1980s and early 1990s, much like the citizens' band (CB) radio craze a decade earlier. In the late 1980s, at least 5,000 BBS operated in the United States.[20] They were also popular in Britain and Australia. By the early 1990s, some estimates put the number of BBS in the United States as high as 40,000, with millions of users. BBS users were not a lunatic fringe (for the most part). Most were computer hobbyists or people with a strong interest in a topic. They showed the same types of behavior as people participating in the more high-end computer conferences. Many read but did not post (lurkers), and some were passionate, almost addicted, to the process of reading and posting. Most BBS allowed users to create handles and post anonymously, which encouraged some uninhibited (and on occasions unwanted) behavior.

BBS had a number of limitations. A user had to dial a BBS directly, which sometimes involved a long-distance call. The operator of a BBS had to tie up a personal computer and a telephone line. BBS computers were not interconnected and generally provided no private e-mail among their users. Popular BBS might have a few thousand users, making it difficult to get through, especially in the evening. The success of a BBS was often tied to the system operator's skills in managing and policing the discussion, which could veer way off topic or degrade into hostile exchanges. When successful, BBS fostered a community among its users, much like modern social networking sites on the Web. Much of the content on BBS foreshadowed the contemporary blog.

Online Terminals in Public Locations and Audiotex

Many users of new media encounter them for the first time in a public location. Examples include public telephone booths in drugstores during the 1920s, TV sets in bars during the late 1940s, and even newspapers in eighteenth-century English coffeehouses. The concept of online terminals in public locations (to access electronic newspapers) was envisioned by Jules Tewlow in the late 1960s.[21] In the early 1980s, online terminals were introduced in shopping malls and hotel lobbies in Toronto, Canada. At no cost, patrons could access shopping information, the location of restaurants, notices about special events, and promotions. The TeleGuide service, developed by Informart, then spread to San Francisco, San Diego, Phoenix, and other U.S. cities. Lee Enterprises set up advertiser-supported public terminals in Davenport, Iowa, Harte Hanks did so in San Antonio, Texas, and Hilton Hotels followed suit in multiple cities. These efforts achieved mixed commercial results. Vandalism was a problem in some locations, advertising revenue was generally insufficient to cover the cost of operations, and in some cases heavy patronage by nontarget users (male teenagers) discouraged use by others. However, other public terminals succeeded, including online coupon-dispensing machines in supermarkets, automated off-track-betting parlors, and online large-screen displays at convention centers. One interesting example was a system of 30 kiosks in a California rural farming community that allowed users to apply for food stamps and Medicare, speeding up the application process and saving the county several million dollars a year in administrative costs.

Observations of terminal users revealed that many people had weak computer skills.[22] Public location videotex terminals, along with ATM machines and computers in offices, helped to teach the broad public rudimentary skills that they would need when computers entered millions of homes during the 1990s.

Audiotex, a term used in the 1980s and 1990s for what are generally now called voice response systems, developed as a hybrid of single-service, dial-it telephone calls (e.g., dial the weather) and traditional videotex. The principal differences between audiotex and videotex were the use of a touch-tone telephone as the access terminal, a relatively limited menu of information in most services, and delivery of the information as spoken words rather than text on a screen. Audiotex services during this period included tax information provided by the Internal Revenue Service, prerecorded information tapes on common medical problems provided by hospitals, information on ticket availability for Broadway plays, and trading prices for specific stocks and bonds. Some audiotex services were free, others used premium-price telephone numbers to bill customers, and still others utilized subscriber account numbers to limit access and for billing purposes.

Audiotex was initially viewed as a weak stepchild of videotex, but it grew into a major industry. Millions of people were willing to pay for audiotex content, and the terminal problem was eliminated—everyone had touch-tone telephones. Many newspapers (e.g., the *New York Times* and *USA Today*) and banks (e.g., Citibank and Chase) offered audiotex services. In addition, audiotex was widely adopted as a way to screen customer service calls by providing a menu of prerecorded information options for those who did not need to speak with a customer service representative.

Audiotex services for which users had to pay for were not without problems: hostility between information service providers and telephone companies (U.S. telephone companies could not control the content of third-party audiotex services); heavy turnover in information service providers; and much negative publicity because of pornographic or otherwise sleazy content on some services and valueless (e.g., out-of-date) content on others. There were concerns that minors would have easy access to inappropriate content and/or would run up very high telephone bills. In Britain, British Telecom banned audiotex chat in the late 1980s because of salacious content. A very close parallel exists between what was popular as audiotex content—weather, sports scores, bank balances, horoscopes, and so forth—and what would become popular on the Web, including sleazy content.

The Transition

By the mid-1990s, the videotex community of consumers and businesses began to merge on the Internet with the latter's community of academics, students, and some corporations. Many trends were favorable. Households had more computers, more people had learned to use computers at school or work, and more clues were available about what ordinary people wanted from online services. Further, a critical mass of people was now online, making it attractive for others to sign on, minimally for e-mail (figure 7.2). Yet the transition had obstacles and ran into potholes. For one, in the mid-1990s, relatively few women were online, though they would come to be crucial to the Web's success. In addition, modems remained painfully slow, and many key groups did not embrace the Web.

Much revisionist history has been written about this period. In some accounts, Bill Gates and Microsoft are said to have been enthusiastic early sup-

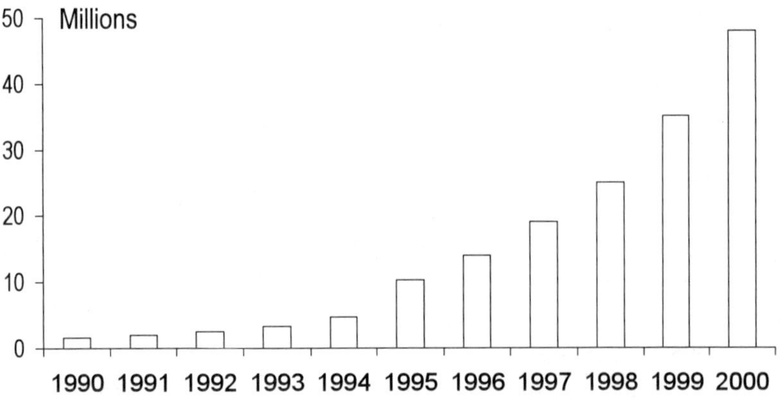

Fig. 7.2. Number of U.S. households subscribing to an online service, 1990–2000. (Data from Gary Arlen, *Interactivity Report* [Bethesda, MD: Arlen Communications, multiple years]; and U.S. Census Bureau, *Statistical Abstract of the United States* [Washington, DC: Department of Commerce, multiple years].)

porters of the Web, whereas in reality, they were cynics who came late to the party.[23] Telephone companies later claimed that they had embraced online services, but these businesses were more interested in interactive television than in the Web (see chapter 8). Indeed, at the time, many local telephone companies viewed the growth in the number of home users of the Internet and the average length of online sessions as a threat: such usage placed heavy demands on switches (previously known as local exchanges) and provided very little revenue.[24] At 21 minutes, the average duration of an Internet session in the mid-1990s was more than five times longer than the average duration of a telephone conversation. Furthermore, most Internet users accessed their ISPs through flat-rate, untimed local calls, so that regardless of length, an online session provided the telephone company with only 12–15 cents in revenue.

The transition to the Internet and its two main attractions, the Web and e-mail, took place in a Wild West atmosphere, with some very successful applications and many failures. Long before the Internet bubble burst in 2001, there was no shortage of excessively hyped and wacky ideas. One was the concept of virtual banks and cybercash. The initial virtual bank, First Virtual Holdings, was founded in 1994. The concept behind virtual banks was that people would convert their dollars or other currencies into a new, branded form of money, known as "e-cash" or "cybercash," and use this Web-based currency for transactions. After decades of marketing efforts to convince consumers that checks, credit cards, ATM cards, and debit cards were acceptable in place of cash because they represented the transfer of real money, these start-ups believed that businesses and consumers would accept electronic scrip or private money issued by virtual banks. The idea was not well received. Even the term *virtual banking*, adapted from *virtual reality*, a term widely used at the time, had strong negative connotations for consumers, whose experience of virtual reality was in theme parks and video arcades, where it involved a game, an illusion, or something frivolous. Why would fledgling financial institutions want to adopt this image, and why would consumers want to place their real money in a virtual bank? Major financial institutions did not support, let alone adopt, this image, and consumers did not put their money into virtual banks. Electronic banking and transactions over the Web ultimately succeeded when people became convinced that they were as secure as dealing with bricks-and-mortar merchants and banks (a reasonable comparison until the latter part of 2008). The concept of virtual cash resurfaced a decade later and again failed.

What Worked: Positive Indicators from Earlier Online Services

Many of the successful Web applications in the transition period of the mid-1990s had roots in earlier online services that had either worked well or provided clues for successful implementation. For example, earlier research clearly demonstrated that many forms of communication, among them e-mail, forums, and chat, would be attractive to Internet users. Communication could also be added to information or transaction services and boost usage, as with consumers' product reviews. Experience with earlier online services had indicated that user-generated content, e.g., readers' comments about newspaper articles, could compete with or complement professional content. Popular content on earlier online services—e.g., weather, sports, news, and games—also proved popular on the Web. Earlier research had indicated that consumers would accept advertising, especially if it helped to reduce the price of services, but that advertisements should not be so graphically intense that they slowed down the user experience. Private sections of online systems such as The Source or CompuServe, which met companies' needs for internal information and communication services, also provided links to other organizations with whom the companies did business. These private sections evolved into intranets and extranets. Earlier online services had clearly shown that consumers preferred flat-rate pricing to metered pricing. Some of the influence of earlier online services on Web applications during this transition period derived from who the Web users were. In 1995, 6.2 million U.S. households accessed the Web through traditional videotex services, such as AOL or Prodigy; only 1.2 million accessed the Web through an independent ISP.

Earlier online research provided many clues about what could be attractive to users if improvements were made. Auctions on The Source and Viewtron were moderately successful, hinting that a more robust and better designed auction service could be very successful. Into this gap charged eBay. Early online databases offered search functions that were too complicated for ordinary users; Prodigy had three forms of search, all of them primitive. Yahoo, Google, and other portals significantly advanced the search process. Earlier research also hinted that multiple forms of online commerce could succeed if transaction services met consumer requirements for security, trusted brands, transparency, quality merchandise, fulfillment, and favorable return policies. Over time, many Web commerce applications met these goals; price comparisons and user reviews offered an added benefit. Research from the early Prestel service through Prodigy indicated that online travel and brokerage services were likely to be popular—and they were.

Failure to attract women had posed a significant obstacle in earlier online services. Prodigy and later AOL made significant progress in this respect, making services more user-friendly, employing attractive graphics, providing services that interested women (e.g., home banking and shopping), and, most important, marketing to women.

What Didn't Work: Things That Should Have Been Learned from Earlier Online Failures

Much of what did not work in Web applications of the mid-1990s had not worked in earlier online services. The lessons from failure were not learned, and mistakes were repeated.[25] One often-repeated mistake was to create Web sites from company brochures or printed marketing materials, with no adaptation for the online environment and its users' expectations. Brochureware, as it was called, represented a fundamental misunderstanding of online services as a distinctive medium. It was accompanied by a failure to update Web content and even by the abandonment (but not removal) of Web sites, deadly mistakes from the videotex era that were repeated on the early Web. In one case, a site promoting a Rolling Stones concert remained online two years after the event. Those who frequently updated their sites often received a nasty surprise when they learned the high cost of doing so. Yet this cost, too, had clearly been indicated by earlier online experience.

Newspapers and magazines struggled with adapting their print products to the Web. Many initially published the same print content on the Web—in the same format and after the print product had been published. This strategy had not worked well for videotex, and it fared no better in the Web transition period. Newspapers and magazines needed to redesign the electronic versions of their products in accordance with how people read online, their expectations of timeliness, and their desire to communicate about news stories. Newsmagazines in particular resisted scooping their print editions by breaking stories online. This practice did not change until January 1998, when *Newsweek* published a story about the Monica Lewinsky scandal online before the print edition had appeared. *Time* magazine, however, waited for its print edition to reach newsstands before publishing the story on its Web site. The dam was broken, and thereafter news magazines began to publish stories online as soon as they were available.

Subscription revenue featured prominently in business plans for Web services during the period. Many commercial organizations believed that new groups of consumers coming onto the Web would pay for content through subscriptions, much as they paid for newspapers and magazines. However, new Web users were similar in attitude to earlier online users in not being prepared to do so. The exceptions were some businesses that had paid for access to online databases and now paid for some specialized online newsletters. Consumers refused to pay subscription fees for content. This barrier was so strong that most organizations that intended to charge these fees changed their plans and never tried to do so. Only a few organizations, including the *Wall Street Journal*

Interactive Edition and *Consumer Reports* Online, generated significant subscription revenue. Many newspapers and magazines offered the bulk of their online content at no cost, although some charged for special sections or tiers of content above the free level. Only modest revenue resulted. Trying to make people pay for content was an understandable decision since the core of their offline business model was a combination of advertising and subscriptions, but many seemed not to have known the history of earlier online services.

User experience with online content was another area where earlier mistakes were repeated. The first issue was designing content to work within the limits of modem speeds. Many videotex applications had been heavy on graphics even though modem speeds were very slow, and the user experience suffered accordingly. Many early Web sites repeated the mistake and had long access times—for example, more than one minute to access a home page.

Research as early as the late 1970s indicated that when people had to choose from menus on successive screens in a tree-and-branch architecture, they made many errors and often abandoned the search in frustration.[26] This common problem in the videotex era was repeated in the transition to the Web. Some Web sites even had welcome pages that merely provided an entrance to the site. Users wanted information to be brought up from the basement of extra screens and presented as close as possible to the initial Web page. Similarly, it was a common mistake in some early online applications to use the tools presented by the technology whether or not they benefited users, a mistake repeated on many early Web sites. One example was watermarks (symbols or icons that could be embedded in the background screen, such as a football team's logo). In a number of cases, text was superimposed over the watermark even though it rendered the text illegible. In these cases, technological bells and whistles, not sensitivity to users, drove application design.

General Lessons

In the widely accepted history of online services, the Web is viewed as a stunning success and earlier online services are seen as failures. The reality is not so simple. Some earlier online services were commercially successful—e.g., AOL for consumers and Lexis/Nexis for businesses. Others succeeded in providing services that users wanted during the interim before the Web emerged (e.g., BBS), and some achieved important service goals with the help of government or foundation subsidies (e.g., Minitel in France and SeniorNet in the United States). The Web has never been a service; it is a platform for services, some successful and others not. Nonetheless, the Web rather than proprietary videotex systems became the platform for a widely used worldwide array of online services.

Some of the advantages of the Web are clear in hindsight. It is an open platform that allows anyone to offer services and has a common suite of protocols that allows information to flow across networks. No one owns it, so no gatekeepers restrict what is offered (though national laws impose some constraints). The Web itself is free. People pay an access provider to link them to it; service providers can charge for content if they wish to do so.

Earlier online services had some but not all of these features. Ownership of a proprietary online system was a key distinction for many of the earlier videotex services. The company or partnership of companies (in the United States, often a telephone company and an information company such as a newspaper) hoped to own a network that would dominate online services. Arguments were put forward on the basis of the "network effect" (see chapter 1) that videotex would sooner or later become a mass-market service to the home. The group controlling a national delivery network, broadly accepted by consumers and businesses, would be well placed to attract and control new service providers that would want to use the network, which they would have to do on the owners' terms. The problem with this strategy was that it sometimes led to restrictions on who could offer a service in a given area (e.g., only one bank), reducing the depth of the offer to the public (and limiting competition among service providers, which might have benefited consumers). Also, rivals were motivated to create competitive online systems, often with different standards, rather than join a consortium that could exploit synergy among service providers.

What analogies underlay the service model for online media? In the case of early online media, two common models were an electronic newspaper and an information database. Both proved too limited. Over time, the accepted model expanded to include four components: communication, games, information, and shopping. AOL and Prodigy followed this approach with some success. The model for today's Web is more like a very large mall, with a wide array of services and these four service components as anchor tenants. So where did the earlier models come from? They often emerged as legacies of service providers' core businesses. A number of early videotex trials were managed by newspapers, which naturally saw the new medium as a way to distribute existing content. The same also held true for many Web services in the transition period described earlier. The Web was perceived as offering a new way to do what they already did. Legacy issues also affected how online services in the videotex and transitional Web eras operated, as when news organizations did not want to "scoop" their print or broadcast output by first publishing a story online. Similarly, legacy print rules prevented publishers from placing an advertisements adjacent to stories relating to the products being advertised.

Research indicated very early that online users liked to read what other users thought about a story, but many news organizations restricted such feedback, viewing it as a form of letter to the editor and hence of secondary importance to articles written by reporters in printed newspapers or magazines. In these respects, start-up videotex and Web service providers had an advantage: they had no rules to break. Start-ups also had some obvious disadvantages: no established brand, no pre-existing customers, and often less funding to build the new services. A general lesson was that online services are distinct from offline counterparts and should not be treated as secondary to them.

Complexity—of pricing, user interfaces, and content design—was a negative attribute for many early online and transitional Web services. Users wanted simple, flat-rate pricing, and all but a few were unwilling to pay for content other than by a flat fee for access to a service. Multiple layers of menus hindered finding content, and complex graphics slowed down access to services. Simpler forms of content such as audiotex and ASCII videotex (without graphics) were often preferable to more sophisticated and complicated online services.

We have discussed user resistance to high prices for terminals that could access only one service and to usage-sensitive pricing for content. In such a context, when does it make sense to subsidize terminals or the cost of creating content? The French government provided more than $1 billion in subsidies to distribute free Minitel terminals to millions of French homes. Presumably, they believed it was worthwihile to jump-start private information services because of anticipated savings in the production and distribution of paper telephone directories. In the United States, AT&T subsidized some of the cost of its Sceptre videotex terminal to reduce its price to a level that users might accept (though even after the subsidy the price was perceived as too high). As discussed in chapter 1, there can be good reasons to subsidize the price of new terminals: for example, a first-year subsidy may allow a company to enter a market, bring down manufacturing costs, and make a profit in subsequent years; or, as with video games, sufficient revenue may be generated from the subsequent sale of content (games) to more than compensate for any loss on the hardware. AT&T may have believed that either or both reasons justified a subsidy.

Information providers were forced to subsidize the cost of content creation in early online and transitional Web services. In a context where consumers would not pay explicitly for content, providers had to rely on advertising revenue, which could be generated only by delivering an audience. It was hoped that subsidizing the cost of content would create an audience sufficient to generate enough advertising revenue to provide some profit after paying for content creation. Information providers struggled for years to survive on just one leg of their business model (advertising), while the other leg (subscriptions for content) was denied them.

Subsidies can be directed at various costs: those relating to terminals, content creation, the backbone network for a service, or segments of users (e.g., those in rural areas, low-income households, or groups such as senior citizens who might need help in getting started with a service). They can be provided by governments or may be funded by specific taxes or fees, by monopoly providers of other services via cross-subsidies, by individual companies through start-up funding, or as grants to particular groups of users. They do not always succeed. It is unclear, for instance, whether the French government ever recouped the cost of its subsidy of Minitel, and AT&T sold only a few thousand of its Sceptre terminals.

The early history of online services can inform our understanding of critical mass (as discussed in chapter 1). The Web enjoyed a most important advantage in its early years: it did not have to create a critical mass from the ground up. A critical mass was already in place as a result of services that had been developed by videotex groups, such as AOL and Prodigy, and because of e-mail; it was relatively easy for service providers to transfer their offerings to the Web. Most important, since communication would become the Internet's core driving force, and a critical mass of people was already communicating online, the Internet—a network of networks—enabled them to expand their reach. Such expansion attracted further users, along with more content and service providers.

Startup videotex services, which lacked such a preexisting critical mass, had to grow from the ground up. Despite its ideological opposition to "industrial policy," the U.S. government heavily subsidized ARPANET and NSFNET, sustaining them for more than 20 years. (The United States has also enacted legislation to provide very favorable tax treatment for e-commerce.) With neither such a subsidy nor a preexisting user base, early videotex services faced a significant challenge in building up to critical mass. Nevertheless, in some cases, operators appear to have discovered what was really needed to develop a critical mass (an emphasis on communication services, use of the personal computers as terminals, and so on), but the knowledge came too late: their parent companies or investors were unwilling to invest more. To use an analogy cited in chapter 2, they did not reach takeoff speed (critical mass) before they ran out of runway (funding).

By the late 1980s, a considerable amount of research showed what worked and what did not in early online services. Much of it was available in academic journals and business publications,[27] so even though the rapidly expanding field was drawing in many newcomers, there was no need to repeat earlier mistakes and every reason to take advantage of lessons already learned. Unfortunately, many people did not read the research; some thought that any knowledge from earlier online services was irrelevant in the new environment. Many mistakes were repeated and opportunities lost. Much of the learning from previous experiences was passed down through people who worked on earlier applications and later moved on to new projects.

Endnote: The Ambiguity of Failure

While it is entirely reasonable to believe that the Web would become the major force it has become without videotex's contributions to the achievement of critical mass and to an understanding of how to create content, earlier online services contributed significantly to the rapidity with which the Web has already achieved such a massive impact. Although it did not achieve commercial success, Prestel's underlying vision of an online utility, open to any service provider and delivering an enormous variety of online services to a mass market, was basically sound: it was actualized two decades later on the Web. Videotex had the misfortune to be slightly ahead of its time technologically. It was launched before the diffusion of personal computers—with, among other things, screens that were far more suitable than television sets for displaying text and keyboards that were virtually essential for entering it. It was launched before the Internet had come to provide an economical and flexible infrastructure for transmission and interconnection.

At an abstract level, electronic media are tied to the concepts underlying their uses. At a concrete level, they are tied to the technologies used both for transmission and the person-machine interface as well as to costs closely associated with technology. At the latter level, the new medium of videotex did not prove itself a success: the real, if latent, need it addressed was not an opportunity it could meet effectively and economically with technology then available or capable of being developed quickly. At the more abstract level, however, it can be regarded as a success.

// EIGHT //

The Long Road to Interactive Television

Treatments of interactive television (ITV) in the popular press could easily lead readers to think that it is an entirely new phenomenon. However, ITV (not to be confused with the British television broadcaster Independent Television, which uses the same abbreviation) has been tested in the marketplace under various guises in each decade since the 1950s and was demonstrated as early as the 1920s. The history of interactive television trials and services offers many lessons about what consumers want from ITV as well as about how to overcome technological and marketplace obstacles to its various forms.

Defining ITV

It is not clear whether the person who coined the term *interactive television* should have been awarded a medal or sentenced to a life term in prison. From a marketing perspective, it was brilliant: for most of half a century, the term has conferred a valuable cachet on whatever it has been applied to (with some exceptions) and has been applied to a very wide range of innovations that had at least some tenuous connection to either the television medium or the television set. However, it has caused and still causes endless confusion: without definition, it tends to mean whatever its users want it to mean.

What does "interacting" with television mean? The answer encompasses a broad spectrum of perspectives: mobile phone voting on who should be eliminated in a reality show; more control over and customization of television content; on-demand delivery of specific programs or movies; real-time interaction between people in different households via game playing and communication. Some observers argue that ITV must include video; others believe that interactive text displayed over a video commercial also qualifies as ITV.

One possibility is to wait and let time as well as the marketplace solve the definitional problem. Or one could use a taxonomy of key ITV characteristics, as shown in table 8.1. Different systems could then be categorized by the types of characteristics they meet.

TABLE 8.1. A Taxonomy of Key ITV Characteristics

Where does the interaction take place?	On TV, PC monitor, mobile device, or videophone only; on two screens (e.g., TV and PC monitor); or on a proprietary device
What types of media are affected by user actions?	Video, audio, text, still image, or animated graphics
Who or what does the user interact with?	Other people through the ITV system; software on a server, computer system, or game console
What is the level of customization in responses?	Each user receives unique content (e.g., game play responses); users choose from a menu that others share (e.g., menu driven news); users see results of what a group did (e.g., responses to a poll).
When are responses sent or displayed?	Live (user sees content or receives feedback immediately) or asynchronous (response is sent or displayed later, as in the results of a poll)
What is the degree of interactivity?	Low (user orders a VOD movie); medium (user searches for programs on an electronic program guide); or high (user plays an action video game)
What types of activities are offered on the ITV service?	Shopping, games, voting, chat, targeted advertising, menu-driven news and sports programs, VOD movies and video programs, interactive fiction, participation in game shows, gambling, program guide, and selectable camera angles in sports, among others

The taxonomy in table 8.1 does not deal with users' perceptions about the ITV experience. When people who have ITV are asked about their experiences, they typically do not use the word *interactive* unless it has been communicated to them in marketing materials. They are more likely to use words such as *control*, *convenience*, and *customization*.[1] The core experience of ITV is a feeling of greater control over content, more convenient access to it, and the ability to alter or customize the content in accordance with individual tastes.

Shortly we will provide a concise history of ITV, with an emphasis on developments in North America. This will be helpful in considering its future prospects—it has had a very long gestation period. The difficulty is that the history is decidedly fragmented, with many unconnected initiatives of a very wide variety of kinds. So, before embarking on the history, readers may appreciate a filter intended to help in separating the more relevant initiatives from the less relevant. The filter can be constructed using the hindsight of today.

It makes little sense to define interactive television in terms of particular technologies used to provide it because users generally are not interested in the technology itself: they care about what ITV provides and what it costs in money, time, and convenience. The user's experience should be key in deciding what ITV is and is not. Another reason for paying little attention to technology in any attempted definition is that two powerful, versatile, and affordable infrastructures have now emerged: digital transmission of television, which can be used in conjunction with set-top boxes of ever-increasing processing power and storage; and the Web, supported by the broadband-accessed Internet. With these two infrastructures, a wide variety of functions associated with ITV have become both technically feasible and increasingly commercially viable.

Central to any definition of ITV should be how it can improve the viewing of television. ITV can improve the TV experience principally in two ways, each of which should be part of a definition of ITV. First, it provides people with options for different viewing experiences. Second, it enables people to select and view content, whether old or new, that they prefer to what they would probably have watched otherwise.

Direct Change in the Viewing Experience

ITV may directly change the actual viewing experience in numerous ways.

- become part of a program by calling in to it;
- participate in polls conducted and displayed during a program; and
- affect how a program will continue. Currently, there are two rather different possibilities. One involves voting, for example, when performers' continuation in a program depends on the cumulative votes of an audience. The other involves making choices about, how, for example, a movie will continue (e.g., the hero recovers or dies) by branching seamlessly through alternative already-filmed segments that correspond to the choices offered them.
- They may be able to chat with other viewers about what they are seeing, with their remarks and others' available either on the TV screen or on a related Web site;
- compete with those on-air, other viewers, or both by taking part in quizzes or making predictions about future action in a sports event.
- They may be able to see additional information about content they are watching or have just watched. When watching Web TV, this is likely to be simply a matter of clicking a link. When watching television not transmitted via the Web, the two main possibilities today are either that, while the program continues on their screen, the information will be displayed as text on part of the screen or (as in some commercials) that viewers will be able to branch away from the program to obtain further information (video or text) about what they have just seen.

- They may be able to conduct some transaction on the television system relating to what they have just seen, e.g., by purchasing a product just advertised in a commercial or, in the United Kingdom, by betting on a contestant in a televised race. Two other possibilities should be included in this category. First with PVRs, viewers can watch television programs with minimal interruption from advertisements by fast-forwarding through them; they can do the same with program segments they regard as boring. The second possibility is the opposite: they can create their own instant replays.

Viewers who do not choose to interact in some of the foregoing ways may be affected by the fact either that they could participate or that that others are doing so.

A Better Choice of Content

ITV can enable people to select and view television content with greater appeal to them in two ways:

- by offering them the opportunity to make more informed viewing choices, primarily through the electronic program guide (EPG) (see chapter 5);
- by offering greater choice of content, most obviously through VOD but also via less ambitious means such as making choices within a program (e.g., camera angles in sports events or segments of a news program) and via recording programs automatically when they are transmitted, for watching at any later time.

What Is Not ITV

From today's perspective, some services probably should not be regarded as interactive television, even though that term was applied to them in the past. In today's context, we would exclude simple video telephony (not video chat over a portion of a TV program) because it typically is a communication exchange with no relationship to TV programming, video services, or other content. We would also exclude technologies in which television is used to deliver services that inherently differ from television as it has generally been known, such as e-mail and electronic banking. Videotex is dead, and the British teletext service is not long for this world (it will be withdrawn in the run-up to the all-digital broadcasting of television in 2012), and we now would consider neither an example of ITV. Television transmission systems can also be used for downloading content to other terminal devices in the home. We would suggest that downloading, in itself, not be regarded as an example of interactive television when what is downloaded is neither television programming nor something to complement television programming on the screen.

These exclusions pose some problems. What about e-mail including video clips? (We would probably categorize them as video e-mail, not as ITV.) Are there murky outliers that could go either way—for example, some forms of video games? Of course. We seek to provide a filter that brings some clarity to an assessment of ITV, not a rigid definition.

There will also be two examples in the following sections in which technology enables viewers, in this case younger children, to experience what they perceive as real-time interaction with what is on television, even though the interaction is an illusion. We would categorize it as ITV because it changes the viewing experience.

In the history of ITV that follows, we include examples of some services that we excluded in our modern definition because at the time they were offered and for many years afterward most industry analysts and scholars regarded them as ITV.

A Concise History of Interactive Television

Early Demonstrations

The first demonstration of what has been broadly viewed as interactive television took place on April 7, 1927. AT&T, which was active in developing both radio and television, created a video link between Washington, D.C., and New York. It was a form of video telephone call with video in one direction (Washington to New York) and two-way audio. Secretary of commerce Herbert Hoover and other Washington dignitaries spoke to AT&T president Walter Gifford in New York. The demonstration conveyed the impression that television would be an extension of the telephone. At one point, Hoover's wife, Lou, commented over the video link, "I don't know if this is a good invention or not. There are times when I talk over the phone and wouldn't want anyone to see how I look."[2] This prescient remark anticipated research findings decades afterward. A few years later, AT&T's Bell Laboratories set up video telephone booths between AT&T buildings in New York and New Jersey to explore further two-way television conversations.[3] At about the same time, the German PTT created a service that linked videophone booths at post office facilities in different cities (see chapter 6). The U.S. pharmacy industry borrowed the concept, demonstrating it with a "Pharmacy of the Future" exhibit at the 1939 New York World's Fair that included a two-way television phone booth. During the 1930s, telephone booths in local drugstores provided a vital communication resource for people who lacked telephones at home, and proponents envisioned that service evolving to include two-way television booths.[4]

Early movies also reflected the vision of interactive television. A 1933 film, *International House*, depicts a Chinese scientist who attempts to find backers for a new invention—television. The movie shows Rudy Vallee and other stars able to see, hear, and respond to people watching them perform on TV.

The fact that a number of early demonstrations of television envisaged two-way service for communication while others believed television would be a one-way service for entertainment and information demonstrates again a lesson of chapter 1: when a medium is new, developers are often unsure of how it will be used or have very different visions of its uses.

1950s

The CBS children's series *Winky Dink and You* (1953–57) created a simple but clever form of ITV. Viewers purchased a basic "Winky Dink Kit" for 50 cents (or a deluxe version for $2.95); it contained a special plastic sheet that was attached to the TV screen by friction and special crayons for writing on the plastic. In each episode of the cartoon, Winky Dink would encounter a problem, such as being chased by a tiger to the edge of a cliff. Children were asked to help Winky Dink by using their special crayons—for example, to draw a bridge on the plastic screen so that he could escape from the tiger. The host, Jack Barry, helped children line up their drawings in the correct spot on the screen by placing his finger on a glass plate in front of the camera and directing children to draw by following his finger. While the technology was crude, children experienced a form of interaction with television content and saw on-screen actions that appeared to respond to their drawings. However, some children did not purchase the plastic sheet and simply drew directly on the glass TV screen. Winky Dink was the first in a long series of ITV applications that was short-lived.

1960s and 1970s

At the 1964 World's Fair, held in New York, AT&T demonstrated a videophone intended for homes, offices, and other locations. Over the next decade, the videophone was tested in a number of market trials and some limited services, but with little success (see chapter 6).

The 1970s saw numerous ITV trials and tests. The U.S. National Science Foundation (NSF) sponsored three major trials utilizing interactive cable televi-

BCTV

Berks Community Television (BCTV) was launched in 1976. It was funded initially by the National Science Foundation and implemented by a consortium of groups from New York University and Reading, Pennsylvania. The project sought to use interactive television to improve senior citizens' understanding and use of public services.[1] It was also hoped that ITV would help senior citizens become more involved in community and political processes. The initial service linked three community communication centers, primarily through talk back and forth across the centers. The system developed the convention of showing speakers from different centers on a split screen, and the resulting programming was transmitted over the local cable system. People at home could participate by calling into a program via a regular telephone and could be heard but not seen.

BCTV is the only ITV service from the 1970s that continues to this day. It survived for a few reasons. First, it was treated more as a social innovation than a technological one. A great deal of effort was made to have multiple community organizations buy into the new service. The equipment used was off-the-shelf, low cost, and could be handled by people with little or no training in television. The programming consciously stayed away from the conventions of commercial television, so it was not likely to suffer from comparison to network television production values. Though it was funded initially to provide information for senior citizens, it quickly added entertainment programs to the mix such as *Singalong,* a very popular program in which people gathered at the different centers sang favorite songs together.

The three original sites were expanded to more than a dozen and incorporated many other groups, including high school and college students, hospitals, and government agencies. Additional groups also helped to provide funding after the initial grant ended. Over time, BCTV evolved into a broad-based community channel. It has continued to use the split-screen ITV format, but its identity is grounded in BCTV's community services and local entertainment, not in interactive television as such.

1. Mitchell Moss, "Reading, Pa: Research on Community Uses," *Journal of Communication* 28, no. 2 (1978): 160–67.

sion for education, community services, and worker training;[5] the U.S. Department of Health, Education, and Welfare supported several tests of ITV for health care;[6] and a large commercial test of interactive cable TV (Warner Amex's Qube system in Columbus, Ohio) received considerable attention.[7]

Qube

Qube was launched in Columbus, Ohio, at the end of 1977 by Warner Amex Cable. Greeted as a television breakthrough, it faced many obstacles. The first was the very expensive cost of its technology. The Qube terminal in homes cost approximately $200—more than four times as much as a regular cable box—and Qube equipment at the cable headend added $2–3 million in plant costs. Also some of the equipment had reliability problems.

Second, interactive program design presented challenges. There was little prior experience on which to draw, and Qube programs had much lower programming budgets than did broadcast programming. Interactivity with low production values could not compete with network programming. Moreover, the technology itself had limitations. All the interaction was based on five extra buttons on the Qube remote control with which viewers responded to choices on the screen. The producers cleverly stretched the limits of the technology. For example, viewers of educational programs could press a specified button to indicate that they did not understand a point.

About three-quarters of cable households in Columbus subscribed to Qube after a few years, but actual use of Qube programming was generally low, with a few exceptions.[1] Some game format programs achieved strong interactive participation.[2] Further, major events attracted large audience participation—e.g., when Qube subscribers were permitted to choose the next play in a live semi-pro football game between the Columbus Metros and the Racine Gladiators.

Cost of the technology and low production values were not the only challenges. Qube had served as a powerful tool for Warner Amex during the franchising wars of the 1980s. Warner Amex showcased Qube as a major technological advance that would be built into the cable system if Warner Amex was awarded a franchise. The strategy helped Warner Amex win franchises in Cincinnati, Dallas, Houston, and Pittsburgh, among other cities. After the franchising battles for major cities ended, the marketing value of Qube for Warner Amex was sharply reduced, and the service was slowly withdrawn.

Qube's principal lesson is not that interactive media cannot compete with traditional one-way mass media. Rather, interactive media must be developed in a viable economic and technical context. Even with these elements in place, producers must learn to create with the new medium, and audiences should not be expected to change their media habits overnight.

---

1. Lee Becker, "A Decade of Research on Interactive Television," in William Dutton, Jay Blumler, and Kenneth Kraemer, eds., *Wired Cities: Shaping the Future of Communications* (Boston: G. K. Hall, 1987), 102–23.

2. Carol Davidge, "America's Talk-Back Television Experiment: Qube," in William Dutton, Jay Blumler, and Kenneth Kraemer, eds., *Wired Cities: Shaping the Future of Communications* (Boston: G. K. Hall, 1987), 75–101.

A number of the NSF and Health, Education, and Welfare projects provide useful lessons. These early tests endured many technical problems. Equipment was often in a prototype stage of development and therefore unreliable. In addition, it was generally expensive, and many user groups could not afford to continue their projects after federal support ran out. Most important, these projects provide a strong reminder that technological innovations are also social innovations. They require significant organizational changes and can meet resistance from entrenched or harried workers (see chapter 3). Nonetheless, some services emerged as success stories—e.g., one NSF-sponsored project in Reading, Pennsylvania, that began in the mid-1970s utilized two-way cable to create programming for and by senior citizens. It was broadly accepted in the community and expanded to include students and a wider group of social service organizations.

Warner Amex's Qube system received a great deal of press attention during this period. It encountered a number of obstacles but was also a showcase of what was possible and served as an important source of learning about a different form of ITV. Qube demonstrated that pay-per-view programming could be viable if the cost of promoting and processing orders could be reduced and if robust content was offered. In fact, Qube led to the development a few years later of a successful pay-per-view service, Viewer's Choice. And Qube introduced a number of interactive formats that have since evolved and been adopted as components of cable and broadcast programming. Two popular U.S. cable services, MTV and Nickelodeon, developed from models that originated in Qube programming (*Video Jukebox* and *Pinwheel*, respectively). In this sense, Qube was an important programming laboratory.

1980s

During the 1980s, U.S. companies and public service organizations launched a large number and wide variety of interactive television services—interactive games over cable, toys that interacted with TV content, and opinion polling during regular TV programs via special 900-number telephone services.

During the early and middle part of the decade, two cable and one broadcast service added new twists to ITV. Launched in 1981, PlayCable, a joint venture of Mattel and General Instruments, offered interactive games downloaded over a cable system to an Intellivision game player and displayed them on a TV set. Subscribers paid $10 to $15 to play up to 20 titles available each month. After two years, the system had approximately 5,000 users, who liked the system, but the high cost of the game player and demands on the bandwidth of the cable system were strong obstacles, and the system was shut down in 1983.[8]

Nabu was launched in the mid-1980s on an Alexandria, Virginia, cable system. It downloaded games and some information services to a special Nabu computer that people rented from the cable company (few people owned a computer during this time period). Arcade-style games displayed on a TV set connected to the computer were the major attraction. Nabu had a promising start, gaining a 5 percent penetration of homes on the cable system within six months, but its Canadian backers pulled out, and the service shut down.[9]

TV Answer was one of the few interactive *broadcast* TV services. The return signal from homes utilized a broadcast radio signal. It worked somewhat like Qube. People used a special remote control and responded to multiple-choice options on the screen, whether answering a polling question or placing a shopping order. By pressing a button on the remote, the unit sent a response back to the cable headend or broadcast station via a radio signal. TV Answer (subsequently called EON) was tested in Fairfax, Virginia, and later received dedicated radio spectrum from the Federal Communications Commission. However, the group of developers from Mexico could not overcome a chicken-and-egg problem. The ITV unit had little value to consumers unless there was a lot of content on programs that used the service; the service had little value to television programmers and advertisers unless a large share of homes had the device. TV Answer struggled for a few years before being discontinued.[10]

Near the end of the decade, trials of interactive TV expanded further in scope. Telaction, developed by J. C. Penney, offered viewers in the greater Chicago area interactive shopping over cable. Viewers used touch-tone telephones to control video still frames and audio transmitted over the cable system. Consumers could choose from 29 stores and then select and order products. Grocery shopping was the most popular. Although only a limited number of people could use the service at any given time, its main problem was the cost of developing and maintaining the service. It was shut down in less than two years.

Captain Power, developed by Mattel, was a 1987–88 children's television program with both live action and computer animation. Viewers could purchase a toy—the Power Jet gun ($35)—that interacted with content in the program. Each show had several interactive sequences in which the viewer could shoot at or be shot by characters in the program. However, there was very little interaction. The video did not change based on the user's actions, though the toy gun reacted to the video and registered the user's score. The game did not catch on with the public and was withdrawn.

NTN Entertainment Network, launched in 1984, took interactive television in a new direction and achieved success. It provided interactive games and trivia contests in public locations such as bars and hotels. Users could compete with people locally or at other locations nationwide. Early NTN programs included *Showdown*, a 90-minute trivia game, and *Power Play*, an interactive hockey game.

It became popular especially in sports bars and spread to more than 12,000 TV screens in public locations by the mid-2000s. In 2005, the company changed its name to NTN Buzztime. Why did it succeed? NTN's strategy of targeting public locations was wise, especially in the 1980s. Further, it offered a complete solution—hardware, network, and content—at a low cost since it was supported by advertising.

During the same period, some very simple interactive television services quietly emerged in education, offered by such groups as the Satellite Educational Resources Consortium, the Public Broadcasting Service, National Technology University, and several state education networks. In some instances, the ITV services utilized full two-way video between teachers and students who were at a distance. However, in most cases, these services utilized one-way video instruction via satellite, cable, or Instructional Television Fixed Service, a microwave frequency, with return audio via a regular telephone call. The interaction was simple: students could ask questions of teachers at different locations, or teachers could ask if students at any location needed further examples to explain the topic. Later, electronic mail, fax, and dedicated data terminals were added as return paths to the instructor and used for polling students, giving exams, and distributing sets of notes. These services reached thousands of primary, secondary, and university students, typically providing courses that would not otherwise have been available in rural areas or small school districts (e.g., advanced mathematics or foreign languages such as Russian or Japanese). The service providers and networks have evolved over time but continue to offer interactive television education services throughout the United States.

Many television news organizations adopted use of an ordinary telephone as the return path for interactivity in regular programming during the latter part of the decade. AT&T established a service in which households could call a special telephone number mentioned during a TV program and use touch-tone keypads to register opinions. Tabulated votes could be displayed at the end of the program or the next day. Users were charged a fee (typically, 75 cents). The system could handle millions of calls and was adopted by many stations and networks.[11]

In Europe and Japan, there were a number of interactive television projects during the 1980s, among them Hi Ovis in Japan[12] and the Biarritz project in France.[13] Both started in the late 1970s and continued through the mid-1980s, using fiber-optic cable to provide videophone calls, interactive text services, better TV reception, and extra cable channels, including movies. The services' primary appeal was improved TV reception and extra cable channels; the videophones and other interactive services received low usage—only 10 percent of households used the videophone to connect to other people or participate in programming in the Hi Ovis project.[14] However, in both cases, much more effort and financial resources went into the development of the technology than in creating interactive programs. The projects were highly visible showcases for advanced technologies that each country was developing, but consumers received little original interactive programming.

During the 1980s there was also a significant growth in the telecommunications infrastructure that could support interactive TV applications as well as increased penetration in businesses, homes, schools, and libraries by a broad array of media that offered limited forms of interaction or greater control over media. The marketplace acceptance of these technologies was complex and dramatic: extraordinary successes (VCRs), extraordinary failures (interactive videodiscs for the consumer market during the 1980s), and a few technologies that had waves of success and decline during the 1980s (for example, console video games). One of the lessons offered by this marketplace history is that the interactive media industries are as volatile as the entertainment and toy businesses. Nonetheless, the overall trend was toward the creation of an environment in which more interactive TV applications could be developed. Further, the adoption and use of these technologies fostered an appetite for interactivity and greater consumer control of media experiences.

The most important of the support technologies entering homes and businesses was undoubtedly the personal computer, which can serve as a terminal for many present and future interactive services. In addition, a very large share of the public gained experience in using interactive media and machines that require interactive responses. Personal computers, automated teller machines, VCR remote control keypads, microwave ovens, information kiosks at airports, and other devices in the home and workplace taught many people important basic skills in using interactive technology.

This infrastructure buildup and the development of greater interactive skills by the general public prepared the way for the 1990s and more ambitious attempts to develop interactive television services.

1990s

The number of interactive television trials and services expanded in the early 1990s. AT&T and Bell Atlantic conducted interactive television trials with groups of employees (AT&T in Chicago and Bell Atlantic in a Virginia suburb of Washington, D.C.). These trials sought to provide experience in operating ITV networks and to learn about the attractiveness of services. Both indicated that reactions to the services were positive, while acknowledging that these had been only preliminary steps intended to lead to larger trials in the future.[15]

RCTV

During 1992–93, AT&T conducted a ten-month trial of ITV in Chicago with 50 households of AT&T employees to learn about the technical requirements of building and maintaining an interactive TV network as well as to test consumer reactions to ITV services.[1] The service, called RCTV (Remote Control Television), included interactive news, weather, sports, shopping, games, music, children's content, and communication services. The research about the trial indicated that the service was used most heavily by people who watched a lot of TV, not computer technophiles. Overall, it achieved a share of viewing time equal to that of a premium movie channel such as HBO. The most heavily used services included shopping (more than half of all households made purchases), games, and sports. In general, competitive activities and content-related communications were very popular.

The trial did not reveal a killer application for ITV. Rather, the trial team, led by Vincent Grosso, identified four key attributes of ITV—communication, transactions, gaming, and information. Adding one of these attributes to a service that lacked it increased usage. For example, when a game element was added to shopping or communication was added to an information service such as news, usage increased.[2] Further, personalities were just as important in ITV as regular TV programs. They also learned that people did not alter their TV behavior or attitudes about TV significantly just because they had interactive television. They sat in the same chairs or couches, at the same distance from the set, and expected ITV to serve the same functions as regular TV—primarily entertainment.

1. Gali Einav, "'I Want My iTV': Content, Demand, and Social Implications of Interactive Television" (PhD diss., Columbia University, 2004).

2. Vincent Grosso, "AT&T's Experiences with Interactive Television" (presentation at the Twenty-Third Annual Telecommunication Policy Research Conference, Washington, DC, October 1, 1995).

In Cerritos, California, GTE conducted another ITV trial beginning in the early 1990s. Its test service, Main Street, consisted of still video images and sound organized as a database with little updating. Services included access to the Mobil Travel Guide, Grolier's Encyclopedia, Money Manager software, and other content that changed little from day to day. Overall usage of Main Street was reported to have been low.[16] Nonetheless, the project generated some useful research findings. GTE found that movies-on-demand were attractive, but consumers were willing to pay only a small increment ($1 extra) more than they paid to rent movies at bricks-and-mortar shops. Further, consumers balked at paying hundreds of dollars for an ITV set-top box and indicated that they would prefer to pay a small rental fee as part of the cable bill.[17]

A number of other groups interested in ITV focused their attention on video-on-demand (VOD). TCI, AT&T, and U S West conducted a trial of movies-on-demand in Denver; Bell Atlantic conducted a similar trial in Northern Virginia. Both had similar results. Test homes purchased 2.5 to 3.3 movies per month, much more than the national average of 0.26 for pay-per-view homes at that time. However, some homes dropped pay services such as HBO to pay for the movies-on-demand.[18] It appears that these households did not increase their entertainment spending for interactive services but rather moved spending from one category of the household's entertainment budget to another.[19] At the same time, the cost of providing VOD (i.e., servers, set-top boxes, and digitizing content) was very high, so neither service moved from trial to full market rollout.

Two interactive television services—Interactive Network (in California and Illinois) and Videoway (in Montreal and Quebec City, Canada)—introduced into the marketplace early in the decade—provided different types of ITV services but ultimately experienced the same outcome. Interactive Network required a special terminal costing a few hundred dollars. It also had a monthly charge of $15 (higher if the subscriber opted for a tier that had prizes), and the interaction took place not on the TV screen but on a small display attached to the terminal. Services consisted of playing along with TV game shows and trying to anticipate the next play in sporting events. It utilized a multiple-choice format, and there was no original content. The number of subscribers was modest, but they were reportedly quite enthusiastic. Interactive Network struggled to increase its market reach and subscriber base. The death knell for the service came not from subscribers but marketing agreements that brought onboard new company overseers who decided to pull the plug rather than support new marketing efforts.[20]

Videoway had no hardware costs for the consumer and a low monthly fee (under $10). Interaction took place on the TV screen, and the service featured extensive original content, including daily interactive news programming, games, interactive ads, and original programming for children. Examples of programming included exercise shows where the viewer could pick the level of difficulty; interactive *Jeopardy*, where viewers competed with contestants on the show; and interactive poker. The service utilized four channels on the cable system. Much of the interaction took place by switching from one channel to another, where different program components were located. For example, Videoway allowed users to choose from four camera angles during coverage of sporting events, with each camera located on a different channel. The service developed a subscriber base of more than 230,000 households, more than 20 percent of the cable households in the markets where Videoway was available, and subscribing households used the service for an average of 13 hours per week, with that time divided roughly evenly between games and interactive programming.[21]

The fact that it required four channels on an analog cable system proved a significant limitation for Videoway. From a business perspective, the cable operator had to weigh the revenue from one interactive service against the potential revenue from four separate channels. In the spring of 1996, the cable operator decided to scale Videoway back to one channel and eliminate the interactive video components. Some interactive text services were retained although these were reduced in number. The Videoway service was also implemented in the United Kingdom. A similar service developed by ACTV was tested in California during the mid-1990s. This form of ITV paved the way for a set of services that would emerge later in digital cable and satellite systems both in the Europe and the United States, when more bandwidth and better compression techniques were available.

These experiences with interactive television collectively indicated that the price of interactive television was important and that users appeared reluctant to pay for expensive terminals. Movies-on-demand, games, children's services,

ITV ON THE CHEAP

Not all ITV trials and services were expensive. A number of groups experimented with low-end ways to create interactive television. In Minneapolis–St. Paul, CBS affiliate WCCO-TV leased time on an independent channel during news broadcasts. The station then transmitted two versions of the news—for example, one with more sports and the other with more local news, or simply changed the order of the stories. Each channel informed viewers what was on the other station, and they could switch back and forth.[1]

A graduate student at New York University, Dan Sullivan, created *Dan's Apartment*, an interactive television show for Manhattan Cable. He videotaped a tour of his apartment and put it on a videodisc at the cable head end. One viewer at a time could call in and use the telephone keypad to control the videodisc and move about the apartment. The show attracted a small cult following. The experiment seemed avant-garde at the time but has since been imitated on a digital cable system that can accommodate a large number of simultaneous users who tour not Dan's apartment but vacation resorts or houses and see properties before deciding to purchase them or make reservations.[2]

1. Andy Meisler, "Custom Made Newscasts for Minnesota Viewers," *New York Times*, January 16, 1995, D6.
2. Georgia Dullea, "For Apartment Voyeurs, Rated G," *New York Times*, March 28, 1991, C1.

and original interactive content were among the most attractive services for users.

A large number of interactive television trials were announced for both cable and telephone environments between 1994 and 1996. These involved a broad range of cable, telephone, and computer companies and many different strategies for delivering services. A half dozen interactive cable TV trials were announced, including AT&T and Viacom in Castro Valley, California; Southwestern Bell and Cox Enterprises in Omaha, Nebraska; IBM, Videotron, and Hearst in Quebec, Canada; and Time Warner in Orlando, Florida. With the exception of the Time Warner service, all of these trials were either cut back sharply from their original plans, delayed, or canceled. At the same time, more than 30 major tests of interactive television in a telephone environment (both DSL and broadband fiber) were announced, including efforts by Ameritech in Chicago and Milwaukee; Bell Atlantic in New Jersey; Bell South in North Carolina; GTE in Virginia; U S West in Omaha; and SNET in Connecticut. The term *video dial tone* emerged to indicate that users would access the associated services by essentially dialing them up. As with the cable trials, all of these telephone company trials were either cut back sharply or canceled.

What led to such grand plans and their subsequent abandonment? Many groups apparently found themselves caught up in the frenzy of trying to corner the ITV market. They did not carefully examine cost issues. The set-top boxes for the trials were very expensive, ranging between $2,000 and $5,000, leading to high per-household costs to develop the necessary infrastructure.[22] Costs for original interactive content were equally high, and none of that content existed. Further, even these very high end systems had limitations. For example, there was latency in calling up some services or responding interactively. This meant that fast-action video games were difficult to implement.

Time Warner stood alone in offering a high-end interactive TV service with shopping, news, banking, and games as well as VOD movies in its Full Service Network trial in Orlando, which lasted from late 1994 to the end of 1997. Press accounts have described this trial as a big disappointment or failure, likely because of the high expectations set early on. Although the trial did not grow into a national service, it was successfully implemented in a few thousand homes and served as a rich learning laboratory about ITV.

Research from the trial indicated that movies-on-demand was the most popular service. In addition, the Full Service Network provided news and sports clips from a menu, replays of news programming on demand, interactive video games among households, an interactive TV guide, home shopping (e.g., ordering pizzas through the TV), and Web-like services such as home banking and classified ads. The interactive news programming, "The News Exchange," was especially interesting. Ten percent of trial homes paid an extra $1.95 or $3.95 per month to receive it. The service offered approximately 100 newscasts, news clips, and full-length news programs on demand, with the content created by a staff of producers and reporters. Further, as with movies-on-demand, consumers could fast-forward, rewind, and pause the on-demand news programming. Viewers also took to doing replays of news events and repeatedly watching news highlights prepared for them, such as key plays in local college football games.[23] However, the high costs associated with production of these segments led the Full Service Network to cut back on original content even before the trial ended. High costs were also associated with the servers and other infrastructure at the cable system as well as advanced cable boxes for homes.[24] The general consensus about the trial, including the assessment of Time Warner management, was that the Full Service Network was ahead of its time and would not be commercially viable on a large scale for some years. However, Time Warner used the trial to plan for the future, including its broadband Web services and a subsequent movie-on-demand service on its digital cable systems.

By the late 1990s, a more realistic picture emerged, and a new evolutionary strategy was born. Both cable and telephone companies developed simpler services with less costly technology and waited for the necessary infrastructure upgrading to take place. This process occurred either through the natural process of replacing old equipment or through an accelerated process financed by the demand for other services, such as high-speed data applications and eventually telephone service over cable.

In the cable environment, many companies decided to offer high-speed Internet services through cable modems and evolve over time to interactive video—e.g., At Home, a service offered by a consortium of cable operators. Some cable companies began to offer interactive program guides and other niche interactive services, such as interactive text accompanying regular TV programs (e.g., Wink Communications), time-shift viewing of TV programs (e.g., Your Choice TV), and still video images with sound (e.g., the Interactive Channel).

Wink Communications conducted a trial with NBC in which text and graphical information were inserted in the TV signal (a form of teletext). The information could be accessed by pressing a special key on the remote control and appeared over video programming. The information included plot summaries, trivia quizzes, and sports scores. Wink gave rise to a new term, *enhanced TV*, as an alternative to *interactive TV*. Wink enhanced regular content with extra information.

Your Choice TV (YCTV) was created by Discovery Communications and was test-marketed in several cities from 1994 to 1998. It provided VOD television programs for 99 cents. The programs were available a few hours to a few days after the program first aired. Approximately 20 to 30 programs were available each day from networks and cable channels such as ABC, Discovery, HBO, and PBS. Research indicated that the concept was appealing, but YCTV struggled to get additional program suppliers to come onboard. Viewers wanted not just ABC but all the major networks, not just one soap opera but all of them. In addition, digitizing programs was expensive at that time. In some ways, YCTV was a precursor to digital video recorders such as Tivo and Web video aggregators such as YouTube and Hulu, which developed different solutions to time-shift viewing.

In the late 1990s, the Web entered the interactive TV environment in a few ways. Some television producers experimented with creating Web content that would accompany or interact with the TV show; other programs let viewers create content on the Web to be inserted in the TV show. MTV was very active with both of these forms of interactive TV. One successful quiz program, *Web Riot*, allowed viewers to compete online with thc contestants on the show and win prizes. Another program, *Yack Live*, had viewers go to an AOL chat room where they could comment about the music video that was playing. The comments were inserted live over a portion of the screen as the video played. Unfortunately, many of the comments were inane or off-color, and the show was soon canceled. The term *two-screen TV* came to describe simultaneous use of the Web and a related TV program (this form of interaction grew exponentially when social networking sites became popular a decade later).

During this period, a number of hardware and software companies, among them Microsoft, Sony, and Philips, backed WebTV, a product that offered the Internet on television. The service was marketed to homes that lacked personal computers but had TVs. By the late 1990s, WebTV found a moderate market of approximately one million households, many of which were older adults who liked to exchange e-mails with their children and grandchildren. Microsoft later purchased WebTV and continued the service under the name MSN TV.

In Europe, many companies watched the withdrawal of high-end interactive television trials in the United States during the 1990s and moved to implement more cost-effective ITV trials, principally offering VOD. In 1995–96, British Telecommunications conducted a 2,000-home trial with movies-on-demand, home shopping, electronic banking, and games in Ipswich and Colchester. The results were sufficiently positive that the company moved forward with an ITV service in London, using British Telecom's Westminster cable company.[25] However, officials ultimately concluded that the cost of VOD was too high and withdrew. ITV trials were also conducted in Sweden by Telia AB and in Italy by Telecom Italia and Stet.

In Germany, Deutsche Telekom AG pulled back from its plan for a 4,000-home ITV trial and replaced it with a smaller test of 50 homes in Berlin followed by a modest trial in Stuttgart. The trial in Berlin offered VOD movies, children's programs, and other entertainment programming along with teleshopping and tele-learning services. It was largely a demonstration project to understand how well the technology performed and what services could be provided.[26] France Telecom, which conducted an ITV trial in Biarritz during the 1980s, adopted a conservative wait-and-see attitude but conducted a 200-home ITV trial in Paris. Many of the European telephone company trials also focused on comparing digital telephone networks and cable as the preferred way to deliver ITV.

Between 1993 and 1997, the technology that was used in the Videoway service in Canada was imported to the United Kingdom and tested with a cable operator, Videotron. The applications closely resembled those in Canada. For example, two commercial broadcasters, Carlton Television and London Weekend Television, created an interactive London news channel with four strands of news programming. Viewers could switch back and forth to choose which segments they wanted to see. Reactions to the service were positive, and it attracted many subscribers, but it experienced the same fate as Videoway because it required so much bandwidth.

By the late 1990s, British satellite operator BSkyB had launched a digital satellite service and began to test ITV. The first project, Open, presented a limited text service. It was not considered a success but paved the way for a wider range of ITV applications in the years ahead.

The ITV activities in Europe during the 1990s were modest in scope and paralleled the evolving efforts by cable and telephone companies in the United States. During the second half of the decade, companies on both sides of the Atlantic exploited the existing telecommunications infrastructure, with modest upgrades, and supported VOD or other forms of ITV that did not require very expensive home terminals or major network overhauls.

2000 and Beyond

By the early 2000s, ITV's prospects appeared to be improving. The cost of set-top boxes and of digitizing analog video had declined significantly. People were getting used to interacting with content through their experiences on the Web, and many new options were available for creating ITV applications such as broadband and PVRs. However, the contexts for developing ITV differed substantially in the United States and Europe.

In the United States, the weak response to ITV trials in the 1990s cast a pall over new high-end ITV applications. Attention shifted from ITV to the Web as the place of opportunity, especially since the penetration of personal computers was high. Consumers initially showed little interest in TV over the Web, but this would change over time. Web development at this time emphasized information, transactions, and advertising.

The atmosphere for interactive television was so negative that most of the groups developing ITV applications dropped the term *interactive television* and instead used terms for specific applications, such as electronic program guides or video-on-demand. ITV applications emerged but as an adjunct of the drive to build digital television systems. The development of ITV services in the United States became driven by competition between cable and satellite operators (and later telephone companies as they returned to the television arena).

In Europe, especially in the United Kingdom, which led the world in the development of ITV, the history and context were quite different from the United States. Far fewer ITV trials had occurred in Europe in the preceding decade, and even though they were no more successful than in the United States, attitudes about ITV were less negative. Many European countries lagged the United States in adopting the Web, so developing Web businesses had less appeal. Europeans also evidenced pent-up demand for more television channels, and private investors stood ready to develop digital satellite services to meet this demand and, in turn, provide a platform for the development of new ITV services.

In the United Kingdom, people had experience with a limited form of enhanced television through teletext, which taught them simple skills about how to interact with television and may have created an appetite for more advanced services. Further, government policies supported the development of ITV applications. The government mandated that 20 percent of the content for a new channel, BBC Three, should be interactive, and TV license fees collected by the government helped fund development of new ITV applications. Competition also spurred the development of ITV. The launch of BSkyB's all-digital satellite service in 1998 prompted cable operators and terrestrial broadcasters to develop advanced services to compete with satellite. Competition led to new ITV services and helped to bring prices down.[27]

By 2000, U.S. satellite television services were completely digital; cable had recently begun a conversion to digital; and some terrestrial broadcasters had begun to transmit digital signals. Also, PVRs had just entered the market, bringing further possibilities for ITV. Little interest in interactive television as such existed; however, with the proliferation of high-capacity digital cable and satellite systems, people faced the challenge of finding programs on systems with more than 200 channels. Interactive EPGs provided a useful tool and within a few years became ubiquitous—and popular—on digital cable and satellite systems. EPGs became an anchor for ITV, though no one except a few people in the industry called them *interactive television*. Video-on-demand became a second anchor service for ITV. VOD was driven by the prospect of additional revenue and by the interests of cable operators who wanted to use VOD to compete with satellite television, which could not offer VOD. The service's popularity at first remained low as a consequence of weak movie offerings and some technical mishaps, but it became a core part of digital cable. Large cable operators such as Comcast, Time Warner, and Cablevision emphasized VOD in their marketing, including paid content such as movies and later free VOD content such as TV programs. An important side effect of EPGs and VOD was a reduction in subscriber churn (the percentage of people who drop a service), which helped secure the future of these services.

A third area of ITV activity since 2000 has been "enhanced" information services, which come in two flavors. One is teletext-like services in which viewers can obtain extra information in the form of text and graphics displayed over the TV picture. The other is extra video information that can be retrieved by selecting an icon on the TV picture or from a menu. The extra video is then provided through VOD or on another channel. Both forms of enhanced information, sometimes called widgets, are used in advertising. In the former case, a window pops up with extra information, such as where to purchase the advertised product locally; in the latter case, clicking on an icon during a 30-second commercial might switch the person to a 10-minute infomercial about the product.

Interactive shopping over digital cable and satellite systems, sometimes called T-commerce, grew slowly in the early 2000s. A number of groups developed technologies that allowed viewers to click on, for example, a sweater worn by a star in a TV program or a football jersey during a televised game and order these items immediately, but consumers showed little interest in interrupting their viewing experience. Although pizza could now be ordered over some digital cable systems (the Holy Grail for some earlier ITV aficionados), the bulk of interactive shopping took place on the Web or on traditional home shopping networks, with people calling an 800 number to place an order.

Web-based ITV grew slowly in the United States from 2000 to 2005, then began to flourish. It has taken a few forms, including downloading or streaming segments from TV programs, entire programs, extra scenes not included in the show, or original made-for-the-Web videos-on-demand. Examples include watching a segment from *NBC News*, an original Web video advertisement from BMW, or a full episode of *Lost*. In some cases—for example, programs on a cable network for children such as Nick Jr.—viewers have been able to download shows before they air on the network. Web viewers can then tell others about the show, increasing the audience when it airs. Viewing TV shows on the Web and viral communication by those viewers to others who will watch on regular TV increase the ratings of the show. The viral communication can be in person or through texts, IMs, and posts on social networking sites.

The Web has also been used to vote about content on TV. Examples have included voting on the dress a bride will wear on an upcoming *Today Show* special and voting on who should advance in amateur talent contests such as CBS's *Star Search* (another instance of two-screen TV). ITV applications for the Web also include choosing endings for TV programs. *Law and Order CI*, for example, let viewers decide if a villain would be killed or live in a future episode. Viewers at the show's Web site could also see both endings. There has been much debate about the appeal of interactive fiction, where the votes of viewers can change an ending or events within the program. Many demonstrations of interactive ITV fiction have taken place, but few applications have been adopted permanently. (It has been tried in online text as well, as in a British videotex service for children in the 1980s, but had limited appeal.) Some observers argue that fiction is a story told by a storyteller to audiences and that people do not want to change the content; others believe that interactive fiction has been widely adopted in the form of video games, which are a form of fiction with plots and many choices as the story unfolds.

From 2000 onward, Web shopping emerged as a multi-billion-dollar business. The shopping information on Web sites initially was primarily text, with graphics later becoming standard, and video eventually added on many shopping sites (e.g., viewers could control a video demonstration of a new car). In this sense, ITV shopping in the United States emerged sooner on the Web than on digital cable or satellite systems.

Another ITV application that has expanded in the United States is telephone voting on a topic posed in a news segment or on the elimination of a contestant on a reality program. This service includes touch-tone votes from wired or mobile telephones as well as the use of text messaging (SMS) from mobile phones. Some two-way cable systems also support remote-control voting. The final 2005 episode of *American Idol* generated more than 25 million phone and SMS votes.

The PVR supported a few ITV applications by the middle of the decade. In addition to their core features of enabling time-shift viewing and providing greater control over television programs, PVRs have been used to download some shows from the Web and to download visuals that appear over television commercials whenever a person uses fast forward to move to the next program segment. By the end of the decade, many services emerged to allow viewers to transfer Web video content on demand to TV sets.

Two services that were tested and failed in the 1980s and 1990s, games and choosing multiple angles during sporting events, returned after 2000 in ITV environments. Game services included low-action games such as solitaire and word games, along with game playing at home in competition to game playing on a TV program—e.g., playing a hand of poker against players on a TV

CABLEVISION'S IO SERVICE

In 2001, Cablevision, a large cable operator in the northeastern United States, launched Interactive Optimum (IO), a two-way digital cable service that supports interactive services along with HDTV, broadband Web access, and VOIP (voice-over Internet protocol, a cable-based telephone service). IO grew very rapidly after its launch and developed a robust offer of ITV services, including VOD, an interactive program guide, games, multiple camera angles for Madison Square Garden sporting events, and walled garden services such as video real estate and automobile ads. Its VOD service includes on-demand movies, pay cable channels such as HBO, selected TV programs, and a micro-niche video magazine service with short program segments on a wide variety of topics. While IO has a number of ITV services, Cablevision does not label the services *interactive,* instead using the terms on-*demand, program guide,* or *enhanced services.*

IO's business model has been to offer a relatively inexpensive digital tier—approximately $10 more than a midlevel cable package—with many extra channels, HDTV, and interactive services. Certain other services incur additional charges. VOD includes some free content as well as monthly subscriptions (e.g., for HBO on Demand) and pay-per-use (e.g., for on-demand movies). Game packages are offered for a monthly subscription. Cablevision bundles IO with broadband Web access and telephony—that is, customers get discounts if they subscribe to two or more of these services.

program. Choosing multiple camera angles in a sporting event was accompanied by watching several sporting events or news segments on one screen, then choosing which game or news segment to watch on the full screen.

In Europe, ITV developed more rapidly than in the United States after 2000. Groups in other parts of the world—most notably Australia and Hong Kong—also developed ITV, but Europe led the way. Many of the European applications were low-end ITV, but they were more widespread than in the United States. Further, the industry in Europe used the term *ITV* as an umbrella for a wide range of applications and services, the most popular of which were gaming, gambling, and voting about content in programs; shopping and banking were less successful.[28] There was much interest in ITV advertising, but it grew slowly. Most viewers used ITV in short sessions (often during commercials or when bored with programs), and awareness of ITV was mixed. The main appeal of digital cable and satellite was more channels and better picture quality, not ITV.[29] A common return signal for ITV was SMS, with a new subcategory of ITV, SMS-TV, emerging.[30] SMS generated a revenue stream for program producers, who split the fee for SMS with mobile phone operators.

One of the more popular ITV applications has been a series of quiz programs, among them *9Live*, a German channel also available in parts of Austria and Switzerland. Viewers participate in quiz programs by calling a special phone number. Cash prizes are awarded to those who answer the most questions correctly. There is a charge for each call, with the proceeds split between *9Live* and the telephone company. SMS-TV is also popular in Norway, the Netherlands, Belgium, Spain, and the United Kingdom. MTV Europe lets viewers vote on the most popular videos, and music awards programs receive as many as several hundred thousand calls from voters. SMS-TV has worked well as a consequence of the very high penetration of mobile phones and the creation of short call-in phone numbers.

The United Kingdom has been at the forefront in applications of ITV, led by BSkyB's digital satellite service. Cable operators such as NTL and Telewest as well as terrestrial broadcasters followed, driving down the price for consumers. Early "walled garden" ITV services (a limited set of mostly textual information services) did not succeed, but over time, operators found applications that generated revenue, including gaming and betting. The United Kingdom has relatively lax gambling laws, enabling the creation of a broad range of betting applications. Gaming applications include both participation in TV game shows with a chance to win prizes and playing games such as Tetris over a digital television service. For example, YooPlay TV, carried on BSkyB, NTL, and Telewest, provides a channel of games and gambling. PlayJam offers a game service in Europe and the United States. Gaming applications had to overcome a number of obstacles, including latency, which makes it difficult to implement fast-action games, and the limits of remote controls versus a controller in a game console such as Sony PlayStation. ITV games also face intense competition from games on the Web, video game consoles, and PC software games. ITV game developers have cleverly chosen games that work within an ITV cable or satellite environment and developed game play that could accompany TV game shows or poker programs.

The BBC has been very active in ITV, though it blemished its image in 2008 by encouraging viewers to participate in phone-in competition when the winners had already been chosen. In more advanced forms of ITV, the BBC has experimented with local news on demand and chat about TV programs, where viewers must opt in to see the comments, thereby solving the earlier problems *Yack Live* experienced. The BBC has also developed many enhanced ITV services, such as extra text or video that users can call up by using their remote control, VOD, and two-screen ITV with Web content that accompanies the video on television. Among the BBC's many interactive programs has been an IQ test in which everyone watching can participate and learn their IQ by answering a series of questions.

BSKYB INTERACTIVE

BSkyB is the parent company of Sky Digital, a major satellite TV service in the United Kingdom and Ireland and an affiliate of DirecTV in the United States. In 1999, Sky Digital launched Open (later called Sky Active), an interactive TV service. Open was a limited service, primarily text, that included e-mail, home shopping, and electronic banking. The return path from the home was via a telephone (and later SMS). By most measures, the early service was not successful: only 50 percent of subscribers used it and only 10 percent made purchases.[1] However, it set the stage for ITV services that would follow.

Sky Digital's primary attraction in these early years was more channels and better picture quality, not ITV. Sky Digital also had cable competitors that were upgrading to digital. In the competition that followed, prices dropped, and Sky Digital offered an affordable digital package that attracted millions of subscribers. Like a Trojan horse, the digital platform allowed ITV services to enter homes, at least initially, as part of other services. For example, a very popular sports package included an ITV service with multiple camera angles that viewers could select. Also, many programs (e.g., news programs) began to include polls on current affairs or voting that allowed viewers to participate (e.g., *Big Brother* let viewers vote on who should be dropped from the competition). The service also offered menu-driven news. The most popular services to emerge were gaming and gambling—e.g., low-end games such as Tetris and gambling on sporting events under the United Kingdom's relaxed gambling rules. Later services included chat with other viewers and My Sky, with customer account information and customer service.

BSkyB was very influential in developing ITV services, many of which were subsequently adopted in the United States and other countries. The company also developed business models that were influential, such as pay-per-play for games and SMS voting, which involved a revenue split between the program provider and the mobile phone company.

---

1. Gali Einav, "'I Want My iTV': Content, Demand and Social Implications of Interactive Television" (PhD diss., Columbia University, 2004).

The United Kingdom has been a major lab for developing and testing ITV advertising, often called red-button advertising after the red button icon that appears on screens when a commercial has extra content available as well as the red button on remotes that is used to retrieve it. The red button has generally come to symbolize ITV in Europe, since it is the method of selection for many ITV applications. ITV advertising supports a number of features that advertisers find attractive. A viewer can call up extra text over a commercial (e.g., a list of where to buy a product) or extra video about a product. Viewers can customize cars, order brochures, request coupons, participate in contests, and order products. In some systems, different commercials can be targeted to different groups of viewers.

Red-button advertising has also been controversial. Some producers have objected that if viewers watch extra video about a product, they will miss part of the regular program. Similarly, advertisers have noted that clicking on the red button during one commercial will cause viewers to miss subsequent advertisements. ITV advertising has also changed somewhat the relationships among advertisers, ad agencies, and broadcasters. Advertisers previously worked with agencies that simply bought time on networks. With ITV, the advertiser or group creating the spot must work with the satellite or cable operator because of the technology requirements for transmitting the spot. ITV advertising also can provide new types of data and feedback about the viewer (e.g., how many people clicked to see more content). Such information is attractive to advertisers and network operators, who can charge more for every person who clicks to get more information, but also engenders privacy concerns among those who worry about how this information is used.

The Future of ITV

One of the unresolved issues associated with the future of ITV is the question of which paths it will follow—digital cable or satellite, fiber-to-the-home telephone networks, the Web, mobile platforms such as MP-3 players or advanced mobile phones, and hardware storage systems such as DVDs, video game consoles, and personal computers. As debate has raged about which path is most viable, some analysts have chosen one horse to ride. In the early 2000s, digital cable appeared to have a commanding lead, at least in the United States. It had a high-speed return path from the home and direct connections between a server at the cable system and homes, both of which satellite lacked. Dial-up access to the Web was too slow to support ITV. However, satellite service providers, led by BSkyB in the United Kingdom and DirecTV in the United States, have devised clever ways around these limitations, and broadband delivery of the Web overcame many of the limitations for Web ITV. Similarly, DVDs developed interactive features; video game consoles entered more homes with interactive games that approached television realism, linked players in different locations, and provided a platform for downloading on-demand movies for display on TV sets. At the same time, personal computers became more powerful, accommodating interactive video. In the long run, applications of ITV are likely to run on all of these platforms.

There is uncertainty about which ITV services will be widely accepted and which will fall by the wayside. Rather than try to pick winners among services, there may be a better way to deal with the issue of content or applications—ITV attributes. Vincent Grosso has identified four general attributes that cut across ITV content: information, transactions, communication, and gaming. Research from the RCTV trial in Chicago[31] and BSkyB in the United Kingdom suggests that adding one or more of these attributes to an ITV content category is likely to make it more appealing to end users. For example, adding a gaming attribute to a transaction service such as shopping or a communication attribute to an information service such as IM chat over a news program may increase appeal.

Uncertainty also exists about how to price content and hardware. Should content be advertiser-supported or paid for by end users? If the latter, should it be based on pay-per-use or a monthly subscription? What price levels will the market support? Will consumers pay for hardware such as advanced set-top boxes, as they do for some PVRs, or will users prefer to lease the equipment, as with many current-generation cable boxes with built-in PVRs? Other alternatives are to bundle the hardware into a tier of interactive television service, in which case users are likely to perceive that they are paying for the content rather than the box, or to give away the set-top box in the expectation that it will generate significant new revenue from content rentals, shopping and other transactions, and targeted advertising. All of these alternatives are being explored.

Will ITV threaten some forms of existing advertising revenue? Potential hazards include viewers' ability to fast-forward through commercials, to superimpose ITV text content over commercials (e.g., superimposing a TV guide on the screen when a commercial starts), and to switch from regular channel content to ITV when a commercial comes on.

The basic costs of providing ITV—servers, digitizing content, and set-top boxes—are much lower than they were in the 1990s. For example, in the mid-1990s, digitizing a movie for VOD delivery cost $300,000, while a set-top box ran $5,000. Ten years later, the cost of digitizing a movie was closer to $3,000, and set-top boxes similar to those used in the Time Warner Full Service Network trial cost approximately $300. If a $300 set-top box is given away, will VOD and other ITV revenue be sufficient to recoup the cost?

Service providers must also deal with issues of scale. Will the models for networks, servers, and user traffic accommodate tens of millions of homes simultaneously using ITV services? Content providers must wrestle with issues of interoperability—that is, can content created for one service work on another provider's system without significant technical or design modifications? Many incompatible boxes now compete for market share, a situation that poses a cost obstacle to content providers that may have to modify their content for each system.

The issue of whether people want to interact with television, which haunted many earlier generations of ITV service, has largely been resolved. With the exception of a group of diehard skeptics, consumers clearly want to interact with television. However, some want to interact a lot, and some want to interact only a little. The current generation of ITV services can accommodate both the frenetic technophile and the relatively passive couch potato.

Questions about consumer demand for ITV center more on price and appealing services. However, television also has a buzz factor—the need for a mass audience to perceive that an innovation is catching on lest it be cast aside. Further, with the high cost of content generation, ITV content providers need large audiences to justify costs. ITV on the Web may have some advantages in these respects. The Web can more readily accommodate niche services such as user-generated videos, and content creation is not as expensive in the Web environment.

The Future of ITV Content and Services

In the mid-1960s, media theorist Marshall McLuhan noted that we tend to fill new media with content from earlier media.[32] Early radio was filled with vaudeville acts, and early television was filled with radio shows that had been converted to a television format. Truly innovative content and viable business models tend to be discovered years after the new medium enters the marketplace.

Virtually every existing service for interactive television is a modified version of content or a service that already exists: movies-on-demand is a DVD rental service directly to the home; interactive home shopping channels are variations on earlier television shopping channels or a video rendition of catalog shopping; interactive games between households are a variation on two people playing in the same room; and user-generated videos are home movies distributed to a much wider audience. These enhancements to existing services appeal to existing media usage habits and content appetites. They are not bold new applications for a new medium. If history repeats itself, genuinely new applications will not emerge until a few years after ITV systems are widely deployed and will not be recognized as creative innovations for an even longer period.

Original interactive programming is expensive. In ITV's early phases, program providers have hesitated to invest heavily in original content. At the same time, some programming, including news, sports, and game shows, can be adapted to interactive formats with only modest increases in production costs. However, original content will be required to fully exploit the new medium.

Who will provide this content? Will experimentation lead to any radical new program formats, and how can this experimentation be encouraged?

Interactive television has finally reached acceptance after many failed trials and services. It is widely deployed in the United States and Europe, through services like VOD, EPGs, PVRs and interactive services on the Web and mobile phones that offer TV or complement regular television programs with interactive applications. Some of the high-end ITV services tested during the 1990s are still waiting to be deployed for reasons of cost. Having finally achieved success, it is not clear whether the term *interactive television* will be widely used except by those in the industry. Consumers know ITV by specific services such as program guides or VOD, not ITV generically.

In the end, interactive television is about control, convenience, and customization of the television experience. Interaction is a mechanism to provide these core values. Gali Einav reminds us that ITV is ultimately television.[33] There is no reason to believe that ITV's functions in people's lives will differ significantly from the well-established functions of television—to entertain, relax, engage, and inform viewers.

// NINE //

Satellite Radio

This is a story about skepticism, challenges, high risks, and the potential for high rewards. It is the story of two upstart satellite radio companies (which later merged) that took on the U.S. radio industry and won acceptance from a large group of listeners but then ran into headwinds of competition from other media and struggled to become profitable. The chapter emphasizes the U.S. satellite radio experience and draws from academic research, industry data, our field research, and historical analysis of more than 80 years of radio.

> WHAT IS SATELLITE RADIO?
>
> Satellite radio, also known by its technical name, satellite digital audio radio service (SDARS), is licensed by the FCC and uses the S-band (2.3 GHz) portion of the radio spectrum to deliver audio and data services directly from satellites to cars, homes, and offices. Radio content is sent from ground stations to the satellites and then retransmitted to radios equipped to receive the signals. The satellite-to-ground signals are supplemented by terrestrial repeater networks in major cities to fill gaps in coverage when tall buildings and other obstructions block the signal.
>
> The United States has two satellite radio services, XM and Sirius, which were independently owned and operated until 2008, when they merged; they continue to operate two services. Both are subscription services that deliver more than 100 channels of audio content such as music, news/talk, and sports as well as data services such as stock quotes and the title of the song being played to subscribers. (Sirius also provides some video services.) Their signals cover parts of Canada and Mexico as well as the continental United States. Receiving the service requires a radio equipped with a satellite chipset or an adaptor that will play through existing radios or stereos.

Skepticism about satellite radio was rampant in the late 1990s and early 2000s. It took many forms: Why would anyone pay for radio when free radio is so widely available. Radio is inherently a local medium, so how can a national satellite service possibly compete? AM and FM stations saturate major markets in the United States, with large cities often having more than 100 stations, so who needs more? Satellite radio technology is untested in the United States and will likely fail to work in large cities with tall buildings and in rural areas with dense clusters of trees? Radio is a dying medium, so why throw good money at an industry that is on its last legs?

The challenges faced by satellite radio included competition from more than 12,000 existing radio stations as well as a range of alternative sources of music in the home and car, including CDs and MP-3 players; how to raise $2 billion for the launch of the satellites and a five-year startup phase; the need to put in place agreements with car manufacturers to install a new generation of radios in vehicles; and the entrenched habits of millions of listeners who already had AM/FM radios in their cars and homes.

The risks associated with satellite radio included the potential failure to overcome any of these obstacles; the possibility of launch failures for the satellites, thereby significantly delaying the startup of services and crippling the companies financially; the real possibility that too few people would subscribe to satellite radio to justify the $2 billion investment; and many industry analysts' argument that it represented another case of a new technology being pushed into a marketplace that didn't need or want it.

New radio technologies had a history of many failures or very long incubation periods. FM radio, launched in the late 1930s, did not win a significant share of the radio audience for 40 years, a startup period that would have killed satellite radio. AM stereo was in the marketplace by 2000 but had failed to attract the public. Digital AM and FM radio was still in a talking phase in the United States, ten years after it was proposed. Further, a new generation of radio services had been introduced over cable and satellite TV systems but had generated little interest among television viewers.

The potential reward for a venture such as satellite radio was significant revenue from a large base of potential subscribers: 200 million cars in the United States already equipped with AM/FM radio, more than 100 million households with an average of five radios each, three million truck drivers who spent several hours each day on the road, and millions of offices that kept radio on throughout the day. But how many of these people would subscribe? We have already discussed the danger of taking such large figures and then making a seemingly conservatively estimate that 30 percent or 20 percent or even 10 percent were likely to subscribe in order to forecast a very large base of users. The reality in the late 1990s, when initial investment bets were placed, was that no one knew if anyone would subscribe to satellite radio.

When satellite radio was launched in 2001, it was a true David facing the Goliath radio industry. Leading the charge against the radio industry was XM's CEO, Hugh Panero, who came from a cable background and shaped the nascent satellite radio industry. At that time, AM and FM radio stations were generating $20 billion a year in revenue. They were owned by two major conglomerates, Clear Channel and Infinity Broadcasting, many smaller multistation owners, and a large group of public and nonprofit stations. At a national level, commercial radio was represented by a powerful lobbying organization, the National Association of Broadcasters, which vigorously fought the introduction of satellite radio. Radio had faced previous challenges for its audience from other media, including television in the 1950s, and AM had been challenged by FM beginning in the late 1930s, but satellite radio represented the first time in 80 years that terrestrial radio faced significant competition from another form of radio.

Measured by its growth in subscribers, satellite radio has generated remarkable success, reaching 19 million subscribers seven years after its launch. Its long-term growth is difficult to assess, though no shortage of forecasts exists. The business case for satellite radio is more complex. The story of how satellite radio took on the terrestrial radio industry rivals an *Indiana Jones* action-adventure movie, with perils and uncertainties at every turn and protagonists willing to take heart-stopping risks.

Satellite Radio Origins and Technological Underpinnings

Satellite radio did not begin in the United States. WorldSpace first offered it in 1998 for developing nations in Asia and Africa. In 1997, the Federal Communications Commission (FCC) held an auction for two U.S. satellite radio services in the S-band section of the radio spectrum. Four bids were received, and two licenses were awarded, one to American Mobile Radio (which became XM Satellite Radio) for $90 million and another to CD Radio (which became Sirius Satellite Radio) for $83 million. These 12.5 MHZ systems would have no further competitors in the S-band.

American Mobile Radio attracted investments from General Motors, Hughes Electronics, Honda, DirecTV, and Clear Channel Communications, while CD Radio attracted investments from Ford, DaimlerChrysler, and Space Systems/Loral. Some of these investors later became very important tools in the marketing and distribution of satellite radio. In particular, General Motors, which had invested $100 million, agreed to sell XM radios exclusively in its vehicles and moved aggressively to install them at the factory where the cars were assembled (rather than at dealerships, where it is much more expensive).

A series of early technical decisions had a major impact on how the two services would develop and ultimately the quality of the user experience. The first of these involved the number of satellites and types of orbit each would deploy. Satellite radio antennas, like their satellite TV cousins, must be able to "see" the satellites to pick up the signal. The placement and power of the satellites affect how frequently and under what circumstances end users may lose the signal. Moving objects such as cars complicate the choices. Sirius chose three medium-powered satellites from Space Systems/Loral that would be deployed in an elliptical orbit at high angles over the United States. XM chose two high-powered Boeing satellites that would be deployed in geostationary orbits south of the United States with a moderate angle beam that targeted the eastern and western halves of the country. As a practical matter, this meant that the Sirius satellites (also lower in orbit) were more directly overhead and therefore less likely to be blocked by tall buildings and would need fewer repeater networks to supplement the signals blocked by buildings. However, the more powerful XM satellites could more easily penetrate light clusters of trees and other nondense obstructions. The XM satellite configuration was also simpler in design. An XM radio could pick up the east or west satellite and stay fixed on it unless the receiver was traveling across the country. The lower-orbit Sirius satellites moved in the sky (at any time, two of the satellites were over the United States), requiring the radio to make more complex adjustments to pick up signals. Within a home, users might even have to move the antenna each day to optimize reception, since the satellite might be in a different location than the previous day. The satellite configuration had an impact on the design of the chipset and contributed to a major delay for Sirius.

In addition to repeater networks, both companies built a few seconds of buffer into the radios to overcome minor signal losses from the satellites—that is, the radio could lose the satellite signal for a few seconds, as when passing under a bridge, without the user noticing any disruption in service.

Both companies took risks in the launch of their satellites. Though all the satellites were insured, insurance never covers all costs, and the delay in launching a replacement could have crippled either enterprise. Sirius launched first, using a Russian Proton rocket, and had all three satellites in orbit by November 2000. XM used a new technique to launch its more powerful and heavier satellites. Working with Sea Launch, a partnership between Boeing and companies from Norway, Russia, and the Ukraine, XM launched its satellites from a barge towed down to the equator, off the coast of South America. Launching closer to the equator enabled the rocket to carry a heavier payload, but the technique was relatively untested. The two satellites, named Rock and Roll, were launched successfully, though one launch was delayed for a few weeks. By May 2001, both XM satellites were in orbit.

With a six-month lead in launching its satellites, Sirius should have been first to market. However, a second major technical issue, the chipset design and manufacturing, came into play. Because of the complexity in the design or simply because of manufacturing delays, the Sirius chipset was not ready in 2001, whereas XM's chipset was ready, and the service launched that November. Sirius inaugurated its service the following July. The head start gave XM a significant early advantage. Chipset design is not a onetime event. Chipsets are redesigned frequently, and each new generation is typically smaller and lighter, has more features, consumes less power, and throws off less heat. These attributes, in turn, affect the size, weight, features, and cost of the radio. Getting a working chipset to radio manufacturers before Sirius enabled XM to stay one generation ahead for the first few years, offering cheaper, smaller, lighter radios with advanced features.

A third significant set of technical issues affecting the end user experience involves the division of bandwidth and the system for compressing signals. With traditional analog AM and FM radio, a station is assigned a fixed bandwidth—generally enough to transmit one regular radio signal (we will not discuss digital terrestrial radio here). With 12.5 MHZ of bandwidth, the satellite radio services had relatively big blocks of bandwidth that could be divided any number of ways—for example, into 75 channels with extremely high quality, 300 channels with low quality, or anything in between. Further, some channels could receive more bandwidth (e.g., music) and others less (e.g., news and talk channels). More channels clearly offered a marketing advantage, but high-quality audio was also an important selling point. Both Sirius and XM launched with approximately 100 channels and later increased to more than 120. A casual listener to either service can hear a clear difference in the quality of the audio on channels that are predominantly talk and those that are predominantly music.

One of the advantages of a digital service such as satellite radio is that it can use compression to squeeze more signals into a defined amount of bandwidth. Compression technology is part science and part art. The scientific part uses complex algorithms to reduce the information that is transmitted while restoring the full signal in the receiver. The art of compression lies in making decisions about which parts of the audio are most important and which can be compromised, with only the best sets of ears listening on the best audio components noticing any difference. The listening environments for satellite radio provided a further wrinkle in the compression decision. Planners anticipated that most subscribers would listen in their cars. A car environment is noisy, and the speaker systems are generally mediocre. Greater compression was therefore possible, since the typical car listener could not distinguish between very high and reasonably good quality. However, the home audiophile with a high-end stereo system (and reviewers) could make such distinctions. Both Sirius and XM's decision makers appear to have struck a reasonable compromise, as most reviewers found the audio quality very good if not quite up to that of CDs.

An additional advantage of compression technology is that it improves over time, as more advanced algorithms are created, enabling satellite radio to deliver more services in the same bandwidth. Collectively, these technological underpinnings determined the quality of satellite radio's end user experience (sound quality and frequency of dropouts), cost, and capacity.

Commercial Radio Opens the Door

When satellite radio was launched in 2001, consumers expressed more interest in the service than many observers had anticipated. But why would people pay for satellite radio when free radio was so widely available?

Decades of research about radio provide strong evidence about its core functions in people's lives, functions that cut across formats and time periods. People listen to radio to keep them company and to enhance or to help change their moods.[1] They use radio to mark their day (wake up, go to sleep, take a break from another activity) and to participate in communities.[2] The community can be the town where the radio station and listener are located, but it can also be a community of Boston Red Sox fans or people who love jazz. Radio research also shows why personalities—e.g., DJs, sports announcers, political commentators—are so important on radio. These personalities perform all of these functions—keeping people company, supporting or changing moods, and building community. Much radio content from the 1920s to the 1970s supported these core functions of radio, but by the 1980s, programmers seemed to forget why people were listening.

Between 1980 and 2000, much radio content bogged down in a stale formula. Driven by myopic research that shoehorned audiences into narrow demographic groups and by corporate consultants who imposed cookie-cutter formats that were supposed to increase ratings, radio began to sound the same all over the country. Conglomerates began to purchase multiple stations and program them in the same way. The number of commercials increased—in some cases to more than 20 minutes per hour. The strategy increased revenue, which doubled between 1990 and 2000.[3]

But programming suffered. The number of available formats shrank. Niche content such as jazz, classical, and folk all but disappeared, while more popular formats—country and talk—proliferated. Many stations played only 30 songs; the top 10 songs on playlists were heard very frequently, and some stations played fewer than 20 songs.[4] If a market had five "soft rock" stations, chances were pretty good that they had nearly identical playlists. At the same time, local news coverage decreased or was dropped completely. The Project for Excellence in Journalism reported that the number of full-time employees in radio newsrooms dropped 44 percent between 1994 and 2000. On the technology front, many stations limited their use of stereo and lowered the rich bass in songs to increase the reach of their signals. From a listener's perspective, the audio experience declined.

In small and medium-size markets, many stations were programmed from elsewhere, and the local flavor of DJ chatter was reduced. This change also affected emergency broadcast services and local radio stations' role as a pipeline to the public in case of disasters. In one notable case, a train derailment in Minot, North Dakota, spilled a large cargo of highly toxic anhydrous ammonia fertilizer. When the police called the local radio station to get help in broadcasting a warning to the public, no one answered, since the station was automated and merely carried a feed from another city.[5]

Innovation also suffered. DJs and station programmers had less freedom to try new songs and new styles of programming. Some sources of innovation outside mainstream commercial radio were stymied. For example, the National Association of Broadcasters fought the expansion of low-power radio stations, arguing that they would cause interference. Low-power radio stations, often run by local colleges, community groups, and other amateurs, are an important source of experimentation. Innovation did not come to a halt, however; many public radio and full- power college stations, along with some commercial stations, tried new forms of programming, but commercial radio in general was stuck in a creativity rut.

By 2001, commercial AM and FM radio remained a mass medium with a very large audience. Radio listening shifted more to cars (70 percent of all listening), and the average listener tuned in to 3.2 stations. Fewer people woke up to radio. Instead, many turned on morning TV shows. The mainstream radio audience was aging, many young people got their music from CDs and later MP-3 players rather than from radio, and the Web was beginning to compete with radio for people's time. The local DJ became less important than in earlier periods, but national radio personalities such as Howard Stern (a shock jock known for outrageous and off-color comments), Rush Limbaugh (a conservative commentator), and Dr. Laura (a psychologist with a call-in program) had very large audiences. National Public Radio also enjoyed a large and loyal following. Overall, however, the enthusiasm for radio that was present in earlier decades diminished, a change reflected in many ways, including the paucity of magazines or newspaper columns about radio. What was there to say? This environment opened the door for satellite radio.

Enter Satellite Radio

Satellite radio did not have an auspicious beginning. XM planned to roll out its service on September 15, 2001. In the preceding months, they had prepared an advertising campaign featuring the theme of objects falling from the sky. After 9/11, however, XM postponed its launch and reworked the campaign to elimi-

TABLE 9.1. Target Groups For Satellite Radio

Expected Characteristics of Groups Adopting Earlier	Expected Characteristics of Groups Adopting Later
Male	Female
25–59	<25 or >59
Rural, then suburban	Urban
Long commute	Moderate commute
Truck/luxury car driver	Non–luxury car driver
Access to few terrestrial radio stations	Access to many terrestrial radio stations
Use in vehicle, then at home	Use in mobile setting
Radio purchased after car	Radio preinstalled in new car

nate any visuals that might evoke memories of the terrorist attacks and rolled out nationally in November 2001. Sirius followed in July 2002.

Numerous questions remained. Would the technology work? What types of content would compete successfully with existing radio stations? Were enough people willing to pay a monthly subscription for radio? Was there a group of early adopters who would buy the first generation of expensive ($300–$500) satellite radios?

Our review of early forums about satellite radio and contemporary industry reports suggests that one key group of early adopters was long-distance truck drivers. Truckers driving 18-wheel rigs from Florida to California pass through many stretches with no radio or a few distant stations. Satellite radio helped them deal with boredom and stay in touch with the world. XM appealed to this group directly with a truckers' channel. Other groups of early adopters included people living in rural areas, those with long commutes, and new technology enthusiasts.[6] Early adopters were also strongly male. Comments about why they adopted XM and responses to a survey indicated that many were strongly dissatisfied with regular radio, especially the number of commercials, and liked the variety of content on satellite radio.[7]

Satellite radio provides an example of how markets for new media often change over time. Early and later adopters can differ markedly. Table 9.1 outlines expected changes between early and later adopters of satellite radio.[8]

Attracting and Keeping Users

Both XM and Sirius lined up sets of car manufacturers, rental car companies, radio manufacturers, and electronics stores to ensure that the public would have access to satellite radio. During the first few years of satellite radio, people could get the service either as part of the original equipment on their car (OEM) or as an aftermarket addition. The difference was crucial. An OEM radio (which includes AM and FM as well as the satellite chipset) is installed at the factory when the car is being assembled. From a user's perspective, it comes with the car, usually with a free trial. The buyer must then decide whether to subscribe after the trial period. In the first few years, more than 70 percent of car buyers chose to subscribe after the trial period ended, with that figure declining to 50–55 percent over the next few years as radios were built into many more cars.[9] Aftermarket radios, obtained from electronics stores or directly from Sirius or XM, can be new radios that replace existing car radios or adaptor units that play through an existing car or home radio. (Stand-alone and mobile radios later became available.) Aftermarket radios represent a much bigger hurdle, since end users must consciously decide to purchase and install the radio before experiencing the service.

As long as three years can pass between the time a manufacturer agrees to make an item an OEM feature and the time cars with that feature start to roll off the assembly line. XM, with General Motors as a key investor and partner, achieved OEM factory installation status in many more car models than Sirius during the first few years, a situation that played a crucial role in gaining XM a larger subscriber base. For the first five years of the service's existence, most satellite radios were aftermarket, not OEM, though the percentage of OEM radios increased each year and dominated by year six.

Early marketing of satellite radio emphasized its variety of music formats, depth of playlists, and relative absence of commercials. Sirius had no commercials on any of its music channels; XM started with commercials on a few music channels but soon eliminated them. News and talk channels had far fewer commercials than did commercial radio. XM initially priced its service at $9.99 per month, while Sirius charged $12.95; XM later matched Sirius's price. Both offered discounts for yearly subscriptions and family plans for users who purchased multiple radios. Marketing campaigns for satellite radio carefully avoided wording that might evoke expectations that radio should be free. XM called its services *channels* rather than *stations* and emphasized that it offered *digital*, *satellite*, and *near-CD quality* service—all words for things that consumers pay for. Sirius initially called its services *streams* but later adopted XM's terminology.

The early growth rate for satellite radio was strong (figure 9.1). The pattern compares favorably with the growth of mass media such as radio, television, and CDs during their early years in the marketplace.

Early adopters of satellite radio liked the services. Both companies reported high user satisfaction and low churn rates—percentage of subscribers who dropped the service—compared to churn rates for mature services such as mobile phones and cable television.[10] Word of mouth was also reported to be posi-

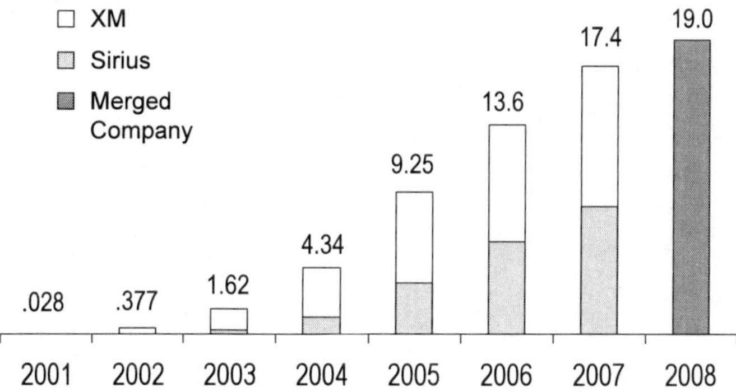

Fig. 9.1. Satellite radio growth: Number of subscribers in millions, 2001–8. (Data from Sirius and XM Annual Reports, 2001–8.)

tive. XM claimed that its early subscribers discussed the service with an average of five friends. As discussed in chapter 2, positive word of mouth is important for the successful adoption of new media but is more influential in later stages of the adoption cycle, when the base of users is larger: 100,000 subscribers spreading positive word of mouth does not have the same impact as 10 million subscribers talking favorably about the service. Early in the adoption cycle, advertising and marketing campaigns carry more of the burden.

The User Interface

Satellite radio's user interface includes the buttons people press to select or change content, the size of the display screen, how content is displayed on the screen, the menus of options, and the general process of navigating through choices. Before satellite radio, the user interface for radios had changed little over the preceding 40 years. Every decade or so, a new feature was introduced (e.g., scan), but most of the changes users experienced involved the size and location of buttons or color of the radio, not functionality. Satellite radio introduced a broad range of new features that required significant changes in the user interface. These changes would make the service more attractive only if the user interface made the new features easy to find and display or play—for example, the name of the song and artist currently playing or direct entry of the channel number from a keypad.

The first generation of satellite radios had relatively few design changes to accommodate new features and received mixed reviews.[11] The radios were designed by the same major manufacturers that had controlled the industry for 40 years. Whether they were rushed to bring the radios to market and lacked the time to redesign the user interface for satellite radio or had no interest in the fledgling service is not clear. However, the radios looked very much like typical AM/FM radios, with small displays that could not show all the information being sent about the song playing. Users had to press two buttons simultaneously to access some features, and engineering-speak leaked into some displays—for example, "Loading DSRP."

XM responded quickly by creating a team of engineers, software designers, and project managers in Florida and Washington, D.C., to create the second generation of radios from the ground up.[12] Team members also worked with outside designers and hardware manufacturers, overseeing the entire process. To maintain a good working relationship with the major radio manufacturers, XM kept its role quiet and simply turned the radios and software components over to traditional distributors, who brought the products to market. The second generation of radios was available in less than a year and received very positive reviews.[13] The initial problem turned into a very important learning experience. XM learned that new features have little value unless the end user can experience them transparently—the hardware should not get in the way. The company also learned to keep a finger on the pulse of all the elements that would ultimately affect its destiny, including hardware. And they realized that satellite radio is an open platform to which they could add many new features and services over time, which they did.

Programming and Features

The launch of satellite radio opened a window of opportunity for innovation. Because the service was new, users had not yet formed expectations about what content would be provided or how it would be presented. Many people subscribed to satellite radio because they were tired of commercial radio and wanted an alternative. There was a great deal of talent available from commercial radio that was unhappy with the status quo and eager to try new things. On-air talent was also available at relatively low cost since the satellite radio service providers could negotiate from the position of a start-up with few subscribers and low revenue.

Satellite radio had the advantage of controlling all of its channels. Competition existed with AM/FM and with the other satellite service provider (for the first six months XM was the sole satellite radio service), but within each provider's lineup of 100 channels, there was in effect no competition. The companies only cared that subscribers found enough benefit in the channels they used to continue subscribing. XM and Sirius thus had freedom to program across channels, to target channels at niche groups, and even to cross-promote among channels.

As first to market, XM had a significant impact on programming content and philosophy. The principal person who guided programming for XM was Lee Abrams, a veteran of the FM revolution in the 1970s. Abrams saw XM as reinventing radio, as FM had done during the 1970s. In the early 2000s, reinventing radio involved a breadth and depth of content, much use of stereo, a new style of DJ, and taking advantage of satellite radio's freedom from content regulation.

Because XM and Sirius offered so many channels, a wide diversity of content could be accommodated. Satellite radio's national footprint aggregated listeners, meaning that formats such as jazz or classical music that could not attract a sufficient audience for a commercial station in one market became viable. And even if national listenership remained low, microniche music formats could be justified if enough people listened occasionally and felt that the channel added benefit to their subscription. Depth of content involved much longer play lists within a music format. Each satellite radio service provider had more than one million songs in its database. If there were five country channels on the satellite radio service, instead of each one playing the same 20 songs to compete for the largest share of country listeners, the five could divide the field into classic country, southern country, modern country, and so on, and provide greater depth in playlists for each niche format.

Stereo provides an important advantage for satellite radio. Many AM stations have stereo capability, but very few radio receivers are equipped to receive it. With FM, many stations minimize their use of stereo to maximize the reach of their signal. With satellite radio, all receivers have stereo, and using it does not affect signal reach. Stereo is also very effective in cars because the speakers are separated and the listener(s) are seated where they can hear the separate signals, unlike many home environments.

As a digital service, satellite radio can transmit audio, data, and even video. The data component of the signal can provide a wide range of information services as long as the radio software and hardware are designed to accept and display them. With sufficient memory, information and even songs can be saved in the radios. The earliest satellite radios provided information such as the name of the artist and song playing. Over time, many other features were added; users could search by categories of content, save information about a song, learn when a favorite song is playing on a different channel, and display customized sports scores or stock quotes.

The use and style of DJs were very controversial in the early days of satellite radio. As its name implied, CD Radio (later to become Sirius) did not believe in DJs at first. This was supported by some user research which indicated that there was broad dissatisfaction with DJs in radio. However, a larger body of research showed that DJs play a very important role in meeting radio's core functions, and Sirius later changed its programming philosophy to include some DJs.[14] XM used DJs from the beginning but sought a different style of DJ. Most took up less on-air time than traditional DJs, and many were experts in the format they played and not simply on-air personalities. For example, a reggae channel was hosted by a leading writer about reggae music.[15]

Satellite radio is free from the content regulations that govern over-the-air stations because providers paid for the spectrum they use and the service is private—only those who pay a subscription and own a satellite radio can receive it. The program lineups of XM and Sirius contain comedy channels with off-color jokes and radio personalities who use off-color language and discuss topics that would not be permitted under FCC content rules. This appeals to many subscribers but could offend others, so XM and Sirius allow users to block channels.

Content

The channel lineups for XM and Sirius started out fairly different but over time became very similar as each imitated what succeeded on the other. However, each struck some exclusive deals with sports groups such as the National Football League and Major League Baseball and major personalities such as Oprah Winfrey and Martha Stewart. Each had core content in the areas of comedy, decades (e.g., music from the 1970s), news, and talk as well as a few niche areas such as radio drama, audio books, and unsigned bands.

Channels have names as well as numbers to communicate a brand image. Whereas AM and FM stations are known by their call letters and frequencies (e.g., WFAS, 103.9), satellite radio channels have numbers and names, for example, Channel 50, Frank's Place. Most satellite radios can accommodate 30 or so preset channels to accommodate multiple users or people who want to group presets such as 1–10 for music channels, 10–20 for news channels, and so on. Channel numbers are grouped by format—for example, all the news channels might be in the 120s. Not all numbers are assigned, so that additional channels can be added to each group over time.

Some of the channels on satellite radio borrow types of content that were popular on commercial radio decades ago. For example, comedy was very popular on radio during the 1920s, 1930s, and 1940s; it found a resurgence of interest on satellite radio in the 2000s. Radio dramas were very popular in the second quarter of the twentieth century but were pushed aside by television drama.[16] Satellite radio has offered such programming a new home, replaying some shows from the 1930s and 1940s and adding others, but it is a much smaller niche than the one for comedy.

Satellite radio also brought back more radio *programs* and specials. In response to competition from television programs in the 1950s, most radio stations developed single-format content and reduced the number of specific programs, although programs remained part of the radio landscape, especially talk shows hosted by Rush Limbaugh, Dr. Laura, and Bill O'Reilly, among others. However, many stations fill most of their day with anonymous or automated DJs and provide no sense of a beginning or end for content segments. Satellite radio offers a mixture of programs and single-format channels with no program segments. However, many DJs and artists (among them Bob Dylan, Eminem, and Tom Petty) host programs.

Many satellite radio channels have content that is targeted to specific groups—e.g., women, truckers, Hispanics, people who were teenagers in the 1960s, gays, evangelical Christians, baseball fans, liberals, and conservatives. Well-known brands from broadcasting and cable are also represented. Channels are programmed by Disney, CNN, MSNBC, Fox News, ESPN, and the Weather Channel, among others. Some of these channels have original content created for satellite radio, while others carry the audio feed from a television channel, for example, the audio feed from CNBC's cable channel. Why would anyone want to listen to the audio component of a cable channel? The concept was borrowed from CBS radio, which for many years has carried the audio portion of the TV program *60 Minutes*. Fans of the program who happen to be in their cars when the show airs can listen, as can people who started watching the show at home and then have to run out somewhere. A similar logic holds for CNBC and people who want to follow business news while in their car.

The decades channels, devoted to content from the 1940s, 1950s, 1960s, 1970, 1980s, and 1990s, are important examples of how satellite radio competes with local radio stations. The decades channels offer multiple ways to build a community of people who identify with a particular period. The DJs on XM's 1960s channel, for example, are named and have strong personalities. They invite call-in requests for songs from the decade, engage callers with small talk about their lives, and promote small competitions such as which state will have the most callers on a particular morning. Each day, they focus on a specific subperiod—e.g., the week of October 10, 1965—and tell listeners about that week's news and television programming. They play vintage commercials and encourage listeners to join fan clubs. Listeners who call in often mention other callers, express loyalty to the program, and treat the DJs like friends. It is a community.

Satellite radio played another card in its battle with local radio stations and the National Association of Broadcasters by creating a national emergency channel, which is turned over to the Federal Emergency Management Agency or state emergency agencies to transmit information about hurricanes, forest fires, or other disasters. Local radio stations have long claimed a special status as a provider of emergency information in local areas, although, as discussed earlier, in at least one case they were not there when needed. Furthermore, local radio stations are reluctant to forgo revenue by turning over the entire station for long periods of time for less-than-major emergencies. Satellite radio services can provide an emergency channel continuously and even create additional channels if needed.

Star Power

Everything changed for satellite radio in the winter of 2003. At this point, Sirius had fewer than half as many subscribers as did XM. Both had relatively low programming budgets, relying on new styles of programming and greater variety rather than major stars to compete with commercial radio and each other.

That December, however, Sirius announced a $220 million deal to acquire the exclusive rights to carry all National Football League games for 7 years. Agreements with the National Basketball Association and the National Hockey League followed. Sirius had enacted a strategy of appealing to male listeners by strongly associating its brand with sports. Wall Street responded favorably, driving up the price of Sirius's stock. XM responded with an 11-year, $650 million deal with Major League Baseball and by concluding agreements to carry Big Ten football and basketball games.

The quest for star power did not end with sports. Sirius signed shock jock Howard Stern and lifestyles expert Martha Stewart; XM inked Oprah Winfrey and shock jocks Opie and Anthony. Each service also had many well known brands, among them CNN, Fox News, and National Public Radio, along with the personalities carried on those channels.

Several issues go along with star power, including the impact on the programming budget, the ability of stars to draw new subscribers, the retention of current subscribers, and the potential loss of subscribers who may be offended by some stars. Fundamentally, what are stars worth? Between 2003 and 2005, the programming budgets for both Sirius and XM more than tripled. And full impact of all of the major deals had yet to be felt. New deals for major stars put pressure on satellite radio service providers when the time came to conclude new contracts with existing content providers: If Stern was worth $100 million per year, what was ESPN now worth? Major new deals can also ignite bidding wars for existing attractions. XM reportedly paid $15 million for the rights to carry the popular NASCAR races from 2001 to 2006; when that contract came up for renewal, Sirius paid a reported $107 million for the next five years of NASCAR races.[17]

Some stars are a plus for the satellite radio service; others are both a plus and a minus. Winfrey and the NFL presumably would attract subscribers but not offend anyone. Opie and Anthony and Stern, however, are attractive to many but offend others. Might some people be so attracted that they would sign up for satellite radio? Might others be so offended that they would cancel their subscriptions? If a star is a mild positive, but not sufficient to motivate a subscription, what combination(s) of stars would provide sufficient motivation to gain subscribers?

What Is Howard Stern Worth?

All of these questions came together in the case of Howard Stern. How many of his commercial radio listeners (approximately 20 million overall, including 8–10 million loyal fans) could he bring over to Sirius? How many subscribers might depart because they found him offensive? How much value did he add to the brand as the home of major talent (Stern plus all the other stars Sirius recruited) and as a controversial figure who would attract free media coverage?

XM reportedly bid against Sirius for Stern but dropped out at a figure much lower than $100 million.[18] Could the two providers possibly calculate a value for Stern? Some industry analysts offered back-of-the-envelope calculations: if Stern brought in 2 million listeners at $13 per month, he would more than cover the $100 million price tag.[19] More optimistically, others calculated, if Stern brought only one-third of his loyal fan base over to Sirius, he would be worth $468 million per year (1/3 × 9 million loyal fans × $156 per year in fees per subscriber), so the $100 million deal was a bargain.

Another rough-and-ready way of looking at his potential value would have been to turn the problem inside out. At the time the contract was signed, Sirius's subscriber acquisition cost (the average cost, mostly for marketing, that a company incurs to obtain each new subscriber) was approximately one year's subscriber fees—i.e., $156. Using this, one could have estimated how many customers (net) Howard Stern would have had to add to cover the cost of his contract. Given the size of his loyal fan base, the question would then have been whether it was likely that the number of fans he would bring to Sirius would exceed the break-even number by a margin sufficient to compensate for all the limitations of the analysis.

Either of these rough calculations might have been rather misleading. Table 9.2 indicates some obvious factors that the former does not take into account; it illustrates the complexity of the problem. If incorporated in the analysis, some of the omitted factors might have had a significant impact on

TABLE 9.2. Factors Omitted from Industry Analysts' Estimates of Howard Stern's Value to Sirius

Net Number of Subscribers Attracted by Howard Stern	
The Following Would Reduce the Estimate of His Value	**The Following Would Increase the Estimate of His Value**
The portion of Howard Stern's fan base who become subscribers to Sirius will include some who would become its subscribers even if Sirius did not carry him.	Howard Stern may attract some new listeners who never heard him on commercial radio but did hear him on the Web, on cable TV programming, or in media coverage about Stern after he joined Sirius.
Sirius may lose some subscribers because they find Howard Stern offensive. Some potential subscribers to either XM or Sirius may decide in favor of XM because they find Stern offensive.	Howard Stern may attract some new listeners on Sirius among existing subscribers who never heard him on commercial radio and decide to keep their subscriptions whereas otherwise they would have dropped them thereby reducing churn.
Some of those who subscribe to Sirius because of Howard Stern will churn out of the service (though probably a smaller percentage than of general subscribers).	
Value of Each Subscriber Attracted by Howard Stern	
These Would Reduce the Estimate of His Value	
Not all the $13 per month in subscription fees will go to the bottom line. New subscribers generate costs as well as revenues: for example, in the setting up of new accounts and in their subsequent maintenance.	
It will take time before all those drawn to Sirius by Howard Stern will have become subscribers. For those who come over after his contract has started, the average revenue generated over the length of his contract will be commensurately lower.	
Indirect Effects on the Sirius Revenues and Costs	
The Following Would Reduce the Estimate of His Value	**The Following Would Increase the Estimate of His Value**
The high value of Howard Stern's contract will drive up Sirius's programming costs as it will cause other content providers to negotiate for higher fees when their contracts come up for renewal.	Contracts with Howard Stern and other major talent add to the value of the brand. Additionally, Howard Stern is a controversial figure who attracts free media coverage, thus benefiting Sirius's marketing.

Stern's valuation. In particular, neither approach considers the two indirect effects—the probable inflationary effect on other contracts and the value of Stern in terms of brand building and free publicity—which are particularly problematic. In one sense, the point is moot: Sirius paid what it did, probably on the basis of pure negotiations rather than a systematic analysis. However, since the company's decision had such a significant impact on the future of satellite radio, it is worth considering some of the factors the analysts likely left out.

The problem of placing a financial value on Howard Stern was even harder than that of placing a value on a high-priced player for whom a sports team might want to bid or on a movie star whom a producer might consider for a role. In the latter instances, figures for other recent deals might provide some guidance; in Stern's case, no such comparisons were possible. Examples from commercial radio, where there are no subscription fees and revenue is based on advertising alone, do not apply.

Satellite Radio Becomes a Mass Medium

By the mid-2000s, satellite radio had established its place in the radio marketplace. If it had not defeated the Goliath AM/FM radio industry, it had clearly won respect. Satellite radio was a success in terms of subscribers—more than 12 million—and could claim the status of a mass medium. But neither XM nor Sirius was profitable, and both faced many challenges. The two rivals engaged in fierce competition and struggled to find successful business models; AM and FM had started to fight back; and new competitors such as Web radio and podcasts were on the scene. It was not a time to rest, but innovation was inevitably more difficult for the two established companies compared to five years earlier, when they were new media start-ups.

New Media and Mass Media

New media companies have many advantages, along with some disadvantages relative to established media companies. They are generally small and nimble, easing the process of changing course and innovating. The financial community does not scrutinize their every move. They can often negotiate with content providers from a position of relative poverty, and they are not locked into traditional ways of doing things, as are many established media companies. Mass media status reduces some of these advantages.

As satellite radio grew, the economic pressures of mass media entertainment increased. Most significantly, satellite radio adopted the star system, paying high salaries for well-known personalities and brands. Subscribers to satellite radio had seemed very happy with the services before the addition of the star power; financial markets, not users, had driven the change. Sirius was first to adopt the star strategy but XM joined them very quickly. It is interesting to speculate whether this was inevitable. What if, in 2003–4, Sirius had been closer to its rival in subscribers and revenue? Would the company have been less tempted to sign the National Football League and Stern, or would they have demanded more modest contracts? Could XM have held its ground with appealing content but fewer well-known brands and personalities? Perhaps not. All other mass media have adopted the star system. But the change added to the challenges the two satellite radio providers faced in finding a successful business model.

Business Strategy: Finding Future Subscribers

AM radio needed several years to find its business model. The appropriate combination of entertainment, news, talk, and commercials that was to become the business model was not obvious in the early 1920s. Satellite radio began with a clearer picture. It would adopt a modified version of the cable TV model: most revenue would come from subscribers to the basic service, with modest additional revenue from premium channels and advertising. As programming costs increased, new sources of revenue were needed. There were many possibilities, such as more premium channels, s-commerce (sale of goods and music over satellite radio), international distribution (both Sirius and XM launched services in Canada during 2005), Web distribution, and video services to cars, among others. But which services were viable? Should satellite radio expend its marketing resources on these opportunities or concentrate on growing its core base of subscribers? There was still a very large pool of potential subscribers in cars and homes. Furthermore, some groups—e.g., women—were not yet represented at expected levels.[20] This scarcity of women may have been linked to the greater sale of aftermarket radios (installed to replace existing car radios or as adapters to play through them) in the first few years of growth compared to satellite radios already built into new cars, which came to dominate in the late 2000s.

A direct parallel exists to the early days of AM radio, when many end users built their radios from kits.[21] At that time, male listeners outnumbered females. Women were interested in radio programs, not in building radios. When radio sets became readily and cheaply available, the technology barrier was reduced, and women quickly adopted radio.[22] It was reasonable to expect a similar pattern for satellite radio once it was easy to acquire a set built into cars, eliminating installation and the messy wires associated with aftermarket radios. There were other core questions such as the demand for satellite radios in homes and mobile settings. Approximately 70 percent of listening to AM and FM radio takes place in cars. Would the percentage shift for satellite radio? Did people want to listen to satellite radio while jogging? Did they want radios that could be easily moved from a car to a home or office? At a fundamental level, assuming that there was at least some interest in all of these options, where should limited marketing resources be assigned?

Competition for Radio Listeners Heats Up

The death knell for AM and FM radio has been sounded many times, only to be wrong in each instance.[23] Commercial radio did not sit idly by as satellite radio scooped up subscribers. AM and FM responded to the challenge by experimenting with new formats, targeting ethnic groups, reducing the number of commercial minutes per hour, and implementing a new version of digital radio. One of the new formats, known as Jack, provided an eclectic mix of music rather than single formats such as soft rock or country. It was intended to make radio more unpredictable and create a feeling of spontaneity. In many cases, however, it used voice-overs that simply promoted the station and did not talk about the music as a DJ would. The effort to target ethnic groups, particularly Hispanics, bore fruit, as the number of Hispanic listeners to commercial radio more than doubled between 1995 and 2005. To recoup revenue lost by reducing the number of commercials played, some broadcasters increased the price of advertising.[24]

Commercial radio also launched a major HD radio initiative during this period. HD radio is a form of local digital broadcasting that was tested in the early 1990s but was not implemented for more than a decade as a consequence of debates about standards and the perception by many in the industry that it was not needed.[25] HD radio allows both AM and FM stations to broadcast one or more additional signals of high-quality audio; HD FM has moderately better quality than HD AM. HD radio transmissions were widely implemented by the mid-2000s, but user adoption of new HD radios was slow because of their high cost and because of a weak understanding of what HD provides. HD radio faces the same hurdles satellite radio encountered when it was first introduced. It needs to find early adopters who will buy expensive radios to pick up relatively unknown services. HD must convince radio listeners that it provides a valuable user experience.

Many other competitors to satellite radio have emerged, including Web radio, podcasts, MP-3 radio, and mobile phone radio, among others. The Web is the most significant, since most commercial and public radio stations have an online presence. International radio stations, amateur radio stations, and podcasts are also available on the Web. Podcasts include individuals giving their opinions on a wide range of subjects; audio files created by other media

DIGITAL RADIO IN EUROPE

Europe has paralleled North America in the development of multiple forms of digital radio, leading in some areas and trailing in others. SKY Digital was the first to offer a satellite radio service in Europe in the late 1990s. WorldSpace, which launched the first satellite radio services in Asia and Africa, offers a satellite radio service for Africa and the Middle East that reaches parts of Europe. It offers many ethnic music channels—for example in Hindi, Tamil, and Arabic—and a dozen news channels, including five from the BBC.

Europe has two forms of terrestrial digital radio, digital radio mondiale (DRM) and digital audio broadcasting (DAB). DRM, first offered in 2003, is a digital shortwave service that creates extra space within the AM shortwave band for digital channels and modestly improves the audio signal. DAB was first tested in the United Kingdom in 1990; by 1995, a service was operating in London. DAB resembles HD radio in the United States, creating extra space for digital channels within the FM band and providing near-CD quality audio. DAB operates in the United Kingdom, Germany, Belgium, Spain, and Denmark, among other European countries. DAB, like satellite radio, supports many forms of data content, such as displaying the name of the artist and song title; some DAB radios can store programming and let users rewind and replay songs.

Digital radio services are also distributed on the Web as well as on some satellite and cable TV services. Germany and the United Kingdom have taken the lead in developing digital radio networks and services. The BBC in particular has been very active in creating new channels that are carried on multiple digital platforms. It is the largest digital audio content provider and has focused on reaching groups that have not been traditional BBC listeners, such as ethnic minorities and young people.

organizations, such as newspapers; and syndicated radio programs, such as Rush Limbaugh's talk show. Web radio and podcasts are viable because people spend so much time at the computer and many PCs are now equipped with good speakers. These services often provide background listening while people perform other tasks on the computer, much as traditional radio provides background listening for other tasks. In some cases, Web radio includes music videos or innovations such as sneak peeks at new songs.

MP-3 radio includes audio services such as Real Networks that create radio programming and allow users to download it to their MP-3 player for listening inside or outside the home. Other new radio services for cars and other mobile environments include WiMax services, which allow Web radio to be picked up in cars, and cellular networks that transmit radio programming to mobile phones anywhere in their coverage areas.

All of these radio services and many nonradio services such as mobile video are competing with satellite radio for people's time. Satellite radio's advantages are its wide coverage area, low cost relative to many other services directed toward mobile settings, relative lack of advertising, and variety without requiring users to do a lot of work to find and obtain program content, as is the case with MP-3 players. Satellite radio's disadvantages are its cost for equipment and monthly subscription, the need for a special receiver, and the end user's relative lack of control over playlists. Another core differentiator is control versus spontaneity. MP-3 players and some other competitors to satellite radio provide more control over content. Satellite radio is a more spontaneous experience and provides more ways to foster a sense of belonging to a community.

The Merger

In January 2007, Sirius and XM proposed a merger of their two companies. After a protracted regulatory review by the FCC, the merger was approved in mid-2008. The new company, Sirius/XM, promised cost reductions through the sharing of facilities, cheaper programming from content providers (which no longer had two companies bidding for their services), and reductions in content duplication (e.g., one jazz channel could be shared by the two services). Some analysts remained skeptical that sufficient cost reductions could be realized.[26]

Satellite radio brings up again the question of what is meant by success or failure for new media. The medium overcame many hurdles and won over millions of users, who enjoy a radically different listening experience. But user acceptance is not sufficient for success as a business.

// TEN //

The Integration of Mobile Phones into Everyday Life

Can you imagine a time when a mobile phone (aka *cell phone* in the United States, *keitai* in Japan, and *handy* in Germany) was a rarity? Most adult readers of this chapter will recall such a time and a subsequent period when mobile phones were used primarily by emergency workers and the business elite. Yet in a relatively short period, mobile phones have been adopted by the mass public and become an essential part of everyday life. Countries in Europe and Asia led the way to this widespread adoption.

This chapter traces the integration of mobile phones into everyday life between roughly 1990 to the late-2000s. It illustrates many of the principles discussed in chapters 1 and 2—for example, how earlier and later adopters of a technology often differ, how the ways a technology is used can change over time, how a decline in price can help spur mass adoption, and how difficult it is to predict the rate of adoption for a new medium as well as the features that will be added to it over time. We treat the core functions of mobile phones, how people use them, etiquette issues, changes in users' perceptions of space and time, the impacts of mobile phones on commerce and on other technologies, nonvoice applications such as texting, and some of the striking ways mobile phones are used in developing countries. The mobile phone is a prime example of how technology can shape social behavior and how social behavior, in turn, can shape subsequent iterations of a particular technology.

We do not attempt to deal with the latest technological advances in mobile phones that have entered the marketplace but are too new for their implications to be fully grasped—4G networks, WiFi-enabled mobile phones, advanced video applications, and many others. We are concerned with the introduction and broad integration of mobile phones into users' lives. Our emphasis, in line with the theme of this book, is the user experience, not regulation, broad societal effects, or technological advances, though we touch briefly on all of these areas to set the stage for developments in user experiences.

We draw on our research along with the rich literature on mobile phones, in particular, the work of Goggin, Katz, and Ling.[1] We give slightly more emphasis to user experiences in the United States but cover applications and uses in many other countries as well. Before tackling how mobile phones became embedded in everyday life and evolved from simple telephones to multi-application devices, it is useful to trace the history of mobile communication devices that set the stage for the mobile phone.

Mobile Communication

One fundamental characteristic of mobile phones is that users can make and receive phone calls anywhere, even in a moving car or train (provided they are located in a covered cell). However, many forms of mobile communication preceded the mobile phone and helped to create a demand for this form of communication. With apologies to fans of carrier pigeons and smoke signals, we will limit our treatment of early mobile communications to electronic technologies. The first notable technology that provided mobile communications was wireless telegraphy, developed by Guglielmo Marconi in the late 1890s. It used the radio spectrum to send telegraph signals over a distance. Many applications demonstrated the technology and gained publicity, such as sending messages across the Atlantic, but its most practical use was as a mobile application: ship-to-ship and ship-to-shore communications. When the *Titanic* struck an iceberg in 1912, a wireless telegraph operator on the ship transmitted a distress signal to other ships and to a Marconi operator, David Sarnoff, in the United States. For a while thereafter, wireless telegraphy captured the public's imagination, much as the Web did in the early twenty-first century. It was celebrated in books and movies; people could now communicate without wires over long distances.

Portable telephones existed in the nineteenth century and were used by technicians installing or repairing lines. At the turn of the century, they were also used in the Boer War. In both cases, the phone had to be attached to an existing telephone line but could then be moved. In 1911, a primitive car phone was developed in Sweden; users had to stop their cars and hook the device to a line on a telephone pole.[2] With a few such exceptions, most telephones were hard-wired to networks and could be moved only by technicians. During the 1970s, telephone jacks came into wide use, enabling people to move phones to any room that had a jack. In the 1980s, cordless or portable telephones were introduced to the general public and became very popular. Though they had a limited range (approximately 200 feet from the base station, which had to be attached to the wired telephone network), they helped to develop an appetite for telephone service that was not hard-wired to a wall. Similarly, speakerphones, telephone extension cords, hands-free headsets, 25-foot handset cords, and other accessories gave people greater freedom of movement than had previously been the case with traditional hard-wired telephones.

The first radio telephone is often attributed to the Detroit police department in the early 1920s, though this device provided only a one-way radio signal from a dispatcher to a police car; policemen then had to find regular telephones to call the dispatcher.[3] In 1924, Bell Labs built an experimental two-way car radio that connected to the telephone network. It was not ready for commercial use but demonstrated that the service was possible. By the 1940s, cars in St. Louis and New York City had radio telephone service, but it was very primitive: the equipment weighed 80 pounds; it was half duplex (meaning that only one person could speak at a time); calls had to be connected by operators; and each system could accommodate only 12 simultaneous conversations. By the 1970s, most of the systems were full-duplex (both parties could talk at the same time) and had direct dialing, but capacity remained very limited and equipment remained very expensive and heavy. Nonetheless, the service had long waiting lists, another indicator of demand.

Europe had similar experiences. The Post Office in the United Kingdom, which operated its telephone service, experimented with the technology in the 1950s, offered limited services in the 1960s and 1970s, but hesitated to offer expanded service given the same limitations of high cost and low capacity. Sweden's state-owned telephone company, Televerket, was more ambitious, developing a mobile telephone system by 1955 and attracting 20,000 customers by 1981.[4]

In 1969, Bell Labs developed a service for Amtrak's New York–to-Washington Metroliner that foreshadowed true cellular telephony. Using existing frequencies and technology, the system had radio zones between which calls were passed as the train moved, as in cellular service. It was implemented as a pay phone onboard the train, with the technology transparent to end users.[5]

A few other types of mobile communications have taken the form of two-way radio rather than telephony. Two-way radio for cars began in the 1920s and was well developed by the 1930s for police cars, taxis, and emergency vehicles. Drivers could communicate in real time with dispatchers and others listening in on the same frequency. During World War II, the walkie-talkie (a portable two-way radio developed by the Canadian government) was used widely by the military. It had the major advantage that it could be carried directly into battle. After the war, two-way car radios as well as walkie-talkies (now used by the public as well as the military) became more common as the equipment became lighter, cheaper, and could transmit over greater distances.

Amateur radio, often called ham radio (the origin of the term is unclear), began with wireless telegraphy operators, many of them amateurs and teenagers. Their numbers grew into the tens of thousands, and they played a significant role in support of the military during World War I. Though most eventually migrated to voice communication, telegraphy remained an important part of amateur radio for many decades, and until early in the twenty-first century, a certain level of proficiency was required to obtain a license. Ham radio has served a dual purpose, providing both public service (e.g., emergency communication during hurricanes) and recreation for its legions of users. Some of the frequencies assigned for its use allow people to communicate around the globe. Beginning in the 1960s, equipment was developed to make ham radio mobile, which led to the creation of a new term, *mobiling*. Ham radio remains a viable service for its core constituents and an important tool for emergency communications.

Citizens band (CB) radio is another form of mobile communication begun in the 1940s but not authorized by the U.S. Federal Communications Commission until 1958. It is a more freewheeling form of amateur radio that became popular initially with truckers, who used it to communicate with other truckers about congested roads, directions, and speed traps. Users originally were supposed to obtain licenses to operate CB radios, but many ignored this requirement, and it eventually was dropped. During the 1970s, CB radio became a fad not just in the United States but also in the United Kingdom, the Netherlands, and many other countries. In the United States, CB users grew from a few hundred thousand at the beginning of the decade to more than 10 million (estimates vary), only to return to a smaller user base of approximately 1 million by the early 1980s.[6] Some observers attribute the rise in popularity to the 1973 energy crisis, when people wanted to find out which gas stations were open, but that is likely only one of several contributing factors. CB was popularized in dozens of movies, TV series, and songs. It also fostered a special code for communicating: users had nicknames (handles) and utilized shorthand terminology to improve efficiency in communicating—e.g., 10-4, meaning "understood," a code borrowed from the police. Communication over CB was an open party line much like Web chat rooms. It also became a forum for much uncivil behavior, which may have contributed to its decline. It is not extinct, however, as truckers and some other groups still use it.

Pagers, also known as beepers, are a nonvoice form of mobile communication that helped set the stage for mobile phones. In its original form, the pager was a one-way radio broadcast to a device that someone wore or carried. The very first pagers did not even have displays but beeped, telling the person to call in and receive a message. Later they displayed the caller's phone number and eventually messages. Users found clever ways to extend pagers' capabilities. In Japan, some people used a number sequence to represent words: 0840, for example, meant "good morning."[7] The two-way pager, in which the receiving device could also be used to send a message back to the sender, evolved later. The first successful pagers for the general public were introduced in the 1970s. More than three million users existed worldwide in the early 1980s, a number that topped 60 million by the mid-1990s. Pagers were popular initially with doctors and other professionals, then tradespeople such as plumbers, and later teenagers. They were also popular with gangs and drug dealers, which contributed much negative publicity.[8] They competed as a cheaper alternative to mobile phones in the 1980s and 1990s. Over time, pager-style communication (i.e., short text messages) was built into mobile phones, and the use of pagers declined.

Another indicator of potential interest in mobile phones was the widespread adoption of other portable media. Newspapers, magazines, and books were, of course, highly portable throughout the nineteenth and twentieth centuries. Other media became portable as the constraint of relying on stationary terminals was relaxed—for example, by the introduction of car radios in the 1930s and the transistor radio in the 1950s. The Walkman (audiocassette and later CD) popularized mobile playback of music, and handheld video game players received widespread use beginning in the late 1970s.

People's collective experiences with portable telephones, radio telephones, the many forms of two-way radio, and pagers had demonstrated a strong interest in mobile communication by the time mobile phones were introduced. It is remarkable, discussed in chapter 2, that some in the mainstream telecommunication industry overlooked the evidence right in front of them and failed to see the growth potential for mobile phones. This clearly was not a case of technology push: users' behavior signaled the demand for mobile phones.

A Brief History of the Mobile Phone

The concept of a mobile telephone system was invented by scientists at AT&T's Bell Laboratories in 1947. In principle, it is a simple concept: clusters of cellular base stations are spread throughout a region. A caller uses a mobile phone to connect over a radio frequency with a base station and through it to the wired telephone network and thus with telephones connected to the wired network or with other mobile phones connected to other cellular base stations connected to the wired network. As the caller moves out of range of one cellular base station, the connection is passed along to an adjacent cellular station. The radio signals are limited in strength, which means that the frequency in use for a particular call in a particular cell can simultaneously be in use for other calls in other cells as long as they are not too nearby. This procedure makes highly efficient use of the radio spectrum. One of the major constraints of early radio telephone services was their very inefficient use of the spectrum: radio calls were transmitted over considerable distances on a single frequency, severely limiting the number of simultaneous calls.

Many technological, regulatory, and economic obstacles needed to be overcome before cellular telephone systems could be implemented, and this process took a few decades. In the United States, mobile phone systems were also delayed by the Federal Communications Commission's slow action in granting spectrum for the service and disputes over standards.[9] The first trial of a cellular telephone service, by AT&T, began in Chicago during 1978, and the first regular service was also offered in Chicago by Ameritech in 1983. The Japanese began a trial in 1979 in Tokyo, but service there developed slowly. The champions in mobile phone service development were Sweden, Finland, Denmark, and Norway, which developed a common standard—the Nordic Mobile Telephone system—and had services operational by 1981. Within a few years, other European countries followed, also developing a common standard, GSM (Global System for Mobile Communications or, in its original French, Groupe Spécial Mobile) that was widely adopted in Europe and elsewhere throughout the world, but not in the United States.

By the mid-1980s, approximately 600,000 people worldwide had mobile phones.[10] Most early mobile phones were installed in cars. Although portable units existed, they were very heavy, expensive, and had limited battery life—as short as 20 minutes of calling time before needing to be recharged. They were appropriately called *luggables.*

Other inhibitors of the growth of mobile phone use in the United States included incompatible standards and the difficulty of building wide area coverage in such a spread-out country. The quality of service not only during the early years but also into the twenty-first century was not comparable to that of wired telephone service. Many customers complained and frequently changed service providers.[11] Some people even dropped service for a while. However, these factors do not appear to have had significant influence on overall adoption, which was boosted by many factors.

First in Europe and later in the United States, early analog systems were converted to digital. Security had been a major problem of analog systems, with criminals finding it relatively easy to intercept mobile phone numbers and use them to make calls, often internationally. Digital networks made such abuses much more difficult.

Most telephone calls, even in the wired network, are short (half are less than one minute, and 70 percent are less than two minutes). As a result, mobile calls seemed less extravagant when per-minute prices were high. Many homes and offices had adopted answering machines, and mobile phones extended similar benefits, since calls could be received at any time in any place. In the 1980s and 1990s, many homes adopted multiple phone lines, some of which were used by only one person in a household. The mobile phone built on this appetite by offering personal phone service for each household member. Prepay plans,

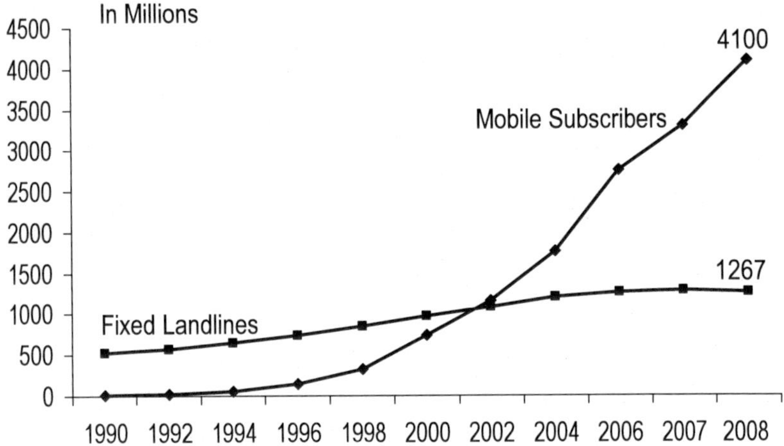

Fig. 10.1. Worldwide growth of telephone service, 1990–2007. (Data from United Nations International Telecommunication Union, *ICT Statistics* [2009].)

where a set number of minutes are purchased in advance and used as needed, were marketed and adopted in Europe much more than in the United States. These plans gave people a feeling of control over their mobile phone bills and extended service to people who lacked strong credit histories. Prepayment also appealed to people who needed only a small number of minutes per month and parents who wanted to restrict their children's usage.

During the 1990s, mobile phones took off.[12] Figure 10.1 shows the comparative growth of mobile and wired telephone subscriptions worldwide from 1990 to 2008. In 1990, the ratio of wired to mobile phones was 50:1. By 2000, that ratio had narrowed to 3:2, and six years later, the world had more mobile phones than wired lines. Adoption rates varied by country. In 2000, the per capita figures for mobile phone penetration were 60 percent in Sweden, 41 percent in the United Kingdom, and 29 percent in the United States.[13] Though mobile growth in the United States trailed many European countries, it was still remarkable. Only 16 years passed from the point when mobile phones were widely available to the point when half of U.S. households had adopted them, one of the fastest growth rates for any communication technology introduced into the United States and more than four times the speed with which wired telephones entered U.S. households.

The adoption of mobile phones was driven by the wide availability of cellular services, price decreases for both mobile phones and service, and a reduction in the size of mobile phones that allowed people to carry them in their pockets. In the 1970s, U.S. mobile phones cost more than $3,000 and weighed a few pounds; in Europe, one early mobile phone, the Mobira Senator, cost $4,500 and weighed more than four pounds.[14] By 1990, phones cost an average of $875 and weighed several ounces; a decade later, they cost less than $200 and weighed only a few ounces. The price of mobile service also decreased dramatically, from 56 cents per minute in the United States in 1995 to 14 cents per minute in 2001.[15] The average monthly bill for mobile phone service declined steadily, reaching its nadir in the late 1990s. The rapidly growing market enabled providers to achieve economies of scale, which drove down costs and hence prices, which, in turn, helped expand the market further (illustrating the kind of positive feedback discussed in chapter 1). Bills subsequently began to increase slightly as telephone companies offered many pricing options and moved a number of customers into higher-priced tiers with the lure of extra features.

One notable change was the transition from mobiles installed in cars to handheld units, a development enabled by smaller, lighter mobile phones and longer battery life. Early use was overwhelmingly for voice calls, but nonvoice applications such as text messaging and later taking photographs began to grow once the networks were converted to digital. As the price of mobile phone service dropped, there were a number of changes in use. Mobile phone use was overwhelmingly by businesses when the price of service was high. As the price dropped, consumer use increased. Businesses did not lessen their use of mobile phones; rather, consumer use grew, accounting for a steadily increasing percentage of the total. Important initial adopters among early business users included emergency repair persons (such as utility company employees) and people who fixed appliances as well as corporate executives.

The value of mobile phones for certain types of workers during this period, when costs were high, was made clear in an interview one of the authors conducted with a refrigerator repairman in 1990. He explained that most of his referrals came from a listing in the yellow pages. Before he began using a mobile phone, he had used an office-based landline with an answering machine. Whenever he checked for messages, he heard mostly clicks—people had called and hung up without leaving messages. He surmised that they did not want to wait for him to return their calls and simply telephoned another repair service listed in the yellow pages. With a mobile phone, however, he could take those calls wherever he was and tell the caller when he would arrive to deal with the problem. Thus, the added business more than justified the mobile phone's high cost.

Most early mobile phone users were men, who accounted for more than 90 percent of U.S. subscribers in 1989.[16] Some observers have attributed this phenomenon more to occupational need (i.e., men dominated the emergency and field-services professions in which mobile phones' value was first recognized) than to gender. Women adopted mobile phones later than men and for somewhat different reasons—most notably, security. By 1997, women accounted for more than half of users, with the surge helped by the drop in prices. By 2000, overall consumer usage had more than doubled from 1993–97 levels; between 2000 and 2002, the average number of monthly minutes of use per subscriber nearly doubled again.[17]

During the 1990s, mobile phones were perceived as lifelines if people's cars broke down or if they felt that they were in dangerous situations and needed to call for help. One woman we interviewed at the time told us of her elevator phobia. Her fear was not that the elevator would drop but that she might become stuck in it and not be able to call for help. With a mobile phone, she felt that she could reach help, and her elevator phobia faded away. By the late 1990s, many U.S. parents began to give mobile phones to their teenage children as a safety device and as a way to keep tabs on them (a use that had already become popular in Europe). With the start of the new century, safety and security remained important motivations for acquiring and keeping mobile phones, especially for older people, but those reasons stood out less amid the many other uses.

We now take for granted the idea that most people keep their mobile phones on at just about all times. In the United States, however, such was not the case for many users in the 1990s, largely because of an artifact of billing. American users of mobile phones pay for both sent and received calls, and when the price was high, many of them used the phones only to make calls, with some users acquiring pagers to receive messages. Many people hesitated to give out their mobile phone numbers even to friends. As prices dropped, more people used mobile phones to both make and receive calls. Keeping mobile phones turned off had an impact on the networking effect discussed in chapter 1. The value of a telephone network is related in part to the number of people it connects. Early in U.S. mobile phone usage, the positive impact of the network effect was limited, since people could not call someone whose phone was off most of the time. There were also reports that in some countries, relatively few people regularly took along their mobile phones when leaving the house, since carrying a phone had not yet become part of a routine, like carrying a wallet or keys, and people consequently forgot.[18] Over time, the number of people who owned mobile phones, carried them outside homes and offices, and kept them on nearly all the time increased, thereby increasing the value of the network. For many, connectivity became almost an obsession.[19]

In Europe and many other countries where mobile phone users do not pay for incoming calls, the billing structure encouraged people to keep their mobile phones on and thereby increased the overall value of the network for users. Such practices encouraged usage, sped up the transmission of messages (which could be received at any time), and supported real-time information services that added value to the service (it is more valuable to receive information about a drop in stock price as soon as the event occurs rather than an hour later). The fact that European countries generally have higher population densities than does the United States eased the process of building mobile phone networks, and prepaid mobile phone service encouraged adoption of mobile phones by those with lower incomes and teens whose parents could control the number of minutes used.[20]

While the caller-pays model adopted in most of the world has promoted a more rapid diffusion of mobile phones, it has come with a cost. When choosing mobile phone companies, consumers tend to focus on their personal charges and to pay little if any attention to what others will pay to call them. As a result, mobile phone operators in countries where the caller pays have imposed high termination charges (charges to the carriers of incoming calls), which are passed on to callers. These high costs reflect the monopoly power of the providers who "own" customers receiving calls for which they do not pay.

Mobile Phone Behavior

To understand the many ways people have come to use mobile phones, it is helpful to list their core functions and attributes. The functions identified by James Katz and his colleagues include personal security; tighter coordination of schedules and more efficient time management; reducing the uncertainty associated with travel; preserving a family network over a distance as family members move to different parts of a country; managing parent-child relationships by staying in touch while physically separated; and freedom for those with medical problems.[21] At a fundamental level, mobile phones allow people to handle more communications and to do so in an environment where they are not tied down by physical connections to a network.

Mobile phones help people feel in control of their lives no matter where they are, enhancing a sense of power. At the same time, they can be an instrument for others to control the mobile phone user—for example, bosses who can reach workers on weekends. Within work environments, some of the core functions of mobile phones include tracking and managing workers; speeding up commercial transactions, which can be conducted while on the road; coordinating schedules; and offering greater access to company-related information.[22] We would add to this list socializing, spreading gossip, killing time, and being entertained.

A mobile phone is generally used by only one person, unlike landlines in homes, which are typically shared. (However, some applications of mobile phones are used by groups or to start conversations between two or more people who are together.) Similarly, a call to a mobile phone is a call to an individual rather than a location as with a landline. Mobile phones are personal devices, a status that leads to a number of behaviors and attitudes. Many people identify with their mobile phones as if they were jewelry or cars. Some people wear mobile phones like articles of clothing, hanging them on belts or attaching them to jackets. Our research found that wearing a mobile phone was more common among men. (By our research, we mean a series of studies conducted by one of the authors in the United States from the early 1990s through the mid-2000s. These studies are complemented by other research.) Some women described wearing phones as more of a "guy thing" and for "techies." However, the mobile phone as a fashion statement about the person is common among both men and women. The color, shape, and style (e.g., a phone with a touch screen) are important for many users. Others who have studied mobile phones as fashion items across many cultures report that important age differences exist, with teenagers more likely to treat mobile phones as fashion items.[23]

Many users personalize their mobile phones. In some countries—for example, Japan—users decorate their mobile phones with tassels or stickers as an expression of personality.[24] Such decorations have not been common in Europe or the United States, though we have observed some of this behavior by teenagers and have interviewed people who said they did it as young teenagers but grew out of the practice. In Europe and the United States, users more commonly customize their mobile phones in other ways—for example, by selecting ring tones, ring backs, or customized screen backgrounds such as personal photographs. Some people see mobile phones as purely functional and do not care about the look. For most, however, some form of personalization is important.

Many users place their phones (often, hooked up to battery chargers) next to their beds while they are asleep; some students have told us that they make and receive calls or text messages during the night. Longer-life batteries (and routines of recharging batteries every night) have enabled mobile phones to be on 24 hours a day. These attributes have contributed to a sense of accessibility—users feel that they and friends, family, or colleagues are available just about any time and anywhere. No other medium matches the mobile phone for accessibility. In addition, because people always have their mobile phones on hand, they are used for things that might otherwise require another technology, such as telling the time or keeping an appointment calendar. Accessibility is not always a positive attribute. When we asked users about the downside to having a mobile phone, the most common answer was that they could be reached anytime and callers expected them to answer or call back as soon as they were free.

Making and Receiving Mobile Phone Calls

People use a number of ways to make calls: direct input of the phone number (dialing); direct input by keying or saying a person's name (the phone recognizes the name from a contact list); calling from the contact list or call history; and speed dialing. The choice is based on the perceived quickness of each method and habit. Perceived quickness varies by mobile phone. For example, with low-end phones, many people say that it is quicker to dial a number (if you know it) than use the contact list (too many steps to get to a name). However, advanced mobile phone users often find that using the contact list is quicker than inputting a number. Many use two or more methods—for example, speed dialing for close friends and family and the contact list for a wider circle of friends. Others use call history when calling someone back (perceived as faster) and direct input or the contact list when initiating a call. A side benefit of automated dialing is that users reach fewer wrong numbers.

People commonly screen incoming calls since most phones display the incoming caller's phone number and often name. Further, some people purchase and assign distinctive ringtones to certain callers, to aid in quickly identifying the caller. The patterns of screening vary considerably but typically involve screening out people they want to avoid—perhaps people who might take up too much time and numbers that are likely telemarketers. The ability to see the number or name of the person calling has had an impact on the opening greetings in a phone call. A mobile phone user can skip the traditional "Hello" and greet the incoming caller by name (e.g., "What's up, George?") or immediately continue previous conversations (e.g., "So, did you get it?") The prevalence of screening also raises some issues for callers. If a call goes unanswered and is transferred to the voice message system, is the person not available or screening? Some people do not care as long as the call is promptly returned.

When first introduced, voice message systems for mobile phones supplemented answering machines attached to landlines. Many people later came to rely solely on voice message systems for mobile phones and discarded their answering machines. This behavior has continued to evolve over time, and the use of voice message systems appears to have declined, but such practices vary by age. Many teens described voice messages as a service for older people, such as their parents. Younger people generally left few voice messages and checked voice mail infrequently or not at all. Simply calling (and thereby recording their names and numbers in the phone's list of recent calls) was enough to generate a return call. Alternatively, some young people sent text messages asking the recipient to call back. Older users were more likely to leave voice messages but many described the process of doing so and subsequently of retrieving messages as a hassle because of the voice message system's design, which involved too many options and too many steps and thus took up too much time.

Socializing and Spreading Gossip

When mobile phone service was expensive, usage was more deliberate—people only called others because they had a specific message to convey. As the price dropped, people began to call others just to keep in touch, often with no specific message. This change has helped mobile phones become a regular habit for millions of users. This pattern parallels the early and later uses of wired telephone lines. In the late nineteenth and early twentieth centuries, telephones were used primarily by businesses and by wealthy people to convey specific messages, but they later came into mass use to convey messages and for chatting or socializing.[25]

The practice of calling friends and family frequently and from many locations has made the mobile phone an important tool for maintaining social cohesion. People previously maintained groups through physical contact and telephone calls from fixed locations. The mobile phone has greatly expanded the ways small groups can stay together. The cohort most affected by this phenomenon is teenagers, who are by their nature more fixated on friends than are young children and adults.

Because they are always on and always present, mobile phones are an ideal medium for spreading gossip, as participants in our studies frequently recounted. After a store in her town burned down under suspicious circumstances, one teenager sent and received dozens of voice and text messages about the incident, and within a few hours, everyone in her circle of friends knew about it and was gossiping about how it might have happened.

Fake Calls

One interesting behavior of mobile phone users first identified by Katz is that many people, at least occasionally, pretend to be making mobile phone calls when they are not speaking to anyone.[26] We have identified three situations where this behavior occurs. The first involves perceived danger: women out late at night who see someone coming toward them flip open their mobile phones and pretend to be talking to other people, hoping that the perception that someone could alert the police would deter a possible attack. The second example, mentioned more frequently, involves deflecting unwanted conversation: when people are not interested in getting involved with approaching acquaintances, they pull out mobile phones and pretend to be talking and therefore unable to chat with the person present. Similarly, when people want to get away from others—for example, an annoying person at a bar—they will pretend that they have an incoming call and walk away. A third example, mentioned by some people in large metropolitan areas, involves using the mobile phone to avoid aggressive panhandlers or people handing out leaflets on the street, who are more likely to leave passers-by alone if they appear to be engaged in a phone conversation.

Scheduling and Coordination

The attributes of "always on" and "always with you" have enabled extensive coordination of activities in a way that was not possible in earlier times. For example, family members going to a mall can split up and coordinate when and where to meet at a later point via mobile phone instead of prearranging a rendezvous before knowing the optimum time and location. Many mobile users in our studies mentioned calling family members from the supermarket to ask about items to be purchased or calling friends to remind them about trivial matters. Some scholars have called this behavior micro-coordination.[27]

Mobile phone use has also evolved to include relaying information about the status of a person in transit to a meeting. In research we conducted in the late 1990s, people frequently used mobile phones to let others know if they were going to be late for business meetings or family events. Over time, some people began to call or text to indicate that they were going to be on time. This behavior further evolved to a point where many people now call or text not just to say that they are on time but where they are along the way to the meeting or event—for example, "I'm three miles away." This process may involve multiple messages along the way.

A related change lies in how some people, especially younger people, schedule meetings or dates. Instead of one call to schedule a specific time and place to get together, a meeting may be negotiated over multiple phone calls or texts. Many teens have reported that if they want to meet up with someone over the weekend, they will first call and see if the person wants to get together. During subsequent phone calls or texts, they will negotiate what day to meet, where, and finally at what time, with the last details sometimes arranged only half an hour before the meeting. Some older people also follow this procedure in certain circumstances—for example, when a meeting time cannot be fixed because of uncertainties in other commitments.

Important age differences generally exist in this use of mobile phones. Older people indicated that if they were running late for a meeting, they would call ahead and indicate their arrival time but would still feel that they were late. When younger people say that they will arrive at 10:00 A.M., they mean around 10:00 A.M. If they then call at 9:30 and say they will arrive at 10:15 and arrive at that time, they do not feel that they are late since they *changed* the arrival time. This strategy keeps options open and builds flexibility into people's lives. The mobile phone becomes a tool in organizing a schedule. But not everyone likes the change.

It is not clear whether these patterns of use will, in the long run, change cultural perceptions of scheduling and time. Some observers have suggested that these developments may "soften" our sense of time.[28] *Soften* is a good term because it does not eliminate fixed time. Trains still run on a fixed schedule, and many meetings must start on time because a room is only available for a specific period. Nonetheless, scheduling has changed since the days when people were generally out of touch for long periods and had to rely on a watch and event calendar to coordinate meetings.

Multitasking

Nearly everyone in our U.S.-based research reported that they occasionally or frequently multitask while on their mobile phones. The accompanying activities included eating, surfing the Web, reading, shopping, doing the dishes, watching TV, and walking, among others. Similarly, everyone of driving age reported using their phones while driving, and some even sent text messages while driving. There have been a number of reports of people texting while driving a car or operating a train, sometimes with fatal consequences. Laws about using a mobile phone while driving vary in different jurisdictions.

Multitasking while driving is not limited to people operating cars or trucks. We have observed many people using mobile phones while on motorcycles and bicycles. Driving when alone was described as free time to catch up with friends or return calls and as otherwise boring down time that people wanted to fill with some activity such as listening to the radio or making calls. Those with long commutes said they have developed routines about who and when they call. Some used hands-free mobile phones in these situations in the belief that doing so reduced the danger, but research suggests that the danger comes from distraction, not from holding the phone.[29]

More generally, during the large portions of the day when people are moving about—walking on the street, running errands, and shopping—they are available to do double duty with a mobile phone by communicating with others. And they do, sometimes to the chagrin of those they encounter.

Etiquette

As with other new media, etiquette for mobile phones has taken much longer to evolve than has simple adoption and use. In the first decade of the twenty-first century, the unwritten rules of social interactions and etiquette for mobile phone use were still being worked out, as a question we have asked a large number of people illustrates: Would mobile phone use on airplanes be a good idea or a bad idea? Many respondents answered that it would be a good idea, since they could use their mobile phones someplace where that use is now restricted; others were appalled at the idea and viewed it as an intrusion on others' right to be undisturbed. When we asked people if they had ever been annoyed by someone making a mobile phone call, most cited numerous examples—individuals who spoke too loudly, conversations that went on too long, inappropriate places to make calls, and topics that they did not want to hear. Specific instances included mobile phone use in enclosed spaces such as trains, in public bathroom stalls, and while engaged with clerks in a store (thereby delaying everyone in line behind them) as well as discussions of very personal topics. People become so absorbed in the call that they do not realize that others are overhearing intimate details. Many people later reported, however, that they engaged in the same behaviors that they previously described as rude or unacceptable when done by others. The acceptability of mobile phone conversations in public places varies by country. According to Heidi Campbell, people in Japan are less tolerant of inappropriate mobile phone behavior in public locations than are people in Western countries.[30]

Help with mobile phone etiquette may come first from businesses—companies presumably can set rules about appropriate behavior at meetings. However, we have observed and many have reported that bad mobile phone behavior is just as prevalent in businesses as in the everyday social world. Some of the people we interviewed told us that their companies had formal rules about mobile phone use at meetings, while others said that unwritten social norms existed; both, however, were frequently violated. Colleagues would receive mobile phone calls during meetings: some would get up and take the call outside the room; some would get up and take the call in a corner of the room (where they could still be heard); and some would take the call at the table, speaking softly or cuffing their hands over their mouths but nevertheless audible. Most respondents characterized these behaviors as poor etiquette, with some wiggle room available depending on the type and level of meeting. Receiving calls was more acceptable if the person left the room. Teens have different views on etiquette issues. When asked where it would be poor etiquette to make or receive mobile phone calls, most had to think long and hard. One teen commented after several moments, "A funeral."

Predictably, teens also reported making mobile phone calls during school by sneaking into the bathroom, a variation of the strategy students used 30 years ago to sneak a smoke. Schools have many rules about mobile phone use, and students devote much energy to figuring out how to break the rules. Our respondents indicated that school administrators have made some progress in restricting mobile phone calls (though some teachers have "mobile phone breaks" to keep students from developing nervous tics at the thought that they might be missing calls).

Ringtones have enjoyed considerable popularity and generated substantial revenue for mobile phone companies and music publishers. They make a statement about the mobile phone owner's personality and about the perceived personalities of callers. However, others perceive "fun" ringtones as more disruptive than simple rings. Over time, many users have switched their phones to vibrate or silent mode to make them less disruptive, and the use of ring tones has declined.

Mobile phone etiquette has many nuances. Many people believed that it was poor etiquette to make or receive calls at tables in restaurants; received calls were more acceptable if the person got up to take the call in the lobby area. Some restaurants have tried to encourage patrons to leave tables when making calls by providing mobile phone booths in their lobby areas. If a person is engaged in face-to-face conversation and he or she answers the phone, does it signify that the person present is less important than the caller? It depends. In our research, if the recipient of the call indicates that the caller is a high-status person (e.g., a boss or a spouse), no breach of etiquette is perceived. Similarly, receiving calls is acceptable if the topic is very important or if the call will be very short. However, in other circumstances, most people consider it a breach of etiquette. Over time, there have been many efforts to develop and enforce rules of etiquette for mobile phone use, such as signs in movie houses, announcements at the beginning of meetings, and designated quiet cars on railroads. The results have been mixed. Devices also exist that can block mobile phone calls within a few hundred feet by jamming transmissions. They are illegal in the United States but are used elsewhere in restaurants and theaters.

At parties, we have observed people taking mobile phone calls and moving away from the group with which they were engaged as a courtesy—but they then were invading the space of other groups. Presumably, it is less offensive to invade the space of strangers. It generally appears that the more someone is connected socially and emotionally to people in a space or to an event, the more the sending or receiving of a mobile phone call is disruptive. Thus, it is perceived as more rude to make a mobile call at church, while dining with a loved one, in a classroom, or in theater and less rude on a train, at a ballpark, on a beach, or walking on the street.

Use in Public Spaces

Several issues are associated with mobile phone use in public spaces. One is noise: many public locations are very noisy. Most people simply accept noise and use their mobile phones anyway, even if parts of the conversation are lost or if they have to ask a person at the other end of the call to repeat something. Only if conditions are very noisy and the call is important do they try to find a quieter place. Most mobile phone microphones pick up sounds from all directions, meaning that background noise is an even bigger problem for people at the other end of the call.

We frequently observed people talking on their mobile phones or texting while walking. Some were fixated on their phones (especially when texting) and seemed unaware of their surroundings—for example, walking across a street against a red light or weaving on a sidwalk and bumping into others.

Though very few public spaces seem to be off-limits for using mobile phones, certain spaces are more popular than other for making calls—for example, any space where people are waiting. The public spaces where people are about to enter or leave dead zones for mobile calls are also prime areas for making calls—e.g., subway entrances/exits. Frequent fliers know that as soon as a plane lands, seemingly everyone onboard gets on their mobile phone. Mobile phones are used frequently at rock concerts, with patrons calling friends at home so they can listen, taking photos and sending them to friends; and using the light from mobile phones to create a sense of community and participation in the music, much as crowds used to wave lighters, lit matches, or candles.

Some people use mobile phones to create private spaces within public spaces—for example, train riders who turn their seating areas into their offices by making multiple calls throughout the train ride. It is as if they have created a bubble around them, separating their seat and themselves from all those around them. As noted in the discussion of etiquette, however, other people are not separated from the mobile phone conversations and often find them annoying if they are too loud, too long, or too personal.

Location

A broader set of issues associated with mobile phones and location involves mobile phone users' desire to know the location of people they are calling or, generally, where friends are located at any given moment; mobile phone calls or texts to others who are at the same location and the ways in which mobile phones can transform space.

One of the most common remarks in mobile phone conversations, especially those of younger people, is "Where are you?" Such statements may constitute the beginning of conversations or the sole purpose of calls. One obvious difference between a call to a landline and a call to a mobile phone is that callers generally know where the landline is located but do not know where the mobile phone is, so asking is natural. Knowing the location can also tell the caller about limitations that may be placed on the call—a person answering in a restaurant may not want to talk at length or about certain topics. Knowledge about another person's location also provides flexibility. For example, if two people are planning to meet at a street fair, neither one has to stay at a fixed location; both can move about and simply compare locations when they are ready to get together. For teens, who seem to have a fixation on the location of friends, it is an opportunity. They want to know with whom they might be able to connect and what is happening at the various locations where their friends are hanging out.

A number of location-based services help mobile phone users locate others. Among other things, such services let subscribers automatically send text messages to friends as the subscriber approaches, see friends' movements over the past few hours, and send text messages to request cabs with the subscriber's location automatically appended. Location-based services, which were popularized in Korea and the United Kingdom but have since spread to many other countries, can also alert parents if their children stray from their normal routes.

It would be reasonable to infer that many location-related uses of mobile phones involve people at different locations, but many mobile phone users have told us that they call or send text messages to people at the same location, for several reasons. One is to find someone at a large gathering—for example, a football stadium. A person we interviewed said he called a friend at such an event who was a hundred feet away and waved his cap so that the friend could find him in the crowd. A young woman said that she often sends text messages to friends at different different tables in a bar, commenting about the people around them.

A mobile phone can transform space in a few ways. It allows people to be present in two spaces—the physical space they occupy and the virtual space they occupy with the person on the call. This situation can create conflicts. Social behavior is governed by unwritten rules for the space we occupy.[31] Different rules cover behavior in theaters, ballparks, bars, and supermarkets. Mobile phone users can occupy two spaces with conflicting behavioral rules, leading to inevitable breaches in etiquette for one of those spaces. Mobile phones also let people leave the physical space where they are located. The term *absent presence* has been used to describe the situation where people are physically present but so absorbed in mobile phone calls that for all practical purposes they are not there.[32] Mobile phones can leak elements of a distant space into callers' physical space when people in callers' physical space overhear conversations that reveal elements of the space at the other end of the call or when callers talk to people in their physical space about what is going on at the other end.

Lee Humphreys has observed that two people can experience the same space very differently.[33] For example, a person who has lived in a neighborhood for 20 years and another person who is passing through for the first time are likely to experience the same space in different ways. Similarly, a person walking through a space and surrounded by strangers (without talking on a mobile phone) may feel isolated, but a person walking through the same space while talking on a mobile phone with friends is likely to feel less isolated. The definition of a space can change according to time of day (e.g., in a school, a large open space might serve as an auditorium in the morning, a lunchroom at noon, and a gym in the late afternoon), the group occupying the space, and the functions taking place. The mobile phone provides another dimension for changing the definition of a space, as when a seat on a train becomes an office. People also use mobile phones to create a verbal diary about the space they occupy, describing for others who are not present the details of their environment—for example, at a beach or in a department store.[34]

The Mobile Swiss Army Knife

When first introduced, the mobile phone was a device for making phone calls. During the 1990s, a few features were added, such as a contact list and clock. From the late 1990s through the early twenty-first century, however, a deluge of applications appeared (table 10.1). Moving people up to a new generation of services was made easier by the quick replacement cycle for mobile phones, which, in turn, has been fostered by a policy of subsidizing the costs of phones and putting those costs into subscription plans. In the United States, the average mobile phone is replaced every 14 months, providing numerous opportunities to place new applications in users' hands. Since replacing a mobile phone is often accompanied by renewing or changing a mobile phone plan, it also provides an opportunity to sell services that have fees above the basic plan.

Many of these features also support a multitude of applications. For example, the Web browser can allow users to obtain maps, do electronic shop-

TABLE 10.1. Features and Services on Mobile Phones

Mobile telephone	PDA
Contact list	SMS (plus text storage)
Calendar	Web browser
Calculator	Game player
Clock	Streaming video player
Still camera	Digital broadcast player
Camcorder	Radio
Alarm	Music storage and player
GPS	Photo storage and display
Voice message box	E-mail
Call history	Credit and debit card
Caller ID	Ring tone
Bar code reader	Electronic ticket
Wallpaper background	Ring-backs
Electronic wallet	Location-based services

ping, get news and weather information, and so on. Attitudes about the mobile phone as a Swiss army knife of telecommunications (and other) features and services vary considerably. Younger people generally are more open to the idea of mobile phones as multiple-application devices; older people are more likely to view them as phones, though many are open to some extra features. We have also encountered many older people and some younger ones who had a low awareness of the extra features on their mobile phones and weak skills in using the devices. Those who have committed to smart phones are more likely to view them as platforms for multiple applications rather than simply mobile phones with extra features. Such people also are more likely to have the skills necessary to use the advanced features or the curiosity to acquire those skills. The availability of features and their adoption rates vary considerably by country.

From a user perspective, some advanced features have important limitations. Many users are concerned about high fees for added features or hidden fees. Moreover, some mobile phone carriers have adopted a "walled garden" approach to content, restricting who may provide content over their network and justifying those restrictions with the argument—some would call it an excuse—that such a policy ensures that only high-quality content is allowed on the network (e.g., blocking pornography). However, many users with experience on the Web want no content restrictions. The user interface on some mobile phones is not well designed, making it hard to navigate through multiple layers of menus.

At the other end of the spectrum are owners of advanced and well-designed smart phones with thousands of applications (apps) available to them. They spend enormous amounts of time with their mobile phones, but making telephone calls is just one activity. They spend more time texting, surfing the Web, checking e-mail, playing games, and watching videos. The smart phone for many of them is a replacement for a laptop computer. These users identify so closely with their mobile phones that some ask for the phone to be buried with them, giving new meaning to the expression *take it anywhere.*

A broad range of text applications have been adopted, including contact lists, calendars, clocks/alarms, and call histories. These features are simple to use, work reasonably well on small screens, and place little demand on the mobile phone battery. One of the most intriguing applications that has become an everyday habit for millions of users is text messaging.

Texting

There are five ways to send and receive text messages using mobile phones, though only advanced smart phones can send and receive in all five of them:

SMS (short message service) or texting, which is limited to 160 characters per message; Web-based e-mail. which can be any length; Web-based IM (instant messaging) offered by companies such as AOL; proprietary IM offered by mobile service providers such as Blackberry (BBM); and proprietary e-mail within certain Web applications such as Facebook. We will concentrate on SMS, or texting, which has become an extraordinary phenomenon.

Texting began in the early 1990s in Europe.[35] It was included in the GSM standard for Europe but was considered a minor component of mobile phone service—a way for carriers to communicate brief messages to business subscribers. No one expected it to become a significant service. As in the case of many new media, however, serendipity entered into the process (in the form of teenagers), and texting eventually surpassed the volume of voice calls in many countries.

Texting took off first in Nordic countries during the middle of the decade. By 2000, nearly one billion text messages were sent in Finland, a country of five million people.[36] Japan was another early adopter of texting, launching a service in 1996. As in Europe, Japan's young people widely adopted texting. Cost was a significant factor in countries adopting the service—text messages cost less than voice calls. The United States was slower to adopt texting. In the 1990s, compatibility problems arose for text messages among mobile phone carriers, and these problems continued well into the present century between some carriers in the United States and others overseas. Also, U.S. service providers offered less of a cost advantage for text messages over voice calls, and pagers had already become popular, meeting part of the demand for text messages.

Many constraints hindered the widespread adoption of text messaging. The length of messages was restricted, and it was difficult to enter messages with the limited number of keys on a typical mobile phone. Many people had difficulty learning "thumb typing" and found its regular use annoying. Older people had trouble reading messages on small mobile phone screens. And early incompatibility among carriers meant that users could send text messages only to people who subscribed to the same service provider. A code was also needed to enable information to be communicated in such a short format.

All of these constraints were overcome for the legion of users, led by teens, who adopted texting, a phenomenon that would have been very hard to predict when texting was first introduced. People learned to thumb type, a shorthand code emerged, preformatted messages and software that filled in partially typed words (called T9) aided in creating messages, and many users came to regard the brevity of the format as an asset. Even the network effect, where the value of a network is related to the number of users, was not a major constraint. Three or four friends who used text messaging was enough to get someone started.

The texting phenomenon was not limited to Europe and Asia. By the 2000s, usage began to take off in the United States and many developing countries. By the middle of the decade, the world leader in the number of text messages per capita was the Philippines.

What is the attraction of texting? In addition to low cost, many people perceive it as convenient, efficient, and unobtrusive: for example, it can be used in situations where it would be inappropriate or embarrassing to make or receive voice calls. Texting also affords greater privacy than voice calls, an attribute that led to its rapid adoption by teenagers—they can make and receive text messages late at night without parents overhearing conversations. David Crystal argues that the restriction of the format to 160 characters is a positive attribute.[37] No penalty is imposed for abruptness; the shorter the better. Texting can be used in clandestine ways, such as in classrooms, undetected by teachers, or as a back channel between two people at a meeting—the electronic equivalent of passing notes under a table. It has also become part of courting rituals; many young couples negotiate a relationship through a series of texts.

Many adults use texting as a shorter alternative to e-mails. It is less personal, which is a positive in some situations—for example, when someone does not have time to fill in the expected opening and closing salutations of e-mail. Texting is often a better way to reach teenage children. Many teens do not check voice messages regularly or at all and can therefore deny receiving voice messages from their parents, but it is very difficult for them to deny having seen text messages—an incentive for parents to learn text messaging. Texting also allows parents to communicate with teens who are with their friends, saving the teens from the potential embarrassment of taking parental calls.

Text messages are generally perceived as less personal than voice calls. As a result, they are less suitable than voice call for certain types of messages. We spoke to a young woman who said that she received a birthday text message from her boyfriend, who was traveling, and felt that it was too impersonal and that he should have called. Newspaper reports have noted understandably negative reactions to incidents in which managers fired employees via text messages or in which spouses learned that they were being divorced. Research in Japan has shown that people who want to avoid intimate social contact prefer text messages over voice calls.[38]

In our research, most text messages were for coordination (e.g., "cu@4") and simple functional tasks (e.g., "call me"), though teens often used it for expressive communication (e.g., "I'm bored"). Nearly everyone we have interviewed said that they were texting more than they had a few years earlier and were making fewer calls as a result. Nearly all the teens we spoke to said that they made more text messages than voice calls.

TABLE 10.2. Txt Speak

b4n	Bye for now
pos	Parent over shoulder
cya	See you later
f?	Are we friends again?
7:-)	Baseball cap
zzz	Sleeping
404	I don't know
sup	What's up?

The style of text messages is closest to instant messages (IMs) but is unique in many respects. Users have developed a set of acronyms, abbreviations, and letter/symbol combinations to communicate more efficiently, as shown in Table 10.2. Many of these are very creative, though some critics view them as a corruption of standard languages. Most scholars view them as no different from many earlier forms of shorthand, such as stenographic symbols, abbreviations common in written communication (e.g., RSVP), or the system of dots and dashes in Morse code.[39] There is little punctuation or capitalization, except for emphasis. Though some teachers have offered anecdotes about students who used text shorthand in essays, these appear to be just that—anecdotes, not the end of standard languages.

The texting format allows only 160 characters and therefore supports some types of messages but not others. One way around the space limitation is to engage in a series of back-and-forth text messages that might span a few minutes or days. This process is common when people are scheduling when and where to meet. A problem sometimes arises when a person text messages another about more than one topic within a few hours and it becomes unclear to what question a response such as "yes" refers.

Texting has accelerated the adoption of some English words in other languages, in part because of the use of English as a second language in many countries and in part because of the brevity of English words compared to, for example, German words. Text messages also have some "code mixing," or mixing of English words with those from other languages—for example, Germans text *mbsseg* to convey "mail back *so schnell es geht*" (as fast as you can).[40] Many other language anomalies have been reported. For example, Richard Ling and Birgitte Yttri report that when Norwegians curse in a text message, they frequently do so in English.[41]

Texting illustrates a few of the principles outlined in chapter 1. For one, those who invent new media services often do not know who will use them and for what applications and whether they will be widely adopted. Also, the most robust service does not always win. If that were the case, mobile phone e-mails would have surpassed text messages.

Still Photos and Video

Still cameras were first built into mobile phones in Japan during the late 1990s, and the technology was deployed a few years later in Europe, the United States and other countries. The camera phone is a good example of a technology for which there was seemingly no prior demand. Cameras were built into mobile phones because the technology to do so existed, and when people replaced their previous phones, they acquired phones with this capability. Early camera phones took poor-quality photos, but many users nevertheless found them fun to use at informal social occasions—locations to which many people would not normally bring digital cameras. The mobile phone camera and the photos it captured became part of events, much as instant Polaroid cameras and photos were part of events a generation or two earlier. People saved photos to view later or show friends, e-mailed them to family members, posted them on social networking sites, or used them as wallpaper backgrounds on phone displays. Phones served as a supplement to rather than a replacement for digital cameras. Over time, the resolution of mobile phone cameras improved, USB adapters were added, and many people adopted them as personal cameras, in place of separate digital cameras.

Video applications on mobile phones fall into two categories: video recorders that capture and save brief clips of live action, and video display of prerecorded content. (We do not treat videophone applications for mobile phones here.) Like early mobile phone cameras, the first generation of mobile phone video recorders were used primarily to capture silly moments at a party, cute actions by toddlers, and other short spontaneous actions. Phones lacked the resolution and capacity to substitute for camcorders. Nonetheless, some users found the recording capability handy, and the brevity of the video was not a serious drain on battery power.

Video playback of prerecorded content falls into three groups: live streaming; download and watch; and over-the-air digital broadcasts. Through the mid-2000s, video playback applications were a work in progress, not a broadly accepted and used feature in the United States and Europe. However, by the late 2000s, many people were watching videos on mobile phones. Usage has been stronger in some Asian countries, especially South Korea, partly as a result of government policies that set a single standard and required some free video services. Among the many early challenges in the United States were the lack of a single standard for mobile phone video, long load times for some videos, heavy consumption of battery power while watching video, high and complex pricing, and poor user experiences when watching videos on small screens. Some of these were overcome by the late 2000s.

The Web, Music, and Other Entertainment Applications

Web content on mobile phones faced some of the same challenges as video applications. An early standard, wireless application protocol (WAP), first introduced in Europe at the end of the 1990s, was decidedly unsuccessful in most parts of the world. WAP was expensive, slow, and hard to use. Web content, even when designed for mobile phones, did not display well on small screens. As a new generation of smart phones with larger screens was adopted, the user experience improved considerably. Japan led other countries with its i-mode service provided by NTT DoCoMo and launched in 1999. The service provided a controlled set of Web applications and content, not open access to the entire Web, and was well received by teenagers. (Computers were available to relatively few Japanese young people at that time.)[42] Other mobile phone providers pursued similar "walled garden" approaches. User interest in Web services clustered around a relatively narrow set of applications, such as maps, weather, sports scores, simple games, e-mail, and news clips, which are more appealing when designed specifically for mobile phones. Faster mobile networks made Web browsing more appealing.

Entertainment applications for mobile phones may also be culturally related, making it difficult to know if a feature that is popular in one country will migrate to other countries. For example, the Japanese, especially young women, have taken to reading novels and Tanka (unrhymed poems with 31 syllables) on mobile phones. Some of these behaviors eventually migrated to Europe and North America. Google attempted to jump-start book reading on mobile phones in the United States with an operating system that extended access to more than one million public-domain books to those using smart phones or other mobile devices, and Amazon began selling books for smart phones.

Mobile phone entertainment applications have not been limited to smart phones in developed countries. In rural India, local mobile phone companies offer radio and other forms of entertainment to consumers as a way to boost revenue. These areas often have no radio, and people are willing to pay extra to hear favorite Bollywood tunes over their mobile phones.[43]

M-Commerce

One of the Holy Grails for mobile phones has been mobile commerce (m-commerce): using mobile phones for a broad variety of transactions, such as buying beverages from vending machines and adding the charge to users' mobile phone bills; buying tickets at movie theaters and using phones as electronic tickets; transferring money to other mobile phone accounts; and using mobile phones to read bar codes in stores and then receiving text messages about nearby locations that offer products at lower prices. All of these applications were first developed outside the United States.

The simplest form of m-commerce has been the use of a mobile phone as a pay phone—for example, vendors in Venezuela let people make calls on mobile phones on a pay-per-call basis.[44] Developing countries have seen the emergence of a number of unique forms of m-commerce, including money transfer. In Kenya and elsewhere in Africa, it is possible to store credit on mobile phones and then transfer some of the amount to other phones. Recipients can then take their phones to gas stations or other vendors and redeem the credit in cash. The service is an alternative to banks and has been most successful in areas where few people have bank accounts.[45]

Japan has developed many m-commerce applications, including use of mobile phones to purchase train and movie tickets, serve as electronic boarding passes on airplanes, purchase items from vending machines, scan bar codes in stores for price comparison information, and even to scan bar codes on food items to learn where they were grown and what kind of pesticides were used by the farmers who grew the items. Nonprofit groups have also developed m-commerce applications. At some universities, students can register for classes and check exam results using their mobile phones.

More widespread adoption of m-commerce will require software interoperability among mobile phones, greater acceptance of these applications (and related equipment) by merchants, a business model for small transactions, and transaction speeds that are faster than face-to-face purchases with regular currency.

Politics

Mobile phones have become integrated into political life. A prominent example took place in the Philippines in 2001, when political activists used mobile phones to organize demonstrators against then-president Joseph Estrada, who was subsequently ousted in a coup. Voice calls and text messages carried news and rumors and helped to gather crowds in Manila. Later, when riot police moved in, mobile phones were used to redirect the protesters away from the police.[46] Mobile phone use for political purposes can also backfire. In 2004, Italian prime minister Silvio Berlusconi sent millions of messages to mobile phone users on the eve of a regional election, but people were annoyed by the messages, and his party lost by a wider margin than expected.[47]

In the United States, candidate Barack Obama made extensive use of mobile phones in the 2007–8 primary and general election campaign. Organizers used text messages to solicit donations, tell people about rallies, provide talking points for supporters, give directions to polling places, and send first-alert messages to supporters—for example, telling them that Joseph Biden had been chosen as the vice presidential candidate. The use of mobile phones for voting has been limited, but in Bulach, Switzerland, citizens can vote via text message after entering their user IDs, passwords, and dates of birth.

Mobile phones have been used in politics in many other ways, not all of them positive. The mobile phone can be a tool for spreading false rumors and deceptive information, as was the case with some mobile phone messages in the Philippine demonstrations. Because mobile phones are always on and always present, they provide a strong channel for reaching people for political purposes.

Mobile Phones and Terrorists

Long before new technologies reach the level of penetration that mobile phones have reached, they tend to be put to use by less desirable elements both in and outside society: in particular, purveyors of pornography, organized crime, and terrorists. Many countries permit people to purchase prepaid mobile phones with cash and without providing identification, thereby offering a level of anonymity that is highly valued by terrorists, who have used mobile phones both for untraceable communication and as detonators. In the 2004 bombings on the Madrid railways, for example, the alarm function on mobile phones was used to trigger the detonators. When detonation is caused by a telephone call, terrorists have flexibility in choosing the time of the explosion, a capability that terrorists in Iraq and elsewhere have used and that has caused some security experts to question the wisdom of proposals to allow the use of mobile phones on planes. In the 2008 Mumbai attacks, terrorists used the global positioning system on their mobile phones to reach their destination by boat and later to coordinate actions among groups spread across the city.

Mobile phones' high value to terrorists has naturally caused concern among security authorities in many countries and in the press. For example, the bulk purchase of 150 mobiles at a store in California and the purchase of 60 mobiles by people who appeared to be of Middle Eastern origin at a Texas store caused alarm. In 2008, the British government proposed that anyone purchasing a mobile phone be required to present a passport or some other form of official photo identification, a requirement that other countries have already instituted. However, mobile phones are often stolen, and they can easily be acquired in one country and used in another, meaning that such measures are unlikely to be particularly effective.

Religion

The mobile phone has become a tool for many of the world's religions. MyAdhan, a service for Muslims in the United Kingdom, sends text messages about prayer and fasting times, provides Muslim-themed wallpaper for phones, and offers a mosque locator. In the Philippines, Catholics can send prayer requests to priests, who read the messages at mass. In Israel, mobile phone users can send prayers to a rabbi, who prints them out and puts them in crevices in the Western Wall. Services in many countries send Bible lessons and passages from the Koran as text messages and e-mails to mobile phones.[48]

For some people, the acceptability of various mobile phone services has become bound up with religion. In Israel, one ultraorthodox group worked with a mobile phone provider to design a "Kosher phone" that supports many of their religious practices. For example, the service discourages the sending of mobile phone calls or texts during the Sabbath by charging high tolls during this period.[49] The integration of the mobile phone into religious practices is another sign of how centrally it has moved into the daily lives of people.

Impacts

The integration of mobile phones into everyday life has had many effects on other products and services, social interactions, and mobile telephony in both developed and developing countries. Its evolution is likely to continue for some time, and such impacts will broaden.

Impacts on Other Products and Services

The mobile phone has affected a broad scope of technologies and services, including landlines, public pay phones, long distance service, area codes, watches, and radio alarm clocks. Many people, especially those in younger age groups, have dropped landlines and use mobile phones exclusively. Others have kept landlines as backups but use them less than before. This trend is likely to continue. Telephone companies that provide landlines have tried to compete with mobile phones by offering new service packages at lower prices, and some have tried to compete by creating innovative new services—for example, landline telephones that can send and receive text messages and can access the Web. The number of public pay phones declined by more than 50 percent in the United States between 2000 and 2006. With such widespread ownership of mobile phones, public pay phones are needed only by people who do not own mobile phones or who are out of range of cell towers.

With the pricing of mobile phone packages, the concept of long-distance telephone calls has in many cases disappeared: a call to a neighbor next door or a friend across the country costs the same, though roaming charges continue to complicate billing. Similarly, area codes have lost much of their geographic meaning. A mobile phone's area code tells us only where it was originally purchased, not where the user lives or is located at any time.

The decline in the use of watches is an example of the broader impact of mobile phones. Since mobile phones tell users the time, and since most users nearly always carry their phones, there is no need for a watch. Many younger people have abandoned watches. Some people continue to wear one because they consider it jewelry; others consider it a part of work attire. Similarly, many people use their mobile phones' alarm feature to wake them up in the morning, eliminating the need for radio alarm clocks and indirectly reducing the time spent listening to radio. In the past, many people set the radio to go on at a certain time and then continued listening to it as they got dressed or ate breakfast. After switching to a mobile phone alarm, they must consciously decide to turn on a radio. As mobile phone cameras have improved, they have affected the purchase and use of digital cameras.

Social Impacts

We have discussed many social impacts of mobile phones—for example, how people have come to use mobile phones to coordinate activities with others and how many younger mobile phone users have become fixated on the current location of friends. The mobile phone has also affected the conduct of politics, the expression of religion, and the methods of terrorists. It has reduced privacy, since users can be contacted virtually anytime and anywhere and feel an obligation to return calls and texts quickly.

It is important to reexamine the core concept of mobile communications. In the past, most thought of mobile technologies as devices used outside the home, office, and school. However, mobile phones are used at home and in the office or school as well as outside these environments. In this sense, they have crossed boundaries between mobile and stationary locations to create a new *living space* for those who use them.

The generation of young people born between 1990 and 2000 may be characterized as the first mobile phone generation. They have grown up with mobile phones all around them, started using them at an early age, and feel that they cannot live without them. They are more likely than older people to personalize their mobile phones. It is difficult at this point to say that their usage patterns—e.g., very frequent texting, large contact lists, and frequent location-based communications—are permanent impacts of being part of a mobile phone generation and not the fleeting behavior of teens. A decade from now we will know which behaviors are permanent.

Impacts in Developing Countries

Mobile phone service has been adapted to meet the needs of people in developing countries and has had strong effects there. As noted earlier, residents of many countries, including developing countries, have preferred prepaid plans to subscription plans (which are more popular in the United States). Prepayment has made mobile phone service affordable for people who lack credit or simply cannot afford monthly plans. Whether the caller or the recipient pays for the airtime component of a mobile phone call also affects usage. In many developing countries where the caller pays, it is common for a person with less income (for example, a young worker) to call another party with greater income (for example, a parent) and then hang up, knowing that the other party will call back. At a broad economic level, many countries with poor telecommunications infrastructures (and no telephone service in some areas) have used cellular technology to *leapfrog* ahead and build mobile phone services that are more advanced than those in many developed countries, enhancing the poorer countries' ability to compete in a global market. In addition, mobile phones are computers and thus bring computing power and applications to developing countries that have low desktop or laptop penetration. In Indonesia and other developing countries, many people who lack broadband Web access at home or work have adopted mobile phone access to the Web.

In many developing countries, mobile phones are shared for both economic and cultural reasons. From an economic perspective, only a few people in a village may be able to afford mobile phones, so they are shared; members of households that use mobile phones in place of landlines often share the phone as they would a landline. Some societies place a strong cultural value on the sharing of resources, which leads to the sharing of mobile phones.[50] Recognizing the shared nature of mobile phones in some countries, one carrier has developed software that allows multiple contact lists on the same handset.

Resourcefulness in bringing mobile phone service to many countries where it might not be expected has been remarkable and demonstrates the strong demand for mobile phones. How, for example, do households with no electricity charge mobile phone batteries? In Bangladesh, solar-powered battery chargers were introduced to meet this need. In other countries, chargers are powered by pedaling bicycles.

This review of mobile phone users and usage demonstrates many of the principles outlined in the core chapters of this book. The mobile phone began as a large, heavy, and expensive device used by a limited group of people. Longer-term uses and users were not anticipated, nor did anyone predict the extraordinarily quick and massive adoption of mobile phones as the price and size declined. The mobile phone began as a technological innovation, but its long-term impacts have been more social than technological. Even as it has become integrated into the everyday fabric of social life, it continues to evolve in directions that are both knowable and hard to foresee.

Notes

INTRODUCTION

1. Brian Winston, *Misunderstanding Media* (Cambridge, MA: Harvard University Press, 1986).

2. Kenneth Lipartito, "Picturephone and the Information Age: The Social Meaning of Failure," *Technology and Culture* 44, no. 1 (January 2003): 50–81.

3. Francis Cairncross, *The Death of Distance: How the Communication Revolution Will Change Our Lives* (Boston: Harvard Business School Press, 1997), 18.

4. Carolyn Marvin, *When Old Technologies Were New* (New York: Oxford University Press, 1988).

5. A Michael Noll and James Woods, "The Use of Picturephone in a Hospital," *Telecommunications Policy* 5, no. 2 (March 1979): 29–36.

6. Robert Johansen, *Teleconferencing and Beyond: Communications in the Office of the Future* (New York: McGraw-Hill, 1984).

7. Everett Rogers, *Diffusion of Innovations*, 4th ed. (New York: Free Press, 1995).

8. W. Brian Arthur, "Positive Feedback in the Economy," *Scientific American*, February 1990, 92–99.

9. Clayton Christensen, *The Innovator's Dilemma: When New Technologies Cause Great Firms to Fail* (Boston: Harvard Business School Press, 1997).

10. John Short, Ederyn Williams, and Bruce Christie, *The Social Psychology of Telecommunications* (New York: John Wiley, 1976).

11. Robert Johansen, Jacques Vallée, and Kathleen Spangler, *Electronic Meetings: Technical Alternatives and Social Choices* (Reading, MA: Addison-Wesley, 1979).

12. Clifford Nass and Byron Reeves, *The Media Equation: How People Treat Computers, Television, and New Media Like Real People and Places* (New York: Cambridge University Press, 1996).

13. John Short, Ederyn Williams, and Bruce Christie, *The Social Psychology of Telecommunications* (New York: John Wiley, 1976).

14. Manual Castels, *The Rise of the Network Society*, 2nd ed. (Malden, MA: Blackwell Publishers, 2000); Sherry Turkle, *Life on the Screen: Identity in the Age of the Internet* (New York: Simon and Schuster, 1995).

15. Harold Mendelsohn, *Mass Entertainment* (New Haven, CT: College and University Press, 1966).

16. Leo Bogart, *The Age of Television*, 3rd ed. (New York: Frederick Unger Publishing, 1972).

17. Lynn Spigel, *Make Room for TV: Television and the Family Ideal in Postwar America* (Chicago: University of Chicago Press, 1992).

18. James Katz, *Connections: Social and Cultural Studies of the Telephone in American Life* (New Brunswick, NJ: Transaction Publishers, 1999).

19. Jay Blumler and Elihu Katz, *The Uses of Mass Communication* (Thousand Oaks, CA: Sage Publications, 1974).

20. Carl Shapiro and Hal Varian, *Information Rules: A Strategic Guide to the Network Economy* (Boston: Harvard Business School Press, 1999).

21. Per Andersson, Ulf Essler, and Bertil Thorngren, eds., *Beyond Mobility* (Stockholm: Studentlitteratur, Stockholm School of Economics, 2007).

22. Eli Noam and Lorenzo Maria Pupillo, eds., *Peer-to-Peer Video: The Economics, Policy, and Culture of Today's New Mass Medium* (New York: Springer Publishers, 2008).

23. Erving Goffman, *The Presentation of Self in Everyday Life* (New York: Doubleday Anchor Books, 1959).

24. Roger Silverstone, *Television and Everyday Life* (London: Routledge, 1994).

25. Shaun Moores, *Satellite Television in Everyday Life* (Luton, UK: John Libbey Media, 1996).

26. Rich Ling, *New Tech, New Ties* (Cambridge, MA: MIT Press, 2008).

27. Ithiel de Sola Pool, ed., *The Social Impact of the Telephone* (Cambridge, MA: MIT Press, 1977).

28. Claude Fischer, *America Calling: A Social History of the Telephone to 1940* (Berkeley: University of California Press, 1984).

29. James Katz, *Magic in the Air: Mobile Communication and the Transformation of Social Life* (New Brunswick, NJ: Transaction Publishers, 2006).

30. Leah Lievrouw, ed., *The Handbook of New Media: Social Shaping and Social Consequences of ICTs* (Newbury Park, CA: Sage Publishers, 2006).

CHAPTER ONE

1. Everett Rogers, *Diffusion of Innovations*, 4th ed. (New York: Free Press, 1995).

2. Malcolm Gladwell, *The Tipping Point: How Little Things Can Make a Difference* (Boston: Little, Brown, 2002).

3. P. G. Holmlov and Karl-Eric Warneryd, "Adoption and Use of Fax in Sweden," in M. Carnevale, M. Lucertini, and S. Nicosia, eds., *Modeling the Innovation: Communications, Automation, and Information Systems* (Amsterdam: Elsevier Science Publishers, 1990), 95–108.

4. Jared Sandberg, "PC Makers' Push into Homes May Be Faltering," *Wall Street Journal*, March 6, 1997, A12.

5. Ithiel de Sola Pool, ed., *The Social Impact of the Telephone* (Cambridge, MA: MIT Press, 1977), 130.

6. Christopher Sterling and Timothy Haight, *The Mass Media: Aspen Institute Guide to Communication Industry Trends* (New York: Praeger Publishers, 1978).

7. Erik Barnouw, *The Golden Web: A History of Broadcasting in the United States 1933–1953* (New York: Oxford University Press, 1968); Catherine Rubio Kuffner, "Legal Issues in Facsimile Use," *Media Law and Policy* 5, no. 1 (Fall 1996).

8. Brian Arthur, "Positive Feedback in the Economy," *Scientific American*, February 1990, 92–99.

9. Everett Rogers, *Diffusion of Innovations*, 4th ed. (New York: Free Press, 1995), 174.

10. Bruce Klopfenstein, "The Diffusion of the VCR in the United States," in Mark Levy, ed., *The VCR Age: Home Video and Mass Communication* (Newbury Park, CA: Sage Publications, 1989), 21–39.

11. Leo Bogart, "Highway to the Stars or Highway to Nowhere?" *Media Studies Journal* (Winter 1994): 1–15.

12. Christopher Sterling and Timothy Haight, *The Mass Media: Aspen Institute Guide to Communication Industry Trends* (New York: Praeger Publishers, 1978).

13. Lee Becker, "A Decade of Research on Interactive Cable," in William Dutton, Jay Blumler, and Kenneth Kraemer, eds., *Wired Cities: Shaping the Future of Communications* (Washington, DC: The Washington Program of the Annenberg School of Communication, 1987), 102–23.

14. Clayton Christensen, *The Innovator's Dilemma: When New Technologies Cause Great Firms to Fail* (Boston: Harvard Business School Press, 1997).

15. William Dutton, Everett Rogers, and Suk-Ho Jun, "Diffusion and Social Impacts of Personal Computers," *Communication Research* 14, no. 2 (1987): 219–50.

16. John Robinson and Geoffrey Godbey, *Time for Life: The Surprising Ways Americans Use Their Time* (University Park, PA: Pennsylvania State University, 1997).

17. A. Michael Noll, *Highway of Dreams: A Critical View along the Information Superhighway* (Mahwah, NJ: Lawrence Erlbaum Associates, 1997).

18. John Carey and Mitchell Moss, "The Diffusion of New Telecommunications Technologies," *Telecommunications Policy* (June 1985): 145–58.

19. Harold Mendelsohn, *Mass Entertainment* (New Haven, CT: College and University Press, 1966).

20. John Carey, "Public Information Terminals," in Martin Greenberger, ed., *Electronic Publishing Plus* (New York: Knowledge Industry Publications, 1985), 13–26.

21. Marsha Siefert, "Aesthetics, Technology, and the Capitalization of Culture: How the Talking Machine Became a Musical Instrument," *Science in Context* 8, no. 2 (1995): 417–49.

22. Harold Innis, *The Bias of Communication* (Toronto: University of Toronto Press, 1951).

CHAPTER TWO

1. John Brooks, *Telephone: The First Hundred Years* (New York: Harper and Row, 1975), 61.

2. Everett Rogers, *Diffusion of Innovations*, 4th ed. (New York: Free Press, 1995).

3. Robert Fildes, "Telecommunications Demand—a Review," *International Journal of Forecasting* 18, no. 2 (2002): 489–522.

4. Willard Zangwill, "When Customer Research Is a Lousy Idea," *New York Times*, March 8, 1993, A-12.

5. Bruce Klopfenstein, "Forecasting the Adoption of New Media," in Jerry Salvaggio and Jennings Bryant, eds., *Media Use in the Information Age: Emerging Patterns of Adoption and Use* (Hillsdale, NJ: Lawrence Erlbaum Associates, 1989), 21–42.

6. A. Michael Noll, "Anatomy of a Failure: Picturephone Revisited," *Telecommunications Policy* 16, no. 4 (May/June 1992): 307–16.

7. *Cablevision Magazine*, December 19, 1983, 30.

8. *Fortune*, March 15, 1999, 118.

9. *USA Today*, October 11, 1998, 2B.

10. "Wounded Birds," *Economist*, May 10, 2001.

11. Clayton M. Christensen, Scott Cook, and Taddy Hall, "It's the Purpose Brand, Stupid," *Wall Street Journal*, November 29, 2005, B2.

12. Daniel Roth, "My, What Big Internet Numbers You Have," *Fortune*, March 15, 1999, 114.

13. Frances Cairncross, *The Death of Distance: How the Communication Revolution Will Change Our Lives* (Boston: Harvard Business School Press, 1997), 18; "The End of the Line," *Economist*, October 23, 1993, 5.

14. H. A. Linstone and Murray Turoff, *The Delphi Method: Techniques and Applications* (Reading, MA: Addison-Wesley, 1975).

15. J. P. Martino, "Looking ahead with Confidence," *IEEE Spectrum*, March 1985, 76–81.

16. Frederick J. Parente, J. K. Anderson, P. Myers, and T. O'Brien, "An Examination of Factors Contributing to Delphi Accuracy," *Journal of Forecasting* 3 (1984): 173–82.

17. J. Scott Armstrong, *Long-Range Forecasting: From Crystal Ball to Computer* (New York: John Wiley, 1985), 91–92.

18. Frank Bass, "A New Product Growth Model for Consumer Durables," *Management Science*, January 15, 1969, 215–27.

19. Everett Rogers, *Diffusion of Innovations*, 4th ed. (New York: Free Press, 1995), 82–83.

20. Robert A. Fildes, "Telecommunications Demand—a Review," *International Journal of Forecasting* 18, no. 2 (2002): 489–522.

21. Vijay Mahajan, Eitan Muller, and Frank Bass, "New Product Diffusion Models in Marketing: A Review and Direction for Research," *Journal of Marketing* 54 (January 1990): 1–26.

22. Ibid., 8.

23. Michael Tyler, "User Research and Demand Research: What's the Use?" in Martin C. J. Elton, David W. Conrath, and William A. Lucas, eds., *Evaluating New Telecommunications Services* (London: Plenum Press, 1978), 3–24; Roger Pye and Ederyn Williams, "Teleconferencing: Is Video Valuable or Is Audio Adequate?" *Telecommunications Policy* 1, no. 3 (June 1977): 230–41.

24. Moshe Ben-Akiva, "Choice of Telecommunications Services," in P. G. Holmlov, ed., *Telecommunications Use and Users* (Stockholm: Teldok, 1990), 53–71.

25. Wikipedia, "Prediction Market," http://en.wikipedia.org/wiki/Prediction_market. (The usual cautions apply. This article provided a useful and accurate summary when last visited in November 2009, but there is always the possibility that it will not be considered accurate at some point thereafter.)

26. "Market, Market on the Wall," *Economist*, Technology Quarterly, December 10, 2005.

27. Nigel Meade, "When Will the Trend Bend?—The Value of Forecasting," Inaugural Lecture at the Business School, Imperial College London, May 2003.

28. Roger Hough, *Pilot Study to Develop a Methodology to Forecast Canadian Demand for New Home and Business Telecommunications Services in the Period 1980–1990* (Ottawa: Department of Communications, 1979); Roger Hough, *A Study to Forecast the Demand for Telidon Services over the Next Ten Years* (Ottawa: Department of Communications, 1980).

29. Maxwell McCombs and Chaim Eyal, "Spending on Mass Media," *Journal of Communication* 30, no. 1 (1980): 153–58.

30. Brian Arthur, "Positive Feedback in the Economy," *Scientific American*, February 1990, 92–99.

31. J. Scott Armstrong, *Long-Range Forecasting: From Crystal Ball to Computer* (New York: John Wiley, 1985).

32. Peter Schwartz, *The Art of the Long View: Planning for the Future in an Uncertain World* (New York: Doubleday, 1991).

33. For explanation of these approaches—and much valuable advice—the interested professional is referred to J. Scott Armstrong's classic book on long-range forecasting. J. Scott Armstrong, *Long-Range Forecasting: From Crystal Ball to Computer* (New York: John Wiley, 1985). The Web site http://www.forecastingprinciples.com/, started by Armstrong in 1997, is also highly recommended.

34. J. Scott Armstrong, *Long-Range Forecasting: From Crystal Ball to Computer* (New York: John Wiley, 1985), 183–86.

35. Jonathan Rosenhead, "Robustness Analysis: Keeping Your Options Open," in Jonathan Rosenhead and John Mingers, eds., *Rational Analysis for a Problematic World Revisited: Problem Structuring Methods for Complexity, Uncertainty, and Conflict* (Chichester: John Wiley, 2001), 181–208.

CHAPTER THREE

1. James Taylor, *Managing Information Technology Projects* (New York: American Management Association, 2004).

2. Everett Rogers, *Diffusion of Innovations*, 4th ed. (New York: Free Press, 1995).

3. Laura Lorber, "An Expert's Do's and Don'ts for Outsourcing Technology," *Wall Street Journal*, May 7, 2007, B8.

4. Jeff Opdyke, "Let the Holiday Videogames Begin. Or Not," *Wall Street Journal Online*, December 10, 2006.

5. Truls Erik Johnsen, "The Social Context of Mobile Phone Use of Norwegian Teens," in James Katz, ed., *Machines That Become Us* (New Brunswick, NJ: Transaction Publishers, 2003), 161–70.

6. Bobby White, "Firms Take a Cue from YouTube," *Wall Street Journal*, January 2, 2007, B3.

7. Ian Miles and Graham Thomas, "User Resistance to New Interactive Media: Participants, Processes, and Paradigms," in M. Bauer, ed., *Resistance to New Technology* (New York: Cambridge University Press, 1995), 255–72.

8. Dimitri Williams, "Virtual Cultivation: Online Worlds, Offline Perceptions," *Journal of Communication* 56, no. 1 (March 2006): 69–87.

CHAPTER FOUR

The quotation at the beginning of the chapter is from Alex Reid, *New Directions in Telecommunications Research* (New York: Sloan Commission on Cable Communications, 1971).

1. S. M. Johnstone, "Research on Telecommunicated Learning: Past, Present, and Future," *Annals of the American Academy of Political and Social Science* 514 (March 1991): 49–57.

2. B. L. Hanson, "A Brief History of Applied Behavioral Science at Bell Laboratories," *Bell System Technical Journal* 62, no. 6 (July/August 1983): 1571–90.

3. For overviews, based on meta-analyses, of the interests of those conducting research on the Internet, see, e.g., Kim and Weaver, which covers journals in the second half of the 1990s, and Rice, which covers the conference programs of the Association of Internet Researchers in 2003 and 2004. Sung Tae Kim and David Weaver, "Communication Research about the Internet: A Thematic Meta-analysis," *New Media & Society* 4,

no. 4 (2002): 518–39; Ronald Rice, "New Media/Internet Research Topics of the Association of Internet Researchers," *Information Society* 21, no. 4 (2005): 285–99.

4. Alphonse Chapanis, *Human Factors in Engineering Design* (New York: John Wiley, 1996).

5. A. Tashakkori and C. Teddle, eds., *Handbook of Mixed Methods in Social and Behavioral Research* (London: Sage Publications, 2002), 308–10.

6. See John Short, Ederyn Williams, and Bruce Christie, *The Social Psychology of Telecommunications* (London: John Wiley, 1976); Ederyn Williams, "Experimental Comparisons of Face-to-Face and Mediated Communication: A Review," *Psychological Bulletin* 84, no. 5 (1977): 963–76.

7. Ederyn Williams, "Experimental Comparisons of Face-to-Face and Mediated Communication: A Review," *Psychological Bulletin* 84, no. 5 (1977): 963–76.

8. Edmund Carpenter, "The New Languages," in Edmund Carpenter and Marshall McLuhan, eds., *Explorations in Communication* (Boston: Beacon Press, 1960), 162–79.

9. J. A. Short, "Effects of Medium of Communication on Experimental Negotiation," *Human Relations* 27, no. 3 (1974): 225–34.

10. Elton and Carey provide an extensive review of the implementation problems that arose in the early field trials and demonstration projects. Martin C. J. Elton and John Carey, *Implementing Interactive Telecommunications Services: Final Report on Problems Which Arise during Implementation of Field Trials and Demonstration Projects* (New York: New York University, Alternate Media Center, 1977) (available from ERIC, No. ED207524).

11. Gregory Hearn, Jo A. Tacchi, Marcus Foth, and June Lennie, *Action Research and New Media: Concepts, Methods, and Cases* (Cresskill, NJ: Hampton Press, 2008).

12. C. H. Waddington, *Operational Research in World War II* (London: Elek Books, 1972).

13. Roger G. Mark, *Final Report of the Nursing Home Telemedicine Project—Submitted to the National Science Foundation* (Boston: Boston City Hospital, 1975).

14. There were some unavoidable compromises in the design of the experiment. Subjects had been invited to participate and offered a small sum of money to do so, though most of those who participated declined the payment; this could have introduced a selection bias. And the fact that the physicians and nurses knew they were participating in the experiment could have affected their actions.

15. David W. Conrath, William G. Bloor, Earl V. Dunn, and Barbara Tranquada, "A Clinical Evaluation of Four Alternative Telemedicine Systems," *Behavioral Science* 22, no. 1 (1977): 12–21; Earl Dunn, David Conrath, Helen Acton, Chris Higgins, and Harry Bain, "Telemedicine Links Patients in Sioux Lookout with Doctors in Toronto," *Canadian Medical Association Journal* 122, no. 4 (1980): 484–87.

16. Allen M. Shinn, Jr., "The Utility of Social Experimentation in Policy Research," in Martin C. J. Elton, William A. Lucas, and David W. Conrath, eds., *Evaluating New Telecommunications Services* (New York: Plenum, 1978), 681–700.

17. Hadley Cantril, *The Invasion from Mars: A Study in the Psychology of Panic* (Princeton: Princeton University Press, 1940).

18. A. Michael Noll, ed., *Crisis Communications: Lessons from September 11* (Lanham, MD: Rowman and Littlefield Publishers, 2003).

19. R. Kohavi, R. M. Henne, and D. Sommerfield, "Practical Guide to Controlled Experiments on the Web: Listen to Your Customers Not to the HiPPO," in Pavel Berkhin, Rich Caruana, Xindong Wu, and Scott Gaffney, eds., *Proceedings of the 13th ACM SIGKDD*

International Conference on Knowledge Discovery and Data Mining (ACM, 2007), 959–67, http://exp-platform.com/hippo.aspx (accessed November 10, 2009).

20. S. Rafaeli, "Constructs in the Storm," in M. Consalvo, N. Baym, J. Hunsinger, K. B. Jensen, J. Logie, M. Murero, and L. R. Shade, eds., *Internet Research Annual*, vol. 1 (New York: Peter Lang Publishers, 2004), 55–65.

21. Martin C. J. Elton and John Carey, "Teletext for Public Information: Research Studies in the Field and in the Laboratory," in J. Johnston, ed., *Evaluating the New Information Technologies* (San Francisco: Jossey Bass, 1984).

CHAPTER FIVE

1. W. Russell Neuman, *The Future of the Mass Audience* (New York: Cambridge University Press, 1991).

2. Ien Ang, "Living Room Wars: New Technologies, Audience Measurement, and the Tactics of Television Consumption," in R. Silverstone and Eric Hirsch, eds., *Consuming Technologies: Media and Information in Domestic Space* (London: Routledge, 1992), 131–45.

3. Harold Mendelsohn, *Mass Entertainment* (New Haven, CT: College and University Press, 1966); Leo Bogart, *The Age of Television*, 3rd ed. (New York: Frederick Unger Publishing, 1972); Lynn Spigel, *Make Room for TV: Television and the Family Ideal in Postwar America* (Chicago: University of Chicago Press, 1992).

4. David Morley, *Family Television: Cultural Power and Domestic Leisure* (London: Comedia, 1986); Roger Silverstone, *Television and Everyday Life* (London: Routledge, 1994); Shaun Moores, *Satellite Television in Everyday Life* (Luton, UK: John Libbey Media, 1996).

5. Robert Bellamy and James Walker, *Television and the Remote Control* (New York: Guilford Press, 1996).

6. Robert Rice, "Onward and Upward with the Arts: Diary of a Viewer," *New Yorker*, August 30, 1947, 47–55.

7. Christopher Sterling and Timothy Haight, *The Mass Media: Aspen Institute Guide to Communication Industry Trends* (New York: Praeger Publishers, 1978).

8. Lynn Spigel, *Make Room for TV: Television and the Family Ideal in Postwar America* (Chicago: University of Chicago Press, 1992).

9. Erik Barnouw, *Tube of Plenty: The Evolution of American Television* (New York: Oxford University Press, 1975).

10. Carrie Heeter and Bradley Greenberg, *Cable-Viewing* (Norwood, NJ: Ablex Publishing, 1988).

11. John Carey and Lee Ann Draud, *An Ethnographic Study of the Philadelphia* S*M*A*R*T *Households* (Westfield, NJ: Statistical Research, 1997).

12. John Pavlik, *New Media and the Information Superhighway* (Boston: Allyn and Bacon, 1996).

13. Paul Lindstrom, "Home Video: The Consumer Impact," in Mark Levy, ed., *The VCR Age: Home Video and Mass Communication* (London: Sage Publications, 1989), 40–49.

14. Donald Agostino, Herbert Terry, and Rolland Johnson, "Home Video Recorders," *Journal of Communication* 30, no. 4 (1980): 28–35.

15. Mark Levy, "Home Video Recorders," *Journal of Communication* 30, no. 4 (1980): 23–27.

16. Alan Rubin and Charles Bantz, "Uses and Gratifications of Videocassette Recorders," in Jerry Salvaggio and Jennings Bryant, eds., *Media Use in the Information Age: Emerging Patterns of Adoption and Use* (Hillsdale, NJ: Lawrence Erlbaum Associates, 1989), 181–95.

17. Paul Lindstrom, "Home Video: The Consumer Impact," in Mark Levy, ed., *The VCR Age: Home Video and Mass Communication* (London: Sage Publications, 1989), 40–49.

18. Bradley Greenberg and Carolyn Lin, "Adolescents and the VCR Boom: Old, New, and Nonusers," in Mark Levy, ed., *The VCR Age: Home Video and Mass Communication* (London: Sage Publications, 1989), 73–91.

19. Russell Shaw, "Cable, Satellite Clash over VCRs at Meeting," *Electronic Media*, December 1995, 1.

20. Amy Jordan, "A Family Systems Approach to the Use of the VCR in the Home," in Julia Dobrow, ed., *Social and Cultural Aspects of VCR Use* (Hillsdale, NJ: Lawrence Erlbaum Associates, 1990), 163–80.

21. John Carey, "New Media and TV Viewing Behavior: Implications for Public Broadcasting," *NHK Broadcasting Studies*, no. 2 (2003): 45–63.

22. Jeffrey Cole, *UCLA September 11 Survey* (Los Angeles: UCLA Center for Communication Policy, 2002).

23. James Von Schilling, *The Magic Window: American Television, 1939–1953* (New York: Haworth Press, 2003).

24. John Pavlik, "You've Got Video: Welcome to Broadband Internet," *TV Quarterly* 35, no. 1 (2004): 29–33.

25. Joel Brinkley, *Defining Vision: The Battle for the Future of Television* (New York: Harcourt Brace, 1997).

26. Tatiana Boncompagni, "The New TV Dinner," *Wall Street Journal*, July 22, 2005, W10.

27. Cited in Nicholas Negroponte, *Being Digital* (New York: Alfred Knopf, 1995).

28. Matt Stump, "On Demand's Premium Evolution," *Multichannel News*, July 25, 2005, 92.

29. Andy Addis, "Why Cable Needs New Navigation Now," *Multichannel News*, July 25, 2005, 97.

30. Gali Einav, "College Students: The Rationale for P2P Video File Sharing," presentation at Columbia University, September 10, 2004.

31. David Waterman, "Business Models and Program Content," in Eli Noam, Jo Groebel, and Darcy Gerbarg, eds., *Internet Television* (Mahwah, NJ: Lawrence Erlbaum Associates, 2004), 61–80.

32. Walter Mossberg, "Device Lets You Watch Shows on a Home TV, TiVo from Elsewhere,"*Wall Street Journal*, June 30, 2005, B1.

33. Russell Shaw, "Cable, Satellite Clash over VCRs at Meeting," *Electronic Media*, December 1995, 1.

34. "Lights, Camera, Brands," *Economist*, October 27, 2005.

35. Robert Kubey and Mihaly Csikszentmihalyi, *Television and the Quality of Life: How Viewing Shapes Everyday Experience* (Hillsdale, NJ: Lawrence Erlbaum Associates, 1990).

36. David Waterman, "Business Models and Program Content," in Eli Noam, Jo Groebel, and Darcy Gerbarg, eds., *Internet Television* (Mahwah, NJ: Lawrence Erlbaum Associates, 2004), 61–80.

37. Harold Mendelsohn, *Mass Entertainment* (New Haven, CT: College and University Press, 1966).

CHAPTER SIX

The quotation at the beginning of the chapter is from Daniel Barenboim, "Meeting in Music," Fourth in the 2006 series of BBC Reith Lectures, http://www.bbc.co.uk/radio4/reith2006/lecture4.shtml (accessed November 2009).

1. Lorne Parker, Marcia Baird, and Dennis Gilbertson, "Introduction to Teleconferencing," in *The Telephone in Education*, bk. 2 (Madison: University of Wisconsin Extension, 1977), 27–53.

2. Robert Cowan, personal communication, July 5, 2006.

3. Michael Luo, "Immigrants Hear God's Word, in Chinese, via Conference Call," *New York Times*, July 21, 2006.

4. Michael Totty, "Prime Time for Teleconferences," *Wall Street Journal*, September 30, 2005, R6.

5. Roger Pye and Ederyn Williams, "Teleconferencing: Is Video Valuable or Is Audio Adequate?" *Telecommunications Policy* (June 1977): 230–41.

6. George du Maurier, "1879 Almanack," *Punch Magazine*, December 9, 1878, http://www.punch.co.uk.

7. Robert Johansen, *Teleconferencing and Beyond: Communications in the Office of the Future* (New York: McGraw-Hill, 1984), 55.

8. Mark Siegeltuch, "A Videoconferencing Case Study: Therapy for an Autistic Child" (manuscript, 1993).

9. Jonathan Glater, "Travel Fears Cause Some to Commute Online," *New York Times*, April 7, 2003, C5.

10. Grace Wong, "Terror Threatens, Traffic Snarls . . . Video Wins," *CNN Money*, August 23, 2006, http://money.cnn.com/2006/08/23/technology/conferencing/index.htm?source=yahoo_quote (accessed February 2, 2009).

11. In the early 1970s, Noll discussed the design of a three-dimensional form of videoconferencing. A. Michel Noll, "Real-Time Interactive Stereoscopy," *SID Journal* (The Official Journal of the Society for Information Display) 1, no. 3 (September/October 1972): 14–22.

12. William Bulkeley, "Better Virtual Meetings," *Wall Street Journal*, September 28, 2006, B1.

13. A. Michael Noll, "Anatomy of a Failure: Picturephone Revisited," *Telecommunications Policy* 16, no. 4 (May/June 1992): 307–16.

14. W. A. Eliot, G. C. Coleman, R. G. Pfefferkorn, L. G. Siegel, L. L. Stine, and A. E. Witter, *The Video Telephone in Criminal Justice: The Phoenix Project*, vol. 1, *Summary of Applications and Findings*, Mitre Technical Report, MTR 7328, August 1986.

15. Elliot Gold, "Happy 25th Anniversary, Picturephone," *TeleSpan*, January 15, 1989, 15–20.

16. While most commentators—e.g., A. Michael Noll—regard Picturephone as a massive failure, Kenneth Lipartito provides a credible challenge to this view in a paper that offers a radical and important criticism of the conceptual framework generally used to assess success and failure. A. Michael Noll, "Anatomy of a Failure: Picturephone Revisited," *Telecommunications Policy* 16, no. 4 (May/June 1992): 307–16; Kenneth Lipartito, "Picturephone and the Information Age: The Social Meaning of Failure," *Technology and Culture* 44, no. 1 (January 2003): 50–81.

17. "Video Phones, in First Public Test, Link Two Campuses in California," *New York Times*, October 15, 1989, 47.

18. E.g., J. A. Short, "Effects of Medium of Communication on Experimental Negotiation," *Human Relations* 27, no. 3 (1974): 225.

19. Roger Pye and Ederyn Williams, "Teleconferencing: Is Video Valuable or Is Audio Adequate?" *Telecommunications Policy* 1, no. 3 (June 1977): 230–41.

20. Everett Rogers, *Diffusion of Innovations*, 4th ed. (New York: Free Press, 1995), 243.

21. M. C. J. Elton, "Visual Communication Systems: Trials and Experiences," *Proceedings of IEEE* 73, no. 4 (April 1985): 700–705.

22. Alma Latour, "Videophones: The New Generation," *Wall Street Journal*, July 26, 2004, R10.

23. Joseph Berger, "What's on TV? A View of Loved Ones from Afar," *New York Times*, January 8, 2005, C1.

24. Elliot Gold, "Freedom Calls Links Families with Their Loved Ones in Iraq," *Telespan*, May 15, 2006, 3.

25. A. Michael Noll, *Highway of Dreams: A Critical View along the Information Superhighway* (Mahwah, NJ: Lawrence Erlbaum Associates, 1997), 16.

26. Everctt Rogers, *Diffusion of Innovations*, 4th ed. (New York: Free Press, 1995).

27. Michael Tyler identified a few projects with this aim; they followed the approach of Roger Pye, Ederyn Williams, and their colleagues. Michael Tyler, "User Research and Demand Research: What's the Use?" in Martin C. J. Elton, David W. Conrath, and William A. Lucas, eds., *Evaluating New Telecommunications Services* (London: Plenum Press, 1978), 3–24; Roger Pye and Ederyn Williams, "Teleconferencing: Is Video Valuable or Is Audio Adequate?" *Telecommunications Policy* 1, no. 3 (June 1977): 230–41.

CHAPTER SEVEN

1. Lawrence Roberts, "Towards a Cooperative Network of Time-Shared Computers" (MIT Working Paper, October 1966).

2. Jerome Aumente, *New Electronic Pathways: Videotex, Teletext, and Online Databases* (Newbury Park, CA: Sage Publications, 1987); Roger Fidler, *Mediamorphorphosis: Understanding New Media* (Thousand Oaks, CA: Pine Forge Press, 1997).

3. Herb Dordick, "The Search for the Electronic Publishing Business," in Martin Greenberger, ed., *Electronic Publishing Plus* (White Plains, NY: Knowledge Industries Publications, 1985), 205–7.

4. Alex Reid, ed., *Prestel 1980* (London: Post Office Telecommunications, 1980).

5. Richard Hooper, "Lessons from Overseas: The British Experience," in Martin Greenberger, ed., *Electronic Publishing Plus* (White Plains, NY: Knowledge Industries Publications, 1985), 181–99

6. Stuart Sutherland, *Prestel and the User* (Brighton: University of Sussex Centre for Research on Perception and Cognition, 1980).

7. Jean-Jacques Servan-Schreiber, *Le Défi américain* (Paris: Denoël, 1967).

8. Martha Williams, "Electronic Databases," *Science*, April 2, 1985, 450–55.

9. Jerome Aumente, *New Electronic Pathways: Videotex, Teletext, and Online Databases* (Newbury Park, CA: Sage Publications, 1987).

10. Jacques Vallée, *Computer Message Systems* (New York: McGraw-Hill, 1984).

11. Martin Nisenholtz, "Information Technology and New Forms of Collective Participation in the Narrative" (paper presented at the Ninth World Computer Congress, 1981).

12. Laura Gurak, *Persuasion and Privacy in CyberSpace: The Online Protests over Lotus Marketplace and the Clipper Chip* (New Haven, CT: Yale University Press, 1998).

13. Robert Johansen, Jacques Vallée, and Kathleen Spangler, *Electronic Meetings: Technical Alternatives and Social Choices* (Boston: Addison-Wesley, 1979).

14. Ronald Rice and Associates, *The New Media: Communication, Research, and Technology* (Beverly Hills, CA: Sage Publications, 1984).

15. J. Tydeman, H. Lipinski, R. Adler, M. Nyhan, and L. Zwimpfer, *Teletext and Videotext in the United States* (New York: McGraw-Hill, 1982).

16. Martin Nisenholtz, "Designing for Teletext and Videotex," *Computer Graphics World* (September 1982): 49–54.

17. Roger Fidler, *Mediamorphorphosis: Understanding New Media* (Thousand Oaks, CA: Pine Forge Press, 1997).

18. Lawrence Day, "Electronic Mail Services in the Information Age" (Bell Canada Business Planning Paper 1, 1972).

19. Katie Hafner, *The WELL: A Story of Love, Death, and Real Life in the Seminal Online Community* (New York: Carroll and Graf Publishers, 2001).

20. *The 1989 BBS Bible* (Collegeville, PA: Bubeck Publishing, 1989)

21. Jules Tewlow, "Time Sharing and the Newspaper of Tomorrow," *ANPA Research Institute Bulletin*, April 15, 1968, 93–108.

22. John Carey, "Terminals in Public Locations," in Martin Greenberger, ed., *Electronic Publishing Plus* (White Plains, NY: Knowledge Industries Publications, 1985), 13–26.

23. Ken Auletta, *The Highwaymen* (New York: Random House, 1997).

24. Richard Sewell, "Not Time to Panic?" *Telephony*, June 2, 1997, 168–74.

25. A. Michael Noll, "Videotex: Anatomy of a Failure," *Information and Management* 9 (1985): 99–109.

26. Stuart Sutherland, *Prestel and the User* (Brighton: University of Sussex Centre for Research on Perception and Cognition, 1980).

27. Jerome Aumente, *New Electronic Pathways: Videotex, Teletext, and Online Databases* (Newbury Park, CA: Sage Publications, 1987); Gary Arlen, *Interactivity Report* (Bethesda, MD: Arlen Communications, multiple years).

CHAPTER EIGHT

1. John Carey, *An Ethnographic Study of Interactive Television* (Edinburgh, Scotland: University of Edinburgh UnivEd, 1996).

2. "Washington Hails the Test," *New York Times*, April 8, 1927, 20.

3. James Katz, "Telecommunications and Computers," *Society* 25 (November/December 1987): 81–87.

4. "Pharmacy of Future to Be Shown at Fair," *New York Times*, February 3, 1939, B2.

5. Charles Brownstein, "Interactive Cable TV and Social Services," *Journal of Communication* 28, no. 2 (1978): 142–47.

6. Ben Park, *An Introduction to Telemedicine* (New York: New York University, Alternate Media Center, 1974).

7. Lee Becker, "A Decade of Research on Interactive Television," in William Dutton, Jay Blumler, and Kenneth Kraemer, eds., *Wired Cities: Shaping the Future of Communications*

(Washington, DC: The Washington Program of the Annenberg School of Communication, 1987), 102–23.

8. George Mannes, "The Ghosts of Cable Past," *Cablevision*, December 26, 1994, 26–31.

9. Thomas Wheeler, "Oral History Interview with Thomas Wheeler," Denver, the Cable Center, 2000.

10. Craig Kuhl, Simon Applebaum, and Wayne Friedman, "A Second Coming of TV," *Cablevision*, October 24, 1988, 28–46.

11. Meg Cox, "Programmers Bet Viewers Want to Interact with TV," *Wall Street Journal*, October 18, 1989, B1.

12. *A Summary Version of the Comprehensive Report on Hi-Ovis Project* (Tokyo: New Media Development Association,1988).

13. Francois Gerin and Nicolas de Tavernost, "Biarritz and the Future of Videocommunications," in William Dutton, Jay Blumler, and Kenneth Kraemer, eds., *Wired Cities: Shaping the Future of Communications* (Washington, DC: The Washington Program of the Annenberg School of Communication, 1987), 237–54.

14. Diana Gagnon, *Interactive Television: State of the Industry* (Bethesda, MD: Arlen Communications, 1990).

15. John Keller, "AT&T's Secret Multimedia Trials Offer Clues to Capturing Interactive Audiences," *Wall Street Journal*, July 28, 1993, B1.

16. John Lipman, "Tuning out the TV of Tomorrow," *Los Angeles Times*, August 31, 1993, A1.

17. William Bulkeley and John Wilke, "Can the Exalted Vision Become Reality?" *Wall Street Journal*, October 14, 1993, B1.

18. William Bulkeley and John Wilke, "Can the Exalted Vision Become Reality?" *Wall Street Journal*, October 14, 1993, B1.

19. Kim Mitchell, "Some Boffo Bell Atlantic Buy Rates," *Cable World*, March 25, 1996, 20.

20. Mark Robichaux, "Innovative Startup Flops, and a Lawsuit against TCI Follows," *Wall Street Journal*, February 26, 1995, A1.

21. Andre Caron, *Interactive Television: Lessons for the Future* (Quebec: University of Montreal New Technologies Research Laboratory, 1996).

22. Dana Cerverka, "Lessons Learned from ITV Trials," *Communication Engineering and Design* (May 1996): 38–42.

23. Peter Zollman, *Interactive News: State of the Art* (Washington, DC: Radio and Television News Directors Foundation, 1997), 43–49.

24. Ken Auletta, "The Magic Box," *New Yorker*, April 11, 1994, 40–45.

25. Jennifer Schenker, "Interactive Television Keeps Waiting to Click with Viewers," *Wall Street Journal Interactive Edition*, September 3, 1996, 1.

26. R. Heidemann, "The IVOD Berlin Project: Access Technology for Service Provisioning," *Alcatel Telecommunications Review*, no. 3 (1996): 196–200.

27. Gali Einav,"'I Want My iTV': Content, Demand, and Social Implications of Interactive Television" (PhD diss., Columbia University, 2004).

28. Gali Einav, "'I Want My iTV': Content, Demand, and Social Implications of Interactive Television" (PhD diss., Columbia University, 2004).

29. Karolina Brodin, Patrick Barwise, and Ana Isabel Canhoto, *UK Consumer Responses to iDTV* (London: London Business School, 2002).

30. Fredrik Nars, "SMS-TV in Europe," *TVSpy.com*, April 21, 2003.

31. Vincent Grosso, "AT&T's Experiences with Interactive Television" (presentation at the Twenty-Third Annual Telecommunication Policy Research Conference, Washington, DC, October 1, 1995).

32. Marshall McLuhan, *Understanding Media* (New York: McGraw-Hill, 1964).

33. Gali Einav, "'I Want My iTV': Content, Demand, and Social Implications of Interactive Television" (PhD diss., Columbia University, 2004).

CHAPTER NINE

1. David MacFarland, *Future Radio Programming Strategies: Cultivating Listenship in the Digital Age* (Mahwah, NJ: Lawrence Erlbaum Associates, 1997).

2. Susan Douglas, *Listening In: Radio and the American Imagination* (New York: Random House, 1999).

3. Lorne Manly, "Satellite Radio Takes Off, Altering the Airwaves," *New York Times*, April 5, 2005, A1.

4. David MacFarland, *Future Radio Programming Strategies: Cultivating Listenship in the Digital Age* (Mahwah, NJ: Lawrence Erlbaum Associates, 1997).

5. Jennifer Lee, "On Minot, N.D., Radio, a Single Corporate Voice," *New York Times*, March 31, 2003, C-7.

6. Robert Score, "An Examination of XM Satellite Radio Subscribers' Perception of Satellite Radio Compared to Traditional AM/FM" (master's thesis, Kutztown University of Pennsylvania, 2002).

7. Robert Score, "An Examination of XM Satellite Radio Subscribers' Perception of Satellite Radio Compared to Traditional AM/FM" (master's thesis, Kutztown University of Pennsylvania, 2002).

8. David Lieberman, Francisco Lume, and Ari Raivetz, *Satellite Radio: Coming of Age* (New Haven: Yale School of Management, 2004).

9. Jason Helfstein and Ofer Elyakim, *XM Satellite Radio* (CIBC World Marketer, 2004).

10. Ellen Sheng, "Sirius's Quarterly Loss Widens on Higher Programming Fees," *Wall Street Journal*, www.WSJ.com (accessed February 17, 2006).

11. Walter Mossberg, "Get 100 Channels—Not on TV, but over Your Special XM Car Radio," *Wall Street Journal*, January 3, 2002, B1.

12. Ashley Fantz, "XM Radio Innovation Center Goes to Infinity and Beyond," *Miami Herald*, August 18, 2004.

13. Walter Mossberg, "Now, Satellite Radio Has the Right Gear to Show off Programs," *Wall Street Journal*, January 23, 2003, B1.

14. Harold Mendelsohn, *Mass Entertainment* (New Haven, CT: College and University Press, 1966); David MacFarland, *Future Radio Programming Strategies: Cultivating Listenship in the Digital Age* (Mahwah, NJ: Lawrence Erlbaum Associates, 1997).

15. Justin Martin, "Radio Heads," *Fortune Small Business*, February 14, 2004, 1.

16. Susan Douglas, *Listening In: Radio and the American Imagination* (New York: Random House, 1999).

17. Sarah McBride, "Two Upstarts Vie for Dominance in Satellite Radio," *Wall Street Journal*, March 30, 2005, A1.

18. Rick Munarriz, "All Hail King Stern," *Motley Fool*, www.fool.com (accessed July 7, 2006).

19. Daren Fonda, "Howard Stern: The $500 Million Man," *Time Magazine*, December 16, 2005.

20. Peter Friedland and Michael Crouch, *Satellite Radio Report* (New York: W.R. Hambrecht, 2003).

21. Erik Barnouw, *A Tower in Babel: A History of Broadcasting in the United States to 1933* (New York: Oxford University Press, 1966).

22. Susan Douglas, *Listening In: Radio and the American Imagination* (New York: Random House, 1999).

23. Marilyn Matelski, "Resilient Radio," in "Radio, the Forgotten Medium," special issue, *Media Studies Journal* 7, no. 3 (1993): 1–14.

24. Sarah McBride, "Clear Channel Scales Back Ad Time," *Wall Street Journal*, July 19, 2005.

25. James Trautman, Steve Rath, and John Carey, *Digital Audio Broadcasting* (Washington, DC: Corporation for Public Broadcasting, 1993).

26. Holt Gollatz, *Sirius–XM Merger: An Answer or Futile Action?* (New York: Fordham University, 2007).

CHAPTER TEN

1. Gerard Goggin, *Cell Phone Culture: Mobile Technology in Everyday Life* (Abingdon: Routledge, 2006); James Katz, *Magic in the Air: Mobile Communication and the Transformation of Social Life* (New Brunswick, NJ: Transaction Publishers, 2006); Rich Ling, *New Tech, New Ties* (Cambridge, MA: MIT Press, 2008).

2. Gerard Goggin, *Cell Phone Culture: Mobile Technology in Everyday Life* (Abingdon: Routledge, 2006).

3. Rich Ling, *New Tech, New Ties* (Cambridge, MA: MIT Press, 2008).

4. Jon Agar, *Constant Touch: A Global History of the Mobile Phone* (Cambridge: Icon Books, 2003).

5. Rich Ling, *New Tech, New Ties* (Cambridge, MA: MIT Press, 2008).

6. John Carey and Mitchell Moss, "The Diffusion of New Telecommunication Technologies," *Telecommunications Policy* 9, no. 2 (June 1985): 145–58.

7. Gerard Goggin, *Cell Phone Culture: Mobile Technology in Everyday Life* (Abingdon: Routledge, 2006).

8. Kathleen Robbins and Martha Turner, "United States: Popular, Pragmatic and Problematic," in James Katz and Mark Aakhus, eds., *Perpetual Contact: Mobile Communication, Private Talk, Public Performance* (New York: Cambridge University Press, 2002), 80–93.

9. There are important geographic and cultural differences between the United States and Europe. The large size of the United States compared to most European countries meant that building a national cellular system would be complex; the cultural preference in the United States for de facto standards versus a preference for de jure standards in Europe encouraged the FCC to be slow in making a decision.

10. Gerard Goggin, *Cell Phone Culture: Mobile Technology in Everyday Life* (Abingdon: Routledge, 2006).

11. Ross Snell, "Fighting the Fickle," *Wall Street Journal*, August 18, 2000, R36.

12. During the 1990s, an alternative mobile phone service based on satellite technology was launched. We discuss this in chapter 2.

13. International Telecommunications Union, *Telecommunication Indicators*, multiple years.

14. Mats Lindgren, Jorgen Jedbratt, and Erika Svensson, *Beyond Mobile: People, Communications, and Marketing in a Mobilized World* (New York: Palgrave Publishers, 2002).

15. P. McGrath, "3G Phone Home," *Newsweek*, March 18, 2002, 38F.

16. L. Rakow and V. Navarro, "Remote Mothering and the Parallel Shift: Women Meet the Cellular Telephone," *Critical Studies in Mass Communications* 10, no. 2 (1993): 144–57.

17. James Alleman and Christopher Swann, "Mobile Communications Business Model in the United States," in Jo Groebel, Eli Noam, and Valerie Feldman, eds., *Mobile Media: Content and Services for Wireless Communication* (Mahwah, NJ: Lawrence Erlbaum Publishers, 2006), 153–64.

18. Leopoldina Fortunati, "Italy: Stereotypes, True and False," in James Katz and Mark Aakhus, eds., *Perpetual Contact: Mobile Communication, Private Talk, Public Performance* (New York: Cambridge University Press, 2002), 42–62.

19. James Katz, *Connections: Social and Cultural Studies of the Telephone in American Life* (New Brunswick, NJ: Transaction Publishers, 1999).

20. Jon Agar, *Constant Touch: A Global History of the Mobile Phone* (Cambridge: Icon Books, 2003).

21. James Katz, *Connections: Social and Cultural Studies of the Telephone in American Life* (New Brunswick, NJ: Transaction Publishers, 1999).

22. James Katz and Mark Aakhus, eds., *Perpetual Contact: Mobile Communication, Private Talk, Public Performance* (New York: Cambridge University Press, 2002).

23. Scott Campbell, "A Cross-Cultural Comparison of Perceptions and Uses of Mobile Telephony," *New Media & Society* 9, no. 2 (2007): 343–63.

24. Laura Forlano, "Wireless Time, Space Freedom: Japanese Youth and Mobile Media" (paper presented at the University of Pennsylvania Digital Media Conference, October 2003).

25. Claude Fischer, *America Calling: A Social History of the Telephone to 1940* (Berkeley, CA: University of California Press, 1992).

26. James Katz, *Magic in the Air: Mobile Communication and the Transformation of Social Life* (New Brunswick, NJ: Transaction Publishers, 2006).

27. Richard Ling and Birgitte Yttri, "Hyper-coordination and Mobile Phones in Norway," in James Katz and Mark Aakhus, eds., *Perpetual Contact: Mobile Communication, Private Talk, Public Performance* (New York: Cambridge University Press, 2002), 139–69.

28. Richard Ling and Birgitte Yttri, "Hyper-coordination and Mobile Phones in Norway," in James Katz and Mark Aakhus, eds., *Perpetual Contact: Mobile Communication, Private Talk, Public Performance* (New York: Cambridge University Press, 2002), 139–69.

29. Rich Ling, *The Mobile Connection: The Cell Phone's Impact on Society* (Amsterdam: Morgan Kaufman Publishers, 2004).

30. Heidi Campbell, "Texting the Faith: Religious Users and Cell Phone Culture," in Anadam Kavoori and Noah Arceneaux, eds., *The Cell Phone Reader: Essays in Social Transformation* (New York: Peter Lang Publishers, 2006), 139–54.

31. Erving Goffman, *Behavior in Public Places* (New York: Free Press, 1963).

32. Kenneth Gergen, "The Challenge of Absent Presence," in James Katz and Mark Aakhus, eds., *Perpetual Contact: Mobile Communication, Private Talk, Public Performance* (New York: Cambridge University Press, 2002), 227–41.

33. Lee Humphreys, "Mobile Sociality and Spatial Practice: A Qualitative Field Study" (PhD diss., Annenberg School for Communication, Philadelphia, 2007).

34. Lee Humphreys, "Mobile Sociality and Spatial Practice: A Qualitative Field Study" (PhD diss., Annenberg School for Communication, Philadelphia, 2007).

35. Rich Ling, *New Tech, New Ties* (Cambridge, MA: MIT Press, 2008).

36. Gerard Goggin, *Cell Phone Culture: Mobile Technology in Everyday Life* (Abingdon: Routledge, 2006).

37. David Crystal, *Txting: The Gr8 Db8* (Oxford: Oxford University Press, 2008).

38. Kenichi Ishii, "Implications of Mobility: The Uses of Personal Communication Media in Everyday Life," *Journal of Communication* 56, no. 2 (June 2006): 346–65.

39. David Crystal, *Txting: The Gr8 Db8* (Oxford: Oxford University Press, 2008).

40. David Crystal, *Txting: The Gr8 Db8* (Oxford: Oxford University Press, 2008).

41. Richard Ling and Birgitte Yttri, "Hyper-coordination and Mobile Phones in Norway," in James Katz and Mark Aakhus, eds., *Perpetual Contact: Mobile Communication, Private Talk, Public Performance* (New York: Cambridge University Press, 2002), 139–69.

42. Kenichi Ishii, "Implications of Mobility: The Uses of Personal Communication Media in Everyday Life," *Journal of Communication* 56, no. 2 (June 2006): 346–65.

43. Eric Bellman, "Cellphone Entertainment Takes Off in Rural India," *Wall Street Journal*, November 22, 2009, B1.

44. Bob Johansen, *Get There Early: Sensing the Future to Compete in the Present* (San Francisco: Berrett-Koehler, 2007).

45. Cassell Bryan-Low, "Time Is Money," *Wall Street Journal*, February 12, 2008, B3.

46. Gerard Goggin, *Cell Phone Culture: Mobile Technology in Everyday Life* (Abingdon: Routledge, 2006).

47. Manuel Castells, Mireia Fernández-Ardèvol, Jack Linchuan Qui, and Araba Sey, *Mobile Communication and Society: A Global Perspective* (Cambridge, MA: MIT Press, 2007).

48. Veethima Chinthammit, "New Services in Mobile Phones" (working paper, Fordham Graduate School of Business, 2005).

49. Heidi Campbell, "Texting the Faith: Religious Users and Cell Phone Culture," in Anadam Kavoori and Noah Arceneaux, eds., *The Cell Phone Reader: Essays in Social Transformation* (New York: Peter Lang Publishers, 2006), 139–54; Adriana de Souza e Silva, "Interfaces of Hybrid Spaces," in Anadam Kavoori and Noah Arceneaux, eds., *The Cell Phone Reader: Essays in Social Transformation* (New York: Peter Lang Publishers, 2006), 19–44.

50. Manuel Castells, Mireia Fernández-Ardèvol, Jack Linchuan Qui, and Araba Sey, *Mobile Communication and Society: A Global Perspective* (Cambridge, MA: MIT Press, 2007).

Index